Crisis Communications

A Casebook Approach

Second Edition

Kathleen Fearn-Banks
University of Washington

LAWRENCE ERLBAUM ASSOCIATES, PUBLISHERS

2002 Mahwah, New Jersey London

Acquisitions Editor:	Linda Bathgate
Editorial Assistant:	Karen Wittig
Cover Design:	Kathryn Houghtaling Lacey
Textbook Production Manager:	Paul Smolenski
Full-Service & Composition:	Gibson Publishing Services
Text and Cover Printer:	Sheridan Books, Inc.

This book was typeset in 10/12 pt. Garamond ITC, Bold, and Italic.
The heads were typeset in Garamond ITC, Bold, and Bold Italic.

Lawrence Erlbaum Associates, Inc., Publishers
10 Industrial Avenue
Mahwah, New Jersey 07430

Frontispiece illustrated by Leonard Rifas

Library of Congress Cataloging-in-Publication Data

Fearn-Banks, Kathleen.
Crisis communications : a casebook approach /
 by Kathleen Fearn-Banks.
p. cm.
Includes bibliographical references and indexes.
ISBN 0-8058-3603-9 (cloth : alk. paper)
ISBN 0-8058-3604-7 (pbk. : alk. paper)
Public relations–Management–Case Studies. 2. Crisis manage-
 ment–Case studies. 3. Advertising–Case Studies.
 I. Title.
HD59.F37 1995
659.2–dc20 95-4122
 CIP

Books published by Lawrence Erlbaum Associates are printed
on acid-free paper, and their bindings are chosen for strength
and durability.

Printed in the United States of America
10 9 8 7 6 5 4 3 2

*This book is dedicated to
Hank Rieger and the late Dr. Edward P. Bassett,
guiding lights in my professional
and academic careers, respectively.*

Contents

Preface

A casebook approach to studying crisis communications means learning from the actions of those who have experienced crises. What did they expect? What actually happened? Were they prepared? What were their strategies? What were their challenges, pressures, and problems? Were the news media adversarial or supportive? If they had to do it again, what would they do differently? These and other questions are answered in the cases presented in this book.

Chapter 1 presents crisis communications theory. What does research say about how organizations can be prepared for crises and about how such organizations can emerge from crises without great loss in reputation and finance. The chapter also includes a mini-case that critiques other communications of White Star Line after its *Titanic* sank on its maiden voyage.

Chapter 2 describes ways of determining the most likely and most damaging crises that may strike an organization. It also contains a list of what should be included in a crisis communications plan (CCP). Chapter 2 in the Student Workbook supplementing this book includes a simple step-by-step plan for developing the CCP as well as examples. Although it is called a "Student" Workbook, it may be valuable to the professional faced with develop-

ing a CCP. The three appendixes in this casebook, present sample CCPs—
for a large company, for a nonprofit organization, and for a small business.

Chapter 3 centers on causes of crisis—rumor which causes crises that is
sometimes very difficult to erase, "gotcha" television news and the nonexpert
expert, and crises caused by the news media which are also difficult to battle.

Chapter 4 gets into the 21st century and cyberspace-caused crises. In-
cluded are mini-cases of rouge Web sites and e-mail rumors. Chapter 5 is
concerned with how to communicate with the news media, lawyers, inter-
nal publics (or audiences) and external publics.

Chapters 6 through 21 are narrated case studies of how spokespersons
and managers used communication effectively, in various types of crises.
Some of the professionals featured are heads of departments and public re-
lations agencies, whereas others are not. These are crises managed by giant
companies as well as organizations with small staffs. Some cases reveal the
work of government agencies and nonprofit organizations. In this book's
case studies, in contrast to many other crisis communications and crisis
management books, many of the professionals talk about the mistakes they
made and about how they would do things different if faced with the same
crisis again.

This second edition of *Crisis Communications: A Casebook Approach*
has five new chapters. Chapter 4 is about cyber crises. Chapter 13 is about
an agency of the government of Canada and of how it handled the concerns
of citizens when boatloads of Chinese immigrants arrived on its shores un-
der suspicious circumstances. Chapter 14 is about Mayor Anthony Wil-
liams of Washington, DC, and the crisis with racial overtones that erupted
during the first month of his administration. Chapter 15 centers on a bon-
fire accident that killed and injured students at Texas A&M University.
Chapter 17 deals with Seattle Metro Transit's handling of a shooting that
caused a bus to fall off a bridge.

Repeated from the first edition are twelve other cases, including the
"textbook cases" on crisis communications—Johnson & Johnson's Tylenol
poisoning (chap. 6) and Exxon's Valdez oil spill (chap. 7). An accompany-
ing chapter describes the Exxon communications few people realize exist
(chap. 8). The table of contents identifies which areas of public relations
and which issues are included in the cases.

ACKNOWLEDGMENTS

My deepest appreciation is extended to the professionals featured in the
cases, the "stars" of the book. All of them are busy people, but they took the
time to endure interviews in person, by phone, and by e-mail. They also pa-
tiently proofread drafts of their chapters and complied, painfully, with my
requests for photographs of them at work.

Lois Reimer of Citizenship and Immigration Canada and Dan Williams of Metro Transit in Seattle both spoke to my Crisis Communications class at the University of Washington and thereby set the framework for new chapters 13 and 17, respectively.

I also thank their staff members who assisted with portions of the tasks, especially Lillian Fickey at Texas A&M and Denny Falls at Citizenship and Immigration Canada. Fickey mailed me clips of every newspaper article written about the Texas A&M bonfire, many hundreds of them.

Colleagues at the School of Communications, University of Washington, are also appreciated, especially Professor Kevin Kawamoto, cyberspace expert, and Daria Sanai, for office support. My favorite critics, Dr. Kayte M. Fearn (my mother) and Professor Albert Sampson, are always appreciated for being both difficult and complimentary. My friend Hal Williams made his home in Kauai a peaceful, relaxing environment for writing.

Last but not least, I thank the students in the upper-division course CMU 452: Crisis Communications, which researched crises as projects. Special thanks go to the students in the team which developed the crisis plan (with a fictitious name in Appendix C) for their favorite local hamburger stand. Their names are on the front page of the plan they developed. Special mention goes to student research assistants who helped in a variety of ways. I expect they are on their way to becoming outstanding professionals: Corey Adams, Kimm Conroy, Meg Hemphill, Stefanie Johansen, Joy Krueger, Jeremy Kuno, Jennifer Northrup, Colin Robinson, Merry Tourtelot, and Mason Yu.

—Kathleen Fearn-Banks

The Nature of Crises

WHAT IS A CRISIS?

"If something can go wrong, it will."

This expression, popularly called Murphy's Law, takes on real meaning for crisis planners. More companies are developing proactive public relations plans and crisis plans. However, in the new century, many large corporations still have no crisis management or crisis communications plans. Management and public relations personnel in these companies are likely to say they acknowledge the need for such a plan; they realize that Murphy's Law is right. However, they lack either the personnel or the expertise to develop a crisis plan, so they hope that the inevitable will not occur until the economy improves and they can hire someone with crisis planning expertise.

Many organizations and individuals go through life saying that they think positively, that somehow if they never have a negative thought, nothing negative will happen. This is absolute balderdash! The slogan should be "Think Negatively."

A crisis can and will happen. "When?" is the question. Negative thinking is more appropriate than positive thinking in crisis management. This book will show that when an organization's leaders think and plan for the worst-case scenario, they will come out of a crisis in better condition than they would otherwise.

A *crisis* is a major occurrence with a potentially negative outcome affecting the organization, company, or industry, as well as its publics, products, services, or good name. A crisis interrupts normal business transactions and can sometimes threaten the existence of the organization. A crisis can be a strike, terrorism, fire, a boycott, product tampering, product failure, or numerous other events (see the list on pg. 23). The size of the organization is irrelevant. It can be a multinational corporation, a one-person business, or even an individual.

Public relations professionals often say, "I have a crisis every day." This is an exaggeration, of course. The term *crisis* denotes something more serious than a "problem." Public relations people deal with problems—solving them or avoiding them. By definition, however, a crisis interrupts the normal flow of business, so a crisis cannot be a *normal* part of this flow.

On the other hand, a crisis is not necessarily so catastrophic that the life of the organization is destroyed. Exxon suffered the crisis of crises after its oil spill in 1989. It still suffers from a bad image, but it continues to thrive in business.

This book advises you to plan for the worst that can happen, whether it be a crisis or problem. This brings us to another expression: "Be prepared." This book shows you how to prepare yourself and your organization to cope with crises that may occur. It deals with preparations made far in advance, as well as with strategies and tactics to be used during a crisis. It examines the experiences of public relations professionals in crises, describing what they did, what they wished they had done, and what hampered their progress. You can learn from their successes and failures.

In a crisis, in contrast to a problem, emotions are on edge, brains are not fully functioning, and events are occurring so rapidly that drafting a plan during a crisis is unthinkable. Simply following one is difficult.

Crisis management is a process of strategic planning for a crisis or negative turning point, a process that removes some of the risk and uncertainty from the negative occurrence and thereby allows the organization to be in greater control of its own destiny.

Crisis communications is the dialog between the organization and its publics prior to, during, and after the negative occurrence. The strategies and tactics are designed to minimize damage to the image of the organization.

Effective crisis management includes crisis communications that not only can alleviate or eliminate the crisis, but also can sometimes bring the organization a more positive reputation than before the crisis.

Public relations deals with *publics.* Publics are the specific audiences targeted by programs. People frequently use the term *general public,* but public relations professionals are usually more specific in their targeting. Examples of corporate publics include the following:

employees
customers
stockholders
community members
board members
unions
retirees

There can be numerous others. An organization depends on these publics for survival because they have some stake in the organization.

Public relations is concerned with reputation. It exists to avoid a negative image and to create or enhance a positive reputation. It is largely the fear of a negative image that causes organizations to develop public relations departments, hire public relations agencies, or both.

Too often, an organization does not consider utilizing public relations until it is in a crisis. Then it wants a speedy recovery.

Research shows (see "Crisis Communications Theories" p. 14) that companies with ongoing two-way communications often avoid crises or endure crises of shorter duration or of lesser magnitude. Research also shows that companies with a crisis management plan come out of a crisis with a more positive image than companies without such a plan.

Whether an organization is a large multinational company or a small business, a crisis communications plan is needed. A *crisis communications plan* (CCP) is preferably a part of a company-wide *crisis management plan* (CMP) that would include sections on evacuation, work sites, equipment, and so on. If a company does not have a CMP, a CCP is still advisable, even urgent.

The media to which you have tried to pitch ideas for news stories, the media that toss "perfect" news releases in the trash, the media that never return phone calls—*that media* will call on you in a crisis. They will probably not telephone in advance. They will show up on your premises—"in your face." The media, seeing themselves as advocates for the people, can be the principal adversaries in a crisis.

This is a time when public relations takes front and center—in a very crucial way. This is not to say that public relations will operate independently—that might be a greater disaster. It is a time, however, when the CEO may listen to the PR guy whose name he can never remember.

Even in a crisis, sometimes, the head of the company or organization does not listen because business schools often teach CEOs to make their own decisions. There are many documented cases of disasters during which CEOs acted independently. The Exxon crisis, again, is an example. Exxon's CEO, Lawrence Rawl, did not respond as the media and environmentalists would have preferred. He did not accept responsibility as rapidly as critics felt he should have. He did not fly to Valdez to express concern. All the moves the public relations experts would advise, Rawl ignored. Rawl is not alone in his response among corporate heads, but the number of bad responses is declining as organizations learn the effects of public opinion.

In a crisis, when everyone else is in a state of panic, public relations practitioners must have a calming attitude of "This is not as bad as it seems," or "This could be worse. We cannot turn crises into catastrophes. This is what we do …."

MINI-CASE 1:
WHITE STAR LINE'S *TITANIC* SINKS

To illustrate terms, let's examine a well-known crisis: the sinking of the *Titanic* in 1912.

Titanic was one of several ships of the White Star Line, which had a primary rival: the Cunard Line. The Cunard Line had two famously fast ships—the *Lusitania* and the *Mauritania*. White Star decided not to compete with Cunard on speed but to surpass it, as far as public opinion was concerned, in size, elegance, sumptuousness, and safety.

The White Star Line planned to launch three ships—the *Olympic*, the *Titanic*, and the *Gigantic*, in that order. In the area of media relations, advance publicity praised the immensely luxurious ships. Postcards went out claiming the *Titanic* was "the largest moving object in the world." A promotional brochure claimed the *Olympic* and *Titanic* were "designed to be unsinkable" (Ziakas, 1999, p. 109). The trade journal *The Shipbuilder* bragged about the *Titanic*'s opulence—its grand staircase, its elevators, its Turkish baths, and, of course, its "unsinkable" construction.

Titanic personnel were chosen to appeal to a celebrated and wealthy clientele, the targeted public. Captain E. J. Smith, called the "millionaire's captain," was the highest-paid captain on the seas and a celebrity in his own right. The musicians were the tops in their field and could play a wide range of music. White Star felt it had thought of everything and had attained the highest form of customer relations.

Crisis management plans and *crisis communications* plans were believed to be unnecessary. After all, if the ship couldn't sink, what could happen? There were medical facilities on board should passengers suffer a heart attack or some other unforeseen illness. The ship had state of the art communication equipment; if help was needed, personnel could radio other ships.

We've learned that it was always possible, though unlikely, that the ship would sink. A long gash in the hull was the worst-case scenario, and that is exactly what happened. So, the nonplanners were short-sighted. What about fires? Certainly the ship could burn. An adequate number of lifeboats would still be needed. In fact, a fire out of control on a ship could have been a worse disaster.

A CMP would have detailed what would be done in the event of fire and other tragedies—how evacuation would take place, how to conduct practice drills for the crew and possibly for passengers, who would lower the lifeboats, who would ensure that passengers were guided safely to the closest lifeboats and ships, who would contact persons ashore by radio, when crew members would save themselves, and so on. A CMP would also include making sure effective insurance policies were in place. In today's crises, one must be sure payrolls can be met; special insurances may be necessary to cover computers.

The CMP would include the crisis communications plan. The CCP would include notification of the home office, where personnel acting as public relations professionals would in turn notify the press, White Star Line executives and employees, and passengers' relatives. These were also key publics. (The term *public relations* was not used at the time, although that management function has always been important to the success of any company or organization.)

The CCP would also include details about who would be spokesperson, once the passengers were brought to safety. If Capt. Smith had survived, he would be the best spokesperson. As it was, Smith went down with the ship. However, the managing director of White Star, J. Bruce Ismay, was aboard, survived, and was rescued from a lifeboat sent from the *Carpathia*. Many felt he should have given his place on the lifeboat to a passenger. But because he survived, he should have been the spokesperson. Instead, he hid in the luxurious quarters of the *Carpathia*'s physician until the ship docked in New York, hoping to avoid the other survivors who huddled on floors and under tables.

There were two persons connected to White Star who participated in the media communications. Harold Bride, a radio operator on the *Titanic* who worked for Marconi Wireless Telegraph Company, was among the passengers picked up by the *Carpathia*. He wrote a first-person account of the tragedy that he sent to the *New York Times* by wire from the rescue

ship. Phillip A. S. Franklin, who had been hired to head White Star's New York office, called together a kind of crisis communications team. This came after David Sarnoff, also a Marconi employee, heard the signal from the *Olympic* that the *Titanic* had run into an iceberg and was sinking fast; Sarnoff gave his story to the Associated Press. Franklin attempted to stop the Associated Press from running the story, saying that even though the ship had run into an iceberg, he had "absolute confidence in the Titanic.... We are not worried about the ship but we are sorry for the inconvenience of the passengers" (Ziakis, 1999, p. 116).

The morning before the sinking, the *New York Times* ran a story announcing that the "The New Giantess *Titanic*" would soon arrive in New York. The story was a PR person's dream, a proactive story aimed primarily at a public of potential passengers and at educating and informing the general public, thereby assuring that when asked, "What is the biggest, most elegant ship afloat?" anyone would say, "the *Titanic*." The *Times* story described the ship's impressive size, luxury, and illustrious passengers aboard its maiden voyage.

On April 15, White Star was in a reactive mode, as is almost always the case in a crisis. Presented with information from the Bride and Sarnoff stories, the *New York Times* ran a story with this headline:

NEW-LINER TITANIC HITS AN ICEBERG;
SINKING BY THE BOW AT MIDNIGHT;
WOMEN PUT OFF IN LIFE BOATS;
LAST WIRELESS AT 12:27 A.M. BLURRED

A later *New York Times* headline read as follows:

TITANIC SINKS FOUR HOURS AFTER HITTING ICEBERG
866 RESCUED BY CARPATHIA, PROBABLY 1250 PERISH
ISMAY SAFE, MRS. ASTOR MAYBE, NOTED NAMES MISSING

Other newspapers' April 15 headlines indicated that the editors were much less aware of accurate details of the story. The *New York Sun's* headline was "All Saved From Titanic After Collision." The *Washington Post* apparently chose to believe the spokesperson for White Star, Franklin. The *Post's* headline was the following:

TITANIC'S 1470 PASSENGERS ARE NOW BEING
TRANSFERRED IN LIFEBOATS TO CUNARD LINE
Twenty Boat Loads Have Already
Been Transferred to the Catania,
Of the Cunard Line ... No loss of
Life Is Feared ... Officials Confident
Throughout Long Period of Suspense ... Halifax Hears that
***Titanic* Is on Her Way to That Port**

(Note that newspapers made estimates of the numbers of passengers rescued and deceased in early coverage. Also, the *Washington Post* thought the rescue ship was *Catania*, not *Carpathia*.)

The *Manchester Guardian*, on April 16, wrote about the miscommunications of White Star. Newspapers love to write about corporate mistakes; it's the stuff of which interesting articles are made. Under the headline "The Day's Strange Reports in America," the story was a timeline of every arrogant message from White Star's Franklin and from other reports. One message from the Government Marine Agency in Halifax said that the *Titanic* was sinking, whereas a message from Franklin said that "all passengers are saved, and the *Virginian* is towing the *Titanic* towards Halifax" (Ziakas, 1999, p. 117).

Franklin finally received a telegram confirming that the ship had sunk, and he later described his reactions: " ... it was such a terrible shock that it took us a few minutes to get ourselves together. Then at once I telephoned, myself, two of our directors, Mr. Steele and Mr. Morgan, Jr. and at the same time went downstairs to the reporters. I got off the first line and a half where it said: 'The *Titanic* sank at two o'clock a.m.' and there was not a reporter left in the room—they were so anxious to get out and telephone the news" (Ziakas, 1999, p. 117).

At Pier 54 in New York harbor, the surviving passengers came ashore and were regarded as celebrities from that point on. An embarrassed and tearful Franklin went aboard *Carpathia* to meet with Ismay, who was in a state of mental and physical collapse. Ismay and Franklin drafted White Star's official reaction to the disaster and came ashore long after the passengers had left. Ismay and Franklin also were present at a stressful media availability event and later issued the formal statement (shown in Fig. 1.1).

The surviving passengers issued their own statement, which read in part:

> We, the undersigned surviving passengers from the steamship *Titanic*, in order to forestall any sensational or exaggerated statements, deem it our duty to give the press a statement of facts which have come to our knowledge and which we believe to be true we feel it is our duty to call the attention of the public to what we consider the inadequate supply of live-saving appliances provided for on modern passenger steamships, and recommend that immediate steps be taken to compel passenger steamers to carry sufficient boats to accommodate the maximum number of people carried on board. (Ziakas, 1999, pp. 120–121)

The survivors were viewed as heroes, as was Capt. Smith, who went down with the ship. Ismay was cleared of any wrongdoing by both British and U.S. inquiries, but his reputation never recovered. In motion pictures about the *Titanic*, Ismay was portrayed as a villain. The denotation of *Titanic* was "huge, colossal," whereas its connotation was "doom." White Star Line became synonymous with bad management. It suffered financial problems during the European Depression and, in the 1930s, merged with Cunard, with Cunard holding 62% of the shares. Both flags were flown on

In the presence and under the shadow of a catastrophe so overwhelming my feelings are too deep for expression in words. I can only say that the White Star Line, its offices and employees will do everything humanly possible to alleviate the suffering and sorrow of the survivors and of the relatives and friends of those who perished.

The *Titanic* was the last word in shipbuilding. Every regulation prescribed by the British Board of Trade had been strictly complied with, the master, officers, and the crew were the most experienced and skillful in the British service.

I am informed that a committee of the United States has been appointed to investigate the circumstances of the accident. I heartily welcome the most complete and exhaustive inquiry, and any aid that I or my associates or our builders or navigators can render is at the service of the public and the governments of both the United States and Great Britain. Under the circumstances I must respectfully defer making any further statement at this time.

FIG. 1.1 Formal statement made by J. Bruce Ismay, managing director of White Star Line, following the sinking of the *Titanic*. Ismay was aboard the doomed ship and issued this statement after consultation with Phillip A. S. Franklin, who headed White Star's New York office (*Source*: Ziakas, 1999, p. 120).

the ships until 1957, when the White Star flag was withdrawn. White Star liquidated its ships and Cunard bought the remaining shares. By 1958, White Star no longer existed. Cunard went on to produce the *Queen Mary*, the *Queen Elizabeth*, and the *Queen Elizabeth II*. The *Queen Elizabeth II* still makes transatlantic crossings.

THE FIVE STAGES OF A CRISIS

A crisis has five stages:

1. Detection
2. Prevention/Preparation
3. Containment
4. Recovery
5. Learning

Detection

The *detection* phase may begin with noting warning signs, or what Barton (1993) referred to as *prodromes* or the *prodromal stage*. Some crises have no noticeable prodromes, but many do.

When an organization in the same business as yours suffers a crisis, it is a warning to your organization. The 1982 Tylenol tampering case was a prodrome to other manufacturers of over-the-counter drugs. Most companies heeded that warning and now use tamper-proof containers. Imagine how many crises were avoided by noticing that what happened to Tylenol could happen to other companies.

On the other hand, Johnson & Johnson itself had little warning before it was hit with this crisis. No one had ever before poisoned an over-the-counter painkiller; it was not a crisis Johnson & Johnson had anticipated. The only warning the company had was a phone call from a journalist from the *Chicago Tribune*, taken by a Johnson & Johnson public relations staff member. The journalist asked questions about the company's holdings, the spelling of names, and so forth. The employee reported the call to supervisors, who called the newspaper and found out that there were deaths attributed to Tylenol (see chap. 6, "Case: Johnson & Johnson and the Tylenol Murders").

The Exxon Valdez oil spill was a prodrome to other companies as well as Exxon itself. Oil companies now know better how to prevent spills, how to clean up spills, and how to react to the public after spills.

There are other less obvious prodromes. Employee discontent over any issue is a sign of a brewing crisis. Perhaps there is an increase in complaints about work hours, work conditions, or unreasonable supervisors. Any one of these and many more issues can be an early sign of a work stoppage. The same prodromes can be early signs of workplace violence.

If you know that your chief executive's salary is especially exorbitant, you also know that this can be fuel for public concern, especially if you are a non-profit organization. This was a prodrome for the United Way of America when its chief executive, William Aramony, was criticized for his salary and perks (see chap. 11, "Case: United Way of America and the Overspending CEO").

An organization should watch for prodromes and make attempts to stop a crisis at this stage before it develops into a full-blown crisis. To detect these early signs, organizations form employee committees that function like lighthouse keepers watching for vessels at sea, watchdogs, or whistle-blowers. These whistle-blowers report warning signs to organization officials who can implement plans to avoid the impending crisis or at least have time to prepare to address the media or other publics.

Roy Betts, media representative for the U.S. Postal Service, speaking of the postal workers' violence prevention program, said "You should be aware of your surroundings. There *are* warning signs if you look for them

and consider them carefully." The U.S. Postal Service installed hotline tele-
phones so workers can report odd or potentially violent behavior. Each
call to the hotline is considered seriously.

Crisis detection also refers to a system within the organization in which
key personnel are immediately notified of a crisis. An organization has a
considerable advantage if it knows about a crisis before its publics do, es-
pecially before the news media get the tip. This gives the organization time
to draft a statement, make preparations for a news conference, notify the
crisis team, and call in spokespersons. As mentioned earlier, the phone call
from a *Chicago Tribune* journalist gave Johnson & Johnson some lead time
before the public knew about the Tylenol murders.

Crisis Prevention

Ongoing public relations programs and regular two-way communications
build relationships with key publics and thereby prevent crises, lessen the
blows of crises, or limit the duration of crises.

The establishment of a corporate culture conducive to the positive and
open interaction of members also minimizes crises, as does including crisis
management in the strategic planning process (see "Crisis Communica-
tions Theories," p. 14).

There are other specific tactics and actions that an organization may
adopt to prevent crises. These tactics must be communicated to appropri-
ate publics. A company must not only do what is right; it also must tell its
publics that it is doing so. *Crisis Prevention* tactics include the following:

1. Fostering the continued development of organizational policies
 that allow for updates and changes based on variances of publics
 and mission.
2. Reducing the use of hazardous material and processes.
3. Initiating safety training and providing rewards for employees with
 stellar safety records.
4. Allowing the free flow of information from employees to manage-
 ment with no punishment of employees who deliver bad news.
5. Following-up on past crises or problems.
6. Attending community meetings.
7. Developing a community board with key outside members who are
 public opinion leaders.
8. Circulating a newsletter to frequent consumers.
9. Offering scholarships for employees and their children as well as to
 other children in the community.

10. Hosting community or employee picnics.
11. Sponsoring community activities, such as Little League teams and charities.

In communications, diligence can sometimes prevent crises. A public relations executive in the Midwest told of a telephone call from a West Coast journalist at 5 p.m., just as she was leaving for the weekend. She could easily have refused the call, but she decided to take it.

The reporter was preparing to write a story for a big-city newspaper about the failure of a product manufactured by the PR executive's company. The story was one that could have sparked a full-scale crisis. The PR person took the time to locate information that proved the information to be baseless. The reporter was satisfied and the crisis-that-could-have-been was averted.

If all members of the management staff are trained to be media savvy, numerous crises can be prevented. Using the same story, the PR executive could have consulted a respected expert on the issue to refute the charges and nip them in the bud. Public relations personnel and key organizational leaders should always be aware of who these experts are and of how to reach them in emergencies. Prompt responses to media inquiries are also a plus.

Crisis Preparation

Crisis preparation is necessary for dealing with crises that cannot be prevented. Pepsi-Cola had no way of anticipating the scare in which hypodermic syringes were found in cans of Diet Pepsi. The presence of these syringes in the cans cried "AIDS," and fear of the illness and death far surpassed brand loyalty. Pepsi could not have prevented the crisis, but it was prepared to deal with it (see chap. 19 "Case: Pepsi and the National Syringe-in-the-Can Scare").

The CCP is the primary tool of preparedness (see chap. 2, "The Crisis Communications Plan"). This plan tells each key person on the crisis team what his or her role is, whom to notify, how to reach people, what to say, and so on. The CCP provides a functioning collective brain for all persons involved in a crisis, persons who may not operate at normal capacity due to the shock or emotions of the crisis event.

Containment

Containment refers to the effort to limit the duration of the crisis or to keep it from spreading to other areas affecting the organization.

Pepsi used an advertisement to end its crisis. After several hoaxes had been exposed without the discovery of one documented case of a syringe

in a can after the original incident, the company decided the crisis was over and told the world so. And it was.

Local United Way agencies managed to contain the effect of the head-quarters crisis with the CEO by publicizing the local organizations as sepa-rate, autonomous entities (see chap. 12, "Case: United Way of King County and the Overspending CEO").

Foodmaker, parent company of the Jack-in-the-Box fast-food chain, was charged by PR critics with delaying resolution of the *E. coli* crisis, which killed several children and one adult in 1993, because the company did not take responsibility for the tainted meat soon enough. On the other hand, as long as people, especially children, were sick and dying, there was no way Foodmaker could curtail the crisis. It was contained to the Pacific Northwest and did not affect all outlets of the chain. Also, Jack-in-the- Box communicated to consumers that other food products in the restaurants were not contaminated.

Recovery

Recovery involves efforts to return the company to business as usual. Or-ganizations want to leave the crisis behind and restore normalcy as soon as possible. Recovery may also mean restoring the confidence of key publics, which means communicating a return to normal business.

Snapps, a fast-food restaurant in Fort Pierce, Florida, suffered from a ru-mor that one of its managers had AIDS and had infected hamburgers. To implement recovery, health department officials participated in a news conference telling the public that all managers had been tested, that none had the AIDS virus, and that the virus could not be transmitted through hamburgers (see chap. 9).

Exxon attempted to recover from the Valdez oil spill by efforts to per-suade tourists that Alaska was still a beautiful place to visit. It is particularly interesting that Exxon looked beyond its own recovery to the way its crisis had affected the tourism industry.

Learning

The *learning* phase is a process of examining the crisis and determining what was lost, what was gained, and how the organization performed in the crisis. It is an evaluative procedure designed to make the crisis a prodrome for the future.

One might think that this is like closing the barn door after the cows have escaped. Any farmer will tell you that once the cows are back in the barn, they will escape again unless you close the door this time. Just because a company has suffered one crisis is no indication that it will not happen again.

Johnson & Johnson, after its second tampering crisis, learned its lesson by selling over-the-counter medications in tamper-proof containers. Other companies followed suit. Public relations personnel set about the task of telling the public about the new safety containers.

Another example of the learning phase is illustrated by the case of U.S. airlines, which had been plagued with hijackings during the 1960s and 1970s. The airlines set up metal detectors at airports for persons boarding planes. The procedure was extended to cover employees after an irate employee boarded a plane with a gun, shot a supervisor, and caused a fatal crash. The airlines' public relations personnel informed passengers of the new safety procedures.

The learning phase brings about change that helps prevent future crises.

PUBLIC OPINION

In a crisis, the public perceives truth to be whatever public opinion says. An organization in crisis must prove to its publics, and often to the general public, that the prevailing opinion is not factual. In contrast to a U.S. court of law where a person is innocent until proven guilty, in the court of public opinion a person or organization is guilty until proven innocent.

Public opinion is difficult to define, but it is based on individuals' attitudes toward specific issues. These attitudes are based on age, educational level, religion, country, state, city, neighborhood, family background and traditions, social class, and racial background. All of these help to form each individual's attitudes, and a predominance of similar attitudes makes up public opinion.

On any given issue, people are in favor, against, neutral, or so disinterested that they could not care less. Most people, unfortunately, fall into the last category. Public relations aims to reinforce positive attitudes, change negative attitudes, and provide information in a way that causes the unopinionated and neutral to form the opinion most conducive to the organization's function.

An organization has no choice in accepting a crisis. A crisis is forced on it, and the organization must cope with it. Organizations can ignore a crisis and hope it will go away. Occasionally, it does. More often, it does not. A crisis ignored is an organization failing.

The essential role of crisis communications is to affect the public opinion process and to be instrumental in establishing and communicating proof that the prevailing "truth" is not factual or not wholly factual.

The news media are a prime tool for changing public opinion. The media can reach the masses in a short period of time because most Americans utilize some form of the news media, primarily television. Radio is popular during prime traffic hours. Public relations experts are trained in knowing how

to reach the media, when and how to call a news conference, when and how to conduct one-on-one interviews, and when and how to disseminate written material.

Crisis communications, like public relations, is not merely the distribution of news releases. Neither is it only media relations. Frequently, community relations, consumer relations, employee relations, investor relations, government relations, and many other kinds of public relations are involved.

MORE *TITANIC* ILLUSTRATIONS

Prodromes for the *Titanic* tragedy were ships that sank previously. White Star thought it had made, in the construction of the ship, all the necessary adjustments to warning signs. The company concentrated on the positives rather than the negatives. It did not examine the worst-case scenario: "What if this doesn't work?" That question was apparently never asked or heeded.

Prevention/preparation would have included making sure there were enough lifeboats and the development of crisis management and crisis communications plans. *Containment* would have meant recognizing the danger as soon as the iceberg was sighted and putting into effect the crisis management and crisis communications plans. However, much arrogance ("This ship is unsinkable") existed. Although there were a limited number of lifeboats, many went unfilled because of poor crisis management. There was apparently time—if there had been a plan to be carried out—to save many more passengers.

Total recovery was not likely in this crisis. The reputation of White Star remained damaged after nearly a century had passed. If the company had done anything right in the prelaunching, the sinking, or the post–sinking, there might have been a possibility of reputational recovery.

In some cases, a company in crisis can seem to be a victim of crises. But this was not true in the sinking of the *Titanic*.

CRISIS COMMUNICATIONS THEORIES

Corporation A owns a chain of clothing stores in a major U.S. city, with catalog sales to other cities nationwide. Its sales total in the millions of dollars. All of its public relations activities are accomplished by one 15-person department, which has as its primary task the writing and distribution of news releases about new products, trends in fashion, and so forth. Each PR practitioner—with a degree in journalism or public relations and a minimum of five years of experience—spends 80% of his or her workday writing news releases. There are quotas each must meet in numbers of well-written news releases.

Corporation B also has a chain of clothing stores in the same city. Its sales total only about one third of the sales of Corporation A, and it has no

catalog sales out of town. The five people in the public relations department write news releases, but they also spend just as much time internally publicizing the *Employees Talk Back* closed-circuit television show shown in the cafeteria and writing brochures and letters for a program through which the best customers get 25% discounts on their birthdays.

Which corporation is likely to suffer most from a crisis? Crisis communications theories tell us the answer (see the end of the chapter).

Public relations professionals, prior to or during a crisis, need to know why they must use various strategies and tactics as well as what strategies and basic organizational practices are successful. Public relations theories explain all of this. Unfortunately, however, few public relations professionals are aware of which theories they actually follow or should follow. As the profession matures, there will be more theorists as well as an increased knowledge of existing theories and of how they fit into the framework of public relations programs.

For many years, practitioners entered the field with a knowledge of journalistic or communications theories if they had academic backgrounds in journalism. Frequently, however, in the past, and to a certain degree today, public relations professionals could be drafted from any position in a company and be anybody from a capable secretary to a frustrated executive. In volunteer organizations, public relations is often the task of the person who says loudest, "That sounds interesting."

As more university students study public relations and enter the field, a knowledge of public relations theory will slowly pervade the profession.

Theories on crisis communications basically explain why various techniques and tactics are or are not successful, whether the same techniques can be expected to work in future crises, and how the techniques can be altered to produce desired results.

Grunig and Grunig

Most of the crisis communications theories build on the public relations *excellence theory* developed by J. Grunig and Hunt (1984) and later expanded by J. Grunig and L. Grunig (1992). The excellence theory is based on types of public relations practices called "models." The four models defined by J. Grunig and Hunt provide a way of classifying the types of public relations that individuals and organizations may practice.

In a spectrum of excellence of public relations programs, Model 1 would be the least desirable. Model 4 would be the most desirable, or could be said to be the "most excellent." Models 2 and 3 fall between these two extremes.

Model 1—Press Agentry/Publicity Model. In this model, public relations practitioners are interested in making their organizations or

products known. They may or may not use truthful statements. False-hoods, half-truths, and incomplete facts are all permissible. The practition-ers' abiding slogan, "All publicity is good publicity," indicates a one-way transfer of information from the organization to the publics. Little or no re-search is required. There is no feedback.

J. Grunig and Hunt (1984) revealed that this model was used by 15% of public relations practitioners. Later, Grunig and Grunig (1992) found the earlier data to be inaccurate and reported that most public relations practi-tioners, unfortunately, still fall into this category.

As practitioners become more knowledgeable and as the profession of public relations grows in respect, the number of practitioners using this model is expected to decrease.

Model 2—Public Information Model. This model is characterized by the desire to report information journalistically. It is different from Model 1 in that truth is essential. Most public relations practice in govern-ment agencies today falls into this category. Companies that simply distrib-ute news releases are examples of this model. The practitioner is often called a *flack*.

This model also involves a one-way transfer of information from the or-ganization to the publics. Little or no research is required. There may be some type of evaluation, such as readership surveys or the counting of news clips. Model 2 is most common in corporations.

Model 3—Two-Way Asymmetric Model. In this model, also called the scientific persuasion model, the public relations practitioner uses so-cial science theory and research, such as surveys and polls, to help per-suade publics to accept the organization's point of view. There is some feedback, but the organization does not change as a result of communica-tions management. In asymmetric public relations programs of this type, the organization rules. It always knows best. Its attitude is that publics should adhere to the organization's viewpoints. An example of asymmetric action is a letter informing a public of a new policy or a recorded telephone message with no technology available for returning messages.

Model 4—Two-Way Symmetric Model. The public relations practi-tioner in this model, also called the mutual understanding model, is an in-termediary between the organization and its publics. The practitioner tries to achieve a dialogue, not a monologue as in the other models. Either man-agement or the publics may make changes in behavior as a result of the communications program.

Research and social science theory are used not to persuade but to communicate. Effective public relations programs based on this model are said to be "excellent" programs.

Symmetrical public relations programs negotiate, compromise, bargain, listen, and engage in dialogue. The organization knows what the publics want and need; the publics, in turn, understand the organization's needs and desires. An example is talking to consumers by telephone or at a public meeting in which the consumers can talk back and changes result.

In crises, organizations are frequently forced, by circumstances, to practice symmetrical communications with adversarial publics. Although most organizations practice Models 1 and 2, research by Grunig and Grunig (1992) revealed that PR practitioners would prefer to practice Model 4 if they had the expertise to do so and if their organizations were receptive to that practice.

The preceding classifications are not precise. An organization, for example, may practice Model 2 and Model 4. If the organization practices Model 2 more than Model 4, it is considered a Model 2 public relations operation.

Before turning to an in-depth discussion of theories, a few terms require definition:

Strategy—An approach on how one handles a problem.

Stakeholders—People who are linked to an organization or who have an interest in an organization and are affected by the decisions made by that organization. Examples of company stakeholders are employees, stockholders, communities, and government officials.

Strategic publics—Stakeholders who are crucial to an organization. The organization cannot function without them. Examples are boards of directors, investors, and unions.

Strategically managed public relations—Communications programs designed to build relationships with strategic publics, the crucial stakeholders of an organization.

Segmentation—The division of a market, population, or a large public into groups whose members are bound by mutual interests, concerns, and characteristics.

Risk communications—An ongoing program of informing and educating various publics (usually external publics) about issues that can affect, negatively or positively, an organization's success. The program builds solid relationships between an organization and its key publics, the publics on which an organization's survival depends. These relationships must be established prior to a crisis. It is too late after a crisis erupts.

Organizational ideology—An organization's philosophy, its working climate, its corporate culture. Each person's experience with the organization—no matter how small or large—puts him or her in contact with that organization's ideology, or corporate culture. The elements of that culture (such as norms of dress, formal rules, informal codes of conduct, taboos, jokes, language, etc.) make up an invisible, internalized whip that cracks and tells people what they can do, what they cannot do, what they can say, and what they cannot say in their dealings with the organization. Researchers disagree on whether organizational culture is harmonious or conflicting, consistent or inconsistent. Nevertheless, it is inescapable that the culture determines to some degree how people within the organization behave. Popular examples of organizational ideology include "Look busy whether you are or not" and "The boss is always right."

Johnson & Johnson (see chap. 6) relied on its organizational ideology in 1982 when, without a crisis management or communications plan, it followed its credo after several people died from poisoned Tylenol capsules. The company's executives credit the credo with getting it through the crisis. In contrast to most organizational ideologies, the credo was written—although it was very brief. More importantly, it was felt and practiced by employees and executives alike. The basic message was that the company had responsibilities to four groups: (1) consumers, (2) employees, (3) communities served by the company, and (4) stockholders.

Communications ideology—The organization's philosophy and attitudes of behavior in communicating with publics. Again, Johnson & Johnson's public relations program during the tampering case is an example. The company's basic rule in coping with the media, and thereby with the consuming public, was "open and honest information." It is difficult for a public relations department of a major corporation to have a communications ideology different from the organizational ideology. A productive public relations operation necessarily suffers from an unproductive organizational ideology and vice versa. (This is further examined in chap. 7, "Exxon and the Valdez Oil Spill.")

Grunig and Repper

J. Grunig and Repper (1992) identified theories on strategic management, publics, and issues as having two primary propositions. Both are conducive to a study of crisis communications programs:

1. Public relations is most likely to be excellent (contribute to organizational effectiveness) when it is an integral part of an organization's

strategic management process and when public relations is managed strategically.

2. Public relations is managed strategically when it identifies stakeholders (separates active publics from stakeholder categories) and resolves issues created by the interaction of organization and publics through symmetrical communications programs early in the development of issues.

These propositions mean that excellent public relations programs, as well as excellent crisis communications programs, have the following characteristics:

1. The public relations head is an important part of the top management of the organization.

2. Programs are designed to build relationships with all key stakeholders of an organization or company.

3. Public relations, through research, identifies who the organization's key stakeholders are and ranks them in order of importance. They may be customers, the media, employees, competitors, unions, special interest groups, vendors, suppliers, environmental groups, consumer advocates, and critics, to name a few.

4. An ongoing public relations plan is developed for each key stakeholder. This necessarily goes beyond media relations into a Model 4 program (two-way symmetrical program). These programs can sometimes prevent crises. At other times, they can help lessen the severity of crises.

5. In *segmentation*, public relations breaks down large publics into smaller subpublics with which it can communicate more effectively about issues or problems. These publics are usually, but not always, active rather than passive. Active publics seek out information and are more likely than passive publics to act on an issue. For example, if an organization wants to gear a program to all public schoolchildren, it might direct its program to the National Education Association or the American Federation of Teachers, organizations consisting of members who are educators and who can reach all public schoolchildren. Organizations that do not segment their stakeholders might send a news release to metropolitan newspapers hoping that teachers will read the article and communicate with children.

6. *Issues management* is part of a two-way symmetrical program that is best handled by the public relations department. (Although issues management is many times handled by public affairs or corporate communications departments, which are separate and apart from public relations departments that only handle media relations, Grunig and Repper's theory does not advise this separation.) A public makes an issue

when it perceives that a problem is brewing or already exists. In issues management, the public relations department anticipates the issues that are potential crises and ranks them in order of possible damage to the organization. Then strategies and tactics are developed and implemented to lessen the likelihood of crises. The crucial element here is early identification of potential crises, like treating a sniffle before it becomes the flu. The treatment might involve making allies with potential adversaries or meeting with community activists to explain a procedure that might be construed as damaging to consumers. Consequently, the odds are enhanced that an issue can benefit the organization rather than hamper it.

Marra

Marra (1992), in an attempt to build on and validate a model of excellent crisis public relations, suggested that organizations develop a theoretically based crisis public relations model that would allow practitioners to identify which variables could be adjusted to make a CCP work and which variables, if not adjusted, would cause it to fail. Marra argued that this knowledge can allow public relations practitioners to know before a crisis what will or will not work. He identified strategies and techniques common to excellent responses to crises with the following hypotheses:

1. An organization having strong and well-developed relationships with its key publics prior to a crisis will suffer less financial, emotional, or perceptive damage than organizations with weak and poorly developed relationships with its key publics prior to a crisis. Key publics would not only be the media, but also employees, customers, community members, and so forth.

2. Marra believed, as the Grunigs and Repper did, that organizations with weak pre-crisis relationships are those with asymmetrical practices; that is, Model 1, 2, or 3. Therefore, an organization that uses two-way symmetrical crisis communications procedures will suffer less financial, emotional, or perceptual damage than the Model, 1, 2, or 3 organization or the organization that uses silence as a crisis response.

3. An organization that establishes and puts into effect continuing risk communications activities and prepares CCPs prior to crises will have stronger relationships with key publics, use two-way symmetrical crisis public relations practices, and as a result suffer less financial, emotional, and perceptual damage than the organization that does not.

4. An organization with communication ideologies that encourage, support, and champion crisis management preparations, crisis communications plans and actions, and two-way symmetrical communications

practices will suffer less financial, emotional, and perceptual damage than the organization that does not.

Fearn-Banks

Two additional characteristics are suggested (Fearn-Banks, 1996):

1. An organization that anticipates, through crisis inventory (see chap. 2), the precise type of crisis will suffer less financial, emotional, and perceptual damage than the organization that does not.
2. An organization that maintains the reputation of having an overall "open and honest" policy with stakeholders and the news media will suffer less financial, emotional, and perceptual damage than the organization that does not. (This is a specific area covered broadly in Marra's fourth characteristic.)

SUMMARY

Various public relations and crisis communications theories suggest attributes and characteristics of programs that are likely either to prevent crises or enable organizations to recover from crises more swiftly than organizations without those characteristics.

Among these characteristics are strong relationships with publics (including the news media), the prominence of public relations within the organization, sound organizational culture, and preplanning for crises.

Persons with public relations savvy are likely to say, "This is obvious. People who are prepared should withstand a crisis better." Nevertheless, the likelihood of a crisis is not seen as obvious by many organizational heads. Most companies still do not plan for crises and take the attitude that "it hasn't happened, so it probably won't happen."

* * *

Answer to question on page 15. Crisis communications theories, so far, do not relate total sales, numbers of employees, education, and experience of PR practitioners, and quantity or quality of news releases to the probability of successful and swift conclusion of a crisis. Company B has ongoing two-way relationships with employees and customers who are key stakeholders. Considering that the PR department of Company A spends 80% of its time on news releases, it is unlikely that there is a two-way symmetrical relationship with strategic publics. Therefore, Company A, according to the theories studied in this chapter, is likely to suffer most from a crisis.

CHAPTER TWO

The Crisis Communications Plan

CRISIS INVENTORY

Before an organization can develop a crisis management plan (CMP) or a crisis communications plan (CCP), it must determine which crisis or crises the organization is most likely to face. A CCP's usefulness is directly associated with how specific it is to a particular type of crisis.

The workbook for this text takes the user through a step-by-step process of developing the CCP. Although there are several items in the plan that are mutual to all types of crises, varying information is needed for each type of crisis for maximum effectiveness. For example, a restaurant chain may decide that food poisoning and fire are its most probable crises. If a food poisoning crisis occurs, the media will want, and the public relations department should have, the following items readily available and in its CCP: recipes, a list of ingredients stocked, a list of vendors used, kitchen precautions and procedures, names and contact numbers of chefs and all other personnel handling food, and a list of medical experts for consultation and as spokespersons.

If a fire occurs, the public relations department should have, in a specific CCP, information about its evacuation procedures, its policy on using

nonflammable decor items (such as window coverings and tablecloths), the floor plan of the structure, and fire experts for spokespersons.

The following list enumerates common types of crises. There are, of course, numerous others. Companies and organizations are advised to consider the list carefully and add types of crises specific to their operations.

Common Types of Crises

acquisition	layoffs
age discrimination	merger
alcohol abuse	murder
bankruptcy	negative legislation
boycott	plant closing
bribery	product failure
chemical spill or leak	protest demonstrations
computer failure	racial issues
computer hacking	robbery
contamination	sexual discrimination
drug abuse	sexual harassment
drug trafficking	strikes
earthquake	suicide
embezzlement	takeover
explosion	tax problems
fatality	terrorism
fire	tornado
flood	toxic waste
hurricane	transportation accident
kickbacks	transportation failure
kidnapping	workplace violence
lawsuits	

Some crises will involve more than one of the types listed, such as "workplace violence" and "fatality," or "boycott" and "sexual discrimination."

Perhaps the involvement of the entire company or of representatives from each department can help determine the crises the company is likely to face. Then each unit's selections could be compared with and compiled into a company-wide list. When done properly, this can be an effective proactive employee relations program, a way of creating "*we*-ness," a way of including all of the employees in the company's decision making. Janitors, executive assistants, blue-collar and white-collar workers, midlevel executives, as well as top executives can have a say. After all, each employee stands to suffer if the company should go under after the most serious of crises. Furthermore, employees in each position classification have unique

perspectives on things that can go wrong. Janitors are more aware of heating and cooling equipment, possible gas leaks, and so on. Workers on an automobile assembly line know more about the quality of cars than managers in carpeted offices.

However, if a company-wide crisis identification program is not feasible, a meeting of key employees familiar with all facets of the operation can determine the crises the company is likely to face. Such a meeting should certainly include more than public relations staff members. You do not want the company blaming the public relations staff for the failure to recognize a possible crisis.

Frequently, ascertaining probable crises can point out problems that prevent crises from occurring. This is the primary reason for company-wide involvement. The second best reason is to be able to manage a crisis once it occurs.

Every company and organization can experience many types of crises. Two questions must be answered: (1) How likely is this crisis? And (2) how devastating can the crisis be? Crisis communications plans should be developed for all crises believed to be both most probable and most devastating. To do this, the public relations department, with its key executives, must take an inventory. Each possible crisis must be ranked as follows:

0—Impossible; that is, the crisis has basically no chance of occurring.

1—Nearly impossible.

2—Remotely possible.

3—Possible.

4—More than possible, somewhat probable; has happened to competitors or similar companies.

5—Highly probable; may or may not have previously occurred in the company, but warning signs are evident.

Each crisis also should be ranked according to its potential damage to the company. The rankings in this category are as follows:

0—No damage, not a serious consequence.

1—Little damage, can be handled without much difficulty, not serious enough for the media's concern.

2—Some damage, a slight chance that the media will be involved.

3—Considerable damage, but still will not be a major media issue.

4—Considerable damage, would definitely be a major media issue.

5—Devastating, front-page news, could put company out of business.

For added security, when in doubt, rank a crisis in the next highest category.

For instance, Company Z determines that there are five crises it could face: workplace violence, fire, protest demonstrations, negative legislation, and tax problems. Each of these crises might be ranked as shown in Table 2.1.

TABLE 2.1
Company Z's Ranking of Crisis Probability and Damage

Crisis Type	Probability	Damage
Workplace violence	4	5
Fire	3	4
Protest demonstrations	2	5
Negative legislation	5	2
Tax problems	2	3

Keep in mind that a crisis you determine to be unlikely simply because it never happened before can happen tomorrow. Both human nature and mother nature are very unpredictable, so natural disasters (e.g., earthquakes, floods, and hurricanes) and human failures (e.g., workplace violence, embezzlement, drug trafficking, and all kinds of discrimination) should be expected to some degree. Frequently, there are no warning signs.

After rankings for probability and damage are made, bar graphs should be made to clearly see and consider each crisis and compare it to others. (Bar graphing can be done on various computer programs or by hand.) At the base of each graph, write the name of each type of crisis (see Fig. 2.1). Plot the height of each bar according to numbers attributed to each crisis in the probability and damage rankings. Choose different colors or shadings for probability bars and damage bars.

When Company Z plots its data on a bar graph, it resembles Fig. 2.1. Considering Company Z's graph, we see that the probability and seriousness of a crisis relating to tax problems is not as crucial as in the other crises. This does not mean that a crisis plan is not important for tax problems, just not as important as for other issues, and not a priority.

According to the graph, the possibility of Company Z's suffering a crisis resulting from negative legislation is likely, though not particularly critical. On the other hand, protest demonstrations are critical, although not very likely. Workplace violence and fire seem both likely and critical.

Most organizations plan for crises ranked high in both probability and damage. In this case, Company Z would probably develop crisis management and communications plans for workplace violence first, then for the

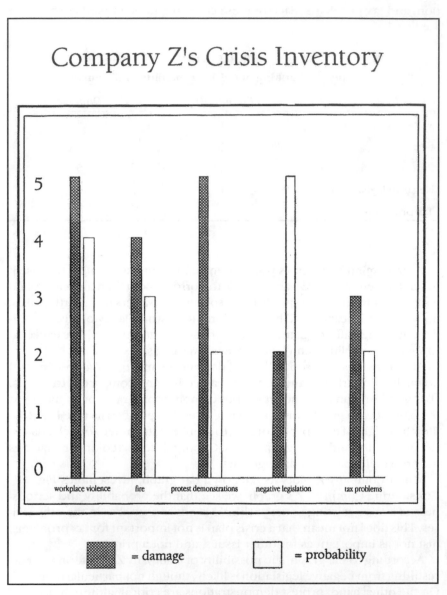

FIG. 2.1. A sample bar graph showing how an organization might assess the probability of and degrees of damage resulting from various types of crises.

other crises in descending order of importance: fire, protest demonstrations, negative legislation, and tax problems.

Sometimes organizations make crisis plans for the most devastating crises no matter how probable or improbable they may be. In this case, Company Z would develop plans for workplace violence first, followed by protest demonstrations, then fire. Naturally, a version of Murphy's Law can be expected: That crisis for which you have no plan will likely happen. Moreover, you will find that any plan, and the process of developing that plan, will make you more prepared for crises generally.

Some organizations, having several crises classified with similar rankings in all categories, make general CCPs with detailed information for all types of crises, although sometimes the detailed information is omitted.

Many companies, fearing all possibilities of crises equally, merely adopt a policy of "open and honest response" with the media and all publics, and plan to be in a total reactive mode during a crisis.

The importance of the crisis inventory is to force organizations to think about the possibilities. Sometimes the most ridiculous crisis occurs, something no one in the company could predict. Pepsi probably never dreamed that it would have a crisis of hypodermic syringes in its cans. On the other hand, Foodmaker and Jack-in-the-Box could certainly have anticipated children dying from eating hamburgers, and Exxon could have anticipated the worst oil slick in America.

The ranking procedure may introduce ideas for prevention programs. You also may realize that your organization is more vulnerable than you anticipated.

Considering that the toll of stress and emotion during a crisis necessarily affects one's thought processes, a carefully developed CCP is the best substitute for a fully functioning brain. Even if you remain cool and calm under pressure, others in the company may not. The CCP alleviates this problem, too.

DEVELOPING THE CRISIS COMMUNICATIONS PLAN

Once likely crises have been identified, the crisis communications plan can be written. A CCP can be part of a larger crisis management plan or it may be a stand-alone document to help public relations practitioners handle crises more effectively.

The CMP includes information such as evacuation procedures; emergency staffing of various departments of a company; and places to purchase or rent emergency equipment, tools, or vehicles—all the things a company may need in a crisis.

Public relations during a crisis focuses on communications with the company's publics during the crisis; for the most part, the same publics to which normal PR activities are directed.

The CMP is sometimes a large volume of instructions, whereas a CCP should be a more manageable, easier-to-read document. After a crisis has erupted, employees are likely to look at a large volume and say, "We don't have time to read this now," and then proceed to handle the crisis by "winging" it. The CCP should be organized in such a way that the practitioners can quickly turn to each section. Some professionals use tabs in a notebook; others use a table of contents. Keeping the CCP on a computer can be dangerous because many crises prevent access to offices (fire, earthquakes, explosives, etc.).

Many companies (such as Johnson & Johnson after the Tylenol crisis) urge employees to keep copies of the plan in various key spots—the office, at home, near the night stand, or in the car. That way, the odds are good that at least one copy will be readily available should a crisis or disaster occur.

If a crisis inventory determines, for example, that there are three likely crises, the organization should draft a CCP for each type. A plan for an earthquake must be different from a plan for a product failure. The publics may be different; the media may be different; the message must be different.

The CCP states purposes, policies, and goals, then assigns employees to various duties. It generally makes communication with publics faster and more effective and should help end the crisis more swiftly than without a plan.

When a CCP is ineffective, it is usually because the type of crisis was not anticipated or because variables arose that were not anticipated. For example, spokespersons or supplies may not be available. The CCP sometimes fails because it is outdated. Such plans should be updated regularly.

Even if unanticipated variables do arise, the CCP should be more effective than having no plan at all. Still, it must be remembered that a CCP is not a manual guaranteeing success, with everything done "by the book," but a guide that must be flexible.

An effective CCP should have the following components arranged in an order that best suits the organization and the particular crisis or disaster:

Cover page
Introduction
Acknowledgments
Rehearsal dates
Purpose and objectives
List of key publics
Notifying publics
Identifying the crisis communications team
Crisis directory

Identifying the media spokesperson
List of emergency personnel and local officials
List of key media
Spokespersons for related organizations
Crisis communications control center
Equipment and supplies
Pregathered information
Key messages
Web page
Trick questions
List of prodromes
List of related Internet URLs
Evaluation form

Cover Page

The cover page of a CCP is similar to the cover page of a term paper. There are as many ways of doing one as there are ways of doing crisis communications plans. It should include at least the date when the plan was written as well as revision dates.

Introduction

The head of the company or organization usually writes the introduction (or the PR practitioner ghostwrites it for the CEO with his or her approval). The purpose of this component is to persuade employees to take the CCP seriously. It stresses the necessity and importance of the plan and it emphasizes the dire results possible when a plan is not followed.

Acknowledgments

This CCP component takes the form of an affidavit signed by all crisis personnel as well as by key executives, indicating that they have read the plan and are prepared to put it into effect. The signatures assure management that its personnel have read the plan.

Rehearsal Dates

Dates of rehearsals for all crises are recorded here. The most damaging and most likely crises should be practiced at least annually if not every 6 months. Rehearsal for any type of crisis is helpful even if an eventual crisis turns out to be somewhat different.

Purpose and Objectives

The purpose statement details the organization's policies toward its publics. It might say, for example, "In a crisis, an open and honest disclosure with the media shall be stressed." The purpose is an expressed hope for a recovery and return to normalcy, to get out of the media. The objectives are responses to the question, "What do you hope to achieve with this plan?" Objectives should not be overly ambitious in difficulty or number. For example, a company may adopt the following goals:

1. To be seen in the media as a company that cares about its customers and employees.
2. To make certain that all communications are accurate.

List of Key Publics

The key publics list should include all publics, both external and internal, with which the organization must communicate during the crisis. The list varies with organizations, but may include the following as well as others:

board members
shareholders
financial partners
investors
community leaders
customers
clients
suppliers
vendors
neighbors of physical plant(s)
competitors
key management
employees
legal representation
media
union officials
retirees
government officials (city, state, county, federal)

Although all publics need not be notified in every crisis, the list of key publics should be comprehensive. It is easier to eliminate unneeded publics at the time of crisis than it is to think of all the crucial publics during the stress of a crisis.

Publics fall into the following categories:

Enabling publics—those people with the power and authority to make decisions: the board of directors, shareholders, investors, and key executives. Notifying enabling publics is a priority.

Functional publics—the people who actually make the organization work: employees, unions, suppliers, vendors, consumers, and volunteers in the case of nonprofit organizations.

Normative publics—those people who share values with the organization in crises: trade associations, professional organizations, and competitors.

Diffused publics—those people linked indirectly to the organization in crisis: the media, community groups, and neighbors of the physical plant.

Notifying Publics

In order to notify publics, a system must be devised for contacting each public, and that system should be described in the CCP. For internal publics, many companies use a chain procedure, such as a telephone tree, in which each person is specifically designated to call others. The person who learns about the crisis first notifies the CEO, the head of public relations, and the head of the department that may be involved. The chain should be clear and error-free, even in the event that certain individuals are not reached.

An appropriate means of notification must be decided on for each public. A news release, for example, is appropriate primarily for the news media, not for other publics.

Board members are often reached by telephone or fax. E-mail or other computerized communications are also used. The media can be notified by way of telephone, wire service, fax, press conference, e-mail, or news release. Other methods used for notifying publics include telegrams, personal visits, letters, advertisements, bulletin boards, and meetings (see Fig. 2.2).

Identifying the Crisis Communications Team

The crisis communications team members, along with backups, should be preselected. The team manager is usually, but not always, the head of public relations. He or she has specific responsibilities: communicating with top management, making decisions, drafting or approving major statements, and notifying the rest of the crisis communications team.

YOUR COMPANY

MESSAGE: There has been an explosion in the plant. There are injured employees. We do not know, at this time, the cause of the explosion or the extent of injuries of the employees. An investigation is underway.

Methods of Communication

	TELEPHONE	E-MAIL	FAX	LETTER BY MESSENGER	LETTER BY MAIL	NEWSLETTER	BULLETIN BOARD	PERSONAL VISIT	NEWS RELEASE	MEETINGS
EMPLOYEES		• J. Naas				• J. Naas	• J. Naas			
EXECUTIVES	• Nelson J.	• Nelson J.						• Nelson J. M. Yerima		• Nelson J.
CUSTOMERS					• Damian L.					
BOARD OF DIRECTORS	• Nelson J.			• Damian L.					•Gina A.	
ELECTRONIC MEDIA	• K. Stone		• K. Stone						•Gina A.	
DAILY NEWSPAPERS	• Gina A.								•Gina A.	
WEEKLY NEWSPAPERS			• Gina A.		• Damian L.					
SHARE HOLDERS		• Ann C.				• Ann C.				
COMMUNITY LEADERS			• Karen N.			• Karen N.				

P
U B
L
I
C
S

* Staff member responsible for communications and followup.

FIG. 2.2. A sample chart showing how an organization might plan to communicate with key publics during a crisis. It includes key talking points and ways of communicating. The lists of publics and types of communication can be longer, shorter, or otherwise different depending on the organization's needs.

The *assistant crisis manager* assumes responsibility when the manager is unavailable (a second backup may be beneficial, if possible). The control room coordinator sets up the room with necessary furniture, equipment, supplies, and tools. An efficient executive assistant can be appointed for this position.

Other PR personnel have the responsibilities of preparing news releases and statements, contacting the media, and reporting all actions to the crisis communications manager. These people may notify employees or volunteers through letters or by writing telegrams to the mayor and governor, by telephoning union officials and others, and so forth.

Crisis Directory

The company should prepare a crisis directory, listing all members of the crisis team, key managers in the company, and key publics or organizations, along with titles, business and home telephone numbers, cellular phone numbers, fax and e-mail addresses, as well as business, home, and vacation addresses. It is also helpful to list the phone numbers of friends, neighbors, and relatives who are frequently in contact with persons crucial to the crisis recovery.

The crisis team should be large enough to get the job done, but no larger. Too many people make it difficult to get tasks completed and decisions made. There is no time in a crisis for egos; each person must be a team player. It is also preferable that crisis team members be generally healthy and capable of working under stress. They should be reliable professionals, whether gofers, interns, or assistants.

Identifying the Media Spokesperson

The media spokesperson must be selected carefully. To the public, this person *is* the company or organization.

Actually, sometimes several persons are spokespersons. This is an arguable point in the public relations profession. Some argue for one spokesperson per crisis, usually the CEO. Others argue for several spokespersons, depending on area of expertise. Clearly, the decision is a matter of what suits the company and type of crisis best.

Even if the CEO is an effective spokesperson, he or she may not be particularly knowledgeable about a technical aspect of the crisis. For example, during an oil spill, the company CEO is not the only important spokesperson; also needed is a person qualified to talk about what will be necessary for the cleanup. Frequently, university professors are called on for their specific knowledge about technical aspects of a crisis and for their credibility.

Another school of thought is that CEOs have no credibility because they have too much to lose. However, if lives are lost or in danger—including the lives of animals—most professionals agree that the company head must be the chief spokesperson.

In all cases, at least one, and preferably two or three, backup spokespersons should be preselected in case the preferred person is unavailable at the time of the crisis. Crises can occur when people are on vacation, on business trips, or sick with the flu. When the 1989 San Francisco earthquake struck, for example, the first two designated spokespersons for the Pacific Gas and Electric Company were at the World Series game at Candlestick Park. The third spokesperson on the list was called and pressed into service.

An effective crisis spokesperson must have some position in the company. It is usually not the PR head, even if the PR person is normally the company's spokesperson. The spokesperson must also be articulate, powerful enough to make decisions, accessible throughout the crisis, able to talk clearly in concise sound bites, and pleasant to the eye of a camera. Moreover, the spokesperson in a crisis must appear rational, concerned, and empathetic. He or she should be pretrained, rehearsed well in advance of the crisis, and briefed prior to the crisis response. The organization's legal adviser should be consulted before statements are made.

If the public relations department is a small or one-person operation, it may be beneficial to have capable, trustworthy volunteers to perform some tasks. Outside public relations firms that specialize in crisis planning and handling might be used. A nonprofit organization can often get PR firms to help pro bono (done or donated without charge). Many nonprofit organizations have PR practitioners on their boards of directors, anticipating the need for their assistance during a crisis.

At times, one person may be required to perform all communications roles. On the other hand, in large companies several people may perform each role.

List of Emergency Personnel and Local Officials

If the crisis is a disaster or emergency, various emergency personnel need to be contacted. A list should be made of contact numbers for police, fire officials, hospitals, the health department, utilities, and paramedics.

If the crisis affects large numbers of people or is a threat to the safety of people, government officials must be contacted. This list should include contact information for the mayor, governor, city council members, county officials, state legislators, and U.S. senators and representatives.

Sometimes union officials must be notified and therefore should be listed, as well as key citizens groups and community organizations.

List of Key Media

After key executives are called, the media are the next most important public to notify of the crisis. A list of media contacts—newspapers, television, radio, wire services—should be completed and listed in order of importance. If particular editors or reporters are important to telling the story to the organization's benefit, a list of their home numbers and emergency numbers will be advantageous.

The media list should contain contact information for morning and afternoon metropolitan dailies, certain weeklies, all TV news stations, the Associated Press, United Press International, Reuters, all radio news stations, and trade publications.

Spokespersons for Related Organizations

If an organization suffers a severe crisis, there may be spokespersons outside the organization who may be questioned. It may be effective to make a list of who these people might be and of how to contact them at any time of day. It also might be effective to meet with them so that they are familiar with your company; with how you will handle a crisis, if it occurs; and with how to reach you.

Sometimes other spokespersons have information you don't have. This information may help you communicate more effectively. So, you need to be able to reach them. Since most people have cell phones, this could be a simple task.

In the case in chapter 17, involving a bus accident and shooting, the news media interviewed the public information officers for the bus company, the police department, the fire department, the hospitals, and spokespersons for county and city officials. The bus company spokesman learned from the news media that a gun was found on one of the victims, and had to scramble to get to the police to find the information. In this case, the spokespersons got together at the site of the accident and determined that they would refer the media's questions to one particular spokesperson. If, instead, the spokespersons had exchanged cell phone numbers, e-mail addresses, or home phone numbers prior to the crisis, they would have been aware of what procedure to follow regarding the media spokesperson.

Crisis Communications Control Center

The location of the crisis communications control center must be determined in case regular office space is unavailable. After disasters and emergencies, offices are often damaged, without power, or they are inaccessible.

Several possible sites should be listed in the CCP, as well as the persons instrumental in gaining access to these locations. Suppose, for example, a local church has offered its conference room. Who gave permission to use the room? Who can unlock the doors of the church and conference room? Does the permission include use of electrical outlets and furniture? Does the site have adequate space for the media to work?

Equipment and Supplies

Determine and list all of the equipment and supplies needed by the crisis team, media, and visiting publics. The list could include, but is not limited to, the following:

chairs and desks

bulletin boards

flip charts and chalkboards

computers or typewriters (perhaps manual typewriters in case power is a problem)

computer printers

telephones and cellular phones

battery-powered televisions and radios

maps of the plant or crisis area

battery-powered flashlights and lamps

police radios

walkie-talkies

company letterhead, pens, and pencils

telephone directories

contact lists and media directories

press kits

CMPs and CCPs

street and highway maps

food and beverages

copying machine(s)

first-aid kits

cameras and film

extension cords and generator power packs

Pregathered Information

Prepare and gather various documents that may possibly be needed during a crisis. Keep identical sets of documents in various locales to ensure availability. The types of documents that can be gathered in advance include

safety records and procedures, annual reports, photos, company backgrounders, executive biographies, company maps, branch office locations, quality control procedures, product manufacturing procedures, and company fact sheets (including such data as numbers of employees, products manufactured, and markets served).

Skeletal news releases can be prepared as long as the PR practitioner anticipates the type of crisis and can make a statement on behalf of the company. As shown in Fig. 2.3, a news release can be written in advance with blank spaces left for data to be filled in (such as the magnitude of the crisis and relevant dates and names).

Key Messages

Under the stress of a crisis, it is easy to forget, or at least fail to state properly, the main points you want to convey to publics or to a specific public. Even when there is no crisis, experienced spokespersons prepare in advance the primary information they want emphasized in what are called key messages or speaking points.

The act of preparing key messages will help you organize your thoughts and will provide consistent information to publics. Each message must be accurate, brief, easy to use in a quote, and memorable. The spokesperson must be easily able to work the key message into responses to questions. Such messages also help reporters—looking for great quotes—to do their jobs.

Effective key messages help avoid misquoting, enable the spokesperson to tell his or her side of the story, and give the spokesperson a way to answer trick questions comfortably. Most of all, they establish credibility for the organization in crisis.

Web Page

Placing news on the organization's Web site and preappointing Webmasters to keep updated information on the site will reduce both the number of phone calls from publics and the amount of time put into crisis recovery. The news put on the site should be brief or detailed depending on the nature of the crisis. In the event of an airplane crash, for example, the airline's Web site would, at first, merely acknowledge the crash. After families of victims are notified, the names of victims would be listed. Regular notices of progress in the investigation would also be posted.

The concern of the company should be expressed and prominently displayed. A statement from the highest executive in the company is expected by the public. The Web site is an ideal venue for keeping safety rules, security precautions, and health policies posted. Restaurants might keep information posted on training new employees about cooking burgers at the proper temperature, using gloves when handling food, or policies that dis-

NEWS RELEASE

For Immediate Release

Date _____

Contact: _____
<center>(name/phone number)</center>

_____ (name of celebrity) DIES

(SEATTLE) _____ (full name and title) _____ died today of _____ (cause of death) at _____ (time of death) _____ at Swedish Hospital Medical Center in Seattle. He/She was _____ (age).

 Further details will be released by _____(name of person to make announcement—family member or professional contact) _____ at a news conference scheduled for _____ (time of news conference), at Swedish Hospital, Glaser Auditorium, 747 Summit Ave.

FIG. 2.3. A sample fill-in-the-blanks news release.

courage employees with colds and other infectious diseases from working with food products.

The Web site is also a bulletin board for informing publics of the organization's community relations projects and other activities that give back to the public. The Web site can afford your organization the opportunity to be a Model 4, two-way symmetric company (see chap. 1). It can encourage feedback, comments, and questions from publics and provide publics with responses and explanations. Finally, the Web site can reveal how the company is making changes as a result of public comment.

Trick Questions

When a crisis occurs, what questions can you predict the news media will ask a spokesperson? Check chapter 5 for types of trick questions. Reporters may not ask certain questions intentionally to trick the spokesperson, but the end result—if a question is not answered carefully—can make the spokesperson and his or her organization look bad.

A spokesperson for a restaurant, for example, might be asked the following trick questions:

1. Off the record, didn't you know this might happen?
2. If the fire happened during the lunch hour, how many people might have been killed?
3. Don't you buy your ground beef from the meatpacker who sold bad meat to the other restaurant?
4. As at most popular restaurants, the work here is very fast-paced and stressful, right?

List of Prodromes

Prodromes are the warning signs that a crisis may occur. List these in the CCP. If any of the prodromes actually happened, log into the plan what the company did in response and when. This helps the spokesperson answer the media question, "Did you have any warning that this might happen?"

As an example of a prodrome, consider the normally good employee who is unusually tardy and seems stressed out and irritable. Management notices the problem and gets help for the employee. Or take another example: several near-accidents in the organization's parking lot. Management takes notice, determines that the parking lot has confusing directional signs, and has the signs redone.

Heeding prodromes carefully can often prevent a crisis and help show that the organization is concerned with resolving problems. The prodromes section of the CCP should be regularly updated.

List of Related Internet URLs

List the URLs of organizations and companies that may have information you need during a crisis. Also include brief descriptions of the data available at the URLs. For example, a restaurant might list the URLs for the National Center for Infectious Diseases, the state department of health, the Food and Drug Administration, and the Center for Disease Control.

Evaluation Form

Evaluation is a crucial step in preparing an effective CCP. As assessment, it is helpful in determining what did and did not work. It also helps plan for, prevent, and cope with future crises by pointing out what needs to be revised in the CCP.

An evaluation form should be developed and placed at the end of the CCP for later distribution of internal publics for input. An environment where suggestions are made freely will add to the effectiveness of the evaluation and CCP.

CHAPTER THREE

Crisis Makers

What causes a crisis? Human failure, terrorism, nature, equipment failure. Any number of things can be the cause. We look at two causes here—rumor and various television news phenomena referred to as "gotcha" journalism, "checkbook" journalism, newsmongers, and the "nonexpert expert."

Although television news programs featured investigative and consumer protection pieces for years, beginning in the 1990s "gotcha journalism" became popular on nonnews talk shows and in TV news departments with experienced investigative units. These programs are often "out to get you" for entertainment and ratings. Television shows that pay handsomely for a juicy story, such as an interesting consumer-protection-type attack, have come to be called "checkbook journalism" because critics believe the participants will say anything if they are paid enough money.

Also beginning in the 1990s, news programs resorted to sensationalism, or newsmongering, in their quest for higher ratings and in the battle for viewers. The term *yellow journalism* used to be applied to such practices.

Rumor is studied because it can happen to anyone; there is often no explanation of why it happened or who started the rumor. Rumors can cause the longest and most damaging of crises. Even outrageous rumors endure or repeat, and they are difficult to battle.

RUMOR

Did you hear?

Children are being kidnapped at K-Mart stores.

Mikey, the little boy in the Life cereal commercials, died after he drank a carbonated beverage containing General Mills' Pop Rocks, an "exploding" candy.

Designer Liz Claiborne, during an appearance on *Oprah,* told viewers that 30% of her profits go to the Church of Satan. Then the video transmission blacked out and when it was restored, Claiborne was gone.

Corona Beer has urine in it.

Procter & Gamble's man-in-the-moon and stars logo was a disguised way of demonstrating the "666" devil-worshiping sign and represented the company's alliance with Satan.

All of the rumors just mentioned are unfounded, untrue rumors. K-Mart is not a kidnapping center. The little boy who played Mikey is an adult. Liz Claiborne never made that statement and Oprah never zapped her off the air. Corona Beer is good and urine-free. Procter & Gamble's logo, which had existed in slightly different designs for over 100 years, was not at all connected with Satanists.

Rumors can spread throughout the United States, turn stomachs, perpetuate negative images, and cost millions of dollars in lost revenue. Corporations have to fight in the press, in the courts, and, in the case of Procter & Gamble, in the churches to stop the rumors.

Incidentally, Procter & Gamble's woes were caused by religious fanatics. The company eventually gave up the battle and altered the logo on its products (Wilcox, Ault, & Agee, 1989).

The Nature of Rumor

Crises can, and often do, begin with rumors. In fact, a crisis can actually be a negative rumor. "Deep-sixing" rumors is an important task in crisis control and crisis communications.

A *rumor* is information usually passed by word of mouth with no verification of fact and no credible source. Rumors can be positive or negative. They can be absolutely false or partly false, or they can be undeniably true or premature facts. "There's a ring of truth in every rumor"—because people know and believe that expression, they tend to believe there is truth in rumors that are patently false and even ridiculous.

A rumor can begin as in the children's game "Gossip" (or "Telephone"), in which Child 1 whispers something to Child 2, who repeats it to Child 3, and so on. By the time the message reaches Child 10, it is usually unrelated to the original message. This is rumor spread innocently, but rumor can also be spread maliciously and intentionally.

The victim of malicious rumor rarely knows how the rumor started or who has heard it. This makes it difficult to curtail its spreading, which happens quickly and often with disastrous consequences.

How Rumors Start

One of the difficulties in establishing the source of a rumor is the realization that each person who passes it on may change it and thus be a contributing part of its source. The sources usually cited for rumors are rarely the actual sources. The rumors themselves may cite a specific person or institution that sounds credible, but the source is not readily available for verification. For example, the teller of a rumor might say, "I read it in last week's paper!" "What paper?" we ask. Not many people will go back and look for an article in last week's newspaper, especially considering that "last week" is also a vague term. Or the rumor teller may insist, "My aunt in Chicago was there when it happened!" This sounds convincing. But who will call the aunt and get specific details? Is there really an aunt at all?

In a psychological study of how rumors start, Ralph Rosnow of Temple University asked research assistants to start a rumor that students in one class were caught smoking marijuana during a final examination. Later, students were interviewed and asked if they believed the story and if they had passed it on. Research revealed that the students who most believed the rumor were more likely to pass it on. Those who did not believe the rumor did not pass it on (as cited in Goleman, 1991).

Rumors are often started innocently. This was the case when comedian Johnny Carson on his late-night show told a joke about a shortage of bathroom tissue. People heard about the shortage but not that it was a joke. There was a run on bathroom tissue in grocery stores. Soon the shelves were empty; the stock was depleted. This rumor was merely annoying to grocery stores and customers who remained tissueless.

However, some innocently started rumors can cause real damage. For instance, consider the Cable News Network (CNN) story about the Individual Retirement Account (IRA) that cited McDonald's as an example of corporations contributing to employee IRAs. In Great Britain, that story circulated as a rumor that said that McDonald's supported the Irish Republican Army—also called the IRA. Members of parliament received numerous letters attacking McDonald's for financing attacks on British soldiers and civilians.

How Rumors Spread

A rumor spreads because people believe it is news and because the "news" has some emotional relationship to their lives. The rumor somehow seems plausible. Often the rumor refers to something causing distress or fear, and the rumor tellers who spread it are hoping to relieve their fear or distress by giving a reasonable explanation or denial.

Dr. Allan J. Kimmel, of Fitchburg State College, in Massachusetts, studied 229 college students. The students passed on rumors about AIDS because they were personally relevant and upsetting. "The more frightened people were by a rumor, the more likely they were to repeat it," Kimmel said. "In repeating something that makes you nervous, you may learn some contrary fact that will calm you. On the other hand, it can escalate your fears if the person you tell believes it" (as cited in Goleman, 1991, p. C1).

Rumors are also spread because people distrust the "establishment"— organizations, governments, and big corporations—or because the rumor tellers want to be thought of as people "in-the know." Information is power. Telling rumors may give people who feel they lack power a sense that they are powerful. Therefore, people who have trouble making a success of their lives and careers are most likely to believe and spread rumors.

Types of Rumor

There are six various types of rumor. The *intentional rumor* is started to achieve a purpose. The financial community thrives on intentional rumor. There are rumors to make stocks rise and rumors to make them decline. People might start rumors to help their own businesses. For example, a young, aggressive manager of a new restaurant getting off to a slow start in a campus community started a rumor at the college—that a famous rock star was related to the owner and that the rock star *might* drop in that night. Needless to say, business boomed that evening, with patrons hoping to see the celebrity who never showed up. When patrons asked if the rock star would show up, the manager responded, "You never know." He offered each patron who asked a free drink. No one left angry. The manager said the ploy was a marketing technique to get people into the restaurant for the first time. He felt the food, the ambiance, and the service would get them back in the future.

The *premature-fact rumor* is an early version of what will eventually become the truth. In the workplace, for example, employees might hear and pass on rumors about layoffs that eventually turn out to be fact. Denying this type of rumor can be more damaging than being silent.

The *malicious rumor* is often started to damage competitors' businesses. For example, someone says, "The stew in the restaurant across the street is

made up of last week's leftovers." This rumor may or may not be true. It may be true of half of the restaurants in town. Yet when told to the right people at the right time, the rumor spreads and causes a decline in patronage.

The *outrageous rumor* is so unbelievable that people react by saying, "It has to be true! Who would create such a story?" The Snapple Beverage Company was the target in 1993 of an outrageous rumor that claimed the *k* on its product labels, which stood for "kosher," actually stood for Ku Klux Klan.

The *nearly true rumor* is so named because it is partly true. People hear it, attach credibility to a part of the story, and then draw a conclusion that the entire rumor must be true. This could have been the case when in the early 1990s a rumor circulated nationally that Reebok, during apartheid, was manufacturing and selling its products in South Africa. This was a crisis for Reebok because the company featured African American athletes in its commercials and marketed to African American consumers. It was true that Reebok once had manufacturing plants in South Africa, but the plants had been closed in 1986.

The *birthday rumor* is one that continues to emerge over and over again. It is as regular as birthdays.

The six primary categories of rumors can overlap. The outrageous rumor may also be malicious. The premature-fact rumor may be intentional, and so forth. One rumor that fits both the nearly true and the birthday categories is the ancient rumor that Chinese restaurants cook dogs. It is true that in China dogs are a delicacy, but that does not mean that owners of Chinese restaurants in the United States are out hunting your pets. This rumor can be traced to the 1850s in the United States and even earlier in Great Britain. The same rumor has now been told of Vietnamese cuisine in Texas, Mexican cuisine in southern California, and Native American cuisine in Wisconsin (Goleman, 1991).

Fighting Rumor

Step-by-step instructions on what to do in the case of rumors is difficult, if not impossible, to provide. Variables such as potential damage, geographic location, type of organization affected, the nature of the rumor, and what crucial publics are affected require each organization's response to be tailored to the situation.

However, some general suggestions can be given for avoiding a crisis brought on by rumors as well as for fighting rumors that are already circulating. Be mindful, nevertheless, that this is not an exact science. Some of the suggestions are conflicting because there are various schools of thought on how to handle the problem.

The following suggestions are general steps organizations may take to minimize the chances of a crisis caused by rumor:

1. Because the victim of a rumor is often the last to hear it, you could establish a rumor center in which various employees or volunteers enlist supporters to be on the alert for rumors.

2. Conduct rumor workshops prior to the circulation of rumors to advise personnel on what actions should be taken in the event of a damaging rumor. Consider what rumors might be most damaging to your organization or company. Study rumors that have caused problems for companies similar to your own.

3. Make sure your company has such strong positive relationships with its key publics that the publics would at least doubt a negative rumor, if not totally disbelieve it.

4. Keep employees informed. Employees left in the dark are fertile ground for the growth of rumors commonly spread by "the grapevine." Even if events that are bad news, such as layoffs, are a possibility in the near future, give employees real information and promise to keep them up to date. This is more advantageous than letting rumors circulate, because the rumors take on imagined and more negative characteristics than the truth. Informed employees can be a company's strongest supporters and loudest defenders.

McDonald's followed this advice when a rumor circulated that there were worms in its hamburgers. It was a well-known rumor that had plagued Wendy's earlier. It did not matter that worms cost more than ground beef per pound; the rumor continued to circulate. McDonald's personnel, on a one-to-one basis with patrons who asked, denied the presence of worms. In addition, the employees recorded the names and phone numbers of those patrons. The strategy was intended to make customers knowledgeable about the company and, therefore, less likely to spread the rumor.

The following suggestions are general steps organizations may take to fight a negative rumor that is already circulating:

1. When a rumor seems to be developing or circulating, disseminate to publics complete, accurate information that is contradictory to the message of the rumor. Do not mention the rumor itself. You do not want to advance its circulation. Your information should imply strongly that the rumor is untrue. This may reduce exposure to the rumor. Be advised, however, that fewer people are likely to see the positive news than the negative news.

2. After a rumor has circulated, analyze it. What is its probable origin? Why was it started? What is its possible impact? Will it go away? Will it mushroom? Where is it centered? Is it national or confined to a particular city or area?

3. Do nothing. Sometimes denial draws more attention than silence. Some rumors do go away. When choosing this strategy, be careful that, if the rumor persists, it will not be damaging.

Gerber Products chose to hang tough and be silent in 1986 when a grocery store charged that a customer had found a fragment of glass in a baby food jar. Gerber's test lab found no traces of glass in the jar, and the store had lost the fragment supposedly found in it. The Food and Drug Administration tested 40,000 unopened jars of Gerber baby food and concluded that no glass existed. Gerber relied on its state-of-the-art equipment designed to filter out any foreign objects larger than four thousandths of an inch. It also X-rayed for possible breakage in the production line. There was no proof that there was glass in the jar. Gerber felt it had proved the rumor false. Although the rumor continued to spread all over the united States, Gerber stood tough on refusing a recall. The rumor eventually died, and Gerber recovered sales, something the company felt it could not have done had there been a recall.

4. Deny the rumor publicly and vehemently, and prove it has no basis in truth. Once the rumor is shown to be unsubstantiated, a person who passes it on might be challenged with, "That is absolutely untrue. I know because …." However, if the rumor is already widespread and potentially serious, a news conference is in order. The purpose is to show how erroneous the rumor is. However, in this news conference, do not repeat the rumor itself unnecessarily.

Popeye's Fried Chicken chain called a news conference when a rumor circulated in Louisiana, claiming that its founder and chairman, Al Copeland, supported former Ku Klux Klan leader David Duke in a political campaign. There were 70 Popeye's restaurants in Louisiana at the time and 900 nationwide. At the news conference, Copeland denied vociferously that he had ties to Duke. To prove the rumor false, he proclaimed his longtime support of Duke's opponent, a point that could be easily disproved if it were not true. He also offered a $25,000 reward for information leading to the source of the rumor and posted the reward signs in his restaurants. The rumor subsided.

Remember that a simple denial is not as interesting or as juicy as the original rumor. Just saying it's not so is boring. Rumormongers expect you to deny it. Why would you admit something so negative? Your denial must be persuasive and convincing.

5. To be convincing, get an outside expert on the subject to discredit the rumor. The expert should be a person with strong credentials who speaks with authority—a university professor, a leading physician, or some other professional.

6. Place ads in high-circulation publications. This is a powerful tool for reaching great numbers of people—if your message is convincing. If

the message is not convincing, the ad may promote the rumor. Before placing an ad, be sure the rumor is totally untrue, not premature. In the latter case, ads can cause more harm than good.

A successful use of ads to fight a negative, unfounded rumor happened when the Life Saver Company encountered a rumor that spider eggs were found in Bubble Yum, a brand of bubble gum that was breaking sales records at the time. After conducting surveys that showed more than half of the children in New York had heard the rumor, the company placed an ad in newspapers with this headline: "Somebody is telling very bad lies about a very good product." The rumors faded. Bubble Yum remained a best-seller.

Some companies use a combination of tactics to fight damaging rumors. Reebok, in its battle against the rumor of doing business in South Africa, purchased ads in more than 200 African American publications, publicized liaisons with major human rights and anti-apartheid organizations, and distributed a brochure to college students containing statements of support from African American leaders. Its chairman wrote op-ed articles and co-hosted the Boston visit of Nelson Mandela.

"GOTCHA" TELEVISION JOURNALISM

Whereas rumor as a source of crises is as old as humankind itself, "gotcha" journalism, often not true journalism at all, is a relatively new source of crises, emerging in the 1990s on television news shows and talk shows. Unlike the reputable investigative news teams that have been doing consumer protection pieces for years, "gotcha" journalism has a new irresponsibility: a drive to entertain the viewer more than to protect the consumer. Because most Americans get their news from television, "gotcha" journalism is a feared source of crisis even for reputable organizations and businesses.

60 Minutes

In 1968, the grandfather of television newsmagazines, "60 Minutes," made its debut. Called "the *Time Magazine* of the Air," it was the first national news program to earn consistently high Nielsen ratings. It is still the premier newsmagazine show, usually in the weekly top 10, and often the highest-rated prime-time show.

A popular feature of "60 Minutes," even in the early years, was its investigative "in-your-face" journalism. Anchors Morley Safer, Dan Rather, Mike Wallace, and others would zero in on a company or organization that had taken advantage of consumers. The investigative practices of the show were considered careful and responsible.

For years "60 Minutes" viewers took pleasure in watching company heads sweat and stumble over explanations. As the camera zoomed in for a close-up of the terrified subject's twitching face, viewers were gratified and comforted to know that television was a watchdog for consumer rights and fairness.

The show still does occasional investigative consumer protection pieces, but somehow it is not so comforting anymore to watch people on the hot seat. Television is now more of an attack dog than a watchdog. There are many programs that thrive on the destruction of individuals, organizations, and companies, and they are doing it for entertainment and high ratings. Sometimes they ruin the lives of innocent people and the businesses of innocent companies in the process. We do not have the confidence in these shows that we have had in "60 Minutes."

Of course, this does not mean that "60 Minutes" had never been guilty of faulty journalism. Washington apple growers will tell you about one incident in 1989 in which a "60 Minutes" investigation based on unscientific evidence cost them about $140 million in loss of sales (Seitel, 1992). The investigative piece cited a study that declared that Alar, an ingredient used in red apple production, caused children to develop cancer later in life. Needless to say, the sale of red apples nearly stopped. Schools removed them from lunch menus. Grocers removed them from their produce departments. Parents were enraged.

The media went into a frenzy, and the issue was covered widely by newspapers, magazines, and the broadcast media. In the meantime, the American Council on Health and Science said publicly that it thought the threat of cancer had been exaggerated. Biochemists at the University of California, Berkeley, said that experts in both toxicology and epidemiology concluded that the amount of carcinogens present in Alar was too infinitesimal to be a threat. No case was ever made against Alar by the government protection agencies.

In 1994, Mike Wallace and a "60 Minutes" news producer were reprimanded by CBS for poor judgment when they secretly taped an interview with another journalist by placing a camera in draperies. Wallace apologized on camera when the segment aired.

"Gotcha" journalism exists in numerous television newsmagazines. As one business owner said, "The only thing worse than '60 Minutes' coming to visit is '20/20' coming to visit." Consultants tell news producers that news programs must be dramatic and exciting to get viewer's attention. Some manufacture the drama, and this is where irresponsibility, poor journalism, and sensationalism enter the picture.

"Dateline NBC," a network newsmagazine, was widely criticized in 1992 for rigging a General Motors truck to explode in one of its consumer protection pieces. Conversely, "Dateline NBC" performed an admirable task

in September 1994 when it criticized the news media's practices regarding President Clinton. In May of that year, the president had been slaughtered by the media for getting a haircut from Beverly Hills hairdresser extraordinaire, Christophe. The complaints were twofold: (1) The presidential haircut took place aboard Air Force One while it was parked on a runway at Los Angeles Airport, thereby causing traffic delays; and (2) the haircut was a frivolous expense to taxpayers. According to the "Dateline NBC" report, the *Washington Post* ran 59 stories about the president's "bad hair day," nine of which appeared on the front page. NBC News mentioned the incident 20 times; other news outlets reported similarly.

The criticism in the "Dateline NBC" update resulted from an investigation by a reporter for *New York Newsday*, who discovered that the president's haircut caused no flight delays, except for an unscheduled air taxi that was delayed for 2 minutes, and that the haircut had cost less than $50 ("Cutting It Close," 1994).

Walter Cronkite partially blamed television newsmagazines for the deterioration of television journalism. He called them an inexpensive way to "give a semblance of public responsibility without bothering with the vast expense of original news gathering" (Rottenberg, 1994, p. 36).

"Checkbook" Journalism and Newsmongers

In the 1980s, the tabloid shows premiered and subsequently were blamed for changing the direction of television news programs. "Entertainment Tonight" first aired in 1981, with celebrity gossip presented in a newscast format. It never pretended to be anything but entertainment, but it looked like news.

Then in 1986, "A Current Affair" premiered on the Fox Network. Although it claimed to be a newsmagazine, the show was a televised version of a supermarket tabloid. Not so coincidentally, Rupert Murdoch, owner of Fox, also owned the tabloid newspaper *Star*.

"Hard Copy" and "Inside Edition" followed in 1989. Both were successful. In 1994, each reached more than six million viewers nightly. Both did investigative pieces. "Hard Copy" vowed to do even more in its 1994–1995 season. These shows and others that have followed are not known for responsible journalism, but they are known for sensationalism and "checkbook" journalism, wherein interview subjects are often paid in the hundreds of thousands of dollars.

Cronkite blamed tabloids for part of the whole degeneration of society: "We've always known you can gain circulation or viewers by cheapening the product, and now you're finding the bad drives out the good" (Rottenberg, 1994, p. 36). In other words, television newscasts attempt to boost ratings by adopting characteristics of tabloid shows: re-created news, sleaze, unconfirmed sources, and misleading teasers. It has become difficult to know where news ends and entertainment begins as a result.

The "Non-Expert Expert"

In the early 21st century, there are innumerable talk shows. The expression "Everyone will be famous for 15 minutes" almost seems to be true. Most of the people who will enjoy 15 minutes of fame will enjoy it as a host or guest on a talk show.

"Meet the Press" is the "high brow" of the talk–interview shows. Then there are the white-collar talk shows such as "Larry King Live." The average viewer of these shows is probably not as informed as the average "Meet the Press" viewer but is considerably more informed than viewers of the blue-collar talk shows such as "Sally." The well-informed viewer demands more responsibility from a talk show in its investigative processes and presentation.

On these talk shows, as well as on newscasts and television newsmagazine shows, the "non-expert expert" has emerged. "People's opinions are often not distinguished from actual facts and evidence," said psychologist Lawrence Balter (Roan, 1994, p. L4). Sociologist Vicki Abt noted that the host-stars "act as pseudoprofessional counselors without suitable credentials to do so" (Roan, 1994, p. L4). Even more alarming, members of the studio audience often take on the position of "non-expert expert," verbally attacking a representative of an organization or company as if they had studied the issues for years.

This phenomenon takes on a particularly damaging aspect when guests on talk shows or newsmagazine shows relate experiences in which they have total belief based on little knowledge. They can be so convinced they are right that the emotion shows in their faces and in their body language. Viewers become compassionate with the subject of such a heart-wrenching scene and never question the facts of the story.

An example of the "non-expert expert" is found in chapter 10, "Cellular Phones and the Cancer Scare."

CHAPTER FOUR

Cyber Crises:
Rogue Sites and E-mail Rumors

A consumer contemplating making a purchase goes to the Internet to search for information about a company or about a product made by a specific company called XCompany. The consumer tries a search engine (such as Yahoo!, AltaVista, WebCrawler, HotBot, or Infoseek) to find links related to XCompany. The search engine produces two choices. One is XCompany's own Web page, which lists all the wonderful products made by the company. The second choice is "Xcompanysucks." Which will the consumer read first?

Or the consumer might go to one of many electronic discussion groups on the Internet and find numerous attacks against XCompany products. The consumer begins to question whether it would be wise to purchase a product from XCompany. XCompany has lost a sale and never had the opportunity to make a pitch.

This is a common scenario duplicated countless numbers of times because more and more people are looking to the Internet for advice. Whereas companies once worried about a few picketers holding placards outside their business, now irate customers, fired employees, and basically

crazed people can attack a company with great ease. They can place their incendiary placards on the World Wide Web for less than $1000. The Internet may be heaven for putting out the company's messages and building the company's reputation, but it can be hell when the message works against the company.

According to Richard Widdows, professor of consumer and textile sales at Ohio State University, "There's an old adage in the consumer affairs offices that if customers have a good experience with a company, they'll tell five or six people. If they have a bad experience, they'll tell 14 to 16 people. But through the Internet, their gripes now could reach potentially hundreds of thousands of people—and for free. That's what companies have to worry about" (Segal & Mayer, 1999, p. A01).

ROGUE WEB SITES

Rogue Web sites are normally created by disgruntled individuals with the intention of bringing attention to an issue or several issues concerning a corporation or organization. The company attacked in the rogue site must consider whether to respond and if it responds, how. Sometimes no response seems appropriate because the site appears to be simply vicious, but the company must determine, as best it can, whether readers will actually believe the claims made. Are Internet users sophisticated enough to realize that information on any Web site, especially a rogue Web site, is not necessarily factual?

Dr. Louis K. Falk, in his research on rogue Web sites, classifies such sites into five categories. Some credit the company for positive moves; others dwell on negativity alone. The five categories are the following:

1. Sites in which consumers are unhappy with the performance of the company:
 - A rogue Web site aimed at United Airlines posted complaints from United customers. It claimed that United Airlines' headquarters accessed the site on average of three visits a day and monitored the site to "fix bad information and to answer questions when [it] can." The rogue site also claimed that all United did was answer questions and that passenger complaints were not resolved.
 - A rogue Web site that targeted WalMart featured complaints and comments from customers and employees and claimed that "a considerable amount of content on this site is from other sites around the world."
 - An irate couple expressed disappointment with Norwegian Cruise Line on a rogue Web site.

2. Sites in which consumers are unhappy with the policies of the company:

- A rogue site aimed at Pepsi-Cola featured complaints that the company supported animal cruelty because it placed ads at bullfights.

- A site protested Home Depot for being "the largest retailer of old growth wood," thereby depleting the rain forests.

- A rogue site criticized Proctor & Gamble for "poisoning animals" by using animals to test products, but it also credited the company for making a change in its policy for color cosmetics, hair care and skin care products, laundry and dishwashing detergents "effective immediately in all countries where the company operates." The rogue site reminds users that the company did not change its policy in the case of oral care products.

3. Sites in which consumers or former employees hate the company:

- A disgruntled former employee of Burger King set up a Web site to complain about creatures in the salad, low wages, and office politics. The information was so rambling that the discerning reader got the impression, "Somebody got fired and has a vendetta against Burger King." Burger King would probably be advised to ignore the site.

- A rogue site complained that McDonald's was not environmentally concerned because it killed animals, damaged the Earth, harmed the health of consumers, and paid employees low salaries. Few McDonald's customers likely cared, as anyone concerned about killing animals for food doesn't order Big Macs.

4. Sites in which consumers create humor pages also called spoof sites:

- A site aimed at making fun of Taco Bell clearly says so. The Webmaster says at the top of the homepage, "I am not Taco Bell. I'm just a freak that likes to eat their food. If you want to write to Taco Bell, please go to tacobell.com. This page is meant to be a fun page." The site's criticism is so minimal, the reader may wonder if Taco Bell might have masterminded the site itself. In one central spot, the hot sauce is criticized for not being hot and the quality of the meat in Taco Bell Lunchables is questioned. But the Webmaster admits that the humor comes from his or her marijuana use as well as his or her relationship with Taco Bell.

5. Sites in which an index is created for complaints of multiple businesses:

- http://www.consumerama.org: An index of companies with links to consumer protest sites, class actions, and government investigations.

- http://www.complainusa.com/index.html: A searchable database of companies where the user can read or post complaints about companies.
- http://www.sprawl-busters.com: Battles large-scale retail stores, and megastores such as WalMart, Home Depot, K-Mart, and Target.

Another type of Internet crisis can develop when a company's own Web site is invaded. This occurred when a medical products company in Michigan discovered that hackers had posted on their own Web site a false news release saying the company was merging with a pharmaceutical firm. Stocks for both companies rose on the NASDAQ index after the fake posting. The medical products company indicated it would pursue the hackers and reassess its security.

The rogue sites that seem designed to destroy a company are often called *attack sites* or *anti-sites.* Many times, the Web address is made up of the company followed by the word *sucks*—as in *yourcompanysucks.com*.

How Do Companies Prevent Rogue Web Sites?

Cyber experts advise companies to purchase several domain names, including buying up the "*suck* sites." This is only a temporary remedy because the clever Webmaster can merely set up a rogue site using "stinks" instead of "sucks," making *Xcompanystinks*. Then there are numerous other synonyms that can be used. The irate Webmaster can also purchase *Xcompanyreallysucks* and *Xcompanystillsucks*.

The suffixes of the domain names are also important. Whereas each domain name identifies one or more Internet provider (IP) addresses, every domain name has a suffix that indicates to which top-level domain it belongs. The number of possible domains is limited, however. The most popular domains include the following:

.gov—government agencies
.edu—educational institutions
.org—organizations
.mil—military
.com—commercial businesses
.net—network organizations

These suffixes were a problem in that whitehouse.gov was the real White House in Washington, D.C. A spoof site was whitehouse.org, and a porno site was whitehouse.com. It would seem that government Internet and Web experts could have prevented that occurrence.

Another Internet address problem occurred when Sno-Isle Regional Library in Snohomish County, Washington, set up a Web site for bibliophiles to reserve books. There is a hyphen in the address. If the hyphen is not typed in the address, the computer user will get a porno site. The address of the porno site is not sexy and seems to have no relevance to its site. The library suspected that the porno site Webmaster wanted the library to purchase the address or merely wanted to play a trick on the library. So the library's legal representative entered the picture.

In November 1999, the federal Anticybersquatting Consumer Protection Act was signed into law. It allows the holder of a copyright or trademark to sue cybersquatters who have registered copyrighted domain names, and it forces them to relinquish those Internet addresses.

The most important prevention is acquiring a federal trademark registration for the company name. The first company or the first person to register the name holds the rights. It is also advisable to register the company trademark and product name under all possible domain name variations (.com, .org, .net, etc.). Companies are advised to register their names with and without hyphens. For example, 1-800-dentists.com and 1800dentists.com are two Web sites owned by two different companies. Confusion is apparent.

If your company has a federal registration for its name, and if another company or Webmaster has taken the name as its domain name, write to the domain name holder and tell him or her that he or she is infringing on your trademark. If he or she fails to transfer the domain name, go to Network Solutions, Inc. (NSI), the organization responsible for the administration of domain names in the United States and Canada. Present NSI with a certified copy of the federal registration and ask to place the domain on hold. Neither party will be able to conduct business at that Web site until the dispute is settled. If the problem continues, a suit in federal court is the next step.

Use a monitoring service. These services help companies track online problems and manage their reputations through online resources and interactions. A Phoenix-based division of WavePhore, called "eWatch," prowls Web sites and assists companies with damage control when criticism hits the Internet.

What to Do After an Attack Site Is Up

If your company is the victim of an attack site, Falk suggests the following tactics:

1. Do not overreact; the problem may not be as bad as it seems.
2. Assess the problem. Consider whether the information is true or false, whether many key stakeholders have seen the site, and whether the persons making the claim are credible.

3. Analyze the attack site.

 a. Do not pretend you are a consumer; webmasters of rogue sites reorganize misleading communications.

 b. Get a picture of how damaging the site is. How are you affected? Learn all you can about the attitudes of your publics and the issues most important to them.

 c. Contact the Webmaster of the attack site by telephone, face to face, or through e-mail. This gives you someone to hold accountable and helps develop a relationship with him or her if that is helpful. It also tends to force people to observe a higher standard.

 d. If the issue is big enough, contact your key stakeholders. This allows you to build a personal relationship with them and educate them about the attack site.

4. Drive the discussion by allowing your employees to be interviewed on the Web site. Make your company the expert on information about your company. Even if there is a negative aspect, admit to it and tell what your company is doing about it.

Kim Bayne (as cited in Janal, 1998, p. 240) suggests the following steps if there is no doubt that the site is an attempt to damage the company's reputation:

1. Make a complete mirror of the attacking Web site for reference purposes.

2. Find out the Webmaster's point of view. Is the Webmaster a disgruntled customer, an ex-employee, a competitor, or a prankster?

3. Create rebuttal pages at the company's Web site to address all accusations and implications. However, don't post the rebuttal pages at the company's site until you have gauged the public's reaction, or you may unwittingly stimulate interest in the attack site.

4. Prepare written statements for your crisis communications team, and make sure all team members agree on how to route inquiries about this particular Web site, should it become an issue.

5. Telephone the Webmaster and explain your concerns about the misinformation. Do not be accusatory, angry, or threatening. Ask him or her to remove the site. Explain that you would like the opportunity to present your company's view in an unbiased manner at the attack site. Use your communications skills first to try to resolve the problem.

6. If for any reason you are unable to communicate with the Webmaster, it's time for your company to draft a nice letter spelling out the situation and asking for resolution by a specific date.

7. Still not getting results? I'd apply the "three strikes" rule here. If after the third attempt to "play nice," you still don't get results, then it's time to get your company lawyer involved (Janal, 1998, p. 240).

The following mini-cases involve rogue Web sites.

MINI-CASE 2: ALASKA AIRLINES

After the 1999 crash of Alaska Airlines Flight 261, two fraudulent Web sites were created to solicit donations for the families of passengers and crew. The Webmaster of the first rogue site used the Alaska Airlines' logo to masquerade his or her site as an official Alaska Airlines page. Visitors who downloaded the fake contribution form unleashed a computer virus that allowed outsiders access to information on their computers.

Company executives were tipped off to the rogue site by an e-mail message. Needless to say, the company, still in shock over the tragedy, was doubly shocked. Company spokesperson Brian Petro said, "We just couldn't understand. It was unimaginable someone would do something like that" (Stiffler, 2000, p. A10). Alaska Airlines contacted the rogue site's Internet provider and asked that the site be removed. The IP, Costa Rica-based Freehomepages.com, complied.

A second rogue site asked for Social Security numbers of Alaska Airlines employees under the guise of donating to co-workers. The site was also purged. It is not known how many Internet users fell prey to the fraud. Alaska Airlines also issued two news releases about the fraudulent sites. The releases warned the public that the sites were fraudulent and vicious and revealed information about the official site, www.alaskaair.com, and fund-raising efforts.

MINI-CASE 3: DUNKIN' DONUTS

The Webmaster of a rogue site aimed at Dunkin' Donuts said he or she had "way too much time on [his] hands" and posted some thoughts about Dunkin' Donuts on a personal Web site. Within a few weeks, the site had "an unusual [but welcome] influx of visitors." The Webmaster learned through the referrer log at Yahoo! that all of these visitors went through Yahoo! to access the site. The Webmaster also learned that Dunkin' Donuts did not have its own Web site, so Yahoo! indexed the rogue site as a "consumer opinion" Web site about Dunkin' Donuts.

The site started getting, it said, "500 hits and a dozen e-mails a week." Then the Webmaster requested and was granted the use of the domain name "dunkindonuts.org" and moved the content previously posted on his personal Web site to the new official Web site. The site made news (Segal & Mayer, 1999, p. A01).

It must be said here that 500 hits are not necessarily 500 complaints. People stumble onto sites. Curiosity leads them to sites. Also, one person may "hit" a site more than once, so it doesn't even mean that 500 people visited the site. And the Webmaster himself admits on the page that some of the hits come from people who "are from Dunkin' Donuts headquarters doing 'damage control,' 'lurking,' or eavesdropping."

Dunkin' Donuts started to respond to the comments on the rogue site. Jennifer Rosenberg, a Dunkin' Donuts spokesperson, on the top line of the rogue site is quoted as saying, "If this was where customers were going to post their comments, we thought it was important for us to go ahead and address them." Soon after, Dunkin' Donuts made arrangements to acquire the site for its own use.

MINI-CASE 4: AMERICA ONLINE

This "*sucks* site" against the largest U.S. Internet service provider charged America Online (AOL) with being "the MTV of the Internet ... competitive on prices, but disastrously poor in service." The site contained several pages of detailed and focused text. James M. Egelhof was identified as the rogue site's Webmaster.

An AOL Webmaster wrote a letter to Cloud 9, the IP of Egelhof's site, saying the site violated the IP's rules: "Both as an Internet user and as an AOL employee, I find his Web page to be offensive and disturbing. Because Mr. Egelhof has chosen to use a noninteractive medium to express his opinions, he is not providing an avenue for an AOL response to these allegations, and thus his communication can be considered harassment [a violation of the IP's rules]."

Another violation was of the IP's rule that users may not use the system to distribute and/or store illegal copies of commercial software. The AOL Webmaster's letter to Cloud 9 continued: "The use of AOL online art in this site is extensive. Please remove the graphics on these pages to avoid possible legal action. I am currently contacting our legal department to determine if they (sic) would consider Mr. Egelhof's opinions to be libelous and to discover precedents for legal action in this medium."

Egelhof maintained that AOL's threats were groundless and that he had broken no law. He said he checked with his attorney about the harassment and libel threats and was told they were "garbage." He said he was also advised "that when a large corporation uses lawsuits (or the threat of them) to try to silence critics, that there are grounds for a harassment suit against the corporation."

At this point, there was much talk about the incident in several newsgroups, and the number of visits to the rogue site increased, Egelhof said, from 20 to 360 daily. As the talk continued, AOL Vice President Lyn

Chitow posted an apology and mailed it to those who complained about the company. The main points of the apology were the following:

1. "We are not in the business of censorship and believe strongly in individual freedom of speech."
2. "We know we are not perfect and welcome feedback about how to make it better."
3. "The author of the [rogue] Web pages was expressing his view of America Online, and I personally found it insightful and helpful as we strive to make it the best service it can be."

Interestingly, the AOL Webmaster who took Egelhof to task offered him a job, saying "we are looking for folks who know (the)Web."

MINI-CASE 5: WALTER CRONKITE

Walter Cronkite, probably the most respected newsman who ever lived, and deemed by a poll in recent years as the most trusted man in America, was the victim of a spoof site. Tim Hughes wrote what he believed to be a humorous spoof in which he claimed that Cronkite was seen in a restaurant spitting in his food. This was a completely fabricated incident and a fictitious essay designed for laughs. Cronkite saw the essay on the Web and contacted his lawyers who convinced Hughes to remove the essay and apologize (Janal, 1998, p. 244).

E-MAIL RUMORS

Where word-of-mouth rumors have put companies in crises for years, electronic rumors have given rumors wings. E-mail rumors can spread to thousands of people in seconds and, just like spoken rumor, they can change elements of the story with each transmission. The culture of cyberspace includes many individuals who apparently believe what they read on the Internet even when just the opposite seems to be the case. Although rules and laws will eventually be put into effect, at the beginning of the 21st century, anybody can write about almost anything on the Internet and even to a greater degree via e-mail. Some people use e-mail rumor with vicious intent, such as competitors; others use it merely to warn their friends. The transmission of e-mail rumors can be extremely damaging to businesses, organizations, and people in public life.

The age old rumors (see chap. 3) about Proctor & Gamble being a Satanworshiping advocate and about Tommy Hilfiger going on "Oprah" and making inappropriate racial remarks continue to circulate on e-mail. When newspaper personnel saw the Hilfiger rumor, they repeated it along with a denial by the company. The company posted denial messages in news-

groups, saying the producer of "Oprah" confirmed that Hilfiger had never been a guest. All this seemed to help. Such rumors seem to rise from the dead periodically and circulate again. The same rumor as the Hilfiger rumor circulated by word of mouth about designer Donna Karen some years ago and about Liz Claiborne and satanism.

An e-mail rumor circulated in the late 1990s claiming that a customer ate chocolate-chip cookies from a café in a Neiman Marcus store. As the rumor goes, she asked the waitress for the cookie recipe and was told it would cost "two-fifty." Thinking that meant $2.50, she agreed, but found later that $250 had been charged to her credit card. According to the rumor, she said the store would not correct the discrepancy because she could have copied the recipe, so she was stuck with the charge. In revenge, she decided to tell everyone she could about the recipe and thereby circulated it by e-mail to people she knew and asked them to circulate it to everyone they knew. In a short time, the recipe and story were everywhere. However, the story is false. The Neiman Marcus store mentioned does not even have a café. Yet the e-mail rumor was widely transmitted and believed.

Another widely circulated e-mail rumor claimed that Kentucky Fried Chicken changed its name to KFC because it could not use the word chicken since what it sells is not chicken, but "genetically manipulated organisms." The rumor asserts that "the so-called chickens are kept alive by tubes inserted in their bodies to pump blood and nutrients throughout their structure. They have no beaks, no feathers, no feet."

As in most e-mail rumors, the writer of the KFC e-mail cited a believable source: "Listen to their [sic] commercials, I guarantee you will not see or hear the word *chicken*. I find this disturbing." The word *chicken* is used repeatedly in the commercials—but the word *fried* is not. Apparently, *fried* is a no-no because health-conscious consumers would be negatively affected and the KFC restaurants do sell products not fried.

KFC officials released the following statement to the news media: "The hoax is intended to destroy the trust that you have placed in KFC to provide high-quality chicken meals at all of our restaurants. Although we hope that readers of the hoax will recognize it as obviously false, we take this or any other attack on the quality of KFC's product seriously" (Noack, 2000).

Spoofs are not limited to Web sites. One writer, obviously in jest, combined all the e-mail rumors he or she could recall, including the Neiman Marcus, KFC, and Proctor & Gamble rumors, into one long, horrific but outrageous rumor and circulated it via e-mail. It, too, was believed.

What Does One Do About E-Mail Rumors

Like word-of-mouth rumors, e-mail rumors are difficult for companies to fight. However, it is sometimes less difficult to determine the source of an e-mail rumor.

In 1999, the Public Affairs Office at the University of Texas Medical Branch at Galveston set up a Web page to fight rumors. Faced with a fiscal problem and a projected deficit, several hundred jobs had already been eliminated and other jobs would be eliminated in the future. The campus rumor mill was abuzz with gossip about which programs would be cut. The Public Affairs office realized the rumors were sapping morale and threatening productivity. "Our biweekly employee newsletter, with its slower response time, didn't seem like the proper vehicle," said Chris Comer, UTMB's director of communications (Lucey, 1999, p. 6).

The university Webmaster and art director worked together to create a Web site called "Rumors and Trumors." Accessed through a flying saucer button on the university's homepage, the site permitted employees to ask about the rumors they heard. The public affairs office then tracked down and posted the answers. The site became a trusted and effective source for employees. Hundreds of rumors were explained or zapped, and morale was improved.

Fighting back with a proactive Web site is one tactic. If the company has a Web site and does not address a circulated rumor on it, it may make the company appear guilty. This happened in July 1996 when TWA Flight 800 went down off the coast of Long Island. The TWA Web site did not address the rumor circulating widely that the plane was shot down by a missile during a nearby U.S. military exercise.

Janal (1998) advised three tactics for fighting all cyber crises, including e-mail rumors: (1) pay attention, (2) read the rumor and think about it, and (3) put up a fight. Companies and organizations should be ever-vigilant, watching for e-mail rumors. Encourage employees to notify the public relations department, or another designated department, when they notice e-mail or word-of-mouth rumors. If the complaint is legitimate, an appropriate solution to the complaint, and perhaps publicity about the correction, should be posted on the company's Web site, through the news media, or through some more appropriate outlet. If the rumor is unfounded and the source of the rumor is known, respond to the rumor. If the source is not known, respond to the listserv or Internet service provider (ISP) associated with the e-mail message that distributed the rumor. Fight in the news media and on Web sites. But do not wait for the rumor to go away. "To many people," said Janal, "silence equals assent" (1998).

At times, a decision must be made between fighting a rumor with public relations or with lawyers. Public relations is the first step. If that does not work or is not feasible, call the lawyers.

Many companies establish a policy forbidding employees from making statements about the company while they are employed or after they depart. Employee comments on an attack site violate that agreement and expose the employees to punitive measures. This may work well in some environments,

but it seems difficult to enforce, particularly with fired or other former employees who are frequently the culprits behind e-mail rumors.

Another tactic is to ignore the problem. Most Internet experts do not embrace this as a tactic and say it would be like a duck sitting in the water hoping the hunter's shot will miss. However, companies have been successful with it—watching and waiting and riding the problem out. If this tactic is taken, ongoing monitoring of the situation is crucial.

Kotcher (1999) advised the following:

1. Your company must respond to the e-mail rumor. If you remain silent, the only side of the story revealed is your enemy's.
2. Think strategically. Devise the best plan for the problem.
3. Speak with one voice. A clear, consistent message is mandatory.
4. Communicate your concern. Even if you are not guilty of the charges, be concerned.
5. Adopt an appropriate tone. Choose formal or informal language depending on the nature of the crisis.
6. Seize the opportunity. This is a chance not only to diffuse the crisis but also to build new alliances and reach goals.

MINI-CASE 6: MICROSOFT AND THE CATHOLIC CHURCH RUMOR

Another spoof was circulated when a comedy writer wrote a news release claiming that Microsoft planned to purchase the Roman Catholic Church. He wrote the following headline and lead:

MICROSOFT BIDS TO ACQUIRE CATHOLIC CHURCH

VATICAN CITY (AP)—In a joint press conference in St. Peter's Square this morning, Microsoft Corporation and the Vatican announced that the Redmond software giant will acquire the Roman Catholic Church in exchange for an unspecified number of shares of Microsoft common stock. If the deal goes through, it will be the first time a computer software company has acquired a major world religion.... (Janal, 1998, pp. 270–273)

The fake news release went on to say that Bill Gates and Steve Ballmer would be invested in the College of Cardinals and that Gates was quoted as saying, "The combined resources of Microsoft and the Catholic Church will allow us to make religion easier and more fun for a broader range of people." The release also claimed that there would be a new software application called "Microsoft Church," that the deal would give Microsoft online rights to the Bible, and that comedian Don Novello, playing his character

Father Guido Sarducci, hosted the announcement which was broadcast by satellite to 700 sites worldwide.

If anything remotely like this were true, which is ludicrous, it would have been a front page, top of the newscast story. So how could anyone believe it on an e-mail transmission? So many people believed it, or, at least, thought it might be true, that they contacted Microsoft for confirmation. The company had to issue a news release denying the rumor. The fake news release also made the news.

MINI-CASE 7: THE KILLER BANANA RUMOR

A rumor circulated both on the Internet and via e-mail claimed that bananas from Costa Rica were infected with "necrotizing fasciitis," or flesh-eating bacteria, and that the entire Costa Rica monkey population had been wiped out because of the bananas. It warned the public to stop eating bananas and to seek medical attention if they had eaten a banana and had come down with a fever. The bacteria, it said, could "eat" 2 to 3 centimeters of flesh per hour, making amputation likely and death possible.

The message, like most e-mail rumors involving food, said the message could be confirmed by the Centers for Disease Control (CDC). Rumors tend to carry an expert's name to make the outrageous rumor seem believable. When contacted, a spokesperson for the CDC said, "This is a false report."

APBNews.com reported on the incident, saying a trade group was trying to squelch the rumor. Tim Debus of the International Banana Association (IBA), an organization directly affected by the rumor, called it "Just another case of Internet terrorism like the recent hacker attacks on popular Web sites." The National Necrotizing Foundation, which researches such diseases and offers support and education services, said it was not possible for the disease to spread in the way the hoax claimed" (Noack, 2000).

Debus indicated that the IBA, concerned that the prank could disrupt the economy, made efforts to get the word out that the allegations were false.

CONCLUSION

Because the widespread adoption of the Internet and the World Wide Web is a relatively new phenomenon, we can expect laws to be passed for the protection of organizations and individuals. Software and Internet piracy, security, and hacking will be among the first laws developed and passed. Laws governing rumors and online attacks will be more difficult to propose and pass because of the anonymity of the culprits and freedom of speech.

CHAPTER FIVE

Managing a Crisis

COMMUNICATING WITH THE NEWS MEDIA

There are three possible results of a crisis: (1) The organization is put out of business, ruined, possibly sued, and key executives possibly charged with crimes. (2) The organization continues to exist, but it has lost some image and respect in its publics' eyes, and perhaps a great deal of financial position. (3) The organization, in a hard-fought battle, has won a war of public opinion and is seen as favorably as before or perhaps more favorably.

Information about a crisis reaches publics through the media more than through any other means. An organization may have to work very hard to get the media's attention during normal times. Its public relations (PR) personnel may struggle even to get a news release used. However, during times of crisis, the media will find the PR personnel.

It is true, unfortunately, that bad news sells. This has always been true. Even Shakespeare wrote about it in *Julius Caesar*: "The evil men do lives after them. The good is oft interred with their bones." A negative story is deemed more newsworthy than a positive one; the media consider your positive news "puffery."

It is the PR practitioner's dream that every news publication and every electronic news outlet will run prominent stories saying, "Company A is the greatest. Its products and services are the greatest, and it has the best PR people imaginable."

Plan a system in advance whereby you are notified of erupting crises. You want to be among the first, if not the first, to know. This can be done by instructing company telephone operators to reach you 24 hours a day, leaving a voice-mail greeting on your personal line during nonbusiness hours, and cultivating friendly relations with key personnel in the media, the fire department, and the police department—people who can notify you in the event of a crisis affecting your organization.

Prevention

Warning signs, called *prodromes*, are crucial because prevention is the best cure for a crisis. Strong community relations programs that get play in the media and endear your company to its publics will help this effort. Actually, ongoing proactive public relations programs of any kind are insurance policies against crises.

A strong people-centered corporate culture, rather than a profit-centered one, is also an effective crisis prevention tool. Corporate culture is the way an organization does business, its unwritten but firmly established values. The corporate culture must be established in such a way that honest, open communication is a basic value. Problems such as the CEO not speaking to the head of public relations and ignoring complaints from consumers are signals of an impending crisis that can be devastating. Employees who are stressed from overburdened workloads can ignite a crisis as well.

Before a crisis, or at the onset of a crisis, you must anticipate what the newsmedia need and want. Looking at the big picture, the media want to sell newspapers and win ratings wars. The media give the public what it wants to know rather than what it needs to know. There is a fine line between news and entertainment, and crises make for entertaining news. The public is perceived to enjoy watching, reading about, uncovering, and hanging organizations, companies, and individuals that *might* have done harm to people, or even worse, to animals.

Never say, "No comment!" To the public, refusing to comment appears to be an admission of hiding information or even guilt. If you do not respond, the public does not hear your side of the story and concludes, "Company X refused to comment and, therefore, it must have done something terrible." If there is some legal reason for not revealing certain information, explain this as much as possible and promise to reveal the information at a specific time. Do all you can to make that information available at the time you specified.

Do not assume that the crisis story will go away. The media can do their stories without you. They can build a case against your organization, portrayed as "the bad guy," by talking with disgruntled employees, volunteers, and customers, and even more often, by seeking out disgruntled former employees, former volunteers, and former customers. The media can also use computer files and call up long-forgotten problems and mistakes and, in a few seconds, regurgitate them and place them before the eyes and ears of the public. The people thus hear the negative story.

In a TV interview, Carl Bernstein (1994), who with Bob Woodward investigated the Watergate crisis for the *Washington Post*, said, "there are always people, if you work hard enough, who will want to tell the truth." In other words, do not wage a war with an enemy who buys ink by the barrel, paper by the ton, and controls the airwaves.

What will the media want to know in the event of a crisis?

What happened?

Were there any deaths or injuries?

What is the extent of the damage?

Is there a danger of future injuries or damage?

Why did it happen?

Who or what is responsible?

What is being done about it?

When will it be over?

Has it happened before?

Were there any warning signs of the problem?

If your organization has erred, it is usually best to reveal the mistake at once, apologize, and make amends. The story may end right away as long as the crisis itself is not continuing. Cover-ups make a crisis persist. Whether your company has erred or not, do all you can to get control of the situation as much as possible and as soon as possible. When you release your own bad news, you decrease the likelihood of rumor, supposition, half-truths, and misinformation.

If the disaster or crisis has already resulted in injury or death, or if it poses a threat to the safety or well-being of groups or individuals, contact the media immediately and indicate that you are looking into the situation, that you "just found out 5 minutes ago." This way, the media representative will realize both the crucial aspect of the problem and that your company cares about people and understands the media's needs. This action may buy you an ally as well.

If the situation is not urgent (be certain of this), it is advisable to look into the situation, to make attempts to fully understand what took place, and to have answers prepared for the media's questions.

If reporters contact you first and you are unaware of the crisis, do not rattle on without knowing details. Ask if you can call back in a few minutes, saying frankly, "I need to find out what's going on." Get the facts and then call the reporter back at the appointed time to communicate them.

Remember that the media and the public are entitled to have the facts about a crisis. The idea is to help the media cover the story accurately and with minimum criticism of the organization or company. The overall goal is to keep or get the public's trust through the media. The media needed you for information for interesting stories. Your organization needs the media to communicate with the public en masse. By keeping this symbiotic relationship in mind, the public relations professional will be in a more proactive position during a crisis and feel more in control of the organization's bad news.

The spirit of cooperation must be established. In a crisis, there are three types of response to a media request:

1. We know and here's all the information.
2. We don't know everything at this time. Here's what we know. We'll find out more and let you know.
3. We have no idea, but we'll find out and tell you.

Give the media access to the material they need: background information, statistics, photographs, and spokespersons.

Spokespersons

Identify one *primary* spokesperson for your company. Designating one primary spokesperson reduces the possibility of conflicting statements, organization values, or explanations being released to the media. Speaking with one voice is more crucial in a crisis than during normal operations.

The CEO is considered by most public relations professionals to be the spokesperson of choice during a crisis, especially if people have been injured, if there is danger of physical harm, or if there are millions of dollars in damage. The CEO usually has the most credibility with publics and the media. He or she is seen as a true representative of the company, as a person who can make decisions and speak for the company. If the company has a heart, it is the CEO's, at least, that's the publics perception.

Alternative spokespersons should be selected in the event the primary spokesperson is not available during a crisis. Supportive spokespersons, people who can speak authoritatively on technical subjects, are frequently of value, too. For example, if patrons of a restaurant get food poisoning, a

physician might serve as a supportive spokesperson responsible for telling the public about symptoms and treatments.

News Conferences

If a news conference is warranted and can be arranged swiftly, arrange one. Be certain to have a prepared statement read and distributed to the media. This assists you in setting the tone for the rest of the session.

Spokespersons, whether the CEO, other top executives, experts, or public relations professionals, should have major talking points. Also called *key messages* and *speaking points*, these talking points are one- or two-sentence summaries used to remind you of messages you want to be sure to get across to the public. They might provide details about the crisis or positive information about the company, such as the company's safety record, safety procedures, evacuation procedures, and other information that says, "We are very concerned; we care."

During the 1993 crisis in which consumers claimed to find hypodermic syringes in cans of Pepsi, the Pepsi-Cola Company, as well as some of its local bottlers, released to the media information about its canning process (see chap. 19). After the public learned of the bottler's precise and cautious procedures, it was difficult to imagine how the syringes could have been placed in the cans during the canning process. The release of this crucial information was credited with shortening the acute crisis stage.

Be mindful during a crisis, however, that it is not the time to bring up unrelated community service projects, no matter how many you have. When lives are in jeopardy, no one wants to hear about how much money you give annually to scholarships.

Spokespersons should rehearse their statements and talking points enough to be comfortable with the information, to be comfortable in front of TV cameras, and so prepared that he or she need only glance occasionally at notes. Preferably, before a crisis, practice sessions should be held in which employees ask the most difficult, rude, pointed questions of the spokespersons to simulate an actual crisis news conference.

Do not prolong the crisis by calling an unnecessary news conference or by engaging in other activities that can keep the crisis in the news. During a crisis, you want to get off the news pages and broadcasts.

Ten *Do's* for Media Interviews

When dealing with the media or when being interviewed by the media, whether in a one-on-one situation or at a news conference, note the following 10 *do's* for media interviews:

1. Do listen to the whole question before answering.

2. Do use everyday language, not the jargon of your business or profession. Even if the reporters use the jargon, use the common vernacular unless the interview is with a professional publication.

3. Do maintain an attitude showing you are calm, courteous, responsive, direct, positive, truthful, concerned, and, if necessary, repentant and apologetic.

4. Do understand the reporter's job. Respect deadlines and return phone calls promptly.

5. Do be accessible and pleasant.

6. Do try to treat the reporter as a partner, an ally in maintaining or restoring the company's good image.

7. Do tell the truth, the whole truth. Misleading or omitted facts are also forms of lying. (Some seasoned public relations practitioners disagree with this position and even insist that no organization in a crisis is ever totally open and honest with the media or anyone else from the outside. This is an arguable point in a moot debate. Even these skeptics would agree that it is important to appear open and honest.)

8. Do look the reporter in the eye. In your response, address each reporter by name if possible.

9. Do use your crisis communications plan.

10. Do keep employees informed of the crisis. They may be volunteer spokespersons.

Ten *Do Not's* for Media Interviews

At the same time, there are *do not's* when dealing with the media:

1. Do not be a wimp! Being concerned and empathetic does not mean that you must shake in your boots.

2. Do not guess or speculate. Either you know or you don't.

3. Do not get overly upset about being quoted out of context. Unless a complete transcript of your interview is printed, you are almost always quoted out of context to a degree. If the quote is completely wrong or libelous, that is another matter. Asking an editor for a retraction or correction is permissible if a reporter has been undoubtedly biased. A friendly letter delivered immediately and followed by a phone call is generally most effective. "Demanding" a retraction should usually be a lawyer's job, as is a charge of libel. Proving libel is difficult and costly.

4. Do not play favorites with the media. Always favoring one newspaper or one television station is bad business. It can haunt you later.

5. Do not pull advertising from a newspaper because reporters are not cooperative. The purpose of advertising is not to help the newspaper anyway.

6. Do not consider your news release "golden." It will be changed except in small-staffed newspapers. If it is written well with real news, you have done the best you can do.

7. Do not stick to a story if it has changed, just to be consistent. The media realize that things change. Johnson & Johnson experienced this during the Tylenol crisis (see chap. 6). It had initially announced there was no cyanide in its plant but later discovered that there was. Johnson & Johnson's public relations staff told the media the truth. No publication made a big deal over it.

8. Do not be trapped into predicting the future.

9. Do not wear sunglasses or chew gum.

10. Do not smoke—unless you are in a place such as Winston-Salem, North Carolina, where the economy is based on cigarette sales and smoking is a way of life.

Trick Questions

A media critic once said, "Being interviewed is like playing Russian roulette. You never know which question will kill you." Sometimes reporters stray from the typical *who, what, where, when,* and *why* questions. Metzler (1994) identified several types of questions that reporters have been known to ask. Metzler's questions as well as a few others follow.

Speculative questions begin with *if.* These can be embarrassing and dangerous. For example, a reporter may ask, "If the earthquake had happened during business hours, how many people would have been killed or injured?"

Leading questions imply that the reporter already has the answer; you are merely to verify it. For example, "You do agree that the company could have avoided this tragedy, right?"

Loaded questions are designed to elicit an emotional response. Some television reporters thrive on these because responses to them make for more exciting videos. A sample might be, "Isn't it true that you knew there was asbestos in the ceiling and failed to do anything about it?" In the case of a loaded question, rephrase it and answer your own question. You could say, "Do you mean, '*Were* we aware there was asbestos?' No, we were not."

Naïve questions indicate that the reporter had not done any homework and does not know what to ask. "Tell me, what does your company do?" is

an example. Reporters who ask such questions are dangerous because they desperately need a story. Make sure they get the story you want them to have. Give them media materials such as press kits, backgrounders, biographies, and news releases.

False questions intentionally contain inaccurate details in them. If the question is, "You fired half of your over-50 staff, right?" the public relations professional, knowing the statistic is wrong, could counter with, "No, only 40%," not realizing the reporter was aiming for that information all along.

Know-it-all questions begin with "We have the story. I just need a few wrap-up facts." The reporter may want you to merely confirm an already formed viewpoint. He or she may not have a story at all but wants you to release only "the dirt."

Silence, or an absence of questioning, is used by reporters who want you to spill your guts, to talk on and on. Many people tend to babble because there is silence. Remember, silence is the reporter's problem, not yours. Use this opportunity to reinforce positive statements or continue to be silent.

Accusatory questions are designed to force you to blame others. Never fall for this. Maintain your innocence if that is true, but do not cast blame on others. The court of public opinion does not react kindly to this.

Multiple-part questions can be confusing to you as well as to the public. Ask which part you should answer first. Then answer each part as a separate question. Also, you can say, "I'll take the first part first." Then restate it yourself the way you want to answer it. Do the same for each subsequent part.

Jargonistic questions are those in which technical words or professional jargon are used. In response, use everyday language. Jargon builds a barrier between you and your publics and erodes their trust.

Chummy questions are those in which the reporter, pretending to be your buddy, may ask, "Say, pal, off the record, what do you think ...?" The PR practitioner should remember that nothing is off the record and should be careful about supposed friendships.

Labeling questions aim to make issues negative or simplistic by seeming to ask for clarity, as in "Would you call the company's work schedule 'stressful'?" You should not accept the reporter's labels unless they are fair and accurate.

Good-bye questions are posed at the end of an interview and may even come after the camera or tape recorder is turned off. The reporter shakes hands and says, "By the way" Watch out for what follows. The interview is not necessarily over.

Remember—in all media questioning—to be positive, concerned, empathetic, and apologetic, if necessary.

Reporters

The preceding discussion of trick questions may seem to be a warning that reporters are sinister creatures whose life goal is to harass public relations practitioners. This is usually not the case.

There are jerks in every profession—including the newsmedia. If you stay in public relations long enough, you will come in contact with them. Know who the jerks and enemies are. Sometimes you can work around them by dealing with other reporters. Other times, you can follow the advice of former President John F. Kennedy: "Forgive your enemies, but never forget their names."

There are also those journalists who apparently make themselves feel better by labeling public relations people "flacks." There is no reason to take this to heart. Reporters do not hate you or your profession. In fact, many of them will seek public relations jobs.

Newspaper and broadcast journalists in record numbers are becoming public relations practitioners. Newspapers are failing. Most on-the-air personnel in television cannot expect to have jobs in their middle age. Everyone is downsizing. Public relations is the fastest-growing communications profession, largely because of crises and the forecast of crises to come.

Reporters are frequently not knowledgeable about or interested in the issues they cover. A story may have been assigned to them. Their task is to bring back an interesting story, a story that will get them a promotion, a raise, an extended contract, an Emmy, or a Peabody. They want their stories prominently displayed in the newspaper or at the top of the broadcast. They want to get this award-winning story back before the deadline. All would rather that you would assist them than be an obstacle to them. Obstacles make awards and raises difficult to obtain.

After reporters have filed stories, they are frequently finished with them. They do not write the newspaper headlines that you hate—that's the job of editors you rarely, if ever, see. Sometimes, if the story continues, other reporters will be assigned.

If you are breaking the news of a crisis or a development in a crisis and you know of reporters who are known to be fair and accurate, you can sometimes give them your story. This does not mean that if you dislike the reporter assigned, you can call another. This works only when no other reporters are involved, and you cannot be charged with playing favorites (see chap. 12).

Choosing the news outlet for bad news is not an unheard-of or new tactic. When death was imminent, physicians attending to King George V injected lethal doses of drugs into his veins in order to hasten his death. They

wanted him to die in time to make the deadlines of the *London Times*, a morning newspaper considered more responsible than what was, in 1936, considered the "inferior news organs of the afternoon."

COMMUNICATING WITH LAWYERS

Lawyers frequently advise clients in crisis to (1) be silent, say nothing, circle the wagons; (2) say as little as possible but reveal what information you have as quickly as possible; (3) deny blame and guilt; (4) shift blame to others or share it with others; and (5) remember that anything you say can be used against you in a court of law.

A public relations counsel suggests that a client be open and honest. "No comment" is perceived by the public as an admission of guilt: Anything you do not say can be used against you in the court of public opinion.

Both professions must be heard and considered. There are times when lawyers are right; spokespersons can speak too much. There are times when speaking up pays dividends in both courts of law and the court of public opinion.

Courts of law proclaim that a person is innocent until proven guilty, whereas the court of public opinion often declares a person guilty until proven innocent. When your company loses in the court of public opinion, it also loses its reputation, good name, and positive image—the very qualities that make for its success.

The public believes that an innocent person can answer a police officer's questions without having a lawyer present. After all, what does the person have to hide? The public also believes that this innocent person can go on the stand and plead his or her innocence, showing emotion in the process. However, lawyers frequently advise clients to refrain from all these actions and reactions. Some lawyers think public relations is publicity, getting somebody's name in the newspaper. Others know what public relations really is, but they choose to ignore it.

Sometimes lawyers may be cautious at a time when public relations professionals feel that open communication with publics is crucial to the positive conclusion of a crisis. The lawyer's job, after all, is to protect the company, organization, or individual. Sometimes public relations counsels may not anticipate threats to their own clients.

Lawyers know that any persons with knowledge of the organization in trouble can be called into court for depositions against the client. Sometimes communication with publics can put the organization in a perilous situation.

A case of law versus public relations occurred in 1985, when a Delta Airlines plane crashed. After the crash, high-ranking Delta employees showed great concern for survivors and families of victims. They sent flowers. They visited. They attended funerals. The company's public relations effort was

so impressive that many lawsuits were avoided as a result. Nevertheless, some lawsuits were filed. In court, the lawyers for Delta were said to be vicious. They accused one plaintiff of being a cocaine addict and of having a child that was not her husband's. They inferred that another victim, a homosexual, might have died soon of AIDS. Irate news stories resulted in calling the company a "monster." At least one newspaper wrote prominently of the airline's "Jekyll–Hyde" behavior.

Delta was upset over the negative publicity, but its lawyers insisted that they had to introduce relevant information, acquired legitimately, to fight money-hungry personal-injury lawyers (Thompson & Hess, 1986). A solution to such a dilemma is a bond of mutual understanding, a marriage of the two fields, a careful balance.

The legal profession is much older than the recognized field of public relations (although, in effect, public relations has been practiced for centuries). As a profession, public relations is moving toward a day when professionals will have to pass a kind of "bar exam." The Accreditation in Public Relations (APR) credentialing offered by the Public Relations Society of America is a step toward this certification.

Lawyers are becoming more adept at public relations. The American Bar Association provides media training for its primary officers. It realizes that a defendant can win a battle in a court of law and lose it in the court of public opinion.

In 1991, for instance, a crisis team consisting of public relations and legal representation for Snapps restaurant in Florida made a decision not to prosecute or sue a teenager who had helped spread a rumor that caused a drastic loss of business (see chap. 9). The members of the team decided that although they might win a victory in court, it would be a case of winning the battle and losing the war. The teenager had apologized publicly and had behaved properly repentant. The public might have boycotted the restaurant had further action been taken against her. It would have been a matter of the powerful restaurant ruining the life of a well-meaning child who made a mistake in judgment.

Conversely, a defendant can lose in court and win in the battle of public opinion. Sometimes the latter offers a brighter future. This was the case when Mayor Marion Barry of Washington, DC, was convicted of a drug charge, served time in prison, and then returned to the nation's capital to resume his political career. Although few voters doubted that Barry was a drug user, there was resounding public resentment of the way he was supposedly "set up" for the arrest. Anger at those believed to be responsible for the "set up" translated into support in the court of public opinion for Barry, who was reelected as mayor in 1994.

More and more, lawyers are influencing public opinion outside the courtroom. We have seen the results of this when a lawyer representing a prisoner

convicted of a serious crime persuades "60 Minutes" or "20/20" to tell a story of the innocence of the client. The lawyer may have exhausted all legal channels or the client may have been unable to afford the legal battle. An effective letter to the television newsmagazine may change everything.

The public is often not aware of how the newsmagazine series got the story; true public relations professionals (or lawyers performing public relations acts) are more concerned with their client's needs than with promoting their own visibility. Thus, a televised account of a "poor, innocent" man imprisoned for years for a crime he did not commit is a public relations tool that appeals to the court of public opinion. In many cases, on the basis of the convincing television profile, viewers appeal to courts for new trials, or judges grant new trials in anticipation of public reaction. Sometimes the prisoner is subsequently freed.

The necessity of merging law and public relations leads to an even greater need for pre-crisis planning by representatives in both fields. Effective pre-crisis planning sets up scenarios for each type of crisis likely to affect the organization. Different strategies and tactics should be outlined for each kind of crisis. Examples are reflected in such statements as these: "If there is a loss of life, we will …"; "If there is no loss of life, we will …"; "If the media is unaware of the story, we will …"; "If the media is pressing, we will …."

A balance between public relations and law should, as much as possible, be determined before the crisis. A balance often cannot be accomplished effectively after the plant has exploded.

Lawyers who have not adapted to public relations procedures should be advised that some key stakeholders can be dealt with personally, whereas others will get their impressions from the media.

Refusing to talk to reporters will not make the story go away. Reporters will get the story—and it may not be the story the company wants to be told. The board of directors of the United Way of America was not aware of this when in 1991 its CEO, William Aramony, was accused of excessive spending (see chap. 11). No one on the board would talk to the media. The story started as a brief section in a long, basically flattering article about Aramony in one newspaper. Editors of other newspapers read the article, focused only on the negative aspects, and soon public perceptions of misuse were nationwide.

The newsmedia is a conduit to the public. The public rarely has any real evidence, at least not as much as juries in courtrooms do. Even though the public is well aware that reporters err, people still tend to believe what they see and read in the media. They make decisions based on sound bites and articles selected and written by reporters.

The court of law and the court of public opinion will remain crucial in deciding the fate of individuals, groups, organizations, and corporations. Both the public relations professional and the lawyer must learn to put

clients in the best light in both courts to gain the best possible outcome to a crisis.

Lawyer Practices Public Relations

Bill Marler is an example of a lawyer who uses public relations in personal injury cases. As part of the firm Marler–Clark, Marler handles cases on a national basis that involve food poisoning. His first client was Brianne Kiner, a little girl from Washington state who sued Foodmaker after she contracted the *E. Coli* virus from hamburgers at a Jack-in-the-Box in 1993. Marler settled that case for $15.6 million. He negotiated an *E. Coli* case with Odwalla, Inc., for a reported $15 million.

Marler is known not only for earning millions of dollars in settlements for his clients, but also for his publicity efforts. According to one reporter, "While many attorneys handle food poisoning cases, few relentlessly court the news media like Marler. When outbreaks occur, he fires off press releases and e-mails offering expertise and interviews" (Leung, 1999, p. A1). The lawyer and his consulting firm give lectures to company officials on the dangers of improper food handling, including videos of children near death from the effects of tainted foods. Marler also lobbies legislative officials urging them to pass laws on food safety: "If you think I pitch newspaper people, I'm merciless when I pitch politicians" (Leung, 1999, p. A1).

COMMUNICATING WITH INTERNAL PUBLICS

Internal publics include all classifications of employees—labor, management, hourly workers, interns—as well retirees and stockholders. In a nonprofit organization, volunteers are also an internal public. Internal publics are crucial in a crisis because they are the most believable spokespersons. Because internal publics may not be hired or paid to speak for the company, the news media seek them out for comment.

In many businesses such as retail stores, employees are a link between the company and the consumer public. They are the principal representatives of the company and have the power to make a potential customer a loyal customer or to make a loyal customer a former customer.

Communication with internal publics before, during, and after a crisis is vital. For each internal public, you must choose the correct message and the correct medium.

Proactive Communications Prior to a Crisis

Companies and organizations are wise to develop programs designed to achieve the following objectives with internal publics, particularly with employees:

1. Employees must learn what positive performance is and how it will benefit the organization and the employee. Employees need job descriptions and perhaps instructions on how their jobs should be done. In some public relations departments, employees admit that they write news releases on a "monkey see, monkey do" system—they use previous news releases and make new ones fit the same format, a kind of formula writing. This may work occasionally, but each news release should have its own unique elements and style. If an employee needs a formula to write a news release, it may be time for writing classes. Demonstrations, practice, and special training or a reference manual may also be helpful.

Employees also need to know the consequences of a job well done and of a job poorly done, including consequences to the company and to the individual employee. It is important for all employees to feel as if they are part of the company. It's a feeling of "we," not "they."

2. Employees must learn what the job priorities are. Employees and management could have various opinions of what jobs or tasks are priorities. It is important for both employees and management to be on the same page. Either side may adjust to the other, but it is important that management and employees agree on priorities. This, again, requires effective communication.

3. Positive performance must be rewarded. Employees perform well when their work is recognized and rewarded. Conversely, they perform poorly when their work is not rewarded. Although managers say the paycheck is enough, they are the very managers likely to suffer crises arising from internal conflict. Research shows that positive reinforcement results in continued effective performance. Rewards may include money, trophies, certificates, an afternoon off, a free lunch, compliments, announcements on a bulletin board, a temporary parking place of honor, and other forms of employee recognition. Even a minor recognition in the form of a letter, memo, or e-mail message can be effective and encouraging when it is provided on a regular, perhaps daily, basis. Such a message might say, for example, "You worked very hard to get that report completed on time and I appreciate your hard work."

4. Poor performance must be punished. Conversely, poor employee performance should be punished. If an employee not doing his or her job well is never reprimanded, the good workers become discouraged. Proper communications with poor performers include formal or informal documents and face-to-face conversations, but they should never include public humiliation.

5. Punishment for good work must be avoided. Many times in companies, an employee who does work well is given more work to do. An employee who makes useful suggestions winds up having to carry out

the suggestions. An employee who comes in early or stays late is despised by other workers. These are examples of punishing employees for exceptional work. First, communication is necessary to reward the good performance; then an effort should be made to provide the training, mentoring, and advising necessary to bring the other employees up to the standard set by the exceptional worker.

6. **Help employees cope with personal problems.** Whether management likes it or not, employees will have personal problems that may interfere with their work. Management should learn to recognize the symptoms of a personal crisis. A personal crisis may exist when an employee does the following: spends an unusual amount of time on the telephone, makes an unusual number of errors, is unproductive, abuses equipment, arrives late or leaves early, stares blankly into space, yells and is otherwise irritable, spends excessive time in the restroom.

Because personal crises can turn into company crises, it is imperative to help employees cope with the issues affecting their performance. Allowing employees time off for personal business (with or without make-ups) is one way to handle these situations; providing on-site psychologists and advisers is another. Some companies even have on-site physicians and dentists available to employees to save time away from the job.

Large companies have employee relations departments to cope with issues surrounding employee problems and employee benefits. Many companies provide outstanding benefits that are a real plus in earning employee loyalty. They may also provide stock options and extensive vacation time. J.P. Morgan grants a free lunch. Fel-Pro pays $3,000 a year to send employees' children to college. Johnson & Johnson has a benefit whereby employees who have worked there for at least 5 years get an extra week's paid vacation when they get married. Johnson & Johnson also has a child-care center and an on-site fitness center.

Communicating With Internal Publics During a Crisis

Once a crisis has occurred, employees and other internal publics must be advised of what has happened early in the notification process (see chap. 2, Fig. 2.2). Whenever possible, internal publics should not learn of the crisis from the news media and they should know about it before external publics do. If the onset of the crisis occurs after office hours, telephone trees are often organized so that perhaps each manager is notified, and the manager telephones some employees and they telephone others. The telephone tree must be in place before a crisis. As a crisis develops, the employee public, called a *functional public,* should be kept apprised of what

is occurring at every step. Common methods for keeping employees informed include meetings, closed-circuit television programs, e-mail, the public address system, and bulletin boards.

Many companies can utilize their Intranet, internal Internets designed to improve productivity and the circulation of proprietary information. The Intranet is better than the Internet in the case of crises because it allows the company or organization to communicate only to its own people, whereas anyone can access the Internet.

During a crisis, internal publics generally want to know what they can or should do. During the Snapps restaurant rumor crisis (see chap. 9), managers volunteered to take AIDS tests to prove that no manager could have spread the AIDS virus through food products. If it is important for employees to make some effort in order to continue the business, convey that to employees and tell them why. If there are crisis tasks employees need to take on, they should be preadvised and pretrained. If the nature of the crisis eliminates jobs—either temporarily or permanently—employees need to be carefully told what options are available and what the future is likely to hold.

As in normal operating mode, it is crucial that employees feel a sense of "*we*-ness" during a crisis, that they are part of the battle. Many companies order employees to remain silent about company issues relating to the crisis; they are especially told not to talk to the news media. They are told to let the appointed spokesperson do all the speaking. Often this is an advisable move; too many people can make for a confusing story. However, some companies and organizations encourage their employees to talk to the media, confident that employees like their jobs and their company and do not fear the news media will get out of hand.

COMMUNICATING WITH EXTERNAL PUBLICS

External publics include consumers/customers, community members, government officials, labor unions, dealers, suppliers, trade associations, competitors, and other outside people related in some way to an organization. As in all types of communications, it is important to strategically plan the correct message and the appropriate medium for communicating with each external public, both before and during a crisis.

Organizations tend to form alliances with key external groups that will make members of these groups feel like they are part of the company. The airlines have been very successful with the frequent-flyer programs, so much so that other businesses are trying "frequent" programs too. Boards of directors and community advisory boards are also popular efforts at bridging the gaps between companies and organizations and the business world and the community respectively.

Precrisis Communications With Customers/Consumers

Generally, a business has five primary objectives designed to build sales and gain loyal customers. These objectives are the following:

1. **Keep the old customers.** Longtime contented customers bring other customers. Programs, like the frequent-flyer programs and exclusive discounts, are examples. Other communications, like newsletters and individual letters, are also frequently used. Assuring loyal customers of the constant effort to have quality products and services as well as competitive prices is important.

2. **Attract new customers.** Good prices, excellent quality, and word-of-mouth referrals from loyal consumers help to attract new customers. Interpersonal contact with sales staff and other employees is also effective in this area. Open houses and other special events bring the company to the attention of potential customers. Publicity about the company's outreach programs also attracts new customers.

3. **Market new services and products.** Customers and consumers want to see that a company or organization is constantly making efforts to better itself in every area. They want to know what the new products and services are, why they are better than the older ones, and that prices are reasonable.

4. **Handle complaints swiftly.** A customer who complains and is subsequently satisfied will return and bring other customers. One who does not complain or is not satisfied after a complaint will switch loyalty to a competitor. If 4 people complain, one can usually assume that there are 24 others who were dissatisfied and did not speak out. Complaints in some organizations are handled by a middle person who mediates between the complainant and the company. He or she may simply say, "We're sorry and will make amends." Or a letter might be written explaining the company's actions. The overall message to the customer is: "We want you to be happy. We want your business."

5. **Educate customers.** Companies develop programs to educate customers about products and services. A store with a new line of cotton garments might inform customers—through ads, publicity, newsletters, Web pages—of the advantages of cotton, how to recognize well-made garments, and so on.

The Nordstrom Consumer Policy

The Nordstrom chain is known for its "customer is first" policy, a prototype and model for other retail stores. A Nordstrom store manager said, "Employees are instructed to make a decision that favors the customer before the

company. They are never criticized for doing too much for a customer, [but] they are criticized for doing too little" (Spector & McCarthy, 2000, p. 88).

The company works on the principle that if it takes care of customers' needs and concern, first, the dollars will come. The corporate organizational chart shows customers at the top of an inverted pyramid and the co-chairs at the bottom. Perhaps the most well-known aspect of Nordstrom customer relations is its returns policy: If a customer is dissatisfied with a Nordstrom purchase for any reason, the store takes it back with no questions asked. Bruce Nordstrom advised his salespeople that "if a customer came into the store with a pair of five-year-old shoes and complained that the shoes were worn out and she wanted her money back, you have the right to use your best judgment to give my money away. As a matter of fact, I order you to give my money away" (Spector & McCarthy, 2000, p. 98). Although the returns policy invites consumer abuse, Nordstrom believes that 98% of its customers are honest and should not be punished for the dishonesty of a few. This policy has forced other retail stores to adopt a more liberal returns policy in order to compete with Nordstrom.

In the area of community relations, companies and organizations adopt outreach programs in an effort to build loyalty among persons in the community surrounding its place of business. This may include making donations to nonprofits, schools, and the like. Or it may mean actually getting involved: A drug store may offer colon cancer screening. The police department might mentor fatherless teens. McDonald's runs the Ronald McDonald Houses providing temporary houses for families while their sick children are treated at nearby hospitals. The Internal Revenue Service includes photos of missing children on its income tax forms. The Alpac Corporation, a bottling company, had the support of the community and the local news media when a customer reported a syringe in a can of Pepsi because the Behnke family, owners of the company, was know for its philanthropy (see chap. 18).

In outreach programs, it is important to publicize your efforts—if your purpose is to build positive relationships with the community. Some organizations feel that publicizing their good deeds is bragging. If you do not publicize, only those people who have benefitted will know about your actions.

Communicating With External Publics During a Crisis

Other than through the news media, organizations should communicate with loyal consumers to inform them of the crisis and progress toward normalcy. Various methods must be evaluated—letters, newsletters, notices on Web sites, telephone calls, and so on. You want customers to remain loyal throughout the crisis and continue to patronize the organization. So tell them all the five Ws of the crisis—who, what, when, where, why. Pepsi, in the

syringe-in-the-can crisis, set up hotlines whereby consumers could ask questions directly of staff members (see chap. 19). Snapps had a hamburger giveaway to show that its hamburgers were not tainted (see chap. 19).

Community members should be reached through key community leaders on advisory boards. Flyers could be circulated in communities and posters could be put up in public places and on bulletin boards. Like consumers, community members will want to know what happened, what was the cause, what is being done, when the crisis will be over, and so forth. The U.S. Postal Service, in response to its workplace violence crisis, organized a symposium on workplace violence attended by corporate, government, academic, and community leaders (see chap. 16).

Labor representatives and government officials should be among the first notified. Key messages should be conveyed because these people, depending on the nature of the crisis, may be called on by the news media to comment.

FACTS TO REMEMBER IN CRISIS INVENTORY
AND DURING A CRISIS

You Don't Learn Much When Your Mouth Is in Motion. When on a fact-finding mission among internal publics to determine likely crises, listen attentively to others. You need to listen to what is said, how it is said, under what circumstances, and who said it. Watch facial expressions; they may be indicative of a story beyond the information you actually gather. Employees may fear reprisals from superiors or want to avoid "ratting" or whistleblowing. There are numerous reasons for omissions, half-truths, and lies. A diligent researcher will see clues and hints of a need for further investigation.

An example of this was exhibited when a specific brand of automobile was found to be dangerously defective. It was discovered, after numerous cars rolled off the assembly line and had been sold, that the workers on the line knew about the defect. They were afraid to pull their supervisors' coattails, afraid of the workplace culture of "Kill the messenger of any news that causes a slowdown."

Never Ask a Manicurist If You Need a Manicure. If possible, when you hire an outside company to evaluate your company for safety, make sure that that company does not do repairs. If you ask a contractor to check for problems, be prepared for a bill for roof repair, a new roof, or some other costly job. Sometimes shady companies suggest costly repairs because they want to benefit financially when actually some inexpensive repairs are ignored. An overlooked crack in a walkway can become a disaster. If the walkway topples and people are injured, the news media and publics will want to know why the problem went unnoticed. Blaming the contractor

for being greedy is not an acceptable response. A good practice is to organize employees and other internal publics to be on the lookout for anything that might escalate into crises—from cracked pipes to the emotional problems of an employee (see chap. 16). This is a form of issues management.

It Is Usually Impressive to Allow Others to Describe Your Good Qualities. When there is an opportunity to let impartial experts speak about your company's diligence, sense of responsibility, or innocence in a crisis, permit them to be spokespersons. In the Snapps restaurant case (see chap. 9), medical officials spoke at news conferences telling the public that AIDS could not be spread to food by an HIV-positive food handler. In the Pepsi syringe crisis (see chap. 19), the FDA told consumers that AIDS could not be spread through contaminated syringes in soft-drink cans. In the cellular phone crisis (see chap. 10), the manufacturer asked an independent bioengineer to participate in a news conference to explain that the power in cell phones was too low to cause damage to human tissue.

No One Listens Until You Make a Mistake (or Have a Crisis). When there is no crisis, it may seem that the news media are uninterested in your organization. When a crisis occurs, many times you have the opportunity to tell what your organization does. This was found to be the case when boatloads of Chinese immigrants arrived in Canada (see chap. 13). Spokespersons for the federal office of Citizenship and Immigration in Canada were then called on to tell the public about their mission and work. After the crisis, Canadians better understood the functions of the federal office.

A Closed Mouth Gathers No Foot: Never Miss a Good Chance to Shut Up. Sometimes companies in a hurry to speak up, be heard, and get the crisis in the news, do not wait until they have gathered enough facts to speak intelligently. Ignoring the news media and publics is not advised, but making statements as if they are facts—before you are very sure—can make you seem unreliable. It is best to answer only the questions you can reliably answer and defer the others until you have answers.

Johnson & Johnson (see chap. 6) initially told the news media there was no cyanide in its plant and, therefore, there was no way Tylenol capsules could have been contaminated during the manufacturing process. Later, the company discovered that indeed there was cyanide in the plant. If the news media had found out about the cyanide through its own investigation, the picture would have been ugly. However, Johnson & Johnson, in an act said to be indicative of the company's overall reputation for integrity, contacted the press and revealed its own lie, thus avoiding the foot in their corporate mouth.

A spokesperson should say just enough to get his or her talking points across effectively—and no more. There is a fine line between overspeaking and underspeaking; planning and practice help the spokesperson determine that line.

Never Underestimate the Damage That Can Be Done by Decisions Made By Groups. At some point in a crisis, there must a decision maker, a person who says, "This is what we shall do." Groups are good for preidentifying issues that may turn into crises and for crisis training. However, when facing an actual crisis, there must be a crisis team leader.

If an organization hires a public relations agency to do the crisis communications and to call the shots, then the agency should have been preselected prior to the crisis. After the plant explodes, valuable time is lost getting a team together to interview and hire agencies.

If You Tell the Truth, You Don't Have to Try to Remember Anything. When there is no time for research, when the newsmedia tell you the news, or when the spokesperson must speak to the news media before there are any real answers, what should you do? In these cases, although you make no definite answers about how or why, the best rule is to tell the truth as you know it, saying repeatedly, "I just learned about this, so I don't have all the answers." If you know, for example, that your company practices safety precautions, say so: "This company is very concerned about employee safety. There are hard and fast rules. There are rewards for safety records. If anything happened, it was not because of a lack of concern for safety. But we are very sorry that it happened." An early, earnest response can sometimes set the tone for how the public will perceive the company in a crisis. If these safety precautions are a part of normal routines, one does not have to worry about recalling them.

Never Mess Up an Apology With an Excuse. Know the difference between an apology and an excuse. An excuse passes blame to others; an apology does not. Do not say, "We didn't realize ..." when you should have realized. An apology is a sincere admission that you are sorry for whatever happened. An excuse was not what the consumer public wanted to hear when people, especially children, were sick and dying from *E. Coli* that had tainted Jack-in-the-Box hamburgers. Saying the meatpacker was responsible for the *E. Coli* infections was not an apology. If your company had sold such a product, you would owe the public an apology: "We are sorry. We will do everything we can to make amends. We take responsibility for medical treatments."

CHAPTER SIX

Case: Johnson & Johnson and the Tylenol Murders

Before September 30, 1982, manufacturers felt that if they made a good product and dealt fairly with consumers, retailers, employees, and other publics, they could maintain a positive image and be considered consumer-friendly, a good company with which to do business.

Johnson & Johnson was one of those companies. It was an old and trusted company. With 165 companies in 53 countries throughout the world, it made baby products: baby powder, lotions, shampoos, cotton swabs, adhesive bandages, surgical instruments, Reach toothbrushes, Ortho-Novum birth control pills, and pharmaceuticals in the World Health Organization list of essential drugs. Johnson & Johnson was a household name.

The corporation also had a positive image among its employees. It was listed as one of the 100 best places to work. The company credo was written by the son of the company's founder in the 1940s (see. Fig. 6.1). The credo said that the company had four responsibilities in the following order of priority: (1) to the consumer, (2) to the employees, (3) to the communities, and (4) to the stockholders.

Our Credo

We believe our first responsibility is to the doctors, nurses and patients,
to mothers and fathers and all others who use our products and services.
In meeting their needs everything we do must be of high quality.
We must constantly strive to reduce our costs
in order to maintain reasonable prices.
Customers' orders must be serviced promptly and accurately.
Our suppliers and distributors must have an opportunity
to make a fair profit.

We are responsible to our employees,
the men and women who work with us throughout the world.
Everyone must be considered as an individual.
We must respect their dignity and recognize their merit.
They must have a sense of security in their jobs.
Compensation must be fair and adequate,
and working conditions clean, orderly and safe.
We must be mindful of ways to help our employees fulfill
their family responsibilities.
Employees must feel free to make suggestions and complaints.
There must be equal opportunity for employment, development
and advancement for those qualified.
We must provide competent management,
and their actions must be just and ethical.

We are responsible to the communities in which we live and work
and to the world community as well.
We must be good citizens — support good works and charities
and bear our fair share of taxes.
We must encourage civic improvements and better health and education.
We must maintain in good order
the property we are privileged to use,
protecting the environment and natural resources.

Our final responsibility is to our stockholders.
Business must make a sound profit.
We must experiment with new ideas.
Research must be carried on, innovative programs developed
and mistakes paid for.
New equipment must be purchased, new facilities provided
and new products launched.
Reserves must be created to provide for adverse times.
When we operate according to these principles,
the stockholders should realize a fair return.

Johnson & Johnson

FIG. 6.1. The Johnson & Johnson credo that guided the company's crisis team through the ordeal of saving the company's image, even as news accounts reported that the company's Tylenol product was killing consumers. (*Source:* Reprinted with permission from Johnson & Johnson.)

The company also had continually good relationships with the media. Little did it realize just how crucial those relationships would become.

September 30 began like any other workday at the headquarters in New Brunswick, NJ. Then a fateful telephone call came in.

A reporter from the *Chicago Sun-Times* telephoned a public relations staff member asking such questions as "How long has Tylenol been on the market?" and "What is Tylenol's share of the market?"

The reporter did not know why he was asked to prepare background information on Tylenol. Someone else was writing the story. An editor had merely assigned him to do background research to use in the main story. The Johnson & Johnson staffer, who then alerted most of the department, thought the call was a bit strange and reported it to Public Relations Director Robert Kniffin. Kniffin called Arthur Quilty, an executive committee member who had responsibility for McNeil Consumer Products Corporation, a subsidiary. Quilty alerted James Burke, CEO. The reporter later called back and explained there had been reported deaths from the intake of Extra Strength Tylenol.

Corporate Vice President Lawrence Foster, who was on vacation, called in, as was his daily practice, and when he learned what had happened, he immediately returned to the office and took charge of the public relations activities.

The corporation had no specific crisis communications plan—few companies did at the time. It did have an emergency plan and call list for such incidents as plant fires. The first step was to notify the chain of command.

There was an immediate meeting in Burke's office with top executives, including Lawrence Foster, head of public relations; David Clare, president and chairman of Johnson & Johnson's executive committee; Joseph Chiesea, president of McNeil Consumer Products Company; and David Collins, chairman of McNeil.

At that meeting, Foster dispatched Kniffin to McNeil's headquarters nearby. Collins, who had been president of McNeil Pharmaceuticals and knew the subsidiary well, was sent to McNeil by Burke. This would actually have been the next step in a crisis communications plan—had there been such a plan.

The executives all said that it was a period of great fear. There were no warnings, no prodromes. Nothing like this had ever happened to them or any other company that provides products for human consumption. What was going on? Was there a psychopathic murderer in the plant?

When the story ran in the media, the public also was afraid. The very idea that a person could take a capsule for a headache and die was terrorizing. People were saying, "I have a terrible headache, but I'm alive." Even con-

sumers outside the Chicago area were afraid of Tylenol capsules, if not also afraid of all over-the-counter pain medications.

Collins immediately set up a 7-member crisis team. The team's first task was to find out what sickness it was actually facing. Then it would determine how to go about the healing process. The crisis team handled decisions in the area of communications and was in charge of all strategies and tactics. With Burke's approval, the team decided to recall all Tylenol capsules from stores in the Chicago area.

The recalled batch was tested and two additional cyanide-laced capsules were discovered. Still, the team and company were uncertain of how the cyanide got into the capsules. It indeed hoped that the criminality was not in the company, but there was no certainty.

Johnson & Johnson had one overriding priority: Warn the public. The company did just that by being completely open and cooperative with the media in getting the news out.

Foster said he believed that three points marked the reason Johnson & Johnson was successful in coping with the crisis:

1. The company was open to the media.
2. It was willing to recall the product no matter what that meant to the company.
3. It appealed to the American sense of fair play and asked for the public's trust.

Foster was responsible for the communications aspect of the crisis team's work. The team was concerned with aiding police and the FBI in finding the responsible party and in dealing with the Food and Drug Administration (FDA).

First, the crisis team identified its key publics:

1. Consumers (through the media)
2. The medical profession
3. Employees and other internal groups
4. The FDA

All publics were notified initially, and the team kept in touch with them throughout the crisis.

The first story appeared in the morning edition of the *Chicago Sun-Times* on October 1. The *Chicago Tribune* ran a story that same afternoon under a banner headline:

5 Deaths Tied to Pills
Fear Killer Put Cyanide in Tylenol

A study of the *Tribune*'s coverage revealed that the newspaper was as supportive of Johnson & Johnson as it could have been in the telling of the bad news, especially considering the usual "in-your-face" coverage of crises in the 1990s. The opening pages of two *Tribune* stories are shown in Figs. 6.2 and 6.3. The company's executives, the police, the FBI, and the newspapers knew from the start that the tampering could possibly have happened at the plant. Nevertheless, there was no insinuation of this in the *Tribune*'s coverage.

The name Johnson & Johnson was not mentioned on page 1. In the continuation of the story on page 2, nearly buried in the middle of 12 column inches of copy, was the following statement:

> A spokesperson for Johnson & Johnson, parent firm of the company that makes Tylenol, said Thursday evening his firm "launched an investigation this morning to track down the capsules."
>
> The spokesman, Robert Andrews, and two other Johnson & Johnson officials met for an hour and a half with Elk Grove Village detectives and evidence technicians.
>
> He said his firm is "collectively shocked." (Houston & Griffin, 1982, p. 2)

There were four *Tribune* stories about the Tylenol crisis in that one issue. Other than in the preceding quoted passage, all other mentions of the company were of McNeil Consumer Products Company, not as familiar a name to consumers as Johnson & Johnson.

The captions for the related photographs on pages 1 and 2 of the *Tribune* also did not mention the company. The caption on page 2 indicated that medical examiners believed "the capsules were tampered with after leaving the manufacturer's plant in Pennsylvania" (Shanker & Grady, October 1, 1982).

On Saturday, October 2, the headline in the *Chicago Tribune* was "Stewardess is 7th Capsule Poison Victim." The page-1 headline was not the dominant headline on the page. A bomb explosion that had killed hundreds of people in Tehran, Iran, took that honor. There were two other stories about the Tylenol crisis: one about the efforts to track the source of the poison, and another about funeral services for the victims.

On Sunday, October 3, the *Tribune*'s front-page banner headline, "Shoplifter Is Sought in Poisoning Probe," referred to a story about a man who had been arrested a couple of months before for stealing Tylenol. The story continued on page 4 with excerpts referring to the Johnson & Johnson plants. The first excerpt read as follows:

Other remedy may be safe, but customers don't buy it

CHICAGO TRIBUNE

Dust is collecting on some drugstore shelves in the Chicago area, and people apparently are learning to live with headaches in the wake of last week's tragedy involving Extra Strength Tylenol laced with cyanide.

An informal survey of drugstores throughout the Chicago area showed that sales of most acetaminophen products have dropped while sales of aspirin have increased slightly. Acetaminophen is the nonaspirin substance used in Tylenol and other pain relievers.

"In general acetominophen products are not selling. Point blank. Done in. Dead. Aspirin products are picking up a bit, but the scare seems to have spread through the shelves," said pharmacist Paul Bablak of the Hinsdale Medical Center Pharmacy. "We're collecting a lot of dust on our shelves. People are scared, and you really can't blame them."

If the fear of cyanide poisoning can be measured by the still-packed medication shelves at drugstores, then the fever is spreading through the metropolitan area, several other pharmacists said.

"I think everybody's walking around with headaches," said Jerry Denny, a pharmacist at Family Pharmacy in west suburban La Grange. "All the acetaminophen products are just sitting on the shelves. Even generic acetaminophen is moving slowly."

The slow sales were found not only in smaller, private drugstores but also in chain stores. Jane Armstrong, director of consumer affairs for the Jewel Foods Co., which operates almost 200 Jewel grocery stores and Osco drugstores in the Chicago area, said, "It's too early to tell what's happening to other acetaminophen products. We have noticed an increase in aspirin sales, although it's not a groundswell at this point."

The results have been the same for major drug wholesalers in the area. Drug buyers from several large wholesalers said they expect orders to increase for aspirin and the substitute acetaminophen products once fear subsides, but they added that it is too soon to accurately measure the effect of the tragedy on drug sales.

FIG. 6.2. One of four news stories appearing in the *Chicago Tribune* on October 1, 1982, the first day of news coverage of the Tylenol crisis. Note that the story did not mention Johnson & Johnson. (Copyrighted Chicago Tribune Company. All rights reserved. Reprinted with permission.)

Stores around nation pull Tylenol capsules

BY BARBARA MAHANEY
CHICAGO TRIBUNE

Stores nationwide quickly ordered personnel Thursday to strip their shelves of Extra-Strength Tylenol capsules and hospital spokesmen reported rashes of phone calls after cyanide-tainted capsules were linked in three deaths and possibly two others in suburban Chicago.

The nation's largest grocery chain, Safeway, in Oakland, Calif., ordered all stores to remove bottles of the over-the-counter pain killer in the 96,000-bottle lot--MC 3000--which was recalled by McNeil Consumer Products Co., of Fort Washington, PA.

All 1,000 Revco Discount Drug Centers and 400 CVS pharmacies in New England pulled every bottle of Extra-Strength Tylenol. "We have pulled it off our shelves completely," said Bernie Thomas of Perry Drug Stores, Inc., which operated 124 stores in five states, including 98 in Michigan.

Meanwhile, poison centers and hospitals were reported swamped with thousands of calls from worried consumers, many of whom said they took Tylenol capsules from the recalled lot, but apparently suffered no ill effects.

"We've had questions ranging from 'Do you know anything about Tylenol being contaminated' to 'Oh my God, I just took Extra-Strength Tylenol, am I going to die?'" said Cathy Piccillo of the Indiana Poison Center, which received 50 phone calls.

FIG. 6.3. Another of the four stories appearing in the *Chicago Tribune* on the first day of coverage of the Tylenol crisis. Again, there was no mention of Johnson & Johnson. (*Source:* Copyrighted Chicago Tribune Company. All rights reserved. Reprinted with permission.)

Consumers nationwide were urged to stop using Extra Strength Tylenol capsules. Johnson & Johnson, parent company of the painkiller's manufacturer, announced it is recalling all Extra Strength Tylenol in the Chicago area (Shanker & Grady, 1982, p. 4)

The second excerpt took the following form:

Investigators have been unable to determine how and where the cyanide capsules were placed in any of the suspect containers—whether the killer infiltrated the drug company's sophisticated manufacturing and distribution system at some point between plants in Pennsylvania and Texas and warehouses elsewhere or whether the killer removed and replaced containers once they had been placed on the shelves of local stores.

Stein said he could not rule out "factory error" because of the reported disclosure by Lawrence Foster, a spokesman for Johnson & Johnson.

Foster said potassium cyanide is used in chemical tests at some of McNeil's laboratories, but not in the manufacturing process. The labs are remote from the manufacturing areas and cyanide would be detected even if someone tried to introduce it during manufacturing, he said ... (Shanker & Grady, 1982, p. 4)

There was another front-page story in the October 3 *Tribune,* this one about a 12-year-old who had died from the poison 4 days before.

Johnson & Johnson installed 33 telephones to communicate with publics during the crisis. Pretaped statements were placed on special toll-free telephone lines to expedite news gathering. The messages were regularly updated. A full-page advertisement was placed in major Chicago newspapers offering consumers an exchange of Tylenol capsules for Tylenol tablets.

During the first week of the crisis, Kniffin handled the media from McNeil, whereas Foster was in charge at headquarters. Approximately 180,000 news stories ran in newspapers nationally. The story was at the top of television and radio newscasts.

Two thousand telephone calls were taken from the media. Thirty thousand calls from consumers came in during the first months following the deaths.

Still there were glitches.

During the first 3 days, as the *Chicago Tribune* articles showed, Foster issued a statement to reporters that there was no cyanide in the manufacturing plants. A few days later, the Associated Press heard that there was cyanide in the plants and called Foster to confirm the report. After checking again, Foster discovered that indeed a small amount of cyanide was used in the manufacturing plant for quality-assurance testing of some kind.

However, the cyanide was kept in a completely separate facility from the production line. Also, none of it was missing. There was no way that it could have gotten into the capsules accidentally. Even if it had, it would have been so dispersed as to be harmless.

Foster called the Associated Press and told it the truth. He has a reputation for being honest, fair, and ethical. He could not afford a cover-up. When he told the wire service that there was no way the cyanide could have gotten into the capsules, the reporters believed him and agreed not to run the story—unless some other news outlet got the information, too.

Sure enough, the *Newark Star-Ledger* got word of the information, called Johnson & Johnson for confirmation, and again Foster said, "Trust me." The reporter agreed.

Keeping his promise to the Associated Press, Foster called and told the wire service that the *Newark Star-Ledger* had the information but had also agreed not to run it. The Associated Press agreed once more not to run the story unless still another newspaper or TV station got the information. After all, the *Star-Ledger* was basically a neighbor to the company.

However, when the *New York Times* got the information, Foster decided to give up. He called both the Associated Press and the *Star-Ledger* and asked them to use discretion in running the story. The resulting stories had very little impact. They were run in insignificant places in the Sunday newspapers, and the facts were not blown out of proportion (as had happened with other crises). The newspapers merely reported the information as Foster had revealed it.

With this Foster realized that his positive dealings with the media over the years had paid off. The story could have made front-page headlines everywhere, but it did not because the media trusted the public relations professional from their past dealings with him.

The FBI and the FDA never found any evidence of tampering at the two Johnson & Johnson plants. They found that the contaminated capsules had come from both plants—one in Texas, the other in Pennsylvania—but for the first time, there was basic proof that the tampering was not an inside job. The finger now pointed to some external, malicious psychopath who bought the Tylenol, laced it with cyanide, and placed it back in the containers and on the selves of stores.

After the crisis team discovered what had transpired, its members were relieved to be assured that the contamination could not have occurred in the plants. The task of the team now turned to saving Tylenol and restoring sales. The team was not worried that Johnson & Johnson would go under because of the company's diversified product line. Sales were not down for other Johnson & Johnson products. There was no boycott against the company. However, there was a fear of Tylenol capsules. The future of Tylenol was at stake.

To reach the employees who had been on pins and needles while the company battled the crisis, CEO Burke spoke to an assembly at McNeil and promised that Extra Strength Tylenol was coming back. Employees wore "We're Coming Back" buttons. Those employees who had been manufacturing Tylenol were given other temporary jobs. Videotaped reports of activities were shown to employees explaining what was going on with the crisis.

Information packages were sent electronically—fax, telegram, other methods—to major distributors who, in a short time, notified half a million retailers and medical professionals.

Up to this point, there was a debate over whether to recall the product. The FBI and the FDA advised against a recall because it would mean giving in to the terrorists.

The decision not to recall would have flown if it had not been for a copycat crime that took place in northern California on October 5. The company decided then that removing the product from all stores was the only way to show the public that it was concerned about the welfare of its customers. On October 5, all Tylenol products were removed from stores nationwide.

Later, there were approximately 250 copycat reports, all of which were found to be groundless.

During the recovery period, a decision was made to repackage the product. A 60-second television commercial featuring the medical director at McNeil notifying consumers of the upcoming return of Tylenol aired in October and November to an estimated 85% of U.S. television households.

The triple-seal safety package devised for the product was announced at a November 11 news conference transmitted by satellite to 29 different sites where reporters were gathered. Burke also announced the availability of coupons that could be used toward the purchase of any Tylenol product and a special toll-free telephone number through which consumers could learn about the special promotion. More than 200,000 calls came in to the toll-free information number. Coverage of the press conference in the *Kansas City Times* applauded Burke and the company for their efforts and described the new Tylenol safety package as having "glued flaps ... which must be forcibly opened. Inside, a tight plastic seal surrounds the cap and an inner foil seal wraps over the mouth of the bottle" (Goodman, 1982). Johnson & Johnson could not have paid for better news coverage.

Johnson & Johnson executives did interviews with network television shows, such as "Donahue," "60 Minutes," and "Nightline," as well as with major newspapers and magazines, such as the *Wall Street Journal* and *Fortune.*

As a result of the crisis, all Tylenol capsules were discontinued, as were capsules of other brand names. Tamper-proof, triple-sealed safety containers were swiftly placed on the shelves of retailers 10 weeks after the withdrawal. Other manufacturers followed suit.

The crisis cost the company more than $100 million. Tylenol regained 100% of the market share it had before the crisis. Seven people died. Other lives were saved by the company's decision to recall all the capsules in the Chicago area. The Tylenol murderer was never found. A $100,000 reward offered by Johnson & Johnson still remains unclaimed.

An October 11 *Washington Post* front-page article praised Johnson & Johnson's crisis response: "Johnson & Johnson has effectively demonstrated how a major business ought to handle a disaster ... what executives have done is communicate the message that the company is candid, contrite and compassionate, committed to solving the murders and protecting the public" (Knight, 1982).

CHAPTER SEVEN

Case: Exxon and the Valdez Oil Spill

In the late 1980s, Exxon was one of the five largest companies in the United States, with sales of $80 billion. Exxon CEO Lawrence G. Rawl had been employed at Exxon for 37 years before getting the top job in 1986. He was considered a strong leader who disliked publicity and the media.

The Valdez oil spill crisis started shortly after midnight on Friday, March 24, 1989. The Exxon Valdez, a 987-foot oil tanker was headed for Long Beach, California, from Prince William Sound off the coast of Alaska. A reporter later described the ship as "longer than three football fields, [and] loaded to the top with enough oil to fill the Rose Bowl almost halfway to the top" (*Turning Point,* 1994).

The weather was calm. The water was beautiful. During daylight hours, an abundance of sea life could be seen. It was the time of the migration that brings to the area the largest concentration of migratory fowl in the entire world. Sea otters, seals, whales, salmon, herring, and halibut inhabited the Sound.

Just before midnight, the local pilot, who had guided the tanker out of the harbor, went off duty. Captain Joseph Hazelwood, in command, put the supertanker on autopilot and headed straight for Bligh Reef, one of

several well-known hazardous areas in Prince William Sound. Hazelwood had sailed the route more than 100 times. Some said he could do it nearly blindfolded. He had been with Exxon for 21 years, 10 of them as captain.

On this night, Hazelwood left his post at the bridge and put Third Mate Gregory Cousins in charge, telling him to keep the tanker on course for 3 minutes, then turn right, thus avoiding the reef. Although Cousins was qualified to take command during normal times, government investigators later said that he was not qualified to take command at that critical period when the ship had to be steered in a very precise maneuver.

Cousins waited too long before ordering the turn, and the Exxon Valdez headed for the submerged rocks. He told Captain Hazelwood, "I think we're in serious trouble." Hazelwood radioed the Coast Guard with the message, "We've fetched up hard aground Evidently, we're leaking some oil" (Smith, 1992, p. 84). Cousins and Hazelwood had just made the two understatements of 1989.

The tanker had run aground on the rocks of Bligh Reef, ripping open a hole in the hull nearly as long as the ship itself. Over the next hours and days, 11 million gallons of crude oil poured out into Prince William Sound. The oil spread relentlessly. Some said the oil slick was 10 feet wide and 4 miles long—the worst oil spill ever in American waters.

Obviously, the beautiful waters were no longer beautiful, but more importantly, sea life perished. It was estimated that 1 million migratory fowl and one third of the sea otter population, about 2,500, died. Also, seals and sea lions fell victim to the slick. Some sources revealed that 2 million animals died as a result of the oil, although this did not include halibut, pink salmon, herring, clams, and worms that remained uncounted. Some scientists claimed that wildlife may still remain poisoned by the oil years later. Others later said Prince William Sound totally recovered from the spill.

The weekend news reports came from local media and through the three major television networks. By Monday, media people from all over the world began to pour into Valdez. The media frenzy had begun. (Examples of the news coverage are shown in Fig. 7.1.) In addition, hundreds of environmentalists arrived in Valdez to help save the animals, the beaches, and the water. Concern was rampant.

Don Cornet, who later became Exxon's public relations manager, was Alaska coordinator for Exxon at that time; he reported to the head of public affairs and rushed to the scene as soon as he got word of the accident. The company's immediate strategy was to focus on the cleanup effort. Exxon's theory was that the initial spill was regrettable, but that at this point the most crucial task was to clean it up as swiftly as possible and restore normalcy to the area.

Frank Iarossi, then-president of Exxon Shipping (the grounded tanker came from its shipyards), was Exxon's main representative at the Valdez

Excerpts from front page news story in *Anchorage Daily News*,
March 25, 1989

Crude oil fouls Sound
Oil officials react slowly to disaster

BY LARRY CAMPBELL
DAILY NEWS REPORTER

VALDEZ - As the largest oil spill in the history of the United States entered
its second day, only a feeble containment effort has been mounted and a
crowd of state, federal and oil company officials remained undecided about
how to clean up the mess.

A 32-square-mile, multi-hued sheen continued to float and spread atop
the waters of Prince William Sound. The Sound is surrounded by land on
three sides. Two large islands, Hinchinbrook and Montague, lie across its
open, southern end. That means that unless the spilled oil can be dealt with,
it is a near-certainty that it will wash ashore somewhere in the Sound.

Valdez residents grew increasingly critical Friday of what seemed to
be sluggish movement by Alyeska Pipeline Service Co., which operates the
oil terminal here, and Exxon Shipping Co. in dealing with the spill. Nearly
24 hours after the Exxon Valdez ran aground on Bligh Reef about 25 miles
southwest of here, officials had done little to contain the spill or clean up
what was beyond containment.

Oil keeps spreading in Sound
State says Alyeska's cleanup effort inadequate, slow

BY LARRY CAMPBELL
DAILY NEWS REPORTER

VALDEZ - State, federal and oil company officials ended Saturday as they
had begun it, no closer to a solution to the problems posed by more than 11
million gallons of North Slope crude oil washing around the fish-and-
wildlife-rich, enclosed waters of Prince William Sound.

But while the oil of the nation's largest spill was left mostly
unmolested, the chief of the state Department of Environmental
Conservation assailed the Alyeska Pipeline Service Co. for its failure to
respond quickly to the disaster.

FIG. 7.1. Excerpts from front-page news stories appearing in the *Anchorage Daily News* on March 25, 1989, the day after the oil spill from the Exxon Valdez.

site. CEO Rawl was nowhere to be found. Iarossi dealt with the logistics of the spill response. Early on, he pointed a finger at Captain Hazelwood. Years later, there was still some confusion over whether Hazelwood had been drinking that night, but it was a fact that his driver's license had been revoked for drunken driving and that he had once been hospitalized for alcohol treatment. He denies he was drunk and no court has ever proven he was. At any rate, Hazelwood was fired. Third Mate Cousins blamed the crisis on "poor seamanship" ("The Big Spill," 1990).

Some Exxon employees placed the blame on Exxon's corporate culture. They said that in order to save money the company had cut crews, and that the short-staffed crews worked long hours and got little sleep. They felt that human fatigue was responsible for the accident. Moving the oil was a cardinal rule, they said, and employees who did not work fast and long enough feared losing their jobs.

Smith (1992) said that in 1986, the Exxon Valdez was designed for a crew of 33. Yet on the fateful night of the spill, the crew numbered only 19.

According to requirements of the State of Alaska, the Alyeska Pipeline Service Company, a consortium of several companies working on Alaska's North Slope, was responsible for the initial response to the spill. Exxon, Atlantic Richfield (ARCO), British Petroleum (BP), and five other companies initially participated in the response. Exxon soon after took over the cleanup efforts from the other companies.

At the start of the crisis, Cornet set up a media center in Valdez, a remote town with limited facilities, equipment, and accommodations. Critics charged that the media center should have been in New York or Chicago, a city that could better accommodate such a large gathering of reporters and photographers. Others insisted that it had to be at the site, regardless of the difficulties. The media said that photographs and videos of the spill, citizens of Alaska, and government officials were all necessary to the stories communicated to the public.

Contradictory statements about the seriousness of the crisis were issued from various news sources. One statement said the damage was minimal. Another said the damage was substantial.

Four days after the spill, local fishermen in the village of Cordova were angry because cleanup efforts had not worked. They and the media were not happy about the response.

Iarossi held a press conference without first being briefed by public relations personnel; he was verbally slaughtered. Brian Dunphy, another spokesperson for Exxon Shipping, said that he would not verify the extent of the damage or what was being done about it, a statement that was not well received.

CEO Rawl still declined to go to the site. He said that he felt "technologically obsolete." The media, the fishermen, the environmentalists, and the public were irate. Customers began to cancel their Exxon credit cards. The

media continued to attack more vociferously. Exxon had not anticipated the intensity of the public's concern about the environmental crisis. Neither had it anticipated such a large spill or the difficulties in cleanup and communications.

Alaska public relations expert George Mason expressed it like this: "The public had been growing more 'green,' but the spill caused a rapid and identifiable leap [in what] I call the 'greening of America.'"

Rawl eventually issued a statement via television telling the public what chemicals would be used to clean up the spill. He made no apologies to the fishermen whose livelihoods had been affected. He showed no emotion over the impact of the disaster.

Ten days after the spill, Exxon released full-page ads expressing concern and vowing to clean up the spill. Still, the company did not accept responsibility for the damage. Three weeks after the spill, the CEO went to Alaska, apparently no longer feeling "technologically obsolete."

All oil companies operating in Alaskan waters now have crisis plans approved by the state. In 1989, Alyeska Pipeline Service Company's plan anticipated a much smaller oil spill and allotted only 5 hours for containment. A primary response in these plans was the use of dispersants as well as *in situ* burning for cleanup. The Coast Guard and the Alaska state government could not decide on the use of dispersants for the Exxon Valdez spill, and this debate prolonged the cleanup. A dispersant test was attempted on Monday following the Friday night spill, but harsh weather prevented its completion. In addition, the spill was so massive that there were not enough dispersants in Alaska to deal with the problem.

A month after the spill, Exxon finally had the equipment for a full-scale cleanup, which was not completed until 1992. Some Alaskans said there was still evidence of the oil in the Sound. In 1994, Exxon issued information to the media showing that predictions of long-term damage resulting from the spill were exaggerated, and that there was oil from other sources in Prince William Sound. Independent scientific studies seemed to confirm this, but oil from these sources was minuscule compared to that from the Exxon Valdez.

Although various controversies about the Exxon spill remained, one thing was certain: The Exxon Valdez was a warning sign, a prodrome for other oil companies. Later, British Petroleum (BP) suffered an oil spill in the Pacific Ocean off the coast of Huntington Beach south of Los Angeles. BP reacted with haste, even getting underwater photographers to capture images of the hole in the ship for the media.

In a few days, the BP accident was no longer news. This spill, however, was in no way as massive or as difficult as the Exxon spill. It should also be noted that Exxon sent personnel and equipment to help work on the cleanup of this BP spill.

Rawl resigned in 1993, and Lee Raymond, second in command, took over as Exxon CEO. In 1989, the position of public relations manager did not exist at the company. In organizational restructuring under Raymond, Carnet took this position. In this new organizational hierarchy, there were fewer layers between the CEO and the public relations department. Cornet reported to the head of public affairs, who reported directly to Raymond.

Although Hazelwood was acquitted of operating the tanker while intoxicated, he was convicted of negligent discharge of oil (a misdemeanor), fined $50,000, and ordered to perform community service. After 8 years of appeals, in 1998 the Alaska Court of Appeals upheld Hazelwood's sentence of 1,000 hours of community work ("Sentence Upheld Over Oil Spill," 1998). After being fired from Exxon and sued, he was unable to find work as a ship's captain, though his credentials and skills were highly praised. He worked for a time in New York as a claims adjuster for his lawyers. In 1999, at 52, he began to do his community service and was scheduled to complete 200 hours a year for 5 years ("Exxon Valdez Captain Finally Will Do Community Service," 1999). Also, in 1999, Hazelwood worked at an Anchorage soup kitchen. Although he resents being fired by Exxon and sees himself as a victim, Hazelwood said, "I felt terrible about my involvement … as any normal human being" ("Serving Time," 1999).

Cousins, the third mate who was left responsible by Hazelwood to steer the ship away from Bligh Reef, continued on his ladder of success to become a second mate on a U.S.-flagged bulk ship (Nalder, 1999).

Ten years after the Exxon Valdez oil spill, the largest marine disaster in U.S. history, scientists announced that Alaska's Prince William Sound was recovering, although full ecological recovery had not been achieved. According to scientists, humans could not do much more to hurry the recovery. Only 2 of the 28 herring were declared recovered. Although sea otters were recovering, it could take decades to make a full comeback in some of the area's most heavily oiled bays (Watson, 1999).

Exxon was ordered by a federal court to pay $5 billion to fishermen and others damaged by the oil spill. Although saying it "deeply regrets" the spill, Exxon argued that there were limits to its deep pockets. It cited the $2.2 billion in cleanup expenses and another $1 billion in civil settlements as sufficient punishments for the damage, saying that a greater amount would send a "perverse message" after all the company had done to mitigate the accident's effects (Connelly, 1999).

Exxon remains fiscally sound. In 1998, it was still the nation's biggest oil company, ranking fourth in profits ("The Fortune 500," 2000). In 1998, when Exxon agreed to buy Mobil Oil for $77.2 billion, the merger created the world's largest oil company, Exxon-Mobil ("Richest Merger of All Time," 1998, p. A1B). Two years later, Exxon-Mobil was number 3 on the *Fortune* 500 list, after General Motors and WalMart ("The Fortune 500," 2000).

CHAPTER EIGHT

Case: Exxon's Other Story—Animal Rescue Centers and Alaskan Tourism

George Mason, APR, in 1989, was vice president of Bradley/McAfee Public Relations, Alaska's largest public relations firm. The firm was part of Bradley Advertising, the state's largest advertising agency. (The company name has since been changed to Bradley/Reid Communications.)

"Alyeska Pipeline Service Company was our largest account, and we'd held it for 14 years," said Mason, who was not personally responsible for the account but had, on occasion, handled crisis communications for the client.

When the Exxon Valdez ran aground on the night of March 24, 1989, Mason contacted Alyeska's public relations director, John Rattermann to offer assistance. One of Alyeska's key public relations staff members was on vacation; two others were at the Valdez site. Mason, as he had on previous occasions, assisted the short staff with duties in Anchorage.

"What is often forgotten in the news stories," he said, "is that Alyeska Pipeline Company, a consortium of several oil companies (including Exxon), was responsible for [the] initial response in the event of a spill."

Although Alyeska and Exxon realized damage had been done and the significance of it, Mason said, "No one knew how much damage had been done and what else *could* happen."

He said that when the Coast Guard arrived at the tanker just after the spill, there were thick fumes from the oil, thick enough to clog helicopter engines and prevent the helicopters from flying overhead. There was, therefore, a fear of onboard fires. In addition, he says, "Captain Hazelwood was smoking."

It was during this period that the media converged on Valdez. As Mason puts it, "In short order, the phones were jammed, and the small airport in Valdez was besieged. General public hysteria, the nightmare dimension of any crisis, was beginning, as was the media feeding frenzy."

In an effort to keep people informed, Exxon held briefings at the Valdez Community Center with representatives of the U.S. Coast Guard and Alaska state government participating. Frank Iarossi, president of Exxon Shipping, represented Exxon. "In an effort to fully cooperate and try to keep information flowing, it had been agreed to allow members of the local communities to participate in the briefings," said Mason.

One of these briefings exploded when angry fishermen shouted their concern and confusion. This was the briefing in which Iarossi was verbally attacked. There was a rumor that a member of Greenpeace planned to toss dead birds at the speakers. That never happened, but there was great concern when a woman with a bag of laundry tried to enter the room.

The day after the angry public meeting, Mason was asked to fly immediately to Valdez to meet with Don Cornet, Alaska coordinator for Exxon:

> I flew out in an eight-passenger plane loaded with workers and contractors hurrying to the scene. I was met at the airport by Alyeska's onsite public relations staff members who gave me a quick tour of the mayhem in Valdez, then to the hotel that had been temporarily set up as Exxon's headquarters.
>
> The hotel was jammed with reporters and others trying to get a story. Security guards were stationed in the hotel's hallway in an effort to provide some breathing and working room for Exxon's staff.

Mason had never met Cornet, and their meeting was brief. As they talked, telephones rang persistently. One long angry caller, he remembered particularly, was the mayor of the seaport town of Whittier, many miles from the spill. "In my opinion," said Mason, "Mr. Cornet had already grasped the futility of the situation as far as the degree of damage Exxon's image had suffered. He seemed to accept this and had begun to look ahead to the long-term future."

At any rate, Cornet, while working on the cleanup of the spill, asked Mason to develop and implement strategies for three areas that he expected would be of future concern:

1. The tourism industry, Alaska's third-largest industry (oil was the state's largest industry).

2. The animal rescue centers Exxon had already begun to set up on Valdez.

3. The seafood industry, Alaska's second-largest industry.

According to Mason:

> I agreed to handle the animal rescue issues and tourism. At the time, I was also the supervisor on the state of Alaska's tourism public relations account, and this arena was a natural one to handle.
>
> However, I explained that I would not directly handle the seafood issues because this was not my area of expertise. Also, the states' seafood public relations account was handled by another agency in Anchorage. I did agree to notify that agency and offer assistance if needed.

Mason then organized the next briefing in Valdez and met with Iarossi and others to plan a briefing strategy. He suggested two separate briefings—one for media, another for the public, including reporters who desired to attend. Prior to making the suggestion, Mason had consulted with reporters at the scene who said they were finding it increasingly difficult to get information over the shouting of the fishermen and environmentalists.

In assembling an agenda for the briefing, Mason included wildlife experts to address animal issues. Security guards checked press passes at the door to ensure that only credentialed reporters were admitted. Mason said that the briefing went smoothly. The media could pose questions without interruptions from persons with personal agendas.

EXXON'S ANIMAL RESCUE CENTERS

After the media briefing, Mason went to the Animal Rescue Center, where there was additional mayhem. Teams of wildlife professionals and their equipment had been flown into Valdez. They were trying to set up the center to help rescue some of the animals.

"Reporters and interested community people were given free access to the facility, again in an effort to cooperate," recalled Mason. "However, the result was impossible. On more than one occasion, eager reporters, mostly freelancers trying to make a buck, were in the way, and in some instances had stepped on injured birds being treated."

Again, Mason, in agreement with the head of the animal rescue center, put secuirty guards to work. This time, it was the media and others not connected with the rescue effort who were kept out. The facility was roped off. Then media tours were arranged and guidelines were constructed to guarantee the protection of the animals.

With the protocols set up, Mason returned to Anchorage to set up long-term systems. He assigned a staff member of his firm, Suzanne Stolpe-Bishop, to the animal rescue effort. She worked in Valdez for 2 months and subsequently won an Aurora Award for her work from the Alaskan chapters of the Public Relations Society of America.

Mason subcontracted a staff member to do the same work with a second animal rescue center in Seward, Alaska. He subcontracted others to act as community liaisons in other communities. "The purpose here," said Mason, "was to ensure credible connection between Exxon and the community, to assist Exxon's local claims offices, and to help in other ways."

ALASKAN TOURISM

Mason headed the tourism campaign himself. He already knew, from previous research, that the greatest concern was that the spill had occurred in spring, the peak time of year when tourists make plans for vacations.

"We suspected," he said, "that the televised reports of thick oil and dead animals would seriously impact decisions of tourists contemplating travel in Alaska. An early survey of vendors statewide confirmed our fears."

Mason said that the tourism industry telephoned from all over Alaska. The fear was that American tourists would think that the spill had marred all of Alaska. Cancellations were also rampant. Some callers asked, "How deep is the oil in Fairbanks?" Fairbanks is a city nowhere near the oil spill.

Mason designed a crisis plan that was further developed and fine-tuned by a team of experts, including public relations heads of Westours and Princess cruise lines. The plan was quickly funded by Exxon and approved by the Alaska Tourism Marketing Council, a combined state and industry group.

The crisis plan involved bringing travel writers to Alaska to witness the conditions and encouraging them to travel within the state in order to report what destinations were and were not affected by the spill. A telephone hotline was also instituted for travel editors to get information swiftly.

News conferences were held in New York, Los Angeles, San Francisco, and Seattle with feeds to major television network programs. The news conferences in San Francisco and Los Angeles were organized by Ketchum Public Relations offices in those cities. Erik V. Peterson, APR, who was formerly Mason's boss in Alaska, did the groundwork for the Seattle news conference. The agency Padilla, Spear, Beardsley set up the New York press conference. Alaska Governor Cooper participated in the news conferences in Seattle and San Francisco and was a very credible participant because he had been so publicly critical of the spill. When he said, "Alaska is beautiful," people believed him.

At the same time, Exxon funded an advertising campaign developed jointly by Mason's agency and McCann-Erickson of Seattle. The public rela-

tions campaign reached an estimated 50 million Americans. The advertising campaign reached even more. Both were successful in diffusing negative travel publicity.

That season, Alaska's tourism set a new record. It was 5% higher than it had been the year before the spill. The public relations campaign won a Silver Anvil Commendation from the Public Relations Society of America as well as numerous other national and regional awards.

"None of it [the tourism and the animal rescue efforts] would have been possible were it not for the cooperation and support of Exxon," said Mason, who went on to become president of corporate communications strategies in Anchorage and an adjunct professor of advanced public relations at the University of Alaska, Anchorage. "Exxon's cooperation and diligence after the spill is a fact that seems to have been lost in the myth of drunken sailors and dead wildlife," reflected Mason.

Mason continued:

The lesson I learned from that crisis and have since applied to other crises is that once the crisis begins and the public hysteria begins, it is too late to worry about your PR. All you can really do is hang on, get on with the work, and continue to do what you think is best and most honest.

However, you must, immediately, plan for the future. Think to the midterm and long-term future to start necessary preparations for those arenas, areas where you can begin to exert some logical controls and protections. Try to get ahead of the curve of events.

CHAPTER NINE

Case: Snapps Restaurant
and the AIDS Rumor

Rarely does a company call a news conference to fight a rumor. There are several reasons why. Companies would ideally prefer to reach only the people who have heard the rumor—and not one person more. This is a difficult-to-impossible task. Nevertheless, many times, the rumor is limited to a specific location. With a news conference, however, the media would wind up spreading the rumor to people who had never heard it. Also, some companies reason that if the rumor is not spread by the media, it is not likely to reach the crucial public by the media either. The people who spread and believe the rumor may not read newspapers or watch television news.

The Snapps fast-food chain departed from both of these tenets in 1991, when it held a history-making news conference to fight a rumor about one of its restaurants. In Fort Pierce, Florida, Snapps confronted a rumor that one of its managers had AIDS and had contaminated hamburger meat. The Ohio-based chain had opened its first Florida restaurant in Fort Pierce in 1990. About an hour's drive north of Palm Beach, Fort Pierce is a middle-class city of 40,000 residents.

The location of Fort Pierce was important in that nearby Jensen Beach, Florida, was where Kimberly Bergalis allegedly contracted the AIDS virus from her dentist. Because Bergalis was the first person known to have contracted AIDS from a health care professional, the incident was widely publicized. Furthermore, because of their proximity to the case, the people of Fort Pierce were probably more concerned with this unique case than many other people. The incident also aroused other questions about how the virus might be spread.

The rumor spread by way of a crudely handwritten flyer (see Fig. 9.1). The flyer was circulated primarily among students in two public high schools, thereby targeting a large chunk of Snapps' clientele. The Fort Pierce Snapps restaurant saw its business drop by 50%. The Snapps corporate office in Columbus, Ohio, sent Regional Vice President Donald G. Gilbert to remedy the crisis.

Gilbert formed a damage-control task force that included a lawyer; a private investigator; and Richard M. Gruenwald, a public relations consultant for Dick Gruenwald Associates of nearby Palm Beach Gardens. The team worked closely with Rod Cardiff, a physician and director of the HRS St. Lucie County Health Unit. Gilbert, the Snapps home office, and Fort Pierce Snapps owners Jack and Jeff Roschman monitored and approved actions of the task force.

The team's first task was to find the source of the rumor. The private investigator felt certain that a student in one of the schools had written the flyer. Police procedure called for a complaint to be filed before the police could enter the case. The investigator and the lawyer were able to collect enough information to file the complaint.

The next step was to have the restaurant's managers tested for AIDS. This decision brought about a necessity for checking legalities. By law, the managers would have to volunteer to be tested; the company could not force them to do so. All seven managers volunteered, including one who had recently been transferred from the Fort Pierce restaurant to one in another city. The law also required that the test results be sent to the people who took the tests, not to the employer. The procedure took a week. The results indicated that all seven managers, as expected, tested negative for the AIDS virus.

Meanwhile, the Fort Pierce restaurant continued to lose business. Layoffs were threatened if business did not improve. "This was a double-edged sword," said Gilbert. "We had to be sure of our facts, have everything in place for the complaint filing and act quickly, as business was continuing to go downhill."

Gruenwald, the public relations counsel, and his associate, John Futch, suggested a press conference. "We all agreed that a press conference would bring everything out in the open," said Gruenwald. "The problem was there. Why hide it?"

FIG. 9.1. The handwritten flyer circulated in Fort Pierce high schools that helped spread the rumor that a manager at a popular restaurant was infected with the AIDS virus and that persons who dined at the restaurant might become contaminated. All managers were voluntarily tested and none tested positive for the virus. The health department cooperated with the restaurant's public relations efforts and, during a news conference, explained that the disease could not be spread in that manner. (Permission of Snapps Restaurant, Inc.)

Snapps made public relations history when it became the first fast-food chain to address an AIDS rumor by going on the offensive and holding a news conference (see Fig. 9.2). "We were most impressed with the way that management accepted our recommendations," said Gruenwald. To add credibility to the occasion, the press conference was held in the St. Lucie Health Unit's office, and the unit's director spoke on behalf of the franchise. At the conference, an announcement was made that the chain was offering a $5,000 reward for information leading to the arrest of the person or persons who started the rumor. The news conference was attended by company executives as well as the county health director, who announced that all Snapps managers had tested negative for the virus. He further stated that AIDS could not be transmitted through food and that it was safe to eat at Snapps.

Two West Palm Beach television stations led their 6 p.m. newscasts with the Snapps news conference story, including interviews with customers. Employees talked about how their jobs were affected. Associated Press and Knight-Ridder News Service picked up the story and used it in newspapers all over Florida as well as in many newspapers out of state.

"The press was most cooperative and news coverage was excellent," Gilbert said. Gruenwald, looking back, said his philosophy was that "if you cooperate with the media, they—for the most part—will cooperate with you."

The *Denver Post* picked up the Knight-Ridder story; its lead emphasized the unusual public relations tactic: "In a highly unusual move, an Ohio-based fast-food restaurant went public yesterday to confront a rumor that one of its managers had AIDS and had contaminated hamburger meat" (Knight-Ridder, 1991). The article went on to comment on the restaurant's denial, the offered reward, and the fact that AIDS could not be transmitted through food. It also pointed out that other fast-food restaurants had been plagued by AIDS rumors, but Snapps was the first to fight the rumor through a news conference (Knight-Ridder, 1991).

The private investigator discovered that a 16-year-old female high school student had written and distributed the flyer, apparently after a class discussion on AIDS. "The girl admitted to writing the flyer," said Gilbert, "but we determined that the student's action came after the AIDS rumor had been circulating in the community and she didn't start the rumor."

"The student, through her parents and attorney, agreed to issue an apology," said Gilbert. "We used the apology in a press release and a full-page ad in the local newspaper."

The minor, who said she wrote the flyer because she was concerned about her friends and wanted to do them a favor, wrote the following apology:

> I apologize to the community in helping to spread a rumor about Snapps, a
> local fast food restaurant. As a young person who has taken a course con-

Store's business cut 50 percent by AIDS rumor

BY PHIL LONG
HERALD STAFF WRITER

FORT PIERCE - In a highly unusual move, an Ohio-based fast food restaurant went public Wednesday to confront a rumor that one of its managers had AIDS and had contaminated hamburger met.

"The rumor is totally false," said Don Gilbert, regional vice president at Snapps, a company with 44 stores, mostly in Ohio.

"All of our managers have been tested and none has AIDS," he said.

But in a little over a month since the rumor started, business in Florida's only Snapps store has dropped almost 50 percent, Gilbert said. Five of the store's 40 positions remain unfilled, and employee hours have been cut. Layoffs are possible, he said.

The firm is promising a $5,000 reward for information leading to the arrest of the person who photocopies or circulated a crude, hand-drawn flier that accuses the manager of having AIDS and contaminating hamburger meat with his blood.

In what may have been the first press conference of its kind involving a national food chain, Gilbert met reporters in the lobby of the health department. He was flanked by the county's health director, Snapps employees, a company attorney and a police detective.

Snapps managers have been tested and they don't have any trace of the virus, said Dr. Rod Cardiff, director of the St. Lucie Public Health Unit.

"There is nothing unsafe about Snapps," he said. "AIDS is not transmitted through food. There is no danger with going to Snapps and eating there."

Fort Pierce police Lt. Irving Hamrick, who suspects that a teenager is responsible because the fliers have been circulated at the county's two public high schools, said his department is investigating.

Prosecutor Linda Craft said the person responsible for the flier could face up to a year in jail on the misdemeanor charge of criminal defamation. it is illegal to publish anything that causes "hatred, contempt, ridicule or obloquy," to an individual, Craft said.

"They are not only affecting my job, but the jobs of many other people employed by Snapps," said Anita Farley, a Snapps worker who has been with the restaurant since it opened in July.

AIDS rumors are not new. McDonald's and Burger King have faced them before. Neither have gone quite so public...

FIG. 9.2. A news story about the Snapps crisis appearing in the *Miami Herald*, May 9, 1991. Note the reporter recognized that the news conference was not a common method of fighting such rumors. (*Source:* Reprinted by permission of the *Miami Herald*.)

cerning aids and having great concern for the people in the community, I took it upon myself to prepare a flyer concerning Snapps without knowing whether the information I received as a rumor was true. I now realize that I was wrong and I apologize to Snapps, its managers and employees. It was not my intent to harm their business and I am sorry that Snapps' business has suffered as a result of the rumor. I have since returned to eat at Snapps and I encourage others to do so as well.

<div style="text-align:center">
Sincerely,

C. J., a minor
</div>

Because the student was a minor, her identity was never made public. State Attorney Bruce Colton said a rumor could violate state laws that made libel a misdemeanor punishable by up to a year in jail. Prosecutor Linda Craft said the person responsible for the flyer could face up to a year in jail on the misdemeanor charge of criminal defamation (Knight-Ridder, 1991).

Gruenwald advised the company not to press charges against the girl. "It was never felt that the girl acted maliciously," he said. "Also, she did not start the rumor. It had been circulating before she wrote the flyer. If we had filed charges, we could win the battle, but not the war of public opinion. The public apology would bring her sympathy and perhaps a boycott to the restaurant. Then, the case might drag out, thus hurting the chances for a return to normalcy."

The media carried the story of the apology with headlines as follows:

Palm Beach Post—"Student Apologizes for Restaurant Rumor" (Reeder, 1991).

Stuart News (Stuart, Florida)—"Student Apologizes for AIDS Rumor About Eatery" (Cheek, 1991).

Miami Herald—"Student Apologizes for Spreading Rumor About Restaurant" (Long, 1991b).

As in most crises cases, recovery stories are not featured as prominently, nor are they as long, as the original stories.

Snapps management continued an aggressive effort to win back customers. Its advertising agency, Haunty & Welter of Columbus, Ohio, launched a strong radio and newspaper, and later, television campaign with a free hamburger weekend, June 1 and 2. "This was a tremendous success," said Gruenwald. "The girl who wrote the flyer, who we called CJ, attended the event." More than 15,000 free hamburgers were served. The event was promoted in a news release and resulting stories using CJ's apology (see Fig. 9.3 and Fig 9.4).

DICK
GRUENWALD
ASSOCIATES
PUBLIC RELATIONS
4362 Northlake Boulevard, Suite 109
Palm Beach Gardens, Florida 33410
(407) 622-3200
FAX: (407) 627-6403

June 3, 1991

SNAPPS SERVES
15,000 FREE HAMBURGERS
OVER WEEKEND

FORT PIERCE --Snapps Restaurant celebrated its first anniversary in Fort Pierce giving away 15,000 free hamburgers Saturday and Sunday.

It was quite a turn-around for the drive-in eatery that saw its business drop dramatically with a rumor that one of its managers had AIDS.

Last week Snapps management announced that a Fort Pierce teen-ager, identified only as "C J", had apologized for writing and distributing a flier stating that a Snapps manager had AIDS. "C J was one of our customers over the weekend," regional vice president Donald Gilbert said.

Since the apology announcment, business has picked up but still has a long way to go to return to normal, Gilbert said.

The weekend event was most encouraging, Gilbert said. There were several large groups including one church with more than 100 kids and a compact car with 13 kids.

\#

For media information: Dick Gruenwald

FIG. 9.3. One of several news releases distributed by the public relations firm hired by an Ohio-based restaurant to manage the crisis in Fort Pierce. (*Source:* Reprinted by permission of Snapps Restaurant, Inc.)

Eatery plagued by rumor fights back

STUART NEWS

FORT PIERCE - A Fort Pierce eatery gave away 15,000 hamburgers last weekend, battling recent rumors that an employee at Snapps restaurant tainted food with the AIDS virus.

Among the many people eating at the restaurant at 25th Street and Orange Avenue was a teenager known only as "C.J." The Fort Pierce Westwood High School student apologized recently for distributing a flier warning fellow students not to eat at Snapps.

Snapps Regional Vice President Donald Gilbert said the weekend promotion was a dramatic turnaround for the eatery, which saw business plummet because of the untrue rumor.

County health officials said food cannot be tainted by the AIDS virus. All the Snapps managers tested negative for the fatal virus.

FIG. 9.4. A news story in the nearby *Stuart News*, June 5, 1991, about the restaurant's crisis recovery process. (*Source:* Reprinted with permission of *Stuart News*, in Stuart, Florida.)

"If we had to do it all over, we would have followed the same crisis management and damage control program. In retrospect, this was an excellent example of crisis teamwork, everyone working together for the common good," concluded Gruenwald.

Gruenwald said the source of the rumor was never found. The restaurant changed names and managed to stay in business, although it never fully recovered its popularity.

CHAPTER TEN

Case: Cellular Phones
and the Cancer Scare

The cellular telephone industry enjoyed rapid growth in the early 1990s. It was averaging approximately 10,000 new customers daily as cellular phones became a necessity rather than a frill.

On January 21, 1993, a Florida widower, David Reynard, still grieving over his wife's death from brain cancer 6 months before, appeared on the Cable News Network (CNN) show "Larry King Live" and told millions of television viewers that he believed his wife's fatal illness was caused by electromagnetic waves from a cellular phone. Following is an excerpt from the transcript:

Mr. Reynard: There were several things that were quite obvious. And a second MRI basically showed she had a large [unintelligible word] type tumor located just behind and above her left ear.

Larry King: When did she die?

Mr. Reynard: May the 24th of last year.

Larry King: When did you start to think, "This has something to do with the cellular phone?"

117

Mr. Reynard: I think when I saw the first MRI and saw the location of the tumor. It appeared that it was in the location directly next to the antenna, and the tumor seemed to be growing inward from that direction.

The show then played a graphic videotape of the dying wife relating her deposition of the matter. To many viewers, this supporting "information" served to verify the claim, despite the fact that no scientific or medical data had been presented. In fact, data were presented to the contrary, but that could not compete with the emotionality of the man whose wife had died.

Here is another excerpt from the transcript as Eleanor Adair, a Yale University scientist, was questioned by King:

Dr. Adair: Yes, I was co-chair of the committee that spent 9 years reviewing the literature and looking into all kinds of questions similar to this one—the possibility of health effects.

Larry King: And?

Dr. Adair: And the standard is set at levels well above those that are emitted by such devices as cellular telephones.

King: Could his wife have been a victim?

Dr. Adair: No, I don't believe so, no.

King: You don't see any connection at all?

Dr. Adair: None at all, because the power output from a cellular telephone is just too low. It can't do that kind of damage to tissue.

King: And they've been sufficiently tested?

Dr. Adair: They have been tested, and the frequencies at which these devices operate have been tested in laboratory experiments for many, many years.

King: To your knowledge, have there been lawsuits?

Dr. Adair: There are lawsuits pending, and one that was just concluded yesterday with respect to the police radar instruments that also had been alleged to cause cancer.

King: Do you make any relationship between the position of the antenna and the position of the tumor?

Dr. Adair: No, I don't. Cancers occur in the brain at many places. People have had cancers as long as individuals have inhabited the earth....

As viewers began to call into the talk show, one claimed to get dizzy when using a cellular phone. One challenged Adair's research, although citing none to the contrary. One asked if a cordless phone was dangerous, too.

Stocks began to fall. Motorola, the largest manufacturer of cellular phones, and McCaw Cellular Communications, Inc., the nation's largest cellular carrier, saw their stocks drop by more than 15% (Kaye, 1993).

Thus, a crisis was born for the cellular telephone industry—in both manufacturing and service companies. Cellular One, a division of McCaw Cellular Communications, Inc., in the Pacific Northwest, was the largest cellular carrier with 3.8 million subscribers, 250 locations in the United States, and 105 markets.

KEN WOO, CELLULAR ONE

Ken Woo, Cellular One's media relations manager, had been with the company for a year and a half when the crisis erupted in 1993. At the company, media relations reported to district public affairs, which reported to the director of sales and marketing. The director of sales and marketing reported to the vice president and general manager of the Washington and Alaska district, who in turn reported to a regional president for Cellular One. The regional president reported to the president and chief executive officer of McCaw/AT&T Wireless Services.

Despite all the layers, Woo said he had "a dotted line relationship to Bob Ratliffe," who reported directly to the president/CEO of McCaw as well as to Marilyn Laurie, the senior vice president of AT&T Public Relations and Employee Communications.

Woo's department, which consisted of nine staff specialists and one administrative assistant, interacted regularly with Ratliffe's division, McCaw Corporate Public Relations. "I talk to Bob regularly. Then, other district public relations people get together via conference call every 2 weeks, more often if there are 'hot issues' to be dealt with, like the cancer scare," said Woo. He went on:

> I heard about the Reynard case from Steve Young at CNN who was preparing a report on it. Then Ron Nessen, vice president of public relations for the Cellular Telephone Industry Association (CTIA) sent an industry alert to all carriers.
>
> My first reaction was to gather facts. I had some knowledge of the technology of cellular phones, but we needed more. We had to understand what we were being targeted for, and we had to find experts to support whatever response we would come up with.

Woo's office contacted Arthur Guy, a University of Washington professor emeritus in bioengineering, asking him to brief the office on the issues. Woo also attended a bioelectromagnetics meeting in Los Angeles to round out his knowledge of the subject.

Reynard filed suit against the manufacturer of his cellular phone, NEC America, and the cellular carrier that provided the phone's service, GTE Mobilnet. Although Cellular One was not in the legal battle, the crisis affected all cellular phone manufacturers and all service companies.

Reynard continued to make appearances on television shows. He told his story on "20/20," "Nightline," "The Today Show," "Donahue," and "The Faith Daniels Show." As each show aired, more and more consumers grew fearful of cellular phones. There were phone calls by the thousands to manufacturers and carriers, including Cellular One and McCaw Cellular. A typical news story is shown in Fig. 10.1.

Woo was concerned about Reynard and people like Reynard, whom he called "nonexpert experts." He said:

> They are the sound bites that are popping up lately on television news regarding people expressing opinions for which they have no expertise. David Reynard was a nonexpert expert making claims unsubstantiated by his own doctors that his wife's brain tumor was the direct result of cellular phone use. His own doctors said they doubted the cause-and-effect claims.

Woo followed the pretrial testimony in the case and said, "[Reynard's] wife's physicians said the size of the growth seemed to indicate the tumor was there long before he claimed she began using a cellular phone."

The case was subsequently thrown out of court, but not before it had frightened cellular phone users and caused damage to the industry.

Woo primarily blamed the media. Once a journalist himself, this was a sensitive point with him:

> These nonexpert experts are handy for reporters on the run with no time to check out their expert credentials. It's a form of "instant public opinion," "instant polls."
>
> In the old days when I was a journalist, we used to call them "man on the street interviews." It is not scientific, does not accurately measure public opinion, does not provide balanced or accurate information, but is used for instant analysis—justification of a particular point of view.
>
> You are seeing more of these kinds of sound bites—quotes as deadlines shorten and writers and reporters file for more editions and broadcasts than in the past. In the O. J. Simpson case there was little public information available and "analysts and consultants" were hired to provide commentary on the guilt or innocence of people.
>
> There was also the invasion of Haiti where retired military officers were called in to second guess where and when an invasion might take place and under what circumstances. Then you have the "Buckwheat" fraud on ABC-TV's "20/20" where nonexpert witnesses "substantiated" a bogus Buckwheat.

Cellular industry waits out a scare

BY MARCIA A. LUDWIG
JOURNAL AMERICAN BUSINESS WRITER

The past two weeks have been rocky for the cellular communications industry.

News reports and talk shows spread fear that portable cellular telephones may cause brain tumors, causing stocks to fall and public-relations personnel to work overtime trying to calm the public.

But analysts say the scare eventually should blow over, leaving no visible scars on the companies or their stocks. Company spokespeople agree.

"We give (the scare) a six- to eight-week life expectancy," said Hershcel Shosteck, a cellular-market consultant and analyst with his own firm in Silver Spring, Md.

The scare first erupted Jan. 21 when CNN's Larry King hosted David Reynard, a St. Petersburg, Fla., man who claims his wife's fatal brain tumor was caused by the cellular phone he bought for her.

McCaw Cellular Communications Inc.'s stock fell $2 in the next day's trading to close at $36.25. The Kirkland-based company's stock rose the following Monday, Jan. 25, but then slid to $32.50 by the end of the week. The stock made two modest gains last week, edging up $2.75, and closed last Friday at $33.75 a share. McCaw is the nation's largest cellular carrier.

Motorola, Inc., of Schaumburg, Ill., one of the largest cellular phone and equipment manufacturers, watched its stock fall from $61.375 the day before the talk show to $53.375 a share last Friday.

"This has been a great example of how one story...got sensationalized by the talk shows. It's impacting business. Motorola lost (11) percent of the value of their company," said Bob Ratliffe, vice president of corporate affairs at McCaw.

To make matters worse, the Federal Food and Drug Administration on Friday issued a statement saying that although there is no proof at this point that portable cellular phones cause cancer, there is no definitive proof that they do not. Therefore, it advised cellular-phone users to limit the length of their calls and possibly to switch from portable phone usage to phones with remote antennas, such as car phones.

(The cellular industry is underwriting a story on portable-phone safety in response to the scare. Cellular carriers point to thousands of existing studies done on different frequencies showing no long-term health effects of cellular phone usage.)

Craig McCaw, chairman and chief executive officer of McCaw, spoke about the FDA's statement to CNN's Lou Dobbs Friday afternoon. He said he was "encouraged" by the FDA's actions so far.

"We believe in our hearts that we're right," that cellular phones are safe, he said.

Ratliffe uses his cellular phone an average of 6,000 to 7,000 minutes a month, far above the average user's call time of 170 minutes a month.

"I'm not worried at all," he said.

Analysts said although cellular-company shareholders have been nervous lately, they should adopt a similar attitude for the long term.

This scare is comparable to the video display terminal scare a few years ago, said Paul Andrews, analyst with AG Edwards & Sons Inc. in St. Louis.

People were worried about the electromagnetic fields generated by computer screens, but that scare "was in the news for six to nine months, then it went away. People are still using video display terminals," he said.

The Eastside's other cellular carrier, US West's NewVector Group in Bellevue, has been busy educating its customers about the scare and has prepared a bill insert for the next billing cycle that details information currently available, said Lisa Bowersock, spokeswoman.

Only a "couple hundred" calls from concerned customers have been received nationwide on the issue, out of roughly 10,000 calls received by U.S. West each day, she said.

US West NewVector is a subsidiary of US West Inc. of Englewood, Colo. Its price has remained stable the past two weeks and closed at $39.875 a share last Friday.

Both Bowersock and Ratliffe said they have detected no increase in sales of their cellular services or cellular phones from their dealers.

FIG. 10.1. News story in *Journal American,* Bellevue, Washington, February 8, 1993, about the cellular telephone cancer scare. (*Source:* Reprinted with permission of *Journal American.*)

Even though a nonexpert expert caused the cellular phone scare, the crisis was still very serious. The only crisis that would be worse is if the charges had been substantiated.

The Cellular One staff benefitted from its corporate culture, which Woo said was in a "we" mode during the crisis: "We have an entrepreneurial spirit that is fed by highly educated professionals working at being the best in their field. We value innovation, making the system work for customers, simplicity, excellence, teamwork, good judgment, and delivering on our promises." Woo felt that his media relations staff had good relationships with the media. He thought that he had good relationships with the West Coast media dating from the time when he was a CBS reporter based in Los Angeles. "There's a good exchange," he said. "I hope it was because of my relationships with people that we had a strong degree of responsible reporting on this issue."

During the crisis, the workday was expectantly busy. It started with reviewing overnight sweeps and opinion polling. The key media were checked to see what new information had been reported on the subject. The corporate team updated the staff on what new information it had. Then Woo shared stories and situations with field communicators. They brainstormed new ideas for dealing with the issues. Next, Woo followed up on work from the previous day, and he ended the day by meeting with key editors and writers to talk about what was known and unknown.

Also during the crisis, an industry and public affairs roundtable was established that consisted of public relations executives from member companies. The roundtable planned an information program aimed at the following publics: Wall Street analysts, government regulators, congressional hearings, general public. Ratliffe of McCaw's corporate public relations operation attended these sessions and reported back to Ken and the staff at Cellular One.

Cellular One was concerned primarily with two publics: consumers and the media. For consumers, the company developed a document called "Communications Guidelines for Questions About the Health Effects of Cellular Phones" for employees who had contact with customers. These employees were instructed not to generate their own materials, but to speak from information in the document. They were also urged to conform to regular company policy and refer calls from the media to public relations personnel.

The communications guidelines had three tiers. The first tier gave employees speaking points, which stressed that cellular phones did not cause cancer or any other health problems, that the company was concerned about customer health and safety, and that people were unnecessarily frightened. The second tier was used for customers who wanted additional information. In this case, a letter was mailed to them along with a position

paper about the safety of cellular phones. The third tier was used for customers still unsatisfied with the company's response. These customers were referred to corporate personnel to be handled personally.

Woo followed a document he had written and refined over a period of years in a previous position with another company. He had input from Jim McFarland and John Renforth, who were, at the time, with Ogilvy and Mather and served as public relations counsel to Woo's company.

Woo was not a great believer in the value of news releases, characterizing them as "the most useless justifications for killing trees." Instead, during the height of the crisis, he conducted briefings with key regional writers and editors and compiled research materials into a booklet titled "Cellular Telephones and Electromagnetic Fields" that explained the health and safety of cellular phones.

TODD WOLFENBARGER, McCAW CELLULAR

In 1993, Todd Wolfenbarger was director of communications at McCaw Cellular. Bob Ratliffe was vice president of communications and there were about a dozen people in the department. As Wolfenbarger explained:

> Unlike Ken Woo, we deal with industry groups, with stock prices, and with issues that affect the company as a whole.
> We have 22 field communicators nationwide, and Ken is one of those. What essentially happened in the crisis is we would develop a message with Motorola and the Cellular Telephone Industry Association (CTIA) and distribute it through our field communicators, who would take it to the media and the consumers.

Wolfenbarger admits that the cellular industry made an early error in that the original Reynard lawsuit was filed months before the "Larry King Live Show" and was a prodrome to the crisis. "In fact," he said, "there was a CNN report that ran a week and a half before (see the McCaw news release in Fig. 10.2) "The Larry King Live Show" gave the crisis legs, and it ran in a way beyond anything we could ever have imagined." He said that at the time of the lawsuit, McCaw had consulted scientists who told them that the risk factor was "unmeasurable." "They said, 'We don't get funding by doing studies that find nothing.' So," said Wolfenbarger, "McCaw believed science and decided it would not be a big deal."

> What was wrong is we had a really complicated message. We had Dr. Arthur Guy from the University of Washington with 30 years of electromagnetic experience. He didn't want to oversimplify things because the functioning of the cellular phone is not a simple process. So, here's this Ph.D. being quoted

NEWS FROM McCAW®CELLULAR...

McCaw Cellular / Cellular One Encouraged by Customer Responses
— Congressional Briefing Re-affirms Cellular Safety —

Kirkland, WA — Feb. 2, 1993 — McCaw Cellular Communications, Inc., which provides cellular phone service in more than 100 markets across the country primarily under the name Cellular One®, said Tuesday it was encouraged by the response of its more than two million customers to the recent stir caused by an alleged link of cellular to health risks.

The company's Customer Care centers reported a confident customer base with customer inquiries at normal levels. "While we understand why our customers might have been alarmed following the news stories, we are encouraged by their response," said Bob Ratliffe, McCaw's Vice President of Corporate Communications. "The scientific community has spoken to Congress and the market has started to rebound as customers get the facts that cellular is safe. I'm happy to report their actions speak louder than other peoples' words," he stated further.

In a representative California market, where McCaw has a customer base of 90,000, only 20 calls have been received about the health-related news stories. In fact, a sales promotion has resulted in a shortage of supply of portable phones.

McCaw Cellular Communications, Inc. (NASDAQ:MCAWA) operating under the name Cellular One® in most of its markets, is the largest cellular service provider in the United States and is developing and marketing a broad range of wireless communications services, including a cellular network that spans the continent, and is capable of transmitting voice and data communications.

McCaw Cellular owns a 52 percent interest in LIN Broadcasting Corp., which is engaged in cellular telephone operations, television broadcasting and specialty publishing. It also has a 32 percent stake in American Mobile Satellite Corporation, which is developing a satellite-based communications network to provide personal communications service to remote areas of North America now out of reach of terrestrial communications systems, and a 51 percent stake in Claircom, Inc., a joint venture with Hughes Network Systems, which is licensed to provide telephone service to commercial and private aircraft. McCaw Cellular is the nation's fifth largest paging service provider.

Contacts:
Bob Ratliffe, Vice President Corporate Communications

Todd Wolfenbarger, Director of Communications

#

McCaw Cellular Communications, Inc. • 5400 Carillon Point • Kirkland, WA 98033 • (206) 827-4500

FIG. 10.2. News release disseminated by McCaw Cellular during the cancer scare crisis. (*Source:* Reprinted with permission of McCaw Cellular.)

about electromagnetic fields and another guy saying simply, "My wife is dead!" Then, the camera cuts to shots of his wife, and then we see that glint of a tear in his eye. It was public perception against science and we couldn't win.

Another incident that was a mistake, according to Wolfenbarger, was a news conference called by Motorola:

Motorola had great information, a lot of research on hand, so we took a back seat to Motorola in the way the conference was run. They had their lead scientist, who is a brilliant guy, but he's not used to reporters firing questions at him. I think he took for granted that he wouldn't go into much detail so he said, "There are a thousand studies out." A reporter yelled, "Can you name two or three of them?" He couldn't, even though he was right; there are many studies. So, it looked bad."

During the crisis, McCaw's communications staff met each day at 6 a.m. in the boardroom to discuss what had happened in the news the previous day.

Numerous inaccuracies were reported, one reporter quoted another reporter, and so on. Wolfenbarger said, "We had one person who was dedicated to calling reporters and correcting errors—'If you write about this issue again, I just wanted to let you know this is not the case. We have some information I can send you that will explain.' This was helpful because few errors were repeated."

The communications staff also developed talking points, which were put together in a customer response book and distributed to field organizations such as Cellular One. "Our talking points were similar to CTIA's talking points," said Wolfenbarger. "There's a real sharp guy running their department, Ron Nessen, who used to be President Ford's press secretary. He has a good feel for dealing with government agencies and how they react."

The government agency that the industry was most concerned with was the Food and Drug Administration (FDA), which neither endorsed nor condemned the cellular phone. The FDA did advise consumers to limit their use of cellular phones. The industry took the FDA's inaction as positive.

Craig McCaw, chairman and CEO of McCaw, appeared on CNN's "Moneyline" with Lou Dobbs and said, "We believe in our hearts that we are right." He also touched on the company's concern that it was suddenly on the wrong side of the health and safety issue. He mentioned that cellular phones reduced stress in business and that stress caused illnesses. Wolfenbarger commented that:

Craig McCaw asked real specific questions of scientists. If the information had been negative and that phones were not safe, Craig, who is very health conscious, would have a problem admitting it.

We do think of ourselves as safety enhancers. Cellular phones save lives dur-
ing earthquakes and hurricanes. Half a million people, each month, call 911
from their cellular phones to report accidents.

McCaw President James Barksdale decided that it was best to offer con-
sumers options. Reporters at *USA Today,* the *New York Times,* and the *Wall
Street Journal* were told that if McCaw customers had a problem with the
safety of phones, they had three options:

1. They could trade in the cellular phones for transportable phones
 with antennas.
2. They could suspend service for up to 3 months, then access it back
 without cost when they felt comfortable doing so.
3. They could cancel their contracts without cost.

Wolfenbarger said fewer than 50 customers canceled. Of those, about half,
he believes, had severely delinquent accounts and were looking for a way
to get out of their obligation.

The story competed for news time and space with other consumer cri-
ses. The Jack-in-the-Box fast-food chain had the *E. coli* crisis that was killing
children who ate its hamburgers. "There was metal in tuna fish, lead in
paint—all within a one-week period," said Wolfenbarger, "and I think all
those crises helped ours die down. I can remember "20/20" debating
whether it would do tuna fish or our story. After a while, people just sort of
decided that [everyone] is out to get you in one way or another."

He said McCaw considered comparing risks in its messages, but decided
it did not want to say that anything was dangerous. "We kind of ditched
that," said Wolfenbarger, "and decided to promote the facts that the
phones are safe, that we had extensive research to prove it, that we are con-
cerned about the safety of our customers, and that we are going to study
this issue for a long time."

AT&T and McCaw Cellular Communications merged in 1995; Cellular
One became AT&T Wireless Services.

Case: United Way of America and the Overspending CEO

One day in late November 1991, in Washington, DC, Tony DeCristofaro, director of public relations for United Way of America (UWA), was told by the organization's senior vice president of communications, Sunshine J. Overkamp, APR, that she had learned from Lisle Carter, UWA's general counsel, that the *Washington Post* was collecting information for a story on United Way.

Persuading the media to do a story on your organization and its "wonderfulness" is a real high in the public relations world. However, when you "hear" through connections and various other routes that a major newspaper is collecting information about you without calling you directly, it is time to worry. Although the story might be full of praise for your organization, it is more likely the opposite case. DeCristofaro recalled Overkamp saying at one point, "The world as we know it is changing."

Charles Shepard, a respected investigative journalist for the *Washington Post*, was digging for information for a story on William Aramony, United Way's CEO for 22 years. While Shepard was at the *Charlotte Ob-*

server in the 1980s, he had uncovered the PLT scandal and subsequently won the Pulitzer Prize for his work.

"He's a very good reporter," said DeCristofaro, drawing out the "r" in "very" in admiration of the man who had made his job difficult for several months.

Neither DeCristofaro nor anyone else on the staff contacted Shepard. "For two months," DeCristofaro said, "we got reports from many people whom he was calling regarding the subjects, types of questions, and directions he was taking." There were indications that there were problems, if not a scandal, brewing.

First let us look at United Way and its place in the minds of Americans in the early 1990s. United Way was among the largest fund-raising organizations in the United States. At the time, there were 2,100 United Way offices nationwide raising more than $3 billion each year for 40,000 large and small charitable organizations.

Most of United Way's money was donated by campaigns in corporations and plants, usually raised by American workers with hard-earned salaries—men and women on assembly lines, laborers, clerks and assistants, and blue-collar workers as well as white-collar workers—who believed in the spirit of helping others. They had been helping others for years through United Way. A scandal at United Way could damage not only the organization itself, but also all the charities served by United Way, all United Way's employees, and the spirit of giving. If you could not trust United Way, could you trust anybody?

In mid-January 1992, DeCristofaro had his first direct link to the *Washington Post:* "Charlie called and we spoke about information he wanted—mostly documents—and he wanted an interview with Bill Aramony," said DeCristofaro, who complied with the reporter's requests. "Charlie would send over 20 questions he wanted responses to. I would give the questions to the lawyers, to Sunshine, to Hill & Knowlton, and to Aramony. We would work on finding facts. I had much more intense contact with Bill than I normally had."

On February 16, 1992, Shepard's article ran on the front page of the *Post*, with the headline "Perks, Privileges and Power in a Nonprofit World." It praised Aramony's brilliance, creativity, and ability to transform the United Way movement into the most successful and respected charity in the country" (Shepard, 1992).

The article also mentioned Aramony's $463,000 annual salary, his hiring of friends and relatives, his using nearly half a million dollars to buy and decorate a New York apartment primarily for his use, and his chauffeured automobiles. It mentioned more than $100,000 spent for first-class air travel, sometimes on the prestigious and expensive Concorde, and sometimes first-class travel with friends to Super Bowl games (Shepard, 1992).

Still, the extensive article was basically balanced with glowing references and with some criticism. The Associated Press did not immediately pick it up; neither did other newspapers.

At the same time, the American people were not in the mood to accept scandals or inequities of any kind. PTL, Oliver North, and John Sununu were fresh in the news; they were not even history yet. The recession had affected the public to the point that it did not accept inflated or lavish salaries, perks, or extravagances of corporate executives of large profit-making companies. This climate made it unreasonable to expect a distrustful public to trust Aramony, considering that he worked for a nonprofit organization raising money for charities. Furthermore, 85% of its funds went to the charities and 15% to United Way's fund-raising expenses.

The 14-member United Way executive committee, headed by LaSalle Leffal of the Department of Medicine at Howard University had hired Hill & Knowlton as public relations counsel in early December 1991. Hill & Knowlton advised the organization to conduct an internal investigation. It engaged Investigative Group International, Inc. (IGI), headed by Terry Lenzner. Lenzner had been a lead investigator for the senate investigative committee for the Watergate scandal. These PR counsels and attorneys put their heads together and formed a United Way crisis team with three leaders:

1. Senior vice president of communications
2. Associate counsel
3. Senior vice president of administration

The team helped IGI gather documents for its investigation and worked with Aramony. "It devised a plan," said DeCristofaro, "on what we were to do, what would be said, and when it would be made public." The plan was based on the organization's original crisis plan but was geared to the specific incident.

In early February, a preliminary report of the internal investigation showed nothing illegal, although it did note some incidents of nepotism and matters of questionable ethics and poor judgment. United Way knew it would have an image problem, but that didn't affect the attitudes of the executive committee members toward Aramony. After all, Aramony had worked tirelessly on behalf of the organization since becoming a volunteer 40 years before. The committee gave him a vote of confidence.

DeCristofaro remembered, "When the story was mild, there was great relief. Nevertheless, I knew there was another story. It was just a matter of when the second story would come out." (For Shepard's views on United Way's public relation's response, see Fig. 11.1).

From the Reporter's Point of View

BY CHARLES E. SHEPARD
WASHINGTON POST

I began researching the United Way of America/Bill Aramony story in mid-November, and we published our first article in mid-February. It was clear from the start that the allegations I was investigating posed a serious threat both to Bill Aramony's career and reputation and to the image of the organization he had run for so many years. Some of those I sought out in my reporting said they were hesitant to talk to a reporter about Aramony for fear that they might harm the United Way movement.

United Way's initial response was guarded; after arriving at the United Way of America to interview Aramony—a process I expected to take several hours—I was told I would get just half an hour. The Post was determined to press for answers to all questions, and we continued, after that truncated interview, to pose questions through United Way of America's communications staff. I was also eventually given a second session with Aramony.

Despite the curious reluctance to make Aramony available for any length of time, United Way of America showed an admirable commitment to answering my many rounds of follow-up questions. That commitment seemed to strengthen as the board grew to recognize that its problem was with Aramony and not an overzealous reporter. At first, it seemed to me, the board just didn't grasp what Aramony had done.

United Way's Tony DeCristofaro, whom I had never met before, displayed a remarkable mix of patience, intelligence, and good cheer in collecting my follow-up questions and coming back promptly with all the answers he could get. I have tremendous admiration for Tony's integrity and abilities, and we've since become good friends. I consider him a model for skilled communications work— he masters the material, makes reporters feel at ease with his friendliness, humor and candor, and comes across as someone who genuinely wants to get the answers the reporter needs.

FIG. 11.1 Charles Shepard, the *Washington Post* reporter whose investigative story on William Aramony ignited the crisis, speaks about the United Way's public relations response.

The public relations department at UWA had a crisis plan concerned with issues of funding controversies, employee issues, embezzlement, local issues, and salaries, including Aramony's . Staff members were aware of Aramonys' salary; such information was made available to the public. Many reporters already knew about it, but it had never been printed in a newspaper as widely read as the *Washington Post*. However, DeCristofaro said that he and other staff members did not know of Aramony's lavish spending until after the crisis erupted.

On February 20, 1992, a second article ran in the *Post*—by Charles Babcock. The headline was "3 Large Locals Ask United Way About President's Spending" (Babcock, 1992). A few days later, the *New York Times* reported what the *Washington Post* had previously reported and stressed the still incomplete investigation—at Aramony's request—as well as the unanimous vote of confidence given Aramony by the UWA executive committee. The *Times* article also indicated that some local United Ways might withhold dues, pending the outcome of the investigation (Teltsch, 1992).

The day following Shepard's second article an onslaught of the media began, including CNN, the Associated Press, NBC, CBS, ABC, Jack Anderson's "Washington Merry Go Round" syndicated column, as well as local media such as the magazine *Regardies*.

The employees and local United Ways learned about the crisis from the media, rather than from the organization. Members wanted United Way out of the media and the issue put to rest. "Everything we did created media attention," DeCristofaro said, "and we couldn't say the charges were not true." He said his department, although it had little information to disseminate, tried to get the facts out as soon as possible to three primary publics: membership, employees, general public. "We had to furnish the member organizations with updates on what was going on," DeCristofaro said. "We asked the AT&T sales department and received a cut-rate price on faxing. True, AT&T's chairperson was on our board and he may have had some influence, but it was not an automatic privilege."

Still there were difficult problems. The stakeholders were upset. There still was not enough information to reveal. The internal investigation was not yet completed. The PR staff members were faxing copies of the *Washington Post* articles to United Way chapters because newspapers in other cities did not cover the situation as extensively as the *Post*. The local media were using stories from the Associated Press, and sometimes those stories were only excerpts. Editorial cartoons were plentiful (see Fig. 11.2 for an example).

United Way board members and top executives of corporations such as IBM, Sears, American Express, and J.C. Penney were not willing to be interviewed. The board members referred these media requests to the PR department.

FIG. 11.2 The United Way crisis was tailor-made for editorial cartoons such as this one by Chris Britt of the *News Tribune* (March 1, 1992), Tacoma, Washington. Reprinted by permission.

Typically, as in any crisis, the media wanted the PR department to be a conduit—to provide them immediately with information and access to people they *wanted* to interview, people with the power to make decisions and speak for the company. However, no one with those qualifications would agree to go on "NBC Nightly News" or "Nightline." Ted Koppel had to say, "United Way would not comment." That was not a good PR move.

Aramony was not talking. The chairman of the board was said to have literally ducked into the men's room to evade the media. DeCristofaro said he could only speculate about why board members refused. It is logical that these people would not want to associate their companies with the scandal. It did not look good for United Way to have no spokesperson.

DeCristofaro felt that the board members might have quelled the journalistic fervor during the time that the public relations department was hampered. "The investigation was incomplete. We couldn't get the story out of the newspapers. We were unable to say Aramony was gone."

On February 26, a satellite teleconference was scheduled for local agencies of United Way. On the podium was Aramony, Leffal, and outside general counsel Berl Bernhard. They answered questions from the audience and basically revealed what was going on. Member agencies were assured that everything would be revealed.

On that same day, Aramony tendered his resignation, but the executive board asked him to stay to maintain stability during the transition. The board accepted his resignation, which would become effective when a successor was named. However, Aramony refused to apologize. According to DeCristofaro, he made a watered-down statement that was entirely too qualified. He dodged the apology and left the public to draw its own conclusions. "Public perception is all we get," said DeCristofaro.

Public perception was indeed the problem. Not very many years ago, the expression "rank has its privileges" was accepted by those with or without rank or privileges. That was not so in the early 1990s. The public was extremely critical of any excesses. The people who made United Way function and the contributors who helped pay for Aramony's extravagances did not, for the most part, have the experience of riding first-class in an airplane.

In a country with few wimps, some outspoken individuals or groups can be expected to object vociferously when an organization supported by public funds is suspected of spending those funds unwisely. Moreover, if the public fails to speak out, the media, in anticipation of the public's interests and concerns, rarely miss making the case known to the masses.

The American public and the member agencies of United Way were furious that Aramony was still with the organization after the news hit the *Washington Post*. The investigation continued. DeCristofaro said that all through the crisis Aramony was in the office daily. Aramony reportedly said, "It's you PR people who are making this a crisis."

The day after the teleconference, Aramony left United Way, and his longtime friend and deputy, Alan S. Cooper, became acting president. After Aramony's departure, the newspaper articles and editorials continued, urging United Way to regain the public trust. Ken Dam took over as temporary head of the organization. Cooper stayed on in his regular position as senior vice president and then retired in June.

Six weeks had passed between the publication of the first news article and the completed investigation on April 2. The report was ready on April 3. The United Way public relations department made a deal with Federal Express (similar to the one it had for faxes with AT&T) and sent the report to all its member organizations. There were complaints after two classes of publics developed—those who received documents overnight and those who received their package later. DeCristofaro said, "It was a matter of budget and numbers. We sent overnight mail to 1,000 cities, and the rest got it in two days." Naturally, the "rest" felt like unappreciated stepchildren.

The report, according to a DeCristofaro news release, continued "a series of recommendations concerning personnel practices, executive compensations and benefits, corporate governance, and affiliated organizations."

During the crisis, DeCristofaro's annual review came up, and he was promoted to vice president of communications. He resigned from United Way in May 1993, and he became vice president of media at Hill & Knowlton in Washington, DC. Overkamp also resigned and (at press time) was vice president of marketing and constituent relations at Council on Foundations in Washington, DC. DeCristofaro stayed on at Hill & Knowlton for 2 years and then became a free-lance public relations consultant. During the summer of 1998, United Way asked to be added to his client list, and soon after, he joined the staff as vice president of marketing. The person in his former position of director of public relations reported to him.

After the Aramony scandal, United Way experienced a budget crisis. "The local agencies had lost trust and confidence in United Way of America," said DeCristofaro. "Some of them withheld dues, and so, because we had a reduction in income, we had to downsize our staff." The previous staff of 320 employees was cut to 220.

In addition, in an attempt to win back the local agencies, United Way reduced dues from 1% of total income before the scandal to .75% in 2000. In 1991, the national income was about $3 billion, which meant that United Way of America, at 1%, had a budget of $30 million. In 1999 to 2000, the income was $3.77 billion, but the dues payments to United Way totaled only about $20 million.

The downsizing made the fired employees victims of the scandal. The remaining staff, DeCristofaro said, was overworked, so they, too were victims. "It will take some time to have an adequate staff," he said.

A positive reaction to the scandal was the new configuration of the United Way board. "We were able to build trust when United Way of America developed a plan whereby 15 seats on the board are designated to be filled by the local agencies. Three persons from each region, who also sit on their local boards, serve 3-year terms. This gives the local agencies a direct vote in the actions of the board, including the appointment of board members at large. The board is larger—45 members instead of 35—and it meets four times annually instead of twice."

DeCristofaro credited Dam with "single-handedly turning the ship around." Dam developed a code of ethics and set up a plan for internal restructuring. His framework was in place when former Peace Corps Director Elaine Chao became CEO in January 1997. The business woman who, according to reporters, served tea to them when they interviewed her, was a completely opposite look from the "good-old-boy" look of Aramony. This contrast was important to building trust and reputation for United Way.

In January 1997, Betty Beene, who had headed two local United Ways, became president and CEO. Under the Chao and Beene leadership, United Way won back all 1,400 local agencies.

In April 1995, a federal jury found Aramony guilty of multiple counts of mail fraud and wire fraud. He lost on all appeals and, as this book was going to press, he was still serving the balance of a 7-year federal prison sentence and was scheduled to be released in October 2001.

Aramony sued United Way of America to get his $5 million pension and salary and retirement benefits allegedly owed to him. United Way of America countersued to recover damages and losses to the organization. Both suits were in federal court and both sides won some appellate battles, but the war in court continues as this book goes to press. DeCristofaro said that, in the end, Aramony may recover some part of the pension.

CHAPTER TWELVE

Case: United Way of King County
and the Overspending CEO

There are approximately 2,200 local United Way organizations in the United States today. Each is autonomous with its own governing body and board of trustees. The money raised by each local organization remains in the community it serves to support charitable organizations.

Most local United Way organizations pay optional dues to national headquarters, United Way of America, based in Washington, DC. In return for dues, organizations receive information resources, research on giving, marketing and advertising materials, and volunteer training.

At the time of the 1992 United Way crisis discussed in Chap. 11, the dues formula was .5% of money raised in campaigns. Organizations that chose not to pay dues still benefitted from operating under the long-respected United Way name. Thanks to William Aramony's relationships with corporations such as J.C. Penney and IBM, local United Ways received monetary donations as well as equipment and supplies.

Diane Turner was director of public relations for United Way of King County, Washington, during the crisis. She reported to Clydean Zuckerman, vice president of marketing and community resources, who reported to

Roberta van der Voort, chief professional officer (CPO). Turner, explaining the United Way headquarters, said, "It's like the headquarters of a trade union. Each local is separate, and headquarters is a unifying element." Turner learned about the brewing problem in December 1991. "We heard a rumbling," she said, "of an investigative reporter from the *Washington Post* looking into the internal workings of United Way of America. At that time, we speculated that it resulted from the actions of a disgruntled employee or group of employees. Bill Aramony had done so much good work over so many years that this will go away. So, let's keep quiet and watch and see."

In the late 1980s, the Washington State United Way had weathered a crisis when member agency Planned Parenthood began offering abortion services against the wishes of the Roman Catholic Church and against United Way's rules of not contributing to agencies that performed medical services. Planned Parenthood subsequently resigned from United Way.

Also in the late 1980s, a crisis occurred when Roberta van der Voort was hired as CPO at a salary of $139,000. Critics felt the salary was too high. The United Way board disagreed. It felt that van der Voort deserved every dime and that no respected or self-respecting chief executive would work for less. Therefore, during the CPO's first year in the position, various corporations chipped in to get her the salary from sources other than the United Way budget.

WASHINGTON POST ARTICLE

A *Washington Post* article had begun the crisis for United Way of America (see chap. 11), but the King County agency did not yet feel the sting of it. "Even when the article came out [on February 16, 1992], we felt it was still possible that it might go away. We knew about Aramony's salary [it was public record], but the extravagance was news to us," said Turner.

United Way of King County decided to withhold dues paid to United Way of America until the investigation was completed. This was communicated to its publics, including the media (see Figs. 12.1 and 12.2).

On March 1, Diane Turner was scheduled for surgery, and Lynann Marcellis, who had recently worked as an account executive for Hill & Knowlton, was hired as public information manager. "I found out when I came out of the anesthesia that the rumors about the investigation and Aramony were persisting," said Turner.

When she returned to work in late March, Hill & Knowlton, the pro bono public relations counsel, was already working with the agency's PR staff. "When you are in a crisis situation, you frequently need an outside perspective, someone who can calmly see the bigger picture of where the crisis can lead and how to contain it," said Turner. Much of Hill & Knowlton's work

```
GENERAL TALKING POINTS
REGARDING UNITED WAY OF AMERICA
APRIL 2, 1992

United Way of King County is continuing to maintain its
position to delay the decision on paying dues until our
Board of Directors has an opportunity to review the report
in its entirety.

We are sensitive to the financial situation at United Way of
America, but at the same time, have a responsibility to the
citizens here in King County.

Our concerns regarding United Way of America revolve around
tighter financial management, greater accountability, and
increased responsiveness to local United Ways.

It's important to remember that United Way of King County
is separate from United Way of America.  Our volunteer Board
of Directors sets local policy and makes decisions based on
what we feel is in the best interests of the citizens of
King County.

Regardless of the outcome of this report, the residents of
King County can feel good about the fact that roughly 90
cents out of every dollar they give stay here, and directly
serves this community.
```

FIG. 12.1. The talking points that spokespersons for United Way of King County used when being questioned by publics about the UWA–Aramony crisis. (Printed by permission of United Way of King County.)

United Way units withhold dues in 'high living' probe

BY DEBERA CARLTON HARRELL
P-I REPORTER

Less than a week after reported allegations that United Way of America officials indulge in high living, local United Way officials say they will withhold dues until an investigation is complete.

United Way groups statewide said this week they are deeply concerned about public perceptions that United Way of America President William Aramony is paid too much and lives in luxury off public donations while supposedly working for the needy.

"We operate in the public trust, and any issue like this that could potentially impact the level of human services in King County is something that concerns us very much," said Lynann Marcellis, manager of public information for United Way of King County.

According to a recent report in the Washington Post, United Way of America paid $20,000 in one year for chauffeur services in New York for Aramony, who earns $463,000 a year. Aramony also flew on the Concorde jet to speed up his schedule, the Post said.

The Post and syndicated columnist Jack Anderson also reported last week that, under Aramony, United Way has created several spin-off companies—one of them run by Aramony's son, Robert—that have engaged in questionable business activities.

One of the companies, reportedly given $900,000 by United Way, used about $430,000 to buy and decorate a New York City condominium for the senior Aramony's use, it was reported.

The King County chapter, like most other agencies throughout the state, will delay paying quarterly dues to United Way of America—usually less than 1 percent of total money raised—until local boards have a chance to review the outcome of the nationally ordered investigation.

An independent first will conduct the investigation, which is expected to take about a month.

Ron Gibbs, executive director of United Ways of Washington State, said the state's 26 United Way charities raised $80.5 million last year.

Marcellis said last year's quarterly dues from the King County chapter to United Way of America were $417,000, generated by 1990 donations of $42.4 million. Last year, the local agency raised $45.5 million in donations and pledges. The dues go for services such as training, staff support, education, governmental lobbying and advertising, chapter officials said.

Bill Dodge, executive director of United Way of Chelan and Douglas Counties in Wenatchee, said his chapter will also defer dues payments "until we get some kind of good news."

He added, "We're very concerned he [Aramony] has access to a condominium and a chauffeur when—my God—we're trying to get money from great-Aunt Martha who's willing to give us $25 and is on Social Security."

Warren Dobbs, executive director of United Way of Spokane County, said his group, too, will defer dues payments, until the investigation is complete.

Chapter directors throughout the state, while wary of defending Aramony outright, credited him with improving the level of training and education services, raising advertising revenues and unifying agencies across the nation.

They cite, for example, Aramony's recent coup in negotiating with the National Football League for $45 million in free public service advertising for United Way.

Chapter directors stressed that local United Way organizations, while paying dues, operate independently of the national group, which does no fund raising.

"They're just allegations at this point," Marcellis said. "People locally should understand that when they donate funds to United Way locally, 90 percent of every dollar goes back into the community to people who need health and human services right here."

FIG. 12.2. This February 21, 1992, article by Debera Carlton Harrell, a reporter for the *Seattle Post-Intelligencer,* was one of several articles she wrote which convinced the United Way public relations department that Harrell be the first reporter to receive the local United Way announcement about cutting dues to United Way of America. Other media received the story by PR Newswire. The public relations department counted on the likelihood that Harrell's story would be complete and accurate and that other reporters would read her article in the morning newspaper and garner much of the information they needed from it. This eliminated a media frenzy over the announcement. (*Source*: Harrell, 1992. Reprinted by permission of the *Seattle Post-Intelligencer*.)

relations department. It was the responsibility of the regular PR staff to communicate with volunteers, media, and staff.

United Way of King County made an early strategic decision that pervaded the entire crisis. Turner said, "Our first strategy was that we decided to separate ourselves from United Way of America, to communicate to our publics that we are autonomous, not a chapter of a larger organization. It was a matter of 'It's them, not us!'"

UNITED WAY PUBLICS

The King County United Way chapter had four external publics and five internal publics with which it needed to communicate about the crisis. Each public had a different interest in the crisis.

EXTERNAL PUBLICS

1. *National media*, seeking a sidebar to the controversy, wanted to know how the crisis affected nonprofit organizations in King County, Washington, serviced by United Way, as compared to how nonprofits in other cities were affected.
2. *Contributors* wanted to know how their monies were being spent or whether they should donate elsewhere.
3. *Charitable agencies* wanted to know if they could count on United Way donations.
4. The *local media* wanted the same kind of information as the national media, but they focused on the local angle; they wanted to know where United Way of King County stood on the issue, what it planned to do, and so forth.
5. *Volunteers* needed to know where they stood, whether their work was worthwhile, and whether the organization was corrupt throughout.

INTERNAL PUBLICS

1. *Employees* needed to know about their jobs. If donations were decreased, jobs would certainly be lost.
2. The *board of trustees* needed to know what its position was in order to guide the organization to normalcy.
3. *Other United Way organizations* wanted to know how other cities were coping with the crisis.
4. *United Way of America staff members at headquarters* wanted to know about actions of local United Ways to determine how their actions would impact them.

NATIONAL MEDIA

"Our second strategy," said Turner, "was to tell our own bad news. We wanted to establish openness and honesty." The agency set up editorial boards with its board chair, the CPO, PR personnel, and editors from key local media.

United Way of King County, which included Seattle, raised more money per capita than agencies in other cities of comparable size, according to Turner. Also, she noted that the organization earned national notice in the fund-raising community with its unique Donor Choice Program that allowed people to choose which charitable institutions received their contributions.

The King County organization's reputation, together with the publicity surrounding previous United Way crises, likely spawned the attention of the national media. "Nightline" and "Prime Time Live" on ABC-TV, *Newsweek*, and the *New York Times* all began to telephone the agency requesting information and on-camera interviews.

The national media did not call with questions about the Aramony investigation, as they did with DeCristofaro at United Way of America. They called instead to ask about how the controversy would affect the local United Ways, whether donations would decrease, and whether charities associated with United Way would suffer. At first, some attempt was made by United Way of King County to respond to these media requests, but eventually the decision was made to decline participation in the national response in order to focus on the local issue. As Turner said, "What was the advantage to respond to an issue for which we were not responsible?" Ultimately, the organization felt that the local publics would decide the fate of United Way of King County; therefore, its time and energy were directed to communicating with these publics.

CONTRIBUTORS AND CHARITIES

"We were concerned," said Turner, "about the charities and the people in the community who need help from United Way. If contributions drop, our assistance to 147 member and affiliated organizations would also drop. Through this entire process, we stressed 'separate' and 'autonomous.' At one point in March, all we did was take calls from the press and the angry public."

Turner and Marcellis took most of the calls. Many were from people who had contributed through company employee plans and who now wanted to withdraw their funds. Some calls were from people associated with member agencies that benefitted from United Way funds. Others were from concerned citizens.

"Our position," Turner said, "was to listen to callers and agree with their anger and concern. We used phrases like 'We are equally horrified,' and

'We feel the same as you.' Then we would go on to say that we are separate; we will continue to serve the public as usual. We made it clear that we were victims, not villains" (see Fig. 12.1).

LOCAL MEDIA

The local media were especially important because they would get the agency's messages out to all the other publics, including future contributors and irate contributors who might cancel their donations.

The local media wanted to know how funds were spent. United Way of King County opened its doors and accounting books, giving explanations for every expenditure. When necessary, the finance manager answered questions. No room was left for misinterpretation.

During the crisis, strategic statements, questions, and answers were prepared in advance. It was decided that van der Voort, the CPO, would not serve as the spokesperson because she had previously worked for United Way of America and that connection could be construed as a conflict of interest. (Amazingly, no reporters made the connection on their own.) Instead, the first vice chairperson of the volunteer board, Karl Guelich, was named spokesperson. Hill & Knowlton, the vice presidents, the chairman of the board, the CPO, and the PR staff all trained Guelich to communicate effectively with the media. He was given the prepared list of questions and answers, speaking points, background information, and the latest news articles. Two 4-hour sessions were held in which every media question or interview situation imaginable was thrown at Guelich for practice in responding to television, radio, and newspaper reporters.

The local media were extremely interested in the controversy. One newspaper had four of its reporters calling about the story. Turner said, "It became overwhelming to tell the same information to various people at the same newspaper who didn't seem to know about each other. None of them had background information, so we had to tell them the entire story. So, finally, we telephoned the assignment editor and asked for one reporter."

INTERNAL PUBLICS

The crisis communications team, in late April 1992, developed a Rapid Communications Plan. Its purpose was to communicate pertinent information to the most important constituents. Together, Turner, the CPO, and each vice president determined which publics would get what information, how they would get it, and who would be responsible for the communication. Board members and executive directors were informed by either fax or phone. Volunteers received communications by mail.

In May, after the results of the investigation at UWA headquarters were released, the local board discussed whether to sever its connection with United Way of America or to make a less drastic response.

Going public with a decision of such importance would usually warrant a news conference, but Wiley Brooks, president of the Wiley Brooks public relations firm specializing in damage control, suggested to Turner that a news conference would be a circus and that the agency should instead announce its response through one reporter.

"We are familiar with the local reporters," said Turner. "We know their investigative style, their interests, how they write, their reputations." Turner spoke of one reporter at the *Seattle Times* as being the type who probably would have insisted on bringing up past crises and problems with the local United Way. *The Seattle Times*, at that time, was an evening newspaper.

The agency's decision to use a reporter at the other Seattle metropolitan daily was based on the fact that it wanted the story to break in the morning. The board meeting was expected to culminate in the evening so that the story could be given to the *Seattle Post-Intelligencer* (called "the PI"), a morning newspaper. "We selected Debera Carlton Harrell, a reporter at the PI whom we knew to be accurate and fair. She had covered a story about us before and nothing, such as a quote, was taken out of context."

Harrell came into the office around 11 a.m. and interviewed Zuckerman to get background information, a chronology of events, and other pertinent facts. Then she agreed to wait until after the board meeting to get final details. For hours, the board hashed over the decision. The meeting ended around 7 p.m., and a news release was immediately prepared.

The board determined that the alliance of United Way of King County with United Way of America was of value in dollars and cents. Its collaborations with corporations (ironically brought about by Aramony) were crucial, as were its research information and its training of volunteers.

Nevertheless, the board decided to cut the dues it paid to the national organization by half. The balance of the funds would be used to fund summer youth programs in Seattle and King County. This decision was spurred by the Los Angeles riots. The board wanted to do its part to avoid a similar disturbance in the Seattle area.

Harrell returned about 8 p.m., after the board made its decision, and a news release was drafted for all media. In addition to receiving the news release, the PI reporter interviewed Guelich, the vice chairperson of the board and the spokesperson. Then she returned to her office to write the story for the morning edition of the newspaper (see Figs. 12.2 and 12.3).

In the meantime, the PR staff distributed the news release to PR Newswire and to all the publics (see Fig. 12.4). Its release was timed so that by the time the media got the wire, the office would be closed for the evening. "What we knew," said Turner, "was that all the media writes from the morning paper, the *Post-Intelligencer*, and the rest of the media had to get that first information from Debera's story, the story we knew would be ac-

From the Reporter's Point of View

BY DEBERA CARLTON HERRELL
SEATTLE POST-INTELLIGENCER

I don't recall all the particulars of the story, but I do remember that I was trying to track United Way's decision closely after we ran the national stories about the Aramony brouhaha. So I kept in touch with the United Way locally, and knew when they were planning to make a decision on whether or not to withhold dues.

I wasn't aware they "selected" me. I do recall pestering them so a decision did not slip through the cracks of my multi-story-juggling schedule. I think they valued the fact that I was informed about social services in the community, since I had covered such services extensively, and that I know how important it was not to misrepresent United Way's role locally—important, not in an image sense (although I'm sure that was part of their criteria), but with respect to potential community impacts because of the broad range of services United Way funds.

They set their own meeting schedule; I hope it's very clear that the time of their meeting wasn't negotiated in any way. No deals were cut, although it was to our advantage that United Way chose to have a night meeting, because we're a morning paper (although it could have worked against us if the meeting had gone too late, since our first edition copy deadline is 8:30 p.m.). Since it wasn't a public meeting, I had no choice but to wait until the meeting had ended and the decision made before turning in the story.

If I recall correctly, and this would make sense given other similar scenarios, United Way suggested and I agreed to come in earlier in the day to interview Board members for background. This worked well for me because it meant I would have time to digest the information and even pre-write some of the story (it's called "A-matter" and we do this, whenever possible, for election coverage and other late-breaking stories) then top it up with the final decision on deadline.

I might emphasize that we were not interested in making United Way look good or bad. Our interest was in the news itself—how the local organization would respond to a crisis at the national level. It was important to us to make readers clear about what the relationship was—and wasn't—between the local United Way and the United Way of America. And because even United Way of King County had taken some past "hits" in media accounts (executive salary and Planned Parenthood controversies), we considered it in the public interest for readers to know about agency accountability and where their donations were going given the current state of affairs.

FIG. 12.3. Debera Carlton Harrell, the *Seattle Post-Intelligencer* reporter who was "invited" to be the first reporter to receive the United Way announcement about dues paid to United Way of America, speaks about her role in the crisis.

News Release

United Way
of King County

107 Cherry St.
Seattle, WA 98104-2223
Phone (206) 461-3700

For Immediate Release

MAY 5, 1992

Contact: Diane Turner
(office) 461-3867
(home) 838-6914

King County United Way and United Way of America

King County United Way Votes to Continue Some Financial Support for
National Association

SEATTLE — The King County United Way board of directors voted today to allocate half
the amount it would normally have contributed to the national United Way association
for 1992, and affirmed its support for the need for a national association. The remainder
of the money will be used to provide needed services in the local community.

"The board's decision today reflects concern over the apparent excess and
mismanagement that have occurred at the national association, but the national board of
governors has demonstrated a desire and an ability to put the organization back on
course and to provide its very valuable services," said King County United Way Board
Chair-Elect Karl Guelich. "It is our belief that the new national association will operate
more economically, but that it needs time and resources to work toward that end. We
hope that this funding level will provide the encouragement it needs to make necessary
changes, keeping it in business long enough for it to do so."

The board will allocate $214,000 to the national association and also authorized
spending an additional $65,000 to purchase services from national. Another $149,000
that would have been paid as dues will be used for employment programs for at-risk
youth, working in collaboration with its affiliated agencies, the business community, the
City of Seattle and other municipalities.

Guelich said the local organization has spent the past three months re-evaluating its
relationship with the national office. "While the recent revelations have caused us to take
a critical eye to our relationship, the intense re-assessment also has renewed our
appreciation for some of the benefits that we get from the national association," he said.

Guelich, managing partner of the Seattle office of Ernst & Young CPAs, also credited the
national board of governors with taking "swift, significant and appropriate action" by
publicly sharing and approving the recommendations of a special independent
investigative report. "The national board of governors has been taking the kind of
positive steps needed to restore confidence in the national office."

continued on back

FIG. 12.4. The news release (continued on next page) distributed by Diane Turner about the decision of United Way of King County to cut its dues to United Way of America by half. (*Source*: Reprinted by permission of United Way of King County.)

PAGE 2

The national board immediately removed United Way of America President William Aramony from the payroll and named Kenneth W. Dam, an IBM vice president and former Deputy Secretary of State, interim president and chief executive officer. A search committee, which includes local United Way volunteers and staff, was established to find a new chief executive. King County United Way President Roberta van der Voort serves on that committee.

The local United Way had withheld its 1992 dues pending today's decision. Responses from other United Way local organizations throughout the country have varied dramatically, from providing no support to the national association to paying national dues in full.

Local United Way organizations, such as King County United Way, are entirely independent from the national organization. However, they traditionally pay dues to the national association and in return receive a number of services and other benefits, including national advertising, staff and volunteer training and national fundraising support.

Guelich pointed out some of the specific steps taken by the national office since the controversy erupted:

- It apologized to local United Ways for the problems created by the Aramony administration.

- It approved implementation of all 45 recommendations made by the investigating team, including that local United Ways will be represented on the national board of governors, which wasn't previously the case.

- It opened regular communication with local United Ways to help determine how the national association can be made more accountable.

King County United Way is a local, autonomous organization run by a volunteer board of 48 directors with representatives from private companies, government, banks, the media, law, medicine, education and churches. For more than 70 years, the King County United Way has raised money for local health and human services agencies. In 1991, the local United Way organization raised $45.6 million, which was distributed to 761 agencies. Those agencies helped one in three people living in King County. Apart from state and federal governments, King County United Way is the largest financial supporter of health and social services in the county.

"More and more people need help today, and there are fewer dollars to go around," said Guelich. "We hope that the thousands of people who have given so devotedly to King County United Way in the past will recognize that we are run independently from national and that 89 cents of every dollar they give goes directly to help those in need in our community.

"We sincerely hope that our action today reveals to our many donors that we are continuing to be accountable for their contributions. Too many people in our county depend on the United Way and they would suffer if the public lost confidence in us and reduced their contributions. That would be tragic."

curate. It was a matter of timing and a way of organizing, not controlling, our own news."

The next morning, there were numerous media calls, but all of the reporters had Harrell's story in the *Seattle Post-Intelligencer* as a foundation. All of the background was in it, so there was no need to ask United Way spokespersons for that information.

The story also stirred calls from the national media. The PR staff stuck to its guns. The disseminated message was, said Turner, "Our job is to raise money locally and to help organizations in our community. The investigation did not change that."

According to Turner:

At no point was there a headline that accused United Way of King County of anything. There were no negative stories about United Way of King County. We had successfully separated ourselves from the controversy plaguing the national office. Our campaign the September following Aramony's resignation was one of the top 10 most successful United Way campaigns in the United States, though we raised less than the previous year.

Turner resigned from United Way of King County in December 1992.

When Aramony was indicted in 1994, Beau Fong, who had been named communication manager of United Way of King County after the crisis, said that the organization was prepared to answer questions from the media. "We had position papers if needed, but we were not called," Fong said, "We still get calls from contributors asking about our connection to the United Way of America. It gives us the opportunity to tell them how the local organization operates. The money raised here, stays here."

United Way of King County's campaign revenue growth, which had averaged 9% per year in the 1980s, slipped to just over 2% in the early 1990s. The donor base also dropped from 198,000 in 1990 to less than 165,000 by 1994. In 1995, the United Way of King County board of directors developed a strategic plan and embarked on a process to remake the organization. The effort was concentrated in reaching the changing workplaces. Whereas the campaign previously was aimed at large companies, the new campaign's goal was aimed at firms with fewer than 50 employees, especially local high-tech companies. In addition, an effort was made to inform contributors of the impacts and outcomes of their donations in the community.

In 1999, United Way of King County raised $82 million, up from $68 million in 1998. Rick Rafael, the agency's public relations head in 2000, said United Way of King County "is recognized as a leader among the 1,400 United Way agencies across the U.S. United Way of King County is the largest United Way on the West Coast in annual campaign revenues. It is the fourth largest United Way agency in the country."

Case: They Keep Coming— Chinese Immigrants in Canada

"The Canadian Coast Guard intercepted a listing cargo ship crammed with about 90 Asians off the coast of Vancouver Island, yesterday … " began a page one story in Canada's national newspaper, the *Globe and Mail,* on July 21, 1999.

On the following day, the *New York Times* wrote, "A ship with no name carrying more than 100 Chinese immigrants without identification papers has been taken into custody by Canadian authorities off the coast of Vancouver Island in what is believed to be the largest interception of immigrants smuggling on Canada's West Coast."

This was the beginning of a crisis for Canadian immigration authorities and a serious problem and perhaps a prodrome of an impending crisis for U.S. immigration authorities. It was expected that most of the Chinese immigrants were ultimately headed for the United States. They entered through Canada because its immigration rules were thought to be less rigorous than those of the United States.

U.S. agents are known for occasionally intercepting immigrants' ships in international waters. Once on board, the agents determine whether the

immigrants have credible claims; if they do not, the agents order the ship to turn around. If a ship arrived on a U.S. shore, the immigrants are treated according to the United Nations (UN) Status of Refugees and given the opportunity to file claims (as is also done in Canada).

However, many Canadians complain that Canada interprets the UN convention too broadly. Furthermore, under Canada's refugee policy—the Charter of Rights and Freedoms—an individual without Canadian citizenship or permanent residence status may ask for refugee status upon his or her arrival in Canada. A person can claim refugee status if he or she fears persecution in the home country because of his or her race, religion, political opinion, social group, or nationality. Smugglers teach their clients how to file a claim, what to say, what not to say, and so forth. For example, Chinese women refugee-claimants can claim gender persecution because of China's one-child rule, and homosexuals can claim persecution due to sexual orientation. Once the claim is made, the refugee-claimant can receive free medical care and apply for work or social assistance while awaiting a process that can take months or years to complete. "Nearly half of the 1494 claims made [in 1998] by Chinese nationals were abandoned after they disappeared, likely into the United States. They go out the front door and into the U.S.," said Don Gracey, a Toronto immigration consultant (as cited in Fennell, 1999, p. 16).

Why do the immigrant smugglers target North America? In 1979, when emigration laws were relaxed by Beijing, an estimated 1 million Chinese fled to seek their fortunes in North America, Europe, and Australia. Today, some do flee the one-child rule in China and homosexual and religious persecution. However, most take legal routes; many refugees (an estimated 100,000 per year) who do not meet the immigration requirements pay smugglers, called snakeheads, about $57,000 (U.S.) for each passage.

The passengers on that ship on July 20 told Canadian authorities they had each paid up to $38,000 (U.S.) for the passage. All 123 passengers (both the *New York Times* and the *Globe and Mail* estimated the number of passengers on the first day of coverage) paid a total of about $4.5 million (U.S.).

Although the cargo ship was equipped with state-of-the-art radar and navigation equipment, the passengers suffered their way through the 38-day journey. Their lodging was in the fish hold of the vessel, where there was no ventilation, no light, and no privacy for the passengers, who included 18 women. The hold was covered in human excrement when the boat arrived in Canada because there were no toilets. The drinking water was contaminated; many passengers were dehydrated. They caught and cooked fish and ate it in shifts on the deck laden with garbage.

Later, other boats arrived after 56 days at sea. Within a few months, four other boats from China had arrived off Vancouver Island. After the required immigration health examinations, including medical and identity processes,

the migrants were held in detention centers, some in a small community that was a 7- or 8-hour drive from Vancouver. Canada's detention policy states that persons may be detained for three reasons: insufficient identity, danger to the public, and unlikely to appear for an immigration process.

After 2 weeks, about 90 of the original 123 passengers were released with reporting terms and conditions attached to their release or, in the case of children, were handed over to the provincial government's Ministry for Children and Families. Some of these migrants who had been released later failed to meet the terms and conditions of their release and arrest warrants were issued for them. The remaining 33 passengers were kept in detention based on one or more of the three criteria. Some of the detainees were suspected of participating in the human smuggling operation. Persons may remain in detention for an indefinite period. An adjudicator (a type of judge), who hears arguments for and against, regularly makes the decision regarding detention or release.

Lois Reimer, manager of regional communications at Citizenship and Immigration Canada (CIC), was part of the chain of command reporting to the minister of the CIC. Between Reimer and the minister were the following positions: CIC regional director general for British Columbia and the Yukon region (one of five regions in the country); CIC assistant deputy minister of operations (responsible for all five regions); and CIC deputy minister.

Reimer noted that the arrival of the boat people in 1999 was not a surprise. There had been prodromes: Boats carrying migrants had previously arrived off the coast of California, and in Australia they had been arriving for at least 7 years. "Because of our international partners, the United States and Australia," Reimer said, "we were very much aware of human smuggling and that it was entirely possible that Canada could receive arrivals of this nature. We knew we had to plan."

The crisis management plan (CMP), entitled *Communications Strategy: Boat Arrivals of Migrants to British Columbia* (1999), involved the CIC as well as "partner" agencies (according to Reimer) that shared responsibility in responding to boat arrivals of migrants in Canada. These partner agencies included the Department of National Defence Coast Guard (DNDcg), Fisheries and Oceans Canada; Canada Customs and Revenue Agency (CCRA); and Royal Canadian Mounted Police (RCMP). Reimer also considered the United States and Australia part of the partnership because the smuggling of people across borders is a global crisis affecting many countries.

RESPONSIBILITIES OF PARTNERS
IN THE CRISIS MANAGEMENT PLAN

The CIC was the lead organization in the crisis planning strategy. According to the CMP, its mission was to ensure a sound immigration and refugee system that was not subject to abuse. At the same time, CIC worked to ensure

that persons seeking entry into Canada were dealt with under the provisions of the country's Immigration Act, respecting Canadian laws. According to the plan, the CIC also took on the role of media spokesperson and was responsible for ensuring that the partner departments and agencies responded to issues within their jurisdiction.

The CMP mandated that the DND (also known as the Canadian Forces) was to "protect Canada, contribute to world peace, and protect Canadian interests abroad. The Canadian Forces defined Canada by protecting its territory and areas of jurisdiction, helping civil authorities protect and sustain national interests, and assisting in national emergencies" (*Communications Strategy*, 1999, p. 3). The DND thus played a leading role in the event of a marine arrival of migrants because it was responsible for detecting and then reporting to the CIC any suspicious vessels meeting the profile of a migrant smuggling vessel in or near Canadian waters.

Coast Guard, Fisheries and Oceans Canada was mandated to "ensure the safe and environmentally responsible use of Canada's waters, support understanding and management of the ocean's resources, facilitate the use of our waters for shipping, recreation and fishing, and provide marine expertise in support of Canada's domestic and international interests" (*Communications Strategy*, 1999, p. 3). In the event of a marine arrival of migrants, the Coast Guard, like the DND, had the responsibility of identifying suspicious vessels. But the Coast Guard had the additional responsibility of leading the search-and-rescue operations at sea.

The CCRA was responsible for ensuring that Canadians were provided with the highest possible degree of protection from the smuggling of drugs and other dangerous goods. In the event of a vessel carrying illegal migrants, the CCRA had a variety of tasks designed to target and identify vessels and containers of drugs (*Communications Strategy*, 1999, p. 4).

"Royal Canadian Mounted Police (RCMP)/Immigration & Passport (I & P) was mandated to combat human smuggling and other criminal violations of the Immigration Act by working with CIC and other organizations in investigating and identifying criminal organizations involved in smuggling illegal migrants into Canada" (*Communications Strategy*, 1999, p. 4). In the event of a boat arrival of illegal migrants, the RCMP played a leading role in the initial response once a vessel or container had been secured and was in the control of Canadian authorities. The RCMP was also responsible for leading the criminal investigation of the smuggling operation (e.g., determining how the migrants got to Canada, identifying the smugglers and whether Canadians were involved, etc.).

STRATEGIC CONSIDERATIONS

All partner agencies took responsibility for media relations when their respective agency or service was at issue. The following were fundamental questions for which the public and the media wanted answers:

1. How did these people get to Canadian shores?
2. Why didn't the government stop the ship before it got into Canadian territory?
3. Why wasn't Canada ready for the arrival of this ship—are there not early warning systems in place?
4. Why didn't Canada just push the ship away from Canadian shores? Why not just let the container go on to the United States where it is destined?
5. What rights do these migrants have once they are in Canada?
6. What responsibility is there on the part of the shipping company bringing containers of stowaways to Canada?
7. Is there enough vigilance of commercial vessels at Canadian ports?
8. How many containers of migrants are you not finding?
9. How much is this all costing Canadian taxpayers?
10. Is Canada being compassionate enough? Is Canada being too compassionate?

There were these additional communications considerations:

1. The need to keep a multitude of stakeholders appropriately informed with a view toward making them communications allies or at least preventing them from becoming critics and possibly using erroneous information.
2. The media's demands for extensive background information on issues related to the crisis.
3. The media's demands for visuals regardless of the operational circumstances.
4. The difficulty of communicating regular updates.
5. Commentary by critics who themselves may be poles apart on the issue and who may create a tension in which operational communications must be carried out—keeping a balanced message on enforcement and facilitation is difficult.
6. Limited CIC communications resources to provide support on site and to ensure that the necessarily limited number of spokespersons throughout the department have consistent messaging.

COMMUNICATIONS OBJECTIVES

The communications objectives of the partner agencies were as follows:

1. To ensure the public knows that the government has the situation under control and is managing it effectively within the scope of Canadian law and the changing circumstances.
2. To ensure the public knows that Canada is working in partnership with other governments and, internally, that its own departments and agencies (CIC, RCMP, DND, Coast Guard, Canada Customs) are working together to combat human smuggling.
3. To respect the privacy of individuals as per Canada's Privacy Act and to respect the confidentiality of ongoing police investigations, while at the same time honoring the communications principles of open and transparent government.
4. To provide the public with information about the challenges faced by the governments of other countries with respect to maintaining open borders, on the one hand, and controlling illegal migration and human smuggling, on the other.
5. To ensure that government communications are carried out in an effective, coordinated manner.

KEY PUBLICS

Internal Publics
 Concerned federal ministers
 Members of Parliament
 The CIC and partner agencies
 Affected provincial government ministries
External Publics
 Other levels of government, including the Province of British
 Columbia and affected municipalities
 The legal community and nongovernmental organizations (NGOs)
 The news media
 The public at large
 Foreign governments and international partner agencies

Regarding key publics, Reimer noted that "Canadian officials regularly discuss the challenges that this activity (the smuggling of people) presents with officials from other concerned countries. To this end, Canada participated in the 20th International Asian Organized Crime Conference that was held in Toronto."

"We were part of the overall plan," said Reimer. "Security was a major part of the crisis plan because no one knew whether we would be dealing

with people who were armed and dangerous." In the crisis communications section of the CMP, Reimer, the lead spokesperson, advised, "You should know, in advance, what your key messages are. What should we say about the health and safety of these people? What should be our first priority as a government agency? This we planned before the first boat arrived, although it was revised several times as more boats arrived."

Reimer remembers the arrival of the first boat: "We had an operational plan that we would activate once a suspicious boat was confirmed. I was planning my usual one-month vacation with my kids. I was thinking, 'I'll just finish this and this and then I'll be on my way.' Then, the alert came in over my e-mail. My first reaction was, 'This is a joke.' But, it was not a joke. There was a boat arrival. We saw the plan become real."

She said the arrival of the Chinese immigrants was big news. Parliament was not "sitting" (not in session) so there were no other major government issues to keep the news media occupied. "We saw unprecedented media interest of this issue. We are used to a fair amount of attention—drug trafficking and other high profile cases, but the reaction to this issue was unprecedented."

The public reaction was mixed, according to Reimer. Some Canadians responded with humanitarian support saying, "This is a tragic situation and these people should be allowed to stay and more of them should be allowed to come. The United Nations High Commissioner for Refugees urged Canada to keep its doors open. Anybody who sets foot on Canadian soil has the right to be defended by counsel, has the right to Canadian processes." Others objected, arguing that "Canada doesn't need this. It's time to toughen the law." People who lived near the area where the migrants were detained complained as well: "Not In My Back Yard [NIMBY] because traditionally immigrants and refugees were not kept there."

Reimer said, "We saw the positioning of special Web sites. We saw surveys come about. There were town hall meetings. Public opinion polls were everywhere. We saw media editorials, forums, and debates of this one issue. Everyone was asking, 'What do you think? Should they come? Should they go? Should we send the boat back? Should we allow them in?'"

The public demand for information was also extensive. Canadian citizens were looking for statistics and background data. They wanted to know how the refugee program worked; how many refugee claims were made across the country; how many were made at the airport, in Quebec, and in Ontario. They asked, "Why do we detain?" and "When do we detain?" They wanted backgrounders.

Reimer was part of a 2-person communications branch, although she had the additional assistance of a co-op student during the summer (see Fig. 13.1). The branch was required to research and come up with answers to questions and develop a wide range of communication tools, including media advisories, backgrounders, and letters to the various publics, and information to the media.

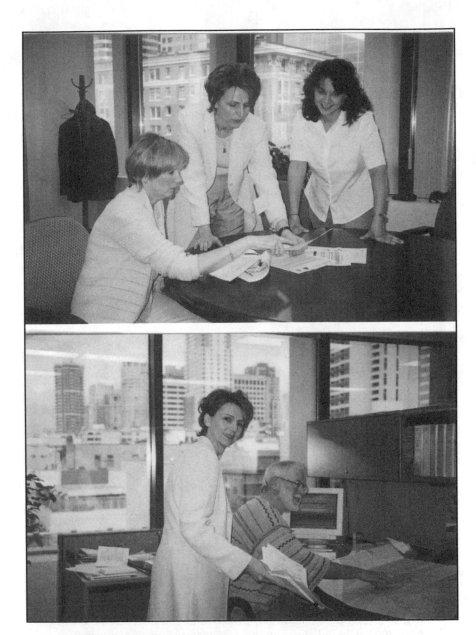

FIG. 13.1. Citizenship and Immigration Canada (CIC). In the top photo, Lois Reimer (*center*), manager of communications, discusses strategies with Janis Fergusson (*left*), communications adviser, and Denny Falls, executive assistant to regional director general. In the bottom photo, Reimer consults with Dan Grant, planning section chief, Incident Command. CIC offices are located in Vancouver, British Columbia, Canada.

Reimer commented on the in-depth media coverage:

We saw media go to other countries to compare the situation in Canada with the situation in these other countries. Our radio and television stations sent staff members to Beijing, Australia, New York. From July to October, less than three months, British Columbia television news had 980 minutes devoted to this issue. A news story is usually 1.5 minutes long, so you can see this was quite phenomenal. The two of us took 1,200 media calls at our regional headquarters alone and each required some significant work and organizing interviews and press conferences. We had 100 front-page stories during that period and 50 editorial cartoons. [See Figs. 13.2, 13.3 and 13.4.]

Then we had calls from the public and the majority of those went to one of three centralized call centers across the country. About 96 percent of the public was against us allowing the boats in. They were against our processing the migrants. So, we got nasty calls like, "Why am I paying your pension? You

FIG. 13.2. Fifty political cartoons published in Canadian newspapers in 1999–2000 reflected the attitudes of Canadians about the arrival of boatloads of Chinese immigrants. The cartoons also reflected questions spokespersons from Citizenship and Immigration Canada had to answer. This cartoon, published in the *Globe and Mail* on September 14, 1999, commented on the complaint that the immigrants found it easier to enter North America through Canada than through the United States. (*Source:* Reprinted with permission from the *Globe and Mail*.)

FIG. 13.3. This political cartoon in the *Vancouver Province* on July 26, 1999, like many others in Canadian newspapers during 1999, expressed the views of Canadian citizens. Many Canadians opposed the arrival of the boatloads of Chinese immigrants, but many others approved. (*Source:* Reprinted with permission from the *Vancouver Province*.)

157

158

FIG. 13.4. This cartoon appeared in the *National Post* on January 5, 2000. (*Source:* Reprinted with the permission of G. Clement and the *National Post*.)

can't manage the program!" Many others went to the Regional Director General's office or the minister's office [Minister of Citizenship and Immigration] and there were letters.

Like many other optimistic crisis communicators, Reimer viewed the crisis as an opportunity—in this case to explain the government's immigration/refugee program and services. However, the crisis communicator must be careful to respond accurately and appropriately to questions. For example, if the crisis involved people who got sick after eating *E. coli*-tainted food and a reporter asked the restaurant owner, "How could the disease have been contracted?" the crisis communicator would not talk about the restaurant's use of low-fat oil for cooking french fries. Reimer, however, was in a situation in which the responses the media wanted were actual descriptions of the work of the CIC.

Reimer said, "A quarter page ad costs $7,000 in the *Vancouver Sun*. This was an opportunity for free advertising. It came down to getting a better understanding of the government program. And our immigration act is very, very technical, very difficult to understand." She had to explain the act in detail to reporters and they had to listen because they had to understand it in order to write their stories.

INTERNATIONAL ISSUES

In addition to the Canadian news media, there was interest from the international news media—CNN, *New York Times, Seattle Times*. The proximity of Canada played a great part in this media interest. Even though Australia had been receiving migrant boats for 7 years when the first Chinese boat reached Canada's shores in 1999, the Australian stories went largely unreported because the issue did not affect life in North America.

In January 2000, when some containers of Chinese immigrants arrived in Seattle and two arrived in Canada, it came to light that the two latter boats were destined for Seattle but had run off course. The primary question asked of Reimer was, "If they were destined for the United States, why did you even open the containers? Why not just let them go there?" Reimer's response was, "First of all, Canada is a humanitarian nation. If we are aware of people inside a closed container, our first concern is the well-being of those people. Secondly, why would we just push the problem to the United States?"

"We saw a lot of comparisons to the United States and Australia," said Reimer, "because we have like systems. One reporter did an in-depth article in which he compared both the American and Canadian systems and what was reported was that, unlike a lot of myth out there, the American system has a 50 percent acceptance rate of refugees and the Canadian system accepts 54 percent. A lot of Canadians, including the media, were saying that Americans are a lot tougher; they do things a lot quicker. This was a real myth buster."

China claimed that if Canada didn't have such a generous refugee determination program, its people would not try to make the trip. "This was not an issue we want to debate in the news media," said Reimer. "It's a very complex issue, and senior officials from both countries meet regularly to discuss concerns such as human smuggling and returning Chinese citizens who are found not to be refugees."

POLITICS

Political debates developed between the current Canadian government and the opposition party. Reimer's position as representative of a government agency was to support current Canadian law, not to debate its merits. Furthermore, the government's Communications Policy required that public servants so restrict themselves.

"We must be very cognizant of the politics around an issue," said Reimer, "but my job as departmental communications manager is to speak to the laws of the land and not to get into conjecture around whether the laws are good or bad; it's not my position to do that. My job is one of explaining how Canada's immigration and refugee legislation works."

INTEGRITY ISSUES

Reimer said the challenge to the integrity of her program was dealing with a discretionary program that at times appeared to be interpreted inconsistently: "While the perception might have been that [the] CIC was treating this group of clients differently from others, the reality is that no two cases are alike and there were significant differences in case facts."

RISK ISSUES

A risk communications strategy was necessary to cope with the Chinese migrant crisis. Canadians were concerned that the refugee-claimants might be carrying such diseases as tuberculosis and hepatitis B. They wanted to know, "Will my kids get sick? Will I get a disease? Are these people criminals? How do I know I'm safe from them?"

One of the important components of the communications strategy was informing the various audiences of the medical and criminal screening that took place immediately after the migrants were brought to Canadian shores.

COSTS TO TAXPAYERS

Like U.S. citizens, Canadians are concerned about where their tax dollars are going and often complain about supporting people they perceive as taking advantage of the government's generosity. The arrival of the boat

people added fuel to that argument: "Why don't we pay for Canadians first? If the Royal Canadian Mounted Police are guarding these migrants, then who is guarding my community? I'm paying taxes to guard them and I am unguarded. I don't have a lawyer, yet these people get lawyers." Canadians also questioned whether Canada could afford to be so generous. The provincial government expressed to the federal government the pressures it had to deal with on the refugee issue.

Canada's Charter of Rights and Freedoms guarantees that "anyone who steps foot on Canadian territory" automatically has basic human rights, such as the right to legal representation and the right to have due process under Canadian laws. During the crisis, it was important that Canadians understood that such rights extended to the Chinese migrants.

Reimer agreed that the detention of the migrants was costly: "We spent about $2.8 million each month to detain about 420 migrants. Citizens want to know what if we get 2,000 or 3,000 immigrants?"

There was an effort made to feed the detained Chinese migrants a diet that was sensitive to their culture. Rumor was that the migrants said their food wasn't hot enough.

Reimer noted:

> There was a negative public reaction when it turned out that the restaurant providing the food was reported to be one of the best in Victoria. We didn't seek the best in town but it turned out that way. An editorial cartoon illustrating the issue of the day was published showing the migrants as demanding and ordering officials around.
>
> Short of a crystal ball, we don't know if more people are coming from China like in 1999. People seem to think that the government knows and ask, "How many are we going to get?" People don't announce their arrivals to us. We may know about twelve hours before they touch down on our shore, but people think we were expecting the boat all along. We are planning for more because we see what's going on in Australia and the United States. I would think that we will get more in the spring, but may get none.

LESSONS LEARNED

Listing her own lessons, Reimer said the following:

> We [Office of Immigration] own the crisis. The RCMP and the Coast Guard are involved, but it's our department's job to communicate. Maybe because the word "immigration" is in our name. We must live with that.
>
> We must anticipate and plan accordingly. For example, we're going to have removals of individuals who are found not to be refugees, so we should plan our communications in advance.

We must consult and compromise with partners. We have no line of authority with the RCMP, for example. There was criticism that the RCMP used police dogs in [its] security work. Was that appropriate for the migrants? So, the RCMP planned to introduce the community to the dogs. There was also a day in which community members could walk through the detention center to see how the migrants are treated.

SUCCESSFUL OUTCOMES

Reimer felt that what made the communications work well was that she was "inside the room where the decisions were made, part of the decision making, not an add-on. We were part of the decision from start to finish. That may mean working at 2 a.m. when they're opening those containers, so you have a real accurate feeling of what's going on. You need to understand the environment. You can't speak from your ivory tower; people won't believe you know or are part of what's going on."

Another successful outcome was feeding the needs of the media and the public. This included preparing tools and strategies, information, and flowcharts.

A third success factor was thinking ahead to be prepared for what might come up. Also, Reimer was able to hire another person so that they could plan for what had not yet happened and develop tools. They planned to prepare communications tools for migrants in their language. They also realized they were fortunate that the first four boats did not have tragic outcomes, such as dead bodies, as the containers arriving in Seattle had. No Canadian personnel, boat passengers, or boat crew members were harmed. These possibilities must be a part of crisis planning.

Finally, Reimer said that "keeping a sense of humor [was a] key." One night while waiting for a boat to come in, Reimer said the boat was expected to arrive "in the next hour," but it didn't come in until 8 hours later. She ended up leaving for home at 11:30 p.m., stopping along the way to get gas for her government vehicle. When the gas station attendant saw her Government of Canada Citizenship and Immigration gas card, he remarked, "You know there's a radio contest going on right now. Anybody can guess how many migrants are on the current ship." Reimer said she tried to keep her composure. Then the attendant said, "If I win, I get a T-shirt that says 'Not tonight, Honey, I have a migrant.'" Reimer laughed to herself, asked for a receipt, and left.

Reimer won the Don Rennie Memorial Award for excellence in government communications for her work on the Chinese immigrants crisis. The award was presented by the Public Relations Society of Canada.

Case: DC Mayor Anthony Williams and Another "N" Word

Mayor Anthony Williams of Washington, DC, is a black man. At least, he always thought so. Yet, some of his constituents in this primarily African American city charged that he was "not black enough." Shortly after he took office in 1999, he suffered a crisis of racial insensitivity when one of his white staff members used the word *niggardly* and caused great debate all over the world. If Mayor Williams can encounter a problem based on race—among people of his own racial group—anyone can.

Peggy Armstrong is the mayor's press secretary (see Fig. 14.1). It is her job to head the crisis communications emanating from the mayor's office, to help him reach his goals, to tackle issues that may hinder reaching goals, to help him communicate with constituents through the news media, and to help build and protect his reputation and image.

First, it is necessary to explain the unique nature of the government of Washington, DC, and how Williams rose to power.

Congress has responsibility for the city, according to the authority of the U.S. Constitution. "In one sense, this is a sleepy little river city," said Armstrong, "while in another, it is a world-class city. The mayor and his ad-

FIG. 14.1 Press Secretary Peggy Armstrong accompanying Mayor Anthony Williams of Washington, DC, at a news conference. Armstrong's position is one of support for the mayor and his staff. Although her contact is primarily with the news media, it also extends to the mayor's constituency. (Printed with permission of Peggy Armstrong.)

ministration serve so many people and types of people worldwide." The actual city has a population of 550,000 who elect the mayor, 62% of them African American. However, there are nearly 2 million people, primarily not African Americans, who come into the city to work, many for the federal government. The mayor must serve not only the DC residents, but also the people who inhabit the city daily yet pay no taxes for the services they expect and demand. He also must communicate and cooperate with the Congress, the White House, and the federal agencies. In addition, Washington, DC, draws much national and international interest because it is the site of the U.S. Capitol and is host to diplomats from every country who reside there but who are not required to obey U.S. laws.

In spring 1995, during the Marion Barry administration, Congress passed the Control Act, which established a Control Board made up of five unpaid members named by the president to help solve the city's financial crisis. The board exists to resolve problems of finance and management. An external measure of the success or failure of the city is the rating of its municipal bonds. The Government Accounting Office (GAO) had declared

the city government insolvent, and its bond rating for municipal bonds had dropped to junk status. The Control Board gave the city's chief financial officer (CFO) position more autonomy and power than it had previously and established the position of inspector-general. The Control Board may be a temporary body; the understanding is that if the city has four consecutive balanced budgets, the board will be dissolved.

Then-Mayor Marion Barry appointed Anthony Williams as CFO to help pull the city out of its serious financial crisis. Williams brought his experience in public management at the local, state, and federal levels to the position in the District of Columbia. It was while he was CFO for the city that Williams first hired Armstrong as his press secretary.

Although he was appointed by Barry, Williams' position was independent of Barry; that is, he reported to the Control Board. Within the first year of his position as CFO, Congress granted Williams personnel authority— every person who worked in a financial job in the District of Columbia government reported to him, and he could go in and tell anybody, "Thank you, but we no longer need your services." This was an obviously controversial authority, but the city was in dire need of financial resurrection. Williams set out to cut and improve financial management, and he did it boldly.

One of the results of the financial crisis was that the city's vendors (people who do business with the city) stopped their deliveries because they had not been paid for months. The city had no money to pay for janitorial supplies for municipal buildings, for example, causing a certain amount of hoarding of toilet tissue for the city's restrooms.

There were numerous district employees allegedly incapable of performing their jobs. Armstrong recalls an incident regarding the public schools: "Our chief financial officer for schools [who reported to Williams] discovered that there were 400 'ghost employees,' employees who were supposed to have been taken off the payroll because of a reduction in force. Their supervisors processed the appropriate paperwork but never sent the employees home. So, they were getting paid even though there was no money in the budget to pay them." The press secretary said she found out about the ghost employees during a media interview of Williams and Abdusalam Omer, the CFO for the public school system. Omer mentioned the problem but neither Williams nor Armstrong knew about it previously.

Armstrong said:

> I just remember sitting there and thinking, "Oh my Lord. What have I gotten myself into?" Nothing I had ever experienced could prepare me for doing that kind of disclosure with a reporter. But what I believe made us successful in the CFO position and as mayor is that Anthony Williams believes that you need to expose and disclose the problems of a troubled organization before you can rebuild the public's trust.

He has said many times, "If we have serious problems, I want to hang out our own dirty laundry all down Pennsylvania Avenue before waiting for a call to come in from a reporter." Because there were a lot of scandals in government aimed at Mayor Barry, the agencies definitely had this bunker mentality. "Avoid the press." "Stick your head in the sand until it goes away." But it won't go away. There were so many stories that could be investigated; it was like shooting fish in a barrel. We were in both a management and a financial collapse.

CFO Williams and his press staff thus started to systematically release the bad news, saying, "Here's the situation. Here are the steps we're taking to fix it." Armstrong noted that they were very aggressive about going forward and getting the information out, "because we believed that one of the problems at the simplest level was that the city's financial investors did not have enough information to trust what the District government said about itself."

At Williams' behest, supervisors carefully evaluated their staffs and terminated superfluous and nonqualified employees. Armstrong recalls one day, in January 1997, when 165 city government employees were fired: "It was absolutely necessary because there were people in jobs who did not have the background, the qualifications for the job. They had been placed in those jobs for a lot of reasons other than qualifications or were promoted into positions without the training or supervision necessary to succeed."

Recalling the bloodbath, Armstrong said:

There was a lot to do the night before. We brought in everybody who had somebody in [his or her] office that [was being] terminat[ed]. We made teams of people go out and tell people. We started in the morning. If employees to be terminated were eligible to retire, they were given that option. We prepared talking points for what to say to the fired employees. You had to be very careful; there were specific guidelines on what you could or could not say based on the recommendation of legal counsel.

All persons on the teams were directed to forward media calls to Armstrong, who did not release the names of the terminated employees but did confirm names if asked specifically. The first inquiries came late in the morning. Armstrong gave the news media a statement from the CFO announcing how many employees in which agencies were terminated. Again, she did not release names. According to Armstrong:

When it was clear this was a big deal, CFO Williams came out and answered questions. It was important to take responsibility for this action and choose to talk to the press for that reason. He spoke to reporters gathered in the conference room next to his office. He basically said, "I am going to stand by my decision. I will not be elusive. Millions of dollars have gone unaccounted for

and we have to change that. My people made these recommendations and I
stand by them."

Gradually the public and investors began to believe in the integrity of
the CFO because of his honesty and straightforward attitude. He would say
openly, "This is a mess. This is unacceptable."

As new managers, deputy CFOs, and agency CFOs were hired, they were
trained in Williams' policy of dealing honestly with the media. "They were
handling press calls and getting quoted in the newspaper, and it really
helped build the public's trust that there are good honest people, good ac-
countable managers," Armstrong said. She did not infer that all managers
before Williams' appointment were dishonest. She merely praised Wil-
liams' threefold policy of building a reputation of integrity, accountability,
and customer service as winning priorities. In a sense, this was a coup for
Barry, who had appointed Williams.

Williams was successful in turning the city's financial woes around. He did
so by clamping down on spending. "No one," said Armstrong, "could spend a
penny without his authorization." Williams was so successful in rescuing the
city financially that all three of its Wall Street bond ratings went from "below
investment grade" to "near investment grade" before he became mayor and
all the way to "investment grade" shortly after he became mayor.

Mayor Barry chose not to run for re-election. Williams, drafted by a di-
verse group of citizens, ran against an assortment of opponents, including
three city council members and a restauranteur. City Councilman Kevin
Chavous and Harold Brazil are African American, and Jack Evans and res-
taurant owner Jeffrey Gildenhorn are white. In the primary election, Wil-
liams won 50% of the votes, whereas Chavous won 35%. Williams went on
to win the general election. His financial success and his reputation for be-
ing honest and open were said to have made the basic difference.

As mayor, Williams soon discovered that being an effective CFO and being
an effective mayor required very different skills. Armstrong believed that it
was Williams' prior success at "shooting from the hip" that got him in trouble
as mayor. The press criticized his willingness to fire and openly criticize Afri-
can American workers, which got him in trouble with some constituents. Af-
ter Williams' second week in office, African American Washingtonian
Anthony Jenkins summed up the anti-Williams sentiment in a byline article
published in the *Washington Post* on January 17, 1999: "There is a concern
that's being discussed in some quarters of the District's African American
community. How black is Mayor Anthony Williams?" He went on to define
"blackness": "There is not one person of color who can separate himself or
herself from the rest of the people of color. Although each person is respon-
sible for the content of their character, some part of their existence is, in
some way, dependent on others of similar background and experience. Not
one of us has made it solely by himself" (Jenkins, 1999, p. 301).

Jenkins' article also criticized leaders with black skin who had lost their "blackness" by claiming to have made it totally alone. He cited "one who wears a justice's robe reversing civil rights with every bang of the gavel and the other rides a 'white' horse through California 'warding' off affirmative action" (Jenkins, 1999, p. B5).

His article went on to discuss the history of the absence of the voice of African Americans in DC political life until the election of Marion Barry: "Against this background comes Williams, with his massive pink-slipping that seemed to some the only way to curb years of bad management. The firings hurt black workers most of all, creating the impression—fairly or unfairly—that he has little or no special concern for people who look like him" (Jenkins, 1999, p. B5).

Similar charges against Williams had circulated even before he was elected mayor. Most of Williams' critics were likely steadfast supporters of Marion Barry who, despite his drug conviction, never lost his "blackness." Some said Barry was "too black," too arrogant for the White power structure, whereas Williams was more palatable. Some said they would rather elect real white people than a person who is black only in terms of skin color. It was clear that Williams was elected by voters who placed a high value on his competence, rather than on his experience in politics or his ability to appear loyal to all constituents.

Also in January 1999, David Howard, director of the mayor's Office of the Public Advocate, was in a budget discussion with two aides—one black, one white. During the meeting, Howard spoke about funds, saying, "I will have to be niggardly with this fund because it's not going to be a lot of money." According to reports, neither of the two aides knew the meaning of the word *niggardly,* and the black aide walked out. Shortly thereafter, Howard's office was deluged with complaints about an alleged racial epithet. Although the word means "stingy and miserly," it was interpreted as a racial insult. Howard felt obliged to submit his resignation.

"He came to me and wanted to write a statement to be released," Armstrong said. "We worked out a statement. We discussed what he would say and what we [she for the mayor] would say. After he left, his resignation became a big story. At that point, he hired for $1 a publicist/friend, Sharon Robinson, to help him with the process. She had done a lot of work in diversity training and became his PR machine."

It should be noted that Howard did not resign to the mayor. His letter of resignation, which was turned in to Chief of Staff Reba Evans, said his ability to serve the administration had been compromised by reports of his use of an insulting word. The mayor was subsequently informed of Howard's resignation by the chief of staff. Williams, who did not want Howard to resign and never asked for his resignation, praised his work. However, as Armstrong commented, Williams "believed in the judgment of his manag-

ers, and if Howard wanted to resign and thought it best, he [Williams] would not argue." (See Fig. 14.2.)

Armstrong prepared a press statement for the mayor's approval. Williams approved the statement but still felt uncomfortable with the director's resignation; he decided not to release it until the news media requested it. In hindsight, Armstrong said she regretted releasing the statement from the mayor: "It should have come from the chief of staff." (See Fig. 14.3.)

The furor that erupted when the mayor accepted Howard's resignation was greater than the furor over the use of the word *niggardly*. People everywhere, including Washingtonians who had voted for the mayor, were upset because there was nothing wrong with the word *niggardly*. They felt the people who were in an uproar had limited vocabularies and that Williams should not have accepted the resignation. In addition, because Howard was Williams' first openly gay appointee, the homosexual community was incensed.

Statement by David Howard regarding his resignation as director of the Office of the Public Advocate

I have resigned my position as Director of the Office of the Public Advocate for the Government of the District of Columbia effective January 25, 1999.

On January 15, in a conversation with two employees, I used the word "niggardly" in reference to my administration of a fund. Although the word, which is defined as "miserly," does not have any racial connotations, I realize that staff members present were offended by the word. I immediately apologized.

Since January 15, I have received many phone calls from individuals who had heard I had made a vicious racist remark, the text of which was actually said and in fact unquotable here. I would never think of making a racist remark. I regret that the word I did use offended anyone. I realize this rumor has severely compromised my effectiveness as the District's Public Advocate and in the best interest of my office, I resign.

FIG. 14.2. When David Howard, director of the Office of the Public Advocate, resigned from Mayor Williams' staff in January 1999, this statement was released to the press. Howard felt obligated to resign, but complaints by numerous persons of all races showed support for him. The mayor, who never asked for the director's resignation, rehired Howard, at his request, to another position. (Printed with permission of Peggy Armstrong.)

Statement by Mayor Anthony A. Williams Regarding David Howard

"I met with David Howard on Wednesday, February 3rd, and asked him to withdraw his resignation as Director of the Office of the Public Advocate and return to work. Mr. Howard indicated he would prefer to serve in another capacity within the Williams Administration. Mr. Howard is working with my Chief of Staff and the Office of Personnel to determine to which position and when he will return to work for the District of Columbia.

"The recently completed review of the incident confirmed for me that Mr. Howard did use the word 'niggardly' but did not use a racial epithet. The review also showed that an employee of the Office of the Public Advocate did misunderstand Mr. Howard to have used a racial epithet.

"The Mayor's Office, in conjunction with the Office of Personnel and Corporation Counsel, are working together to ensure that we have effective operating procedures in place so that managers and employees can resolve issues such as this in a productive manner.

"As I said at American University on Sunday, I've been doing a lot of listening since last Tuesday. While it is important for a mayor—or any leader—to act decisively, make bold decisions, and create a sense of urgency, it is not always necessary to act hastily. I believe I acted too hastily in accepting David's resignation."

FIG. 14.3. Mayor Williams, in office only a few weeks when the "N"-word incident occurred, issued this statement regarding his rehiring of David Howard. The mayor admitted that he had acted "too hastily in accepting" Howard's resignation. (Printed with permission of Peggy Armstrong.)

Julian Bond, NAACP chairperson, said, "You hate to think you have to censor your language to meet other people's lack of understanding" (*"Julian Bond Remains Critical of DC Mayor in Word Flap,"* Jan. 28, 1999, p. 2). The press joined the condemnation, reporting unanimously that the word had never carried a racial meaning during its centuries of use. Colbert King, a black columnist for the *Washington Post*, pointed out that the word had been used 65 times in the *Post* in the past several years. "It has been used by reporters in practically every section of this newspaper," wrote King, "by prominent nationally syndicated columnists and the U.S. Supreme Court's most liberal justice" (King, Jan. 30, 1999, p. A19).

In an interview with Linton Weeks of the *Washington Post*, Howard said, "It was my decision to resign. Any criticism should be voiced to me. I

used poor judgment in using that word. I regret it deeply. I hope this is a signal flag to all of us" (Weeks, 1999, p. C01).

Following Howard's resignation, Mayor Williams was scheduled to appear at two events in the city. At one of these events, there was a *stakeout*. A stakeout is when members of the press are waiting in an ambush situation to ask questions. There were about 15 members of the press present, including a few television cameras and radio personnel. No print media reporters were present.

Williams was quoted as saying that Howard had used poor judgment, although he had used the word *niggardly* correctly, and that "[i]f you work in an oil refinery, you need to be careful with matches." He further said that many words can easily be misunderstood.

Howard went on to say, in the *Washington Post* interview, "I resigned, not because I used poor judgment in using the term 'niggardly,' but because of the rumors that spiraled out of that." Although the rumors were that he was racist, numerous black associates came to his defense claiming there was no sign of racism in his behavior. "Being gay," Howard said, "gives me an extra layer of sensitivity when it comes to dealing with minority groups" (Weeks, 1999, p. C01).

Armstrong, who is not African American, stated that during this period she learned that there is a colloquial expression used in African American culture, *niggerly,* which means "like a nigger," when the word is used in its most negative sense. The people were hurt because they believed Howard had used that word.

After the furor erupted over Howard's resignation, he and the mayor met and shared what they had learned from the experience. The mayor asked him to return to the administration; Howard said he could not return as public advocate because the incident compromised his ability to serve in that capacity. Williams praised Howard's work, saying he had done a great job, but that he, again, accepted his professional judgment. Howard accepted a position as special assistant to the mayor and the chief of staff as director of scheduling.

The African American staff member who misunderstood Howard's words remained in the Office of the Public Advocate. He was an alumnus of the Barry administration, but he had also worked as field director in the Williams campaign during the primary and as a general staffperson during the general election. "He knew everybody," said Armstrong. "A person like that is valuable in the public advocate's office. I do know that he felt badly about what happened."

To prevent similar crises in the future, Armstrong said a plan was developed to ensure that personnel issues would be handled by the chief of staff, not the mayor. The chief of staff was made responsible for doing an informal review of an issue or problem and making recommendations to the

mayor. Media inquiries were to be handled on a case-by-case basis by the chief of staff or the press secretary depending on the judgment of the press staff. Staff members involved in disputes were to be instructed not to talk to the media.

In response to the charge that he was an inexperienced politician, Williams said, after a year in office, "I was elected as a non-politician, but I'm being held to the standards of a veteran politician. That's personally a difficult adjustment to make." He compared the experience to being a non-skier and being pushed off a mountain (Abeyta, 2000, p.1).

"The mayor believes that he will have to deliver results to win people who did not vote for him," said Armstrong. "We knew that people want to see him, talk to him, touch him. They want him in their communities. The early perception was that he cared about dollars and business more than the real people who live in the city. After all, he fired 165 of the real people." To combat this reputation of being uncaring and aloof, the mayor made 1,100 public appearances, most in neighborhood gatherings, during his first year in office. Everywhere he went, he talked with the people, listened to people, shook their hands. Whereas Williams always had what Armstrong called "broad support," as months passed, she said, "his support deepened." News columns and reports in the local papers testified to that.

In November 1999, near the end of his first year as mayor, Williams held a 2-day event called the Citizen Summit, a planning session for the citizens of the city and an opportunity to discuss neighborhood action. Whereas the city expected about 1,500 constituents to attend the Citizen Summit, more than 3,000 people from all eight of the city's wards and from every race, gender, and income level attended. "The only disappointment," said Armstrong, "was that the majority of the people attending did not have children in the D.C. Public Schools." The school system is, of course, a very important concern in Washington, DC, as it is in most other large cities.

Another effort at making people feel closer to the mayor involved Williams' mother. Virginia Hayes Williams, in her 70s and a typical, loving, warm mother-type, took on projects dealing with seniors, children, and the arts community. She also served meals to seniors and the homeless and, in general, served as a very good substitute for the mayor (in much the same way as the Royal Family of Great Britain does when it makes special appearances in place of Queen Elizabeth). The mayor's wife, Diane Williams, employed as a financial manager for the Greater Washington Urban League, also accepts limited obligations to the city. "Her effort was to choose activities she can remain committed to," said Armstrong. "If she were to take on more than she can handle, she would wind up disappointing people. Her special cause is the battle against breast cancer."

In 2000, the mayor developed a unique program for informing constituents of his administration's pledges and goals for the city. Dubbed a form of "baseball cards" for "Team DC," 14 flashy cards were developed, one for each of the mayor's top deputies. One card, for example, includes a photo of a deputy along with the promises to renovate 1,000 apartments and houses and to help bring two new grocery stores to Southeast neighborhoods. Another card with the photo of a different deputy promises to cut wait times in lines at the Department of Motor Vehicles. "Clearly we've put ourselves on the spot," said Williams. "It's not a lot of platitudes. You're talking about miles of road resurfaced, a certain number of cops on the streets. These are things people can really see, touch, and feel" (Leonnig, 2000, p. A33). The cards are posted on the city's Web site (www.washington.gov) and displayed in city government offices.

Also in 2000, Williams assembled an inner circle of young, talented black Cabinet members to help him better connect with certain segments of the black community. The mayor spoke of his plan as including "people who are the very best, who represent the District, look like the District, and, if at all possible, are from the District." Although the mayor also said that the plan was not meant to put to rest the "black-enough" issue, his aides admitted that the move would help silence some critics who say that he too often relied on white advisers (Cottman, 2000, p. C01).

In a *Washington Post* survey of DC residents after the mayor's first year, Williams was "viewed unquestionably as the most popular and powerful figure in DC government. Three in four residents said they approved of the job he had done as mayor; an equally large majority say they personally liked him. ... Of all residents, 77% approved. Of white residents, 88% approved. Of African Americans, 72% approved" (Morin & Cottman, 2000, p. A1).

Ellen Johnson Finney, a lifelong resident of the DC area, commented that "Mayor Williams has gone through baptism by fire. From the beginning, he was not a politician; he thinks in financial terms, logical terms. We know he has a good heart and that he knows what he wants to do. He's a good mayor."

On April 30, 2000, CBS's "60 Minutes" profiled Williams, praising the work he had done in his first year as mayor and his diligence in overcoming adversity.

(This book went to press during Mayor Williams' second year in office.)

CHAPTER FIFTEEN

Case: Texas A&M University
and the Bonfire Tragedy

Eleven Texas A&M University students and one alumnus were killed and 27 others were injured when the traditional Aggie bonfire they were building collapsed at 2:42 a.m. on November 18, 1999. The burning of the bonfire and the celebration surrounding it were part of a detailed two-day time line of events leading to the November 26 football game with the University of Texas. The bonfire would represent the Aggies' burning determination to defeat its archrival, commonly called (in lowercase letters) "t.u."

The tragedy made big news in Texas but also made newspapers and broadcast news nationally and internationally. *USA Today* quoted the university's president, Ray C. Bowen, as expressing "unspeakable grief." The *Philadelphia Inquirer's* headline read, "Collapse Kills 11 at Texas A&M." The 12th victim died the next day. And in France, *Le Matin* had the headline "Une pyramide meurtriere" (a pyramid of death).

The 32-page *Bonfire Briefing Book* detailed the history of the event as well as the precautions, maps, charts, and diagrams for erecting the 55-foot tall, 45-foot wide log monument. The erection of the bonfire pyramid had

begun on October 3, 1999, with the cutting of trees from land that farmers needed cleared; an estimated 6,000 to 8,000 logs were to be used. On October 30, the center pole, made of two utility poles, arrived, and on November 6, the center pole was raised and anchored 10 feet in the ground, 55 feet above. "Stacking" logs would take 2 to 3 weeks. There would be six stacks with the fifth and sixth stacks wired together on the day before the bonfire (see Fig. 15.1). The book included a detailed time line of the festivities planned for November 25, down to the arrangement of the media vehicles, the football team's arrival, when the torches would be thrown and the bonfire lit, and which yells the cheerleaders would do. But in 1999, the day of festivities never came. The accident occurred during the stacking phase.

TRADITION AND CULTURE

The bonfire tradition at Texas A&M began in 1909, with the first bonfire made from a simple trash heap. *Tradition* is the operative word; it is capitalized in some Texas A&M publications. Many, especially non-Texans, wondered, "All these years of building the bonfire and there's no expertise?" "What's the big deal?" "What a wasteful reason to die!" "Students are a university's most precious resource. How can we risk them?" "Why waste people and trees?" "Start a new tradition—build a house for Habitat for Humanity." "It's simple—People were killed; stop the tradition." But it was not so simple because the bonfire was part of the Texas A&M culture.

Five thousand students put in 125,000 work hours each year to build the bonfire. Aggies participated every year, and from 1935 on, the bonfire was a monument of logs, growing bigger every year until 1970, when a limit was placed on its size. University alumni and community members returned each year to see the bonfire blaze. In 1963, the bonfire was canceled because of the assassination of President John Kennedy, so in 1994 the class of 1964 was invited to participate in the lighting of the bonfire; the students came in large numbers, eager to have their moment.

Some students risk their grades to take time to build the bonfire. A&M student John Comstock, the last accident victim to be released (in April 2000) from the hospital, had been pinned under the rubble for 7 hours. His injuries left him partially paralyzed, and his left leg had to be amputated above the knee. Still, he said he wanted the bonfire tradition to continue. Some parents of students who were killed also wanted the tradition to continue. Former U.S. President George Bush, whose library is located on the Texas A&M campus, was asked if the tradition should continue. He replied, "Absolutely" (Kirsch, 1999b).

Aggies say "you have to be there" to understand the spirit and the tradition of the bonfire, that the experience is beyond words or description. They

FIG. 15.1. An artists' sketch of the bonfire built by students shows the telephone poles spliced together to make the center pole which supports the structure. The spliced poles are also embedded underground. The logs on each stack are held together in groups of three with baling wire. (Drawing by Gina Arnold.)

call it the "Spirit of Aggieland." They say it keeps Aggies of today and yesterday in a tight bond.

There had been prodromes to the 1999 bonfire tragedy. In 1955, an Aggie on all-night duty at the bonfire construction site was hit and killed by a truck. He is called the "first Bonfire hero," not its first victim. In 1957, a few days before the scheduled burning, the bonfire stack fell while the Aggies were lunching. No one was hurt. In 1981, an Aggie was killed after he rode a tractor to the cutting site; he hit a bump, was thrown off the tractor, and was crushed beneath its wheels. In 1994, following heavy rains, the stack of logs shifted and had to be rebuilt.

Proponents of the bonfire discount that the 1999 tragedy is a warning of what could happen again. They argue that the bonfire can be built more safely and that the tradition must continue. After all, in Texas in 1999, 11 students died in traffic accidents. University students die playing football, but there is no move to abolish the game. Accidents happen (Tang, 2000).

EXTERNAL AND INTERNAL COMMUNICATIONS

In 1999, it was not Cynthia Lawson's decision to continue or not to continue the bonfire tradition. As executive director of university relations at Texas A&M University, it was her job and her staff's job to head external and internal communications. Lawson reported directly to President Bowen, who reported to the chancellor of the Texas A&M system. The chancellor reported to the Board of Regents.

Lawson's staff consisted of 21 persons whose duties included national, international, state, and local news and information, institutional communications, strategic planning, photography, graphic design, video services, and other public relations and communications duties (see Fig. 15.2).

Texas A&M University, located in the small college town of Bryan/College Station, is among the top-20 U.S. universities and a major research university. The Office of University Relations disseminates to national outlets research findings in the Second Chance Cloning, news releases about genetically altered crops, NASA, the ocean drilling program, and so on. News releases vary from local and state media to wire services and national media. Lawson said that before her arrival at Texas A&M, "There had been a few other national stories about hazing incidents or the relocation of a pig farm to make room for President Bush's library, and Presidential Conference Center."

Having been in her position for only 5 months, Lawson had not been a part of the longtime bonfire tradition and had not seen the actual structure, although everyone on campus and in the College Station vicinity could watch the daily building of the bonfire on the Web. A digital camera

FIG. 15.2. Cynthia Lawson, executive director of university relations at Texas A&M University, had been in her position only 5 months when the bonfire accident occurred. She has since come to understand the "Traditions" that are so important to the university. (*Source:* Printed with permission of Texas A & M Office of University Relations.)

was focused on the construction most of the time. Most residents of the state are aware of the bonfire after it is lit.

On November 18, 1999 around 2:50 a.m., Lawson got a call from the university's Critical Incidence Response Team, telling her there had been an accident, the bonfire had fallen, and students were injured. She did not know, at that time, that there were deaths. "I had no idea of the magnitude of the project nor could I place any meaningful significance [symbolic or otherwise] as to what the collapse actually meant," she said.

Lawson's first task was to telephone selected members of her staff; then she headed for the site of the tragedy. She did not have to call key administrators because the Critical Incidence Response Team had that responsibility. The university president told Lawson to make all the communications decisions, saying that she was "the expert" and that it was "her call." Lawson saw this as an act of faith on Bowen's part, because even though she had been highly recommended for the position, they did not know each other. She was appreciative.

A&M had only a skeletal crisis communications plan in place, a 1-page document advising personnel of the critical nature of effective communications during a crisis and mentioning what it called "one-minute manager" admonitions, such as "Be honest. Be accurate. Do not speculate." As Lawson explained, what helped her to a greater degree was her prior experience with crisis planning:

> I worked in Public Affairs at the Detroit Edison Company back in the 1970s and 1980s. During that time, Detroit Edison was constructing a nuclear power plant. Part of my responsibilities was being involved with and ultimately managing the Joint Public Information Team.
>
> This team was created to handle a media crisis in the event of an accident at the nuclear power plant. As I recall, a "mock crisis" was created once or twice a year. County and state officials, as well as FEMA and Edison employees were involved in the effort. Even the news media participated in the effort by asking tough questions. The purpose was to coordinate the information released during a nuclear crisis. I recall that we used to be called in the middle of the night. We knew the week, but not the day or time.
>
> The drill was gruesome—all day long. The circumstances of the accident were never the same. Sometimes [in the drill] no one was hurt; other times, people were killed. We never knew the direction of the nuclear plume and what the consequences of that particular scenario were. Mock press conferences were held; faxes were released. An entire Joint Public Information Center was set up with equipment, etc. It was as real as one can get and yet not be real. I even remember vice presidents getting angry at me for pushing them to release "pretend information" that the press would want and need.
>
> The skills I learned in these practices long ago were ingrained in me. I knew what I had to do. It was automatic.

However, as we will see later, Lawson said she would make some changes if she had to do it again.

Another factor that helped Lawson with the crisis communications was that she had spent the first months of her position connecting with key community leaders. There was no organized advisory board, but there were these community leaders who she said "were invaluable during the crisis." One of them was Royce Hickman, president of the Bryan/College Station Chamber of Commerce. He came to the fallen bonfire and asked what he could do to help. Hickman helped arrange for food for student workers and the news media. He also arranged for a masseur/masseuse to treat workers who were becoming weary.

Home Depot contacted Hickman to offer its services. Houston Cellular offered cell phones and backup batteries to the Office of University relations, and before the day was over, these phones were being used by the

fire department, police department, and rescue workers whose cell phone batteries had died.

Relationships with the news media also paid off. "There were many 'media types' on campus who had connections with media throughout the state. Lane Stephenson, Deputy Director for University Relations, and Sherylon Carroll, Associate Director for University Relations, had extensive contacts and relationships. I had developed relationships with the local media, but national and regional contacts were virtually nonexistent," Lawson said.

As at most universities, a number of people at Texas A&M had public relations expertise. Lawson estimated that there were about 20 such people, and they deferred to her and her office for media response. "This cooperation was a first at the university," she said. "This is important in a university setting. Unlike a corporation that may send forth an edict ordering that no one talk to the news media except the public relations officers, in a university, academic freedom seeks to prevail to its fullest extent. Everyone has something to say and a need to talk. With a few exceptions, this did not happen. And I am glad. Otherwise, we could not have controlled the message as well as we did."

Most of the first day of the crisis was spent answering media questions and arranging interviews for reporters. There was a never-ending parade of news personnel. "Since they did not arrive at the same time, it required repetition of information to bring them up to speed throughout the early morning hours of the crisis," said Lawson. "Key members of my staff and I tried to do this one-on-one. So, to keep some control of the scene and to keep from having a 'circus' atmosphere, I advised the media that I would come back every hour on the half-hour to advise them of new developments. Also, I told them that if new information developed before the appointed time, I would immediately come and advise them. Then, I was careful to keep my promise."

VOLUNTEER HELP

Lawson held four or five news conferences throughout the first day and brought with her, at various times, President Bowen, Vice President of Student Affairs J. Malon Southerland, Bonfire Adviser Rusty Thompson, Student Body President Will Hurd, and Bart Humphreys, a public relations official representing the joint city–county rescue operations. Because there were students by the thousands around the site, the media had easy access to students. Hurd made himself available throughout the day of the crisis and during the aftermath. He was also helpful in identifying for reporters those students who were especially effective at being interviewed and could be counted on for helping to get the types of messages the university wanted conveyed.

The key messages were the following: (1) concern for the parents of the injured and dead students, (2) facts about the bonfire tradition, (3) facts about the bonfire accident, and (4) an understanding of and appreciation for the "Aggie Spirit" and the "specialness" of the Texas A&M family.

In addition to getting warm clothing for the workers, newspeople were helpful in numerous other ways. When university officials needed to urge students to telephone their parents to tell them they were not injured, the electronic media got the word out. They also urged the community to refrain from needless telephone calls to avoid jamming phone lines. When a hotline was installed for parents, the news media announced it. When night fell and the temperature dropped, the media put out a call for coats and sweatshirts for workers, and more than enough soon arrived. Then the call went out to stop. Lawson said, "the media was a tremendous asset in so many ways to the success of the rescue operation. We were truly indebted."

Another asset was the cooperation of university legal representatives. "General counsel were on the site, and I spoke to them briefly," Lawson explained. "They did not try to counsel me with respect to what I or others should or should not say. Texas A&M, fortunately, takes the position that we must do the right thing. We must be truthful regardless of the consequences. There was no attempt to cover-up or be deceitful. If inaccurate information went out, we corrected it as soon as it was brought to our attention."

OTHER FORMS OF COMMUNICATION

An instance of incorrect information being disseminated occurred when Rusty Thompson, the bonfire adviser, estimated the height of the stack at the time of the collapse. The truth was, according to Lawson, that no one had gone out and measured the stack, so the actual height was not known. As it turned out, Thompson's guess was inaccurate. It was corrected.

The university has an ongoing communications vehicle called the "Aggie Hotline." It began as a means of communicating with faculty and staff via the Web. On the first day of the crisis, the Office of University Relations immediately developed a Web page for the bonfire accident. The Association of Former Students also had a Web page that it used to communicate with its constituents. The hotline and the two Web pages were used to update information on a regular basis throughout the bonfire crisis and for months afterward. All internal publics with Internet access—students, faculty, staff, parents, community leaders, the Board of Regents, government officials—could and did access these electronic sources on a regular basis.

In addition, the Texas A&M University PBS television station, KAMU-TV, was at the site to provide coverage of the crisis. Students tuned into the university TV station as well as to other local stations. Informal systems of com-

munications, such as residence hall councils, the student government, and student activity leaders, were used to inform students of a candlelight vigil, a Thursday night memorial service, and other events. The aftermath of the crisis was covered by the student newspaper, the *Battalion*, a morning daily. In its first edition following the start of the crisis, the *Battalion* reported the names of the deceased and injured students, but because the why and how of the crisis were not known, no other hard news was included. Other coverage included eyewitness testimony and feature material or "soft news."

The chronic stage of the crisis, when the accident made front-page national news, lasted about 2 weeks. However, the story remained in the news until the Christmas break. There were inquiries almost daily for several months. Although the national and regional coverage soon subsided, coverage in Texas continued daily for many months more.

Texas A&M University made all documents, memos, and other pertinent information available to the press through the university library. "Initially," said Lawson, "general counsel was not comfortable with the decision to release the information to the public in the library. The reality was that the president made the decision that this was the right thing to do. General counsel was given the task of logging and disseminating all of the information. Everything was released except pictures from the morgue of the deceased students. The media can get those, too, upon request."

The most important public, during the first days of the crisis, was the parents of the deceased and injured students. Once a deceased or injured student was identified, his or her parents were telephoned and informed. If the parents lived close enough to the university, a personal visit was made. It was only after parents were notified that student information was given to the news media and posted on the Web site. Parents of injured students were visited frequently in the hospital. Periodic visits were made months later to student John Comstock, who remained in rehabilitation, and to other students and parents as needed.

SPECIAL COMMISSION ON THE 1999 AGGIE BONFIRE

As days passed, information was provided to parents via phone calls, visits, or letters depending on the nature of the information and the urgency. The types of information the university needed to send included instructions for receiving special funds available for funeral arrangements, hospital bills, lodging, announcing the creation of the Bonfire Commission, meetings of the Bonfire Commission, and so on. The parents also were informed of negative or hurtful stories in the press (e.g., there were stories that some students were under the influence of alcohol). All of this communication to parents was disseminated by the vice president of the Office of Student Affairs.

Texas A&M at College Station is a member of a consortium of 12 universities that make up the Texas A&M University system. The system has its own public relations director who, according to Lawson, "came to the site, stayed by my side, and kept the regents informed, primarily by cell phone." Some of the regents came to the crisis site. They also were kept apprised by accessing the Web page and watching and listening to news reports. After the first day of the crisis, the president and chancellor kept the Board of Regents informed through phone calls and board meetings.

Both Texas A&M University and the university system have vice presidents of governmental affairs. Both officers came to the crisis site and stayed throughout most of the day. They communicated regularly to state legislative leaders by phone. After the crisis ended, the legislature was updated via memos from the two governmental affairs officers, personal visits, phone calls, and the Web site.

Within a few days of the start of the crisis, University President Bowen made a decision to appoint a person outside the university to head an independent commission to investigate the cause of the bonfire accident. There were discussions about who that person should be and what qualities the person should have. University officials felt this was the right thing to do no matter what the commission's report might reveal. The independent commission, later called the Special Commission on the 1999 Aggie Bonfire, would be more credible to the public, alumni, parents, community, and taxpayers than if the university conducted its own internal investigation.

Leo E. Linbeck, Jr., a trusted Houston businessman with a stellar reputation who was active in civic affairs, was asked to head the commission. Four other members were chosen by Linbeck; they were from El Paso, Dallas, Austin, and Fort Worth. Lawson's office sent out media advisories under commission letterhead announcing the meetings. The advisories told the press the agenda of each meeting and gave details as to how the press might cover it.

The media began to line up interviews for the commission report months before the report was due. Lawson's office prepared for the national media attention she knew the report would bring. She also geared up for the national media attention after the announcement was made about the future of the bonfire. Either way, it was expected to be good news—bad news—welcome news to some, disappointing news to others. Lawson's staff also realized it would again be sought after on the 1-year anniversary of the bonfire accident, November 18, 2000.

PSYCHOLOGICAL COUNSELING FOR STAFF MEMBERS

University President Bowen strongly urged psychological counseling for all university employees who were at the bonfire site at the time of the acci-

dent. Others within the university community were also urged to seek such help. "I had encouraged all of them to make personal appointments with a counselor. But none of them did; none of us did," said Lawson. "Then, about a month passed, and I asked a psychiatrist to come to one of our meetings to talk with us as a group. As it turned out, there were a lot of issues that needed to be addressed. Individuals had visual images, disturbing images they could not get out of their minds. Others had feelings of being left out of the loop."

One of the problems was that when the accident occurred, Lawson, not knowing the full extent of the tragedy, telephoned two members of her staff immediately. One of them picked up another en route to the site. Hence, there were four members of the Office of University Relations involved from the beginning. The rest of the staff arrived at the office at 8 a.m., as usual, to find that things were already in progress without them. "Some of them had difficulty finding tasks that were useful or helpful," said Lawson. "They felt left out. Somehow, getting lunch for everyone or doing what they called 'menial tasks' made them feel guilty because they were not pulling their weight."

Although no task is meaningless in a crisis, Lawson said almost 4 weeks passed before these staff members realized their value to the crisis communications. One of the most important functions of a CCP is often overlooked—that everyone has a valued role in the communications process. Before the crisis, each person on the crisis communications team should know what his or her role will be in the event of a crisis and how important that role is in the management of a crisis.

All of these issues had to be addressed by the psychologist. In addition, Lawson spoke about the sheer exhaustion they experienced: "I cannot begin to describe the pressure 'not to lose it' because you are in a managerial position, because you must appear before the news media, and because you are simply a professional. A time to cry is critical. A time to mourn is mandatory."

Lawson recognized her personal breaking point on the Sunday following the Thursday accident. She told the following story:

> I was walking out of church when a young A&M student came up to me. Physically, he looked like a linebacker. He shook my hand and thanked me for representing the university and the students so well. As he said this, his voice trembled. Then, he wrapped me in his arms and sobbed from deep inside his soul. Then, I broke too. I buried my head in his chest and cried. There we were … two strangers brought together by an unbelievable tragedy, two people who felt the need to be so strong for others at the expense of our own personal needs. We cried together for 15 minutes. He had his release; I had mine. I was okay after that. People need to take time to cry. I feel I should have taken this release earlier, even if privately.

Another problem Lawson related was being in the middle, between grieving parents and the news media. The news media wanted all the information they could get. When you are in the position of providing or not providing information to the news media, providing it is usually the right thing to do. People have a right to know. It is our right under the First Amendment. But, it is not always the thing you want to do. Although most reporters are very responsible and do not speculate or resort to sensationalism, some others are not. Some documents can easily be taken out of context by irresponsible or unprofessional news personnel. This can cause additional pain to families of an accident's victims.

One example of misquoting occurred when University President Bowen was interviewed by Kelly Brown, a reporter for the *Eagle* in College Station. The reporter asked, "If the Commission's report were to find that the administration was at fault, and if the Board of Regents asked for your resignation, would you resign?" Lawson was present and heard the question and the answer. She said Bowen simply answered, "Yes." It was the only answer to the question. If the Board of Regents asks for a resignation, nearly anyone employed by the university would resign. But some newspapers did not print the first part of the question, "If the Board of Regents asked for your resignation." They ran the headline, "Bowen to Resign." That was not what he said. As Lawson explained:

> Not wanting to bring undue attention to the whole issue, I did not attempt to correct the quote. However, my concern was that in the aftermath of the report, the misquote could create some problems for us. If the report were to cite any administrative oversight, the news media would attempt to pressure Bowen into resigning. They can be relentless about these things. President Bowen has provided exemplary leadership for this institution prior to the bonfire as well as during the crisis. His absence would be a great loss for Texas A&M.

Lawson added that phone calls and e-mail messages primarily supported Bowen.

Another media problem occurred when the *Arizona Republic* published an editorial cartoon that compared the Texas A&M bonfire accident with both the 1993 Branch Davidian inferno and the 1999 brutal murder of a black man in Jasper, labeling all three events "Texas Bonfire Traditions." The university community and Aggies everywhere were incensed. The newspaper pulled the cartoon from its Web site and apologized for having published it. Then the editorial page editor apologized and sent Bowen a $10,000 peace offering to be placed in two memorial funds. Bowen returned the checks, saying "it would do violence to our ethical standards to accept it from the *Arizona Republic*" (Kirsch, 1999a). It didn't end there. A

columnist for the *Arizona Republic*, whose column was published in other newspapers as well, charged that Bowen, "other grownups," and the university could have prevented the bonfire tragedy, but "[Bowen] wants people to be upset about an editorial cartoon" (Montini, 1999).

NEGATIVE NEWS STORIES

As stories negative to the university or to the bonfire tradition emerged, the University Relations Office rarely responded other than simply stating that the university did not want any responses that could potentially influence the commission's report (see Fig. 15.3).

On December 3, a headline, primarily in Texas newspapers, was "A&M Student's Use of Crane May Have Violated Bonfire Rule." There was an apparent rule that only professional operators could run the crane. University spokesperson Lane Stephenson, on Lawson's staff, was quoted in the story as saying the student "had 200 hours of experience, sufficient to satisfy federal requirements for operating the equipment." Because there was no information that the operation of the crane had anything to do with the collapse, Lawson told another reporter, "The commission will delve into each aspect of the incident" (Slover & Lee, 1999).

On December 5, when headlines read, "2 Bonfire Victims Were Legally Drunk," Lawson told reporters, "There's a real danger of getting off point. It isn't that these things aren't important or shouldn't be looked at. But the major issue is, what caused this thing to fall?" (Ball, 1999).

On December 10, news stories, in Texas and nationally, related allegations made by e-mail from members of the engineering faculty at A&M to the president that the bonfire design was unstable. Certain faculty members admitted they kept quiet and ignored colleague T. J. Hirsch, a former member of the faculty, who had been complaining for years that the structure was "fatally flawed." Stephenson did not comment on the e-mail messages and was quoted as saying, "Basically, we're going to let the commission appointed to investigate the accident do its work" (Haurwitz & Copelin, 1999).

When the headline on December 15, was "Photos Show Bonfire Leaning Before Fall," Stephenson was quoted by the Associated Press as saying, "Now that the commission is at work, everything having to do with the bonfire accident will be deferred to the commission" (Associated Press, 1999). After repeatedly referring reporters to the commission, the university noticed that news articles began to include sentences like the following one: "University officials have referred all questions to the commission, which will not speculate on a potential cause until the investigation is complete" (Brown, 2000).

Lawson took a stand on January 7, 2000, when reports circulated that the investigation of the collapse would cost more than $292,000. She was

A&M bonfire
safety rules
were broken

**A&M student's operation of a crane may
have violated Bonfire rules**

2 bonfire victims were
legally drunk

Faculty doubted bonfire's stability
A&M engineering faculty doubted bonfire's stability

Photos show bonfire
leaning before fall

Texas bonfire surpassed 55-foot limit

**A&M's tab for Bonfire aftermath:
$292,000 and growing**

Report: Bonfire
ropes were cut

Bonfire logs
appeared to
be leaning,
report says

FIG. 15.3. Headlines from several negative news stories, which Cynthia Lawson and her staff had to contend with during the Texas A&M bonfire crisis.

quoted as saying, "We're committed to do what needs to be done under the circumstances. I haven't heard anyone asking, 'How much will it cost?' or 'How are we going to pay for it?' or 'Who's going to pay?' We're doing it because it's the right thing to do" (Ward, 2000).

LESSONS LEARNED

When asked if she would do anything differently if she had to endure the crisis again, Lawson listed the following:

1. "I would have called all of my staff out immediately."
2. "I would have called in a lot of other PR folks on campus to assist us with answering media calls."
3. "I would have had one or two staff members dedicated to watching the media reports and providing me with any inaccurate information being disseminated."
4. "I would have had one or two staff members developing 'other' stories for the media and lining up prospective interviewees for the immediate aftermath of the crisis. During a crisis, there is such a feeding frenzy of information.

 When the crisis is over, there is immediate famine. But the media still needs to continue the story. I would prefer to have provided a bunch of stories for them that I wanted to 'get out,' thereby not forcing them to 'go get any story' they could to keep the momentum going."
5. "There will be a crisis communications plan. Once it is written, we will 'exercise' the plan, just like we did at Detroit Edison."

In May 2000, the commission reported that the bonfire collapsed due to a combination of factors: Students cut corners; school officials failed to adequately supervise students; organizational failures; and structural problems. Student drinking and horseplay were not deemed direct causes. The commission's leader said a safe bonfire would have been possible had school officials taken necessary precautions. The latter pronouncement met with "whoops" from students who filled a basketball arena to hear it.

Lawson said that, now that she has been at the university through this crisis, she understands the "Traditions" (always capitalized in Texas A&M publications) at the core of Texas A&M University. The notion "Tradition" has its roots not only in the longevity of the university itself, but also in the fact that many of the opportunities for student involvement are major events or projects that involve a large percentage of the student body. These students thus have many "shared experiences"—Bonfire, Fish Camp, Muster, Elephant Walk—where lifelong bonds are created. Texas A&M probably offers

more opportunities for shared experiences than most other higher education institutions. And the students probably do a better job perpetuating those Traditions than do their counterpart schools less rich in tradition.

President Bowen announced, in June 2000, that the traditional bonfire would continue but not before the year 2002 and only with greater school supervision and a professionally engineered design.

In November 2000, the university community observed the 1-year anniversary of the accident with a ceremony attended by 25,000 people in a pouring rain. All gathered on the muddy polo fields at 2:42 a.m., the exact time and place of the collapse. Family members of the students who died sat together in a circle. There were 6-foot pillars bearing the name of each victim and the year he or she was to graduate.

As the 40-minute ceremony began, the lights on the field were turned off and a memorial flame atop a platform in the center of the circle of family members was lit. A cannon was fired 12 times.

CHAPTER SIXTEEN

Case: U.S. Postal Service
and Workplace Violence

Roy Betts, media relations representative for the U.S. Postal Service, stands in the little square-shaped cubicle that is his office and disseminates information about the new electricity-powered Postal Service trucks. If his cube had been situated just a bit differently, he could see a magnificent view of Washington, DC, from the office windows of the headquarters building nicknamed the Pink Palace, but he is not concerned with views just now.

In addition to the outgoing news on trucks, he is thinking about a story already in the local papers about a gunman on a rampage in San Francisco. "My first thought when I heard about it," he says, "was 'I hope he's not a postal employee.' But even though he's not, I guarantee you I will get at least one phone call from the news media about the incident."

Many Postal Service employees are experts on violence, particularly workplace violence. Between 1983 and 1993, there were 10 incidents of violence in which postal employees or former postal employees murdered 34 people, most at a work site.

The most notorious incident, staff members simply called "Edmond." Part-time letter carrier Patrick Sherrill, about to be terminated from the Edmond, Oklahoma, Post Office, brandished a gun and shot 14 people. When it was over, all of them were dead and Sherrill killed himself. It was August 20, 1986. "Edmond," said Betts, "seemed to be a bizarre, rare incident. I believe institutions, like individuals, go through a period of denial before reality sets in. The Postal Service was in denial after Edmond, but Royal Oak shocked us into reality."

The Royal Oak incident happened on November 14, 1991, when postal employee Thomas McIlvane killed four people in the Royal Oak, Michigan, Post Office, injured eight others, and killed himself (see Fig. 16.1).

"Once the trigger is pulled, you've lost; the battle is over," Betts said. "You go through posttrauma and then do what you can to prevent another incident" (see Fig. 16.2). "You can't erase the incident from people's minds or delete words from the media. The media is very interested whenever there's an incident of violence." (Examples of U.S. Postal Service communications with employees and the media are shown in Figs. 16.2 and16.3.)

Following the Royal Oak incident, the U.S. Postal Service issued its Joint Statement on Violence and Behavior in the Workplace to postal employees (see Fig. 16.4). It was a response, not only of Postal Service management, but also of the unions and the management associations—all working together to prevent further tragedy.

In the early 1990s, departments reported to then-Postmaster General Marvin Runyon. Each department somehow dealt with the issue of preventing workplace violence. Betts reported to Frank Brennan, the manager of media relations, who reported to Corporate Relations Vice President Larry Speakes (yes, the same Larry Speakes of the Reagan administration), who reported to Runyon (see Fig. 16.5). Among its other duties, the media relations department was faced with getting information to the media and to employees about violence prevention programs. It was also instrumental in keeping the media away from grieving employees, families, and eyewitnesses to incidents of violence.

Ann Wright, manager of employee health and services, collaborated with others to set up the national strategy for violence prevention.

Dave Cybulski, manager of management association relations, served as a liaison with four principal unions of postal workers and three management associations. Workplace violence became a point of unusual accord between the labor associations and the Postal Service. "We have very collegial relations with the unions on this issue," said Cybulski.

Employee Relations Specialist Bradley Johnson was hired by Suzanne Henry, former vice president of employee relations, to coordinate all the various violence prevention efforts. He was responsible for the develop-

Violent tendencies targeted
Postal chief orders screening, replaces Royal Oak director

BY WYLIE GERDES AND MIKE BETZOLD
FREE PRESS STAFF WRITERS

In the wake of a fired worker's rampage that left four employees of the Royal Oak post office dead, federal officials on Friday ordered a sweeping review to pinpoint current and former employees with violent tendencies.

The toll from the Thursday shootings reached five Friday as postal supervisor Rose Marie Proos, 33, and the gunman, 31-year-old Thomas McIlvane of Oak Park, died at William Beaumont Hospital in Royal Oak. Five other people remained hospitalized.

McIlvane's shooting spree was the fifth such assault at a post office in the last six years. His attack, sparked by his firing for swearing at a supervisor, came just over a month after four people were killed in Ridgewood, N.J. by a fired postal employee,.

At a news conference in Birmingham, U.S. Postmaster General Anthony Frank said the five shootings formed no pattern. Nevertheless, he said, records of nearly 750,000 current postal employees, along with those of former employees, will be examined.

In addition, the Postal Service will review its hiring process and begin contacting law enforcement and military agencies about potential employees.

Local police and postal inspectors had investigated allegations of threatening behavior by McIlvane, who had a history of aggressive behavior while a marine, officials said.

Frank also has asked for an examination of the circumstances that might lead up to such violence, and directed postal officials to contact private firms that have had similar tragedies.

"Together, we begin the long process of healing. And we are resolved to do all that we can to assure that senseless carnage never again strikes our postal family," he said.

FIG. 16.1. A news story in the *Detroit Free Press*, November 16, 1991, about a gunman's shooting rampage at a U.S. Postal Service facility in Royal Oak, Michigan. (*Source:* Reprinted by permission of the *Detroit Free Press*.)

Newsbreak

10 p.m. (EDT) postal shootings update

Three postal employees were killed and three others wounded today in two separate shooting incidents at facilities in Dearborn, Michigan, and Dana Point, California. Crisis response professionals are on the scene in both locations providing counseling and support for all employees and their families.

At approximately 9 a.m., employee Lawrence Jaison, 45, allegedly entered the main floor of the Dearborn, MI, Vehicle Maintenance Facility (VMF) and opened fire on fellow employees with two small-caliber handguns, killing automotive mechanic Gary Montes and wounding two others before taking his own life.

VMF employee Sandra Brandstatter was critically wounded with gunshot wounds to the head and back while VMF Manager Bruce Plumb is in serious condition after being shot in the back. Another VMF employee, Glen Gay, suffered an injured hip in a fall while fleeing the facility and also reported chest pains. All three were admitted to Oakwood Community Hospital.

Jaison, a 26-year postal veteran, had filed an EEO complaint alleging discrimination on the basis of sex in the selection of Brandstatter for a position he had applied for at the VMF. The final decision denying Jaison's EEO claim was issued on April 19, 1993.

Almost four hours after the first incident, former postal employee Mark Richard Hilbun entered a rear door of the Dana Point, CA, Post Office. He allegedly shot and killed letter carrier Charles Barbagallo and wounded a clerk, who was grazed in the head by a bullet. The clerk was treated and released.

Hilbun, who was fired last September and had been arrested previously for assault, then went to the postmaster's office and fired a shot through the door, failing to wound the postmaster. After shooting at, and missing, a private citizen outside the building, Hilbun escaped and still is being sought by Orange County Sheriffs. A search of Hilbun's mother's home following the shootings led to the discovery of his mother and her dog, both dead. The stabbing of Hilbun's mother occurred approximately one hour before the post office shootings.

 UNITED STATES POSTAL SERVICE

PLEASE POST ON ALL EMPLOYEE BULLETIN BOARDS

Published by Corporate Relations, U.S. Postal Service Headquarters, Washington, DC 20260-3100

FIG. 16.2. U.S. Postal Service announcement informing employees of two workplace shooting incidents on May 6, 1993. (*Source:* Reprinted by permission of the U.S. Postal Service.)

POSTAL NEWS

UNITED STATES POSTAL SERVICE Washington DC 20260-3100

Media Advisory

<u>Who</u>: Postmaster General and CEO Marvin Runyon

<u>What</u>: The Postmaster General will discuss actions to be
 taken by the Postal Service in the aftermath of yesterday's
 tragedies at the Vehicle Maintenance Facility in Dearborn,
 Michigan and the Post Office at Dana Point, California.

WHEN: Friday, May 7, 1993

TIME: 10:00 a.m.

WHERE: Hyatt Regency Dearborn
 Fairlane Towne Center
 Franklin Suite, 2nd Floor
 East Atrium
 Dearborn, Michigan

BACKGROUND At the Press briefing also will be Ken Hunter, Chief Postal
Inspector, Washington, D.C.; Joseph Mahon, Vice President of Labor Relations,
Washington, D.C.; Ormer Rogers Jr., Area Manager, Customer Services,
Chicago, Ill.; and Jim O'Beirne, Postmaster will be in attendance.

A press briefing on the investigative aspects of the Dearborn tragedy will be
conducted at the Dearborn Police Headquarters at 11 a.m. In attendance will be
local and federal law enforcement officers.

CONTACT: Jim Mruk, (313) 271-0041

FIG. 16.3. U.S. Postal Service urging the press to attend a briefing at which
Postal Service officials would discuss the workplace violence in Dearborn,
Michigan, and Dana Point, California, that occurred on the same day in
May 1993. (*Source:* Reprinted by permission of the U.S. Postal Service.)

JOINT STATEMENT ON VIOLENCE AND BEHAVIOR IN THE WORKPLACE

We all grieve for the Royal Oak victims, and we sympathize with their families, as we have grieved and sympathized all too often before in similar horrifying circumstances. But grief and sympathy are not enough. Neither are ritualistic expressions of grave concern or the initiation of investigations, studies, or research projects.

The United States Postal Service as an institution and all of us who serve that institution must firmly and unequivocally commit to do everything within our power to prevent further incidents of work-related violence.

This is a time for a candid appraisal of our flaws and not a time for scapegoating, fingerpointing, or procrastination. It is a time for reaffirming the basic right of all employees to a safe and humane working environment. *It is also the time to take action to show that we mean what we say.*

We openly acknowledge that in some places or units there is an unacceptable level of stress in the workplace; that there is no excuse for and will be no tolerance of violence or any threats of violence by anyone at any level of the Postal Service; and that there is no excuse for and will be no tolerance of harassment, intimidation, threats, or bullying by anyone.

We also affirm that every employee at every level of the Postal Service should be treated at all times with dignity, respect, and fairness. The need for the USPS to serve the public efficiently and productively, and the need for all employees to be committed to giving a fair day's work for a fair day's pay, does not justify actions that are abusive or intolerant. *"Making the numbers" is not an excuse for the abuse of anyone.* Those who do not treat others with dignity and respect will not be rewarded or promoted. Those whose unacceptable behavior continues will be removed from their positions.

We obviously cannot ensure that however seriously intentioned our words may be, they will not be treated with winks and nods, or skepticism, by some of our over 700,000 employees. But let there be no mistake that we mean what we say and we will enforce our commitment to a workplace where dignity, respect, and fairness are basic human rights, and where those who do not respect those rights are not tolerated.

Our intention is to make the workroom floor a safer, more harmonious, as well as a more productive workplace. We pledge our efforts to these objectives.

D.C. Nurses Association

Federation of Postal Police
Officers

National Association of Letter
Carriers

National Postal Mail Handlers
Union

United States Postal Service

National Association of Postal
Supervisors

National Association of Postmasters
of the United States

National League of Postmasters of
the United States

National Rural Letter Carriers'
Association

Dated: February 14, 1992

PLEASE POST ON BULLETIN BOARDS IN ALL INSTALLATIONS

FIG. 16.4. The U.S. Postal Service Joint Statement on Violence and Behavior in the Workplace, a document issued to postal employees after the Royal Oak, Michigan, incident in 1991. (*Source:* Reprinted by permission of the U.S. Postal Service.)

FIG. 16.5. Roy Betts (*left*), media relations representative at U.S. Postal Service headquarters in Washington, DC, gets advice from Media Relations Vice President Larry Speakes.

ment and implementation of the Postal Service's corporate strategy on prevention programs for workplace violence. Johnson developed a leadership awareness program on workplace violence prevention for 40,000 supervisors, managers, postmasters, and local union officials. Regarding the program, Johnson said, "The issue is too massive and the credibility of the program too important for me to do it alone. So, I consulted with several of the nation's leading clinical psychologists. These consultations provided me with the strategic direction and foundation for the development of this program."

Ask any one of them about the violence and you will be told that the incidents, although tragic, are not as common as they seemed. The U.S. Postal Service is the largest civilian employer in the United States (at times, General Motors is larger), with 730,000 employees. With that many employees, problems develop, conflicts occur, and violence can happen.

The media, even today, still seems especially interested in incidents that take place in post offices. The crimes committed by postal workers make much greater food for the news-hungry reporter than crimes committed against postal workers. Mail carriers are mugged, shot, stabbed, and bitten by dogs, but rarely do these incidents make news.

At the same time, crimes committed at non-postal work sites may be unreported, underreported, or reported as something other than workplace violence by the media. Cybulski noted one such tragedy in which an irate airlines employee walked onto a plane, shot his supervisor, and caused a fatal crash. The story was reported as a plane crash, but the incident was also an act of workplace violence.

Then-Postmaster Runyon maintained that, despite the news media's concentration on postal issues, the U.S. Postal Service had a lower rate of violent worker death than industry in general (Fields, 1993). Betts said the staff thinks of the Postal Service as a family operation despite its large number of employees. He said:

> At some point in time, somebody in every family works for the post office. Most of the postal workers are mail-handlers—sorters, clerks, carriers, truck drivers—in all the various facilities around the country. As we talk, they are collecting and delivering the mail.
>
> When we go home, the night shift is going to work. Mail approximating 650 million pieces a day [177 billion in 1993] is being dumped on conveyer belts, sorted, and sent to its destination the next day. These people are valuable to us. The purpose of this organization is to get the mail out, and they do it.

In order to protect these valuable employees, Runyon and other Postal Service officials first admitted that workplace violence was a problem. Violence in the workplace was increasing. The Bureau of Labor Statistics revealed that more than 1,000 U.S. workers were murdered at work in 1992, and these were not just postal workers. Most were victims of highway crashes and robberies, but the prevailing publicity centered on the U.S. Postal Service. The staff saw the Postal Service as a mirror of society; hence, the problems of American society were also the problems of the U.S. Postal Service. Cybulski said he input four keywords into the Nexus computer program: employee, violence, homicide, and workplace. "The printer kept going and going and going. It's what's going on in society," he said.

"Violence is a part of everyday life," said Betts. "Either you are victimized by violence or you recognize it for what it is and develop strategies to cope with it." To prevent the growth of violence, the U.S. Postal Service developed a 6-part national strategy for violence prevention.

VIOLENCE PREVENTION STRATEGY

The prevention strategy was developed by a national committee consisting of postal management, union officials, and management associations. Rank-and-file employees were also consulted through focus groups to determine their ideas on the issue. The result is a violence prevention strategy with these six sections:

selection
security
policy
climate
employee support
separation

Selection

The U.S. Postal Service's hiring procedure is designed to select the right person for the right job. To that end, one outside firm is contracted to do thorough background checks of all job applicants. The firm has access to national databases to investigate job applicants' criminal and driving histories, credit records, and physical and mental health backgrounds.

Ann Wright, a Postal Service manager who has held several high-level managerial positions, said, "Because we have a unique population in that we're across the entire country and we have mobile people, it's been difficult for personnel to do thorough checks on the local level." Wright noted that the outside firm frees up Postal Service employees to do other screening processes, such as getting references from former employers (Anfuso, 1994, p. 70).

Competency examinations are also used in the new hiring procedure. However, the Postal Service has declined to use behavioral tests in the screening process. Management looked into the possibility and could not identify a test that was effective for its purposes. Critics of behavioral tests say they invade privacy and may not be a predictor of violent behavior.

Security

Wright said that in order "to protect people from homicide and other violence, a certain amount of security is necessary."

Security procedures vary at U.S. Postal Service facilities, depending on their size. There are 38,000 such facilities nationwide. Some have a single employee; others have as many as 4,000 employees and operate on a 24-hour schedule. The Postal Inspection Service, the law enforcement department of the U.S. Postal Service, coordinated security measures with the management at each facility.

Some facilities have security guards. Some require employee badges for admittance to the premises. Some have surveillance cameras. There are also awareness programs in place with guidelines on how to report incidents of workplace violence.

Policy

A policy of "no incident of violence," not even a minor incident, is promoted at Postal Service locations. All such incidents are to be reported. No weapons are permitted on Postal Service premises, including in parking lots. There are to be no threats of any kind and no pushing, cursing, yelling, or other aggressive behavior.

"We're trying to promote a clear, direct, absolute, and well-known policy related to violence," Wright said. She also said that seemingly small incidents are forbidden because they can escalate into something major.

"An employee's chances of being terminated for bearing firearms are greater than ever before," said Betts. "We cannot afford the risk."

Climate

Positive changes in the culture of each Postal Service facility are aimed at ensuring an environment conducive to safe, productive work. Managers and supervisors participate in a series of training sessions designed to make them knowledgeable about conflict resolution, positive reinforcement, and employee empowerment.

The employee unions are also working with the Postal Service to improve the process of addressing workers' grievances. Both union and Postal Service officials agree that alleviation of stress is the key factor in improving the relationship between employees and management.

The American Postal Workers Union (APWU) represents 366,000 postal employees, who join voluntarily. In 1994, Tom Fahey, APWU communications director of the union, noted that "the relationship between labor and management of the Postal Service has not been good at all, to put it mildly" (Browning, 1994, p. 24). Communications publications emanating from Fahey's office were concerned with employees' complaints about a militaristic management style that they felt contributed significantly to the violence.

Henry claimed progress had been made, although she admitted that the complaints and the stress had not been totally eliminated. "We're doing a lot of things jointly with our unions that wouldn't have been possible before," she said (Browning, 1994, p. 24).

The Postal Service issues an annual employee-opinion survey to measure employee satisfaction and promote positive interaction between employees and managers. In the 1994 survey, half a million employees participated and expressed that they had better authority to do their jobs, that they were kept more informed on important matters, that union and management worked better together, and that the quality of service had im-

proved. They were generally happy with their salaries and job security, and they were enjoying their work..

However, they were concerned that improvements be made in job safety, that the pace be quickened in changing the work culture and in preventing problems like sexual harassment. As an example of changes resulting from the survey, one third of performance compensation for managers is now based on employee satisfaction.

Employee Support

Founded in 1986, the Employee Assistance Program (EAP) was originally for the recovery of alcoholics. Dr. John Kurutz is manager of the EAP, which is a short-term counseling and referral source that helps employees overcome any problem dealing with work or personal issues that can cause stress and physical, mental, or emotional duress.

The EAP has counseled more than 600 employees. Also, improvements have been made in teaching employees how to use the EAP. All Postal Service employees participate in some kind of orientation program that includes an explanation of the EAP.

Two 24-hour hotlines and toll-free numbers were installed for employee use in reporting threats or other concerns to headquarters. One line connects to the U.S. Postal Inspection Service and is for the reporting of threats or other illegal activity. The second line takes calls reporting almost anything employees want to vent. Wright said all calls are taken seriously. According to Betts:

> Employees know about the hotlines. A worker can talk too loud and another will call the hotline. This can be an early sign of a crucial problem. We try to do this without a witch-hunt atmosphere. But we use common sense in defining acceptable and unacceptable behavior. We do not ignore any calls.
>
> Sometimes people just call with personal problems. And that's okay. If a caller contacts us and needs some sort of counseling, then counseling is available on that phone line.

The U.S. Postal Inspection Service investigates threats from both hotlines. During the first year of operation, the hotline logged 1,790 calls. Paul Griffo, national spokesperson for the Postal Inspection Service, said, "If you are threatening others or if you are exhibiting threatening behavior, it's going to be followed up on right away" (Browning, 1994, p. 23).

In certain regions of the Postal Service, crisis intervention teams have been organized to address threats and behavior believed to be potentially violent. Jim Merrill, a human resources executive with the Pacific Area, heads such a team in California. Each district creates its own crisis intervention

team made up of key employees as well as others from outside sources. "The teams provide an organized way of addressing potentially dangerous situations so that we can have control and respond appropriately," said Merrill (Anfuso, 1994, p. 76).

Merrill recalled an incident in which a former employee wrote a threatening letter and sent it via computer to the Antioch, California, Post Office. The letter read in part, "I have post-traumatic stress disorder. I haven't been properly treated; I'm enraged and I wake up at night thinking that I want to kill the postmaster" (Anfuso, 1994, p. 76). The crisis intervention team went into action. The former employee hired an attorney to deal with the issue, so the team met with the attorney. A physician on the team met with the former employee's therapist. A permanent restraining order was filed against the former employee. Additional security was added, and the postmaster was temporarily moved to a different site.

> "You don't have control of that person [the former employee] because he's outside your work force," said Merrill, "but through these efforts we were able to put him on notice, determine that he wasn't dangerous, that he was just blowing off steam, and defuse the situation." (Anfuso, 1994, p. 76)

Also, in California, 5,000 postal managers were trained in how to report threats and how to recognize the warnings of violence.

Separation

"We're trying to make the point with our managers and supervisors that firing people doesn't necessarily solve the problem," said Wright. "Quite a few of our most violent incidents have been [committed by] terminated employees who come back and shoot people" (Anfuso, 1994, p. 69).

An employee who places all hope in his or her job is one type of worker at risk for violence. This employee, if terminated after many years on the job, suddenly realizes loyalty is a myth, or at best a one-way street.

Nevertheless, termination is sometimes necessary, so the Postal Service has created policies and procedures for terminating employees effectively and for making assessments of potentially violent consequences.

THE DEARBORN PREVENTION PROGRAM

In addition to the various programs emanating from the U.S. Postal Service headquarters, individual postal facilities may have their own programs. Following the May 1993 shooting at the Dearborn, Michigan, Post Office, the staff adopted the following violence prevention program:

1. A suggestion box was installed in each of four area post offices to promote employee feedback.

2. Two work teams were formed: a communications committee and a leadership committee. Each consists of 8 to 10 workers, a union representative, and a manager. The work teams discuss suggestions made by employees and make recommendations to the joint labor–management committee.

3. An employee picnic helps raise funds for victims of the shooting incident. The city police and firefighters are invited to attend.

4. An employee-of-the-month program rewards employees with engraved plaques, gift certificates for movies and dinner, and special employee parking places.

COMMUNICATIONS

Without question, employees are the target public for the Postal Service's violence prevention program. How do policies and programs developed at headquarters in Washington, DC, get communicated to nearly three quarters of a million employees?

According to Betts, there is competition for the attention of employees on the issue of workplace violence. There are Postal Service communications along with communications from unions, the media, and peers. "Each may have a different slant but the messages are the same," Betts said. "It would be naïve to expect anything different. Our best bet is to communicate early, often, and accurately. Credibility is all we have."

Various newsletters and bulletins are circulated nationwide, including *Postal Life,* a national newspaper for postal employees. Newsbreaks are posted on bulletin boards in postal facilities nationwide. *Video Focus* is a video that is issued monthly describing new policy decisions. There are television monitors in rooms where employees take breaks and have meals. The supervisors ensure that everyone has the opportunity to view the videos.

Special "Town Hall" meetings are held once every 3 or 4 months at selected locations. Former Postmaster General Runyon headed a 2-hour session attended by about 250 employees. At these meetings, issues pertinent to employees are discussed and questions are answered by the postmaster general. Videotapes of each session are distributed to facilities throughout the country.

One-on-one meetings with supervisors are also considered important, as are group meetings with supervisors.

The unions have made it possible to segment the employee public further. Cybulski says all the unions and management associations have newsletters and bulletin board messages widely read by their particular workers.

The American Postal Workers Union communicates with approximately 330,000 window clerks and mail processors. The National Association of Letter Carriers communicates with 300,000 people who deliver mail. The Mail Handlers Union communicates with 51,000 workers who do heavy lifting, loading, and unloading of mail. The National Rural Letter Carriers Association communicates with 60,000 workers in rural areas— carriers who deliver to street boxes.

According to Cybulski, management associations also are a source of communications with their members. The three associations are the National Association of Postal Supervisors, the National Association of Postmasters of the United States, and the National League of Postmasters of the United States. Cybulski said that the Postal Service formed a leadership team in April 1993:

> Every officer of the Postal Service and the presidents of the unions and management associations meet for a full day, twice a month. There are no substitutes for the presidents because we need the person with authority to make commitments and decisions. Workplace violence is a subject all members of the team believe is crucial, and participants take information and decisions back to their members.

OTHER EFFORTS

In December 1993, the U.S. Postal Service sponsored a symposium on workplace violence in Washington, DC. It was attended by academic and professional experts on the subject, in addition to corporate and government executives.

There is also a National Committee on Workplace Behavior headed by Joseph Mahon, vice president of labor relations.

The Postal Service's communications program got a boost when the Center for Disease Control (CDC), in August 1994, published statistics that said despite extensive media coverage to the contrary, neither the Postal Service nor postal occupations are among the groups at increased risk for work-related homicide. The report further found that "the occupational fatality rate for U.S. Postal Service workers is approximately 2.5 times lower than that for all workers combined." The CDC report went on to say, "Although the occupational homicide rate for the Postal Service is similar to the national rate for all industries, co-workers appear to be disproportionately responsible for homicides that occur in the Postal Service" (Center for Disease Control and Prevention, 1994, p. 594).

The CDC statements were good news and no news, respectively, to Betts and the rest of the headquarters staff. "We were aware that people from employee relations had been working with the CDC on the study,"

said Betts. "The results confirmed what we were saying all along." When re-leased to the media, the information was more credible to the public com-ing from the CDC than from the Postal Service. If the Postal Service had released the information, it could have been accused of attempting to im-prove its image with questionable data. The CDC, however, had nothing to gain from the release of the information.

The CDC information was reported on the Associated Press wire and ap-peared in positive stories by many newspapers, including the *St. Louis Post-Dispatch* (August 21, 1994), *Washington Times*, the Denver *Rocky Mountain News, Commercial Appeal* (Memphis), *Houston Post, Newsday*, (New York), *Orange County Register, Sacramento Bee, Newark Star-Led-ger, Denver Post*, and *Seattle Post-Intelligencer* (see Fig. 16.6).

An employer does not cause violence. Circumstances on a job can, how-ever, contribute to stress levels, which cause violence. The Postal Service is looking for solutions and, by these efforts, it is making significant contribu-tions to corporate America.

Betts says of the Postal Service, "We are coming of age. We are an organi-zation which tries to define and redefine our mission, our purpose. We are looking for new innovative ways of handling mail, but 80 cents of every dol-lar in our budget is spent for labor. Our operations remain labor-intensive."

In the middle of these words, Betts got a phone call from a California re-porter asking about the possibility of doing a series of articles on violence and wanted suggestions and cooperation from Betts. "See what I told you," Betts responded after the call. "I knew that the incident in San Francisco would cause some media connection to us. I knew it!"

Two murders occurred at Postal Service locations in the late 1990s. In 1997, in a Milwaukee post office, a worker shot and wounded a supervisor and killed another employee before killing himself. In the Dallas area, in 1998, a postal clerk was fatally shot by a letter carrier.

In October 1998, Postmaster General William J. Henderson formed the U.S. Postal Service Commission on a Safe and Secure Workplace. Chaired by Joseph A. Califano, Jr., former secretary of the U.S. Department of Health, Education and Welfare, the 6-person independent commission in-vestigated and analyzed workplace violence within the Postal Service. It gave special attention to several factors, including work-related stress, sub-stance abuse, and the workplace environment.

At the same time the commission was formed in 1998, Suzanne Milton was hired in the newly created position of manager of workplace environ-ment improvement (part of the Human Resources Department). Among her tasks were improving the employee awareness program and generally bringing a better focus to the Postal Service's many other programs. "We are also trying," she said, "to concentrate on the positive, ignoring the un-

From the *Newark Star Ledger*, Friday, August 19, 1994

Postal workers' death risk found to be low

ATLANTA (AP) – The risk of death on the job for postal workers is far less than gory headlines about post office shootings would suggest, federal health officials said yesterday.

In fact, the risk of death for the U.S. Postal Service's 892,000 employees is 2.5 times less than that of all workers nationwide, according to the Centers for Disease Control and Prevention.

Taxicab drivers and dispatchers have the most risky occupation, with a death rate of 26.9 per 100,000 employees, said CDC epidemiologist Dawn Castillo. The Postal Service rate is 2.1 per 100,000.

The rate for all U.S. industries combined was 5.4 per 100,000 in the period studied by the CDC, 1983-89. The CDC has not yet compiled figures for the 1990s.

The CDC researchers found that motor vehicle-related accidents were the leading cause of death on the job both nationally and in the Postal Service.

From 1980-89, 43 percent of the postal workers killed on the job died in motor vehicle accidents. Nationally, the figure was 23 percent.

Murder was the second highest cause of death on the job for postal workers and the third leading cause for all workers, the CDC said. Machine-related injuries are the second leading cause of death on the job for all workers.

Firearms were the most common murder weapon, and postal employees were more likely to be killed by a co-worker than by people not employed by the Postal Service, the researchers found.

From the New Orleans **Times-Picayune**, June 16, 1993

Postmaster ponders rash of violence

WASHINGTON (AP) – Postmaster General Marvin Runyon is trying to pin down the causes and solutions for workplace violence.

Recent killings by postal workers in Michigan and California are just the most recent of many such incidents that have affected the post office and other businesses around the nation.

"Images of grieving family members and shocked employees during my visits to the sites of both tragedies will remain with me forever," Runyon said in a commentary Monday in the Los Angeles Times.

Runyon said he is considering trying to organize a panel of corporate executives and researchers "to explore what the nation's businesses can do to curtail workplace violence."

In addition, he said, the Postal Inspection Service is launching a study to try and determine what connects workers who turn to violence.

Runyon said his agency has tightened screening procedures for job applicants, operates hotlines to report threats and is trying to improve communication.

"All kinds of jobs in our economy come with built-in stress. Yet the vast majority of managers don't push employees too hard. Moreover, 99.99 percent of postal employees don't do violent things to fellow employees when they face job disappointments and frustration," wrote Runyon.

As for the causes of specific incidents, Runyon concluded, "I don't have all the answers and probably never will. I wish I knew what causes irrational behavior by irrational individuals."

FIG. 16.6. Excerpts from news stories with a positive slant about workplace violence at the U.S. Postal Service following the 1994 CDC report. The *Star-Ledger* story was one of many that followed the report from the Center for Disease Control and Prevention.

205

fortunate slang slogan, 'going postal.' We know that people think posi-
tively of their letter carriers and the people they see at their local post
offices, so we build on that positive feeling."

Betts said, "The whole idea of 'going postal' is a myth. To us, going
postal means delivering billions of cards, letters, and packages on time.
That's going postal."

CHAPTER SEVENTEEN

Case: The Metro Transit Accident:
Driver Shot, Bus Flies Off the Bridge

It was Nov. 26, the day after Thanksgiving, 1998. Dan Williams, media relations specialist for Metro Transit in Seattle (a division of the King County Department of Transportation) was preparing to take his children to an afternoon movie when the phone rang. It was a reporter from the *Seattle Post-Intelligencer* asking if Williams knew anything about an accident involving a bus on the Aurora Bridge. (See Fig. 17.1.)

Williams had been with the county agency for 15 years, 12 as media relations specialist in the office of the director of Metro Transit. He was one of only two media relations specialists who reported to Ron Posthuma, assistant deputy director of Metro Transit, who reported to Director Paul Toliver.

Williams first thought was that the call was routine. In a city where buses are so crucial, accidents happen. Metro Transit had 1,600 full-time drivers and 750 part-time drivers. Also it was after 3 p.m., peak traffic hours. Approximately 1,000 buses are in operation during peak hours, most of them heading into or away from the downtown area. Because of the holiday weekend, traffic was somewhat less congested. Williams told the reporter he hadn't heard anything, but promised to get back to him. It also was not

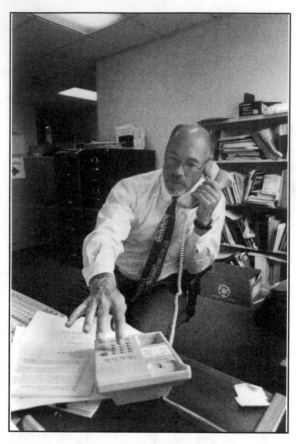

FIG. 17.1. Dan Williams, media relations specialist for Metro Transit, served as primary spokesperson during the 1998 bus tragedy, in which a Metro bus driver was shot and the bus plunged off Aurora Bridge in Seattle. (*Source*: Printed with permission of Dan Williams.)

unusual to get calls about accidents from reporters because newsrooms regularly monitor (police) radio scanners.

"I called our control center not really expecting anything out of the ordinary," said Williams. "Our coordinators have a lot of people to notify in case of an accident, and they must also communicate by radio to personnel at the scene of the accident. Calmly, the coordinator told me that the driver of a bus southbound on Aurora Avenue had been shot, the bus veered off the bridge, the driver had been ejected and was receiving medical treatment on the roof of a building where he fell, and there were multiple injuries to passengers."

Aurora Bridge is one of the tallest bridges in Seattle, a city of bridges. It is commonly called Suicide Bridge because it is the bridge of choice for people who want to take their own lives. There were so many suicide jumps from the Aurora that the news media stopped covering them for fear that the victims, through jumping, were seeking a strange kind of publicity or fame. The bridge is also part of Aurora Avenue, a major thoroughfare connecting the northwest section of the city to the downtown area. On both

ends, the bridge spans houses and other structures; in the center, it towers 175 feet above Lake Union (see Figs. 17.2 and 17.3).

After learning of the accident, Williams said, "My immediate reaction was to suppress whatever shock I was beginning to feel and do whatever was necessary to get to the scene as soon as possible. I made a quick call to neighbors and dropped my kids at their house. Television news helicopters were circling the accident scene, just a half mile from my house. I didn't call the reporter right away because I didn't have enough information."

Williams arrived at the scene about 30 minutes after the time of the accident. He described the scene as follows:

> The bus was resting upright in the front yard of a house. Emergency medical crews were removing victims from the bus and laying them on blankets and stretchers under the bridge; two or three of the most severely injured had already been taken to hospitals. The rest were being evaluated and treated at the scene. The bus driver was still receiving treatment on the roof of the house [where he had landed]. The Seattle Police Department had taped off the area, keeping media and onlookers about a block away. Detectives were beginning their investigation.

Williams learned that an assailant had shot the bus driver, sending the southbound 60-foot-long (so long it bends in the middle), 40,000-pound bus across oncoming northbound traffic, traffic that would have been heavier at that time of the afternoon had it not been for the holiday. The bus crashed through two sections of iron and concrete guardrails and shot through the air, temporarily landing on top of a 2-story apartment building near the bridge, where the driver was ejected. But then the bus bounced off the roof and broke in two: The front part of the bus landed on the steps of the apartment building, and the back part landed upright on a front lawn.

The driver, 44-year-old Mark McLaughlin, died of his injuries. The assailant apparently died of a self-inflicted bullet wound, but his identity was not known until the next day. The 33 passengers had various injuries; one later died of his injuries. Miraculously, no nonpassenger was injured.

The Friday following Thanksgiving is normally a "slow news day." Very few events, press conferences, or speeches are scheduled because many people take the day off as part of a 4-day Thanksgiving weekend. Newscasts usually consist of soft news and features; it's a good day for public relations professionals to get their video news releases aired. But this was not a typical holiday weekend. Soft news, features, and video news releases were bumped by this breaking news event. Because the combination of a shooting, an accident, a bus off a bridge, and relatively low loss of life was so unusual, the story was carried by news outlets all over the United States.

FIG. 17.2. Sketch of route of bus headed over the bridge embankment The 60-foot Metro Transit bus was traveling southbound toward downtown Seattle when a passenger in the front of the bus shot the driver. The bus then swerved into oncoming traffic on Aurora Bridge, crashed through a guardrail, and plunged about 45 feet, striking the roof of an apartment building before coming to rest on the front lawn of that building. The driver, the assailant, and another passenger died of injuries. (*Source:* Drawing by Gina Arnold. Used by permission.)

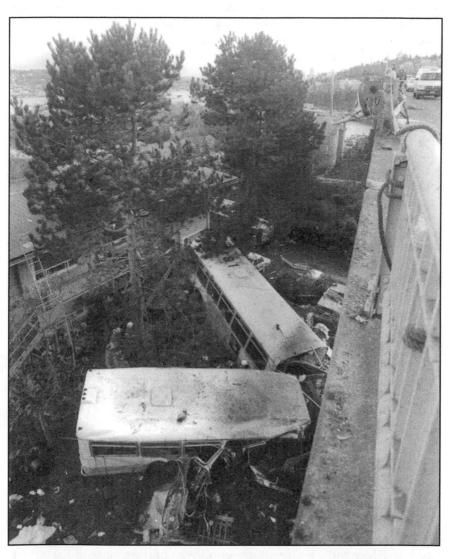

FIG. 17.3. The 40,000-pound Metro Transit bus broke into two after it fell from Aurora Bridge in Seattle. Three people died and 29 passengers were injured, some seriously. Fortunately, no one on the ground was injured. (*Source*: Reprinted by permission from the *Seattle Post-Intelligencer.*)

The accident occurred at 3:15 p.m., and shortly thereafter local television news operations began covering the accident with live breaking news reports. Some stations preempted regular broadcasting and were on the air continuously through their evening newscasts. After the network news programs (some of which also ran the story), the local stations returned to air more live coverage from the scene.

PRE-CRISIS CUSTOMER RELATIONS

Before the accident, Metro Transit had established a customer relations program that included three separate phone lines: (1) a 24-hour telephone service providing bus route information and trip planning called "Rider Information," (2) an automated phone system that provided bus schedule information called "Bus Time," and (3) a Customer Service Office that handles customer complaints and commendations.

Customers using the Rider Information service were routed to a recorded menu of options without talking to a real person, although it was also possible to talk to a real person. The system was designed to free operators to respond to more complex questions about the transit system. Customers could listen to the recorded information and then stay on the line to speak with a live operator.

Metro Transit received more than 2 million calls in 1998. Williams believed the system contributed to customer loyalty. He also said the drivers were considered an integral part of the customer relations program: "They are the agency's main connection to customers. They are the 'face' of Metro to the public. Metro's philosophy in hiring and training is that driving skills can pretty much be taught to anyone, but it is people skills that are of primary importance."

PRE-CRISIS EMPLOYEE RELATIONS

Metro Transit bus drivers are members of the Amalgamated Transit Union Local 587. Metro's contract with the union stipulates processes for grievances, complaints, and so on. In addition, there are committees on which employees can serve to work with management on such issues as security and safety. From each of seven bus operations/maintenance bases, a driver and a maintenance employee of the month are selected. At the end of the year, those employees select the bus driver and maintenance employees of the year from among the monthly winners. The winners' photographs are posted on all the buses, along with a blurb citing their outstanding work.

PRE-CRISIS COMMUNITY RELATIONS

At the time of the accident, Metro Community Relations was in the midst of conducting a hands-on planning process in communities throughout King County. In addition, Metro Community Relations developed and staffed the Public Safety Partnership program, wherein volunteer bus drivers attended community meetings to discuss ways to make buses safer for customers and drivers, what people could do to protect themselves, and how they could help Metro Transit identify and prosecute people who committed crimes on the bus.

PRODROMES

Metro's history of assaults and robberies during the 1980s resulted in demands from the drivers for better security. Metro then developed its own security force for its buses, patrol cars, and bus stops. There were seven traffic-related fatalities involving buses in the 1990s, prior to the accident; none involved passengers. There were serious bus accidents causing injuries to passengers. In 1978, 5 people were hospitalized and 67 were injured in three buses involved in a sequence of rear-end collisions on a freeway. In 1981, a bus with defective brakes crashed into a collapsible barrier, slightly injuring 20 passengers. In 1979, two cars collided with a bus, hospitalizing six people. In 1967, a driver was shot and killed after an assailant had committed a robbery on a bus.

Williams said that Metro took security issues very seriously and was continually improving its programs: "Our system is relatively safe, compared to similar systems in other cities. Assaults are rather infrequent, considering the amount of service on the streets and the number of passengers carried. We consider crime a community problem, not just a transit problem." Following the 1998 crisis, Metro Transit distributed a chart to the media showing the relative safety records of public bus systems in Seattle and other cities (see Table 17.1).

MEDIA RELATIONS IDEOLOGY

Williams had established relationships with news media personnel and believed he and his office were known for their credibility. Many of these relationships developed over years of working for the same agency, whereas others Williams intentionally developed with key news media personnel. He described his media relations ideology as follows: "Honesty and responsiveness are key to good media relations. If you adhere to those two concepts, you develop trust and credibility with reporters and editors."

TABLE 17.1
National Transit Database—1996 Security Statistics

Transit Systems (Comparable Cities/Fleets)	Aggravated Assault		Robbery	
	Drivers	Passengers	Drivers	Passengers
King County Metro (Seattle)	1	0	0	3
Phoenix	7	4	2	0
Oakland	8	11	1	35
Houston	3	2	3	17
Salt Lake City	5	0	0	0
San Diego	18	48	0	8
Boston	63	18	0	10
Minneapolis	45	11	2	26
Pittsburgh	16	3	0	6
Portland	1	7	0	7
Tacoma (Pierce Transit)	1	0	3	3

Note. This chart was effective in getting positive coverage of Metro Transit's security system after the 1998 bus tragedy. Reporters and editors were able to see how the city's bus system compared to other bus systems in cities of comparable size. (Printed with permission of Dan Williams.)

CRISIS MANAGEMENT PLAN

In 1998, Metro Transit did not have a crisis communications plan. However, its emergency procedures included a plan for notifying top management and media relations personnel in the event of a crisis. The media relations personnel were to take appropriate action: notifying the news media, reporting to the scene of the emergency, contacting other staff members, identifying a spokesperson, and so on. The Media Relations Department followed its own guidelines, which stated that its personnel would be available to respond to emergencies 24 hours a day.

STEPS AFTER THE TRAGEDY

Williams said that at the accident scene, his first step was to find Metro personnel who could give him details of the accident:

After about ten minutes, I learned that the driver was dead. After establishing some very basic facts—bus route number, direction of travel, circumstances of the accident—I went to look for the police department public information officer, Christie Lynn Bonner. Bonner told me that the fire department had established the initial command post, so together we went to look for the fire department public information officer, Sheila Strehle.

Williams, Bonner, and Strehle met briefly to share information about the cause of the accident, the crime involved, the number of injured passengers, and so forth. They knew that each of them would be approached by the media and that it was imperative that they all had the same information. It would have been disastrous if they had told different stories; the reporters would then not trust any one of them.

Together, the three PR people for Metro Transit, the police department, and the fire department faced the media. Each answered questions specific to his or her respective agency. This was an excellent professional move. No one was trying to be the star of the crisis; their shared goal was to get the story told accurately and to help ensure that each agency would be perceived well by the media and the public for effective communications. As Williams explained:

> Our initial news conference was held around 4 p.m., about 45 minutes after the accident. The five local television stations—KING-5 (an NBC affiliate), KOMO-4 (an ABC affiliate), KIRO-7 (a CBS affiliate), KSTW-11, and KCPQ—each had at least two crews at the scene. The local papers—*Seattle Times, Seattle Post-Intelligencer, Tacoma News Tribune*—were present, as was the *New York Times,* the Associated Press, the television newsmagazine "Dateline NBC," and several radio stations.
>
> After the initial news conference, I spent the rest of the evening gathering information as it became available, communicating with agency personnel at the scene and by cell phone, conferring with the other agency public information officers at the scene, doing interviews with reporters, and making plans for the next day. I communicated with Rochelle Ogershok, public affairs coordinator for [the] King Country Department of Transportation, by phone. She worked with Elaine Kraft, communications director for King County Executive Ron Sims, to issue a statement from Sims expressing sorrow for the victims. Sims and Transit General Manager Rick Walsh visited victims at Harborview Medical Center and spoke to reporters there.

The primary demand for information was in three areas—the homicide, the rescue-medical operation, and transit security. After the initial news conference, Williams said, the three primary spokespeople—fire department, police department, and Metro Transit—responded to media ques-

tions about their own areas and issues in separate interviews. He said, "The three of us would get together throughout the evening to compare notes and exchange information. We had an agreement that we would stick to our own areas of expertise and refer reporters to each other rather than answer questions about each other's areas."

Most of the printed material that Williams distributed to the media in the days following the accident included statistics from the transit security database, in response to specific requests from reporters. The statistics covered things like bus routes with the most security incidents, the frequency of particular kinds of incidents, and the number and categories of incidents that occurred on Route 359 (the route of the bus in the accident). Williams said he turned over the entire security database to the *Seattle Times*.

Some of the written documents included the following: (1) a security program fact sheet, (2) security statistics from the National Transit Database (see Table 17.1), (3) a joint management–union statement on transit security, (4) incident reports by a Metro bus driver who identified the assailant as a person who had pulled a gun in a previous incident, (5) reports from Metro agents detailing follow-up surveillance work after that incident, and (6) an op-ed piece written by Metro Transit Manager Rick Walsh summarizing Metro's security improvements over the past years.

There were also impromptu briefings of the media at the accident site and at Harborview Medical Center, where most of the injured passengers were taken. There was a joint news conference on Saturday, the day after the accident, with Walsh and Barry Samet, president of the Amalgamated Transit Union Local 578. On the following Monday, there was another news conference for the distribution of the joint statement on transit security.

NEWSPAPER COVERAGE

On Saturday, November 27, the day following the shooting and accident, coverage in the city's two major daily newspapers, the *Seattle Times* and *Seattle Post-Intelligencer* was extensive.

The *Seattle Times' front page, which was devoted primarily to the incident, featured this banner headline:*

Rider Shoots Driver; two dead, dozens injured
Bus falls from bridge

Two related stories began on the *Times'* front page: One told what happened; the other told what happened from the point of view of the passengers who were on the bus. The front page also included a large 5-column color photo (roughly 10" by 6") of police and firefighters rescuing victims from the mangled bus, a 2-column color photo (4" by 3½") of the bridge site where the bus went through the guardrail, a half-column headshot of the bus driver, and a series of three drawings showing the route of the bus from the point that it entered the bridge to where it landed after the fall.

At the bottom of the *Times'* front page were two unrelated stories: One on the President Clinton–Monica Lewinsky situation (with a half-column color headshot), which probably would have been the major story had the accident not occurred, and another about an accountability system set up by the Washington legislature for judging how well the state's six public universities served students. Both of these stories were continued on other pages.

Inside the *Seattle Times,* on pages A19, A20, and A21, following world and national news, was a feature piece entitled "The Aurora Bus Tragedy." On these three pages were (1) seven black-and-white photos, which dominated the pages; (2) the jump stories continued from page 1; (3) a long story about security on the buses, quoting Barry Samet, president of Local 587, Amalgamated Transit Union (the bus drivers' union); and (4) a list of the passengers on the bus, including their names, ages, conditions, and which of six hospitals treated them. In addition, there was the expected article about the driver and what a wonderful person he was.

Also in the *Seattle Times,* TV critic Kay McFadden's column was on the "human touch" of KOMO TV's coverage of the tragedy. She noted that KING-5 was first on the air with the news that the bus had plunged off the bridge, but that KOMO-TV was first to break the news that someone had been killed and, later, that the driver had been shot. Various KOMO-TV news personnel were praised by the columnist for their "dogged reporting, superior productions and rock-of-Gibraltar-like narration by anchor Dan Lewis." One reporter was praised for "buttonholing officials as they arrived on the scene" and for seeming like an old friend of the police department spokesperson, Christie-Lynn Bonner. The columnist wrote that all the other stations' reporters seemed to get to people of interest only after the KOMO-TV reporter had already done so. McFadden praised Lewis and his staff at KOMO-TV for being armed with data, keeping the story going "even when there [was] nothing to report," and for maintaining a "human touch." Lewis apparently signed off the newscast with this comment: "A quick prayer for the people involved would probably not be a bad idea right now" (McFadden, 1998).

In the *Seattle Post-Intelligencer,* the front page was similar to the *Times,* with the Clinton–Lewinsky story at the bottom. The banner headline read as follows:

A Horror Scene in Fremont

Shooting triggers bus plunge off Aurora Bridge; 2 dead, 33 hurt

There were three stories about the accident beginning on page one. One was about the bus driver and his family; another on the story from inside the bus. The lead story was the basic five W's and H (who, what, where, when, why, and how). As in the *Seattle Times*, there were a color drawing showing what happened to the bus on the bridge, a 3½-column (7" by 8½") color photograph showing the damaged bridge and the bus broken into two pieces, and a map of the accident site.

Inside the *Seattle Post-Intelligencer*, following the national and international news, on pages A4 and A5, was a spread entitled "Aurora Bridge Bus Plunge." This 2-page spread included (1) the jump stories continued from page 1; (2) an entire column listing quotes from witnesses; (3) an article on how disaster drills helped prepare the Harborview Medical Center staff to handle the disaster (a very positive story for Harborview); (4) a story about how residents near where the bus fell described the accident; (5) a history of Metro Transit bus accidents, marking this one as the worst in Metro's 30-year history, but showing a relatively good accident record and few injuries to passengers; (6) a story on how traffic was affected by the accident; and (7) a list of victims' names, ages, and conditions, as well as the hospitals at which they were treated. There were also six black-and-white photographs.

Both newspapers included quotations from Dan Williams, Christie-Lynne Bonner, Sheila Strehle, spokesperson for the Seattle Fire Department; Elaine Kraft, spokesperson for King County Executive Ron Sims; Tina Mankowski, spokesperson for Harborview Medial Center; and L. G. Blanchard, spokesperson for the University of Washington Medical Center. Although they all had important jobs to do and they could all be criticized if the communications did not go smoothly, Williams was more in the hot seat than the others and was quoted most often. After all, it was his agency's bus that crashed and killed people, and it was one of his employees who was killed. In addition, all of the spokespersons scrambled to get representatives of their respective organizations—firefighters, police officers, bus employees and officials, witnesses, victims willing to talk with the media—to make sure the public knew they were all on their toes and doing the best possible job.

Saturday's news coverage also indicated that the bus driver had been shot but that the identity of the assailant was still unknown. On Sunday,

November 28, the accident story had become second in importance to a story about the death of the charismatic public school superintendent, John Stanford, who had lost a long and well-publicized battle with leukemia. However, two new developments about the bus accident were reported: the name of the assailant—Silas Cool—and the bad news that another victim had died.

In both Seattle newspapers on Monday, November 29, the accident shared front-page prominence with the death of Stanford. The articles on the bus accident in both newspapers were concerned with painting a picture of Silas Cool: Who was he? What was his problem? Who knew about his problem(s)? A spokesperson for the Union Gospel Mission, Bill Whipple, came forward to provide some of the answers. Although not homeless, the unemployed and troubled Cool had frequented the mission for food. Security on buses was also an important story for several days.

As expected, on the 1-year anniversary of the tragedy, the Seattle newspapers revisited the crisis. The *Seattle Post-Intelligencer's* front-page story ran the following headline:

**Bus crash nightmare
Won't let itself be forgotten**

One lengthy article included extensive interviews with survivors—who talked about their inability to sleep, nightmares, and recurring injuries—in its retelling of the story of the accident. Another article was about how the driver's family had worked to adjust to life without him. Both stories were predictable but nonetheless heart-wrenching. Neither article was critical of Metro. There were a few paragraphs that mentioned claims and suits and that noted the county had settled some claims and had "helped some victims financially." The two most critically injured passengers got lump-sum settlements and would receive monthly payments as long as they lived. One had his right arm and leg amputated; the other suffered a very serious brain injury. There were also claims from residents who had some simple complaints such as broken windows (Sunde, 1999, A1).

The article about the survivors mentioned that some of the victims argued that the State of Washington, not Metro Transit, was responsible for the bridge, that the guardrails had not been strong enough, and that the northbound and southbound traffic should have been divided by concrete barriers. Some victims filed suits against Cool's estate.

In January 1999, *Seattle Weekly* praised Metro Transit in an article entitled "King County—Too Nice to Sue" (Fefer, 1998).

COMMUNICATIONS WITH LAWYERS

Williams said he had no contact with legal counsel until several days after the accident. Metro Transit's legal counsel was provided by the King County prosecuting attorney's office. "At no time did legal staff try to prevent me from media contact," said Williams. "When they did get in touch with me, it was to brief me on the county's plans for providing financial assistance to the victims. Naturally, there was concern over liability issues, and they did suggest ways that the county could express regret and sorrow without admitting liability. But they were sensitive to the media's and public's need to know, and they agreed it was in the county's best interest to be as forthcoming as possible."

CHALLENGES

Williams described his primary challenges as follows:

Responding in a timely and effective manner to the overwhelming number of requests for information, getting the information quickly from internal sources and passing it along to the media with appropriate explanations and interpretations. I received an estimated 500 media inquiries in the 10 days following the accident.

Television reporters created problems by showing up on buses and at bus bases, wanting to interview employees. They were focused on getting their stories and didn't seem to understand that they might be causing disruptions for employees and customers. It was also difficult to be patient with reporters and editors who keep their ears glued to their police scanners and wanted to pursue every security-related incident on the transit system, no matter how routine or trivial. It was a challenge to make the media understand the routine nature of those incidents without coming across as trying to discount or minimize the importance of security.

Williams also said it was a challenge throughout the crisis to find the time to produce good written material that would shed light on Metro's security program, to convince the media to analyze rather than sensationalize, and to remain patient and unemotional. Even so, he said he never felt—or allowed himself to feel—traumatized at the scene:

It was in the week to 10 days following the accident, while media pressure was intense for an extended period of time, that I had periods where I couldn't think clearly enough. I overlooked important details and had trouble controlling my emotions, post traumatic stress. I think I gained some insight, because I was very much in control at the scene of the accident. I have even felt very

emotional at times since then while writing or talking or viewing television coverage about the accident.

EVALUATION

Customer Service. According to Williams, the Customer Service office's effort to respond to customers' inquiries contributed to customer support after the accident. Tom Randall, chief of customer service, reported that about 80% of the hundreds of callers to the office following the accident expressed sympathy with Metro and/or the driver and his family. About 10% of all callers expressed anxiety about bus security and safety, and another 10% said rude bus drivers were to blame for most altercations. Overall, however, Williams pointed out that "the rapport between drivers and customers contributed to public support for Metro after the accident. Some drivers complained that Metro management failed to protect drivers adequately, and I'm sure that influenced some people, but I think that generally people saw the whole agency as a victim of this crime."

Media Relations. Williams noted that Metro's pre-established relationships with the news media paid off, but he added that quick response to media requests was probably more crucial to the satisfying symbiotic pairing with the media during the crisis:

Most of the reporters sympathized with what Metro was going through. And I think, in the aftermath, it was important to have credibility with the media as I tried to make the case with reporters and editors for the effectiveness of our security program. For the most part, I believe reporters accepted the information I provided at face value. I can think of only one reporter who was suspicious and antagonistic, and it was a reporter I had never [before] worked with on a regular basis.

Williams feels certain that if the news media could not get the on-site information they needed on that first day, the negativity would have carried over and made it harder for Metro to deal with reporters and editors in the aftermath of the accident:

Getting the union and management together to face the media early on was good. It minimized finger-pointing. It avoided having reporters running back and forth between the various camps, repeating accusations and denials. I think that, while far from perfect, our general ability to respond to the media went well. There were no stories about Metro's unwillingness or inability to respond. I think that Rick Walsh and Ron Sims both were excellent at being available and willing to talk to reporters. Both came across well and

established good rapport and credibility with the media and, through them, [with] the general public as well.

Community Relations. "I think the improvements we were in the process of setting up before the accident added to our already-strong community relations, public outreach program," Williams said.

Government Relations. Williams noted:

Since we are a government agency, the contact between Metro management and County Executive Ron Sims was [a kind of] government relations as [was] the contact with ... 13 members of the County Council. The latter communication included members of the County Council's Transportation Committee, primarily to chair Rob McKenna and Greg Nickels, who had been active for years in transit security matters. I worked directly with Sims and his staff and with staff from the prosecuting attorney's office. I also had at least one conversation with an official from the Federal Transit Administration.

Employee Relations. Williams was not involved in activity with employees, but he knows that funds were established for the crash victims and the family of the slain bus driver. "There was quite a bit of communication about that through e-mail and the county's Intranet Web site," recalled Williams. "I also know there were meetings at the seven bus bases with operations managers, security personnel, and drivers to discuss the incident and Metro's security program. Each base already had a security committee and, within a week after the accident, these committees were assigned tasks to work toward some long-term security improvements."

Williams went on to say that "Amalgamated Transit Union Local 587 was instrumental in establishing a fund for [the bus driver's] family and organizing a memorial service for [him] that took place 10 days after the shooting. The union and management worked together on a plan for continued improvements to the transit security program."

Williams said, "I think that communication and coordination among our department, the prosecuting attorney's office, and the county executive's office went very well. This was critical in dealing with sensitive questions about liability and victims' claims."

"IF I HAD TO DO IT OVER ..."

Williams said, "If I had to relive the experience, I would be better prepared and have better knowledge of our security program, with up-to-date hand-

out material readily available and better access to the security database. I would also take the time at the very beginning to assemble a team—probably four or five people at the most—which would devote itself to external and internal communication on the issue for as long as necessary."

The team, he said, would be based on a kind of corporate communications model:

I would like at least one person for internal communications, probably two or three for external communications (media, public affairs, publications), and one person to develop and maintain a Web site. There would also be a supervisor or manager to oversee everything, and a[n] ... administrative assistant. This team would be centralized in the director's office. It seems like a good way for the same messages/information to get out simultaneously to multiple audiences.

CHAPTER EIGHTEEN

Case: Alpac Corporation and the Original Syringe-in-the-Can Scare

Steve Bryant as vice president and deputy general manager of EvansGroup Public Relations in Seattle, Washington had handled many crisis management problems for clients. The agency had handled more food-related crises than other types, but the 1993 crisis of hypodermic syringes reported in Diet Pepsi cans was, as Bryant reflects, "the most spectacular crisis in which we had been involved at the time."

The Alpac Bottling Company, based in Seattle, was the principal Northwest bottler of Pepsi-Cola products. It was, at the time, a family-owned business, but it was later acquired by the Pepsi-Cola Company. EvansGroup had handled advertising for Alpac on an ongoing basis for many years and its public relations on a project basis.

Like many companies, Alpac had a recall manual that had elements of a crisis management plan but not an actual crisis management or crisis communications plan.

THE PROBLEM AND STRATEGIES

On Thursday, June 10, 1993, at about noon, the corporate attorney for Alpac telephoned EvansGroup, indicating that KSTW-TV News in Tacoma, Washington, had called about a report from another attorney charging that his clients found a syringe in a can of Diet Pepsi. The station wanted a spokesperson to be interviewed by reporter Steve Williams, on camera, in about 2 hours.

John Eastham, then-president of EvansGroup, and Bryant, as well as personnel from Alpac, assembled and prepared a response for Alpac spokespersons. The crisis communications team consisted of Bryant; Eastham; Susan Hebert, then-director of public affairs for Alpac; Al Call, Alpac CEO; and Paul Elliot, director of operations who directed production and was the initial spokesperson. Doug Hoffman, an attorney from a local firm representing Alpac's insurance company, was also an integral part of the team. Carl Behnke, president of Alpac, was out of town but communicated by car telephone.

In the early stages of the crisis, Pepsi's New York-based national public relations team, led by Rebecca Madeira, served in an advisory capacity. Anne Ward from that team kept in contact with the Alpac team. Pepsi-Cola eventually took over the helm.

The crisis communications team reviewed the situation, decided that Call would be the spokesperson for the first interview, and established principles that would be stressed in interviews. The team prepared Call by giving him a list of media interview tips, posing sample questions to him, and critiquing his responses.

Earl and Mary Triplett said they had found what appeared to be a used hypodermic syringe in a Diet Pepsi can after drinking its contents. They were afraid that the needle might have been contaminated and believed that it was important to warn the public that "somebody" might be intentionally placing syringes into the soft-drink cans. The can that the Tripletts possessed was bottled at Alpac on April 7, 1993.

"Visible top management is essential. This was a key part of our strategy," said Bryant. "When something serious like this is reported, people don't want to hear from the PR practitioner. They want to hear from the people who are ultimately responsible."

Call, the Alpac spokesperson, indicated that his company was investigating the situation, that Alpac was concerned about consumer safety, and that it would take all the appropriate steps to clear the matter. It was primarily a question of showing concern and compassion for consumers in general, and for the Tripletts in particular. This is an essential early position on the part of any company in a crisis resulting from product tampering or product failure.

There were two very serious aspects to this crisis:

1. The Tripletts, in their 80s and said to be a very devout Christian cou-
ple, were especially credible. Neighbors, friends, and the media compared
them with the Pledge of Allegiance, the Boy Scout Oath, and the Pope.

2. In his first televised interview, Earl Triplett said the presence of the
syringe in the can made him worry about acquired immune deficiency syn-
drome (AIDS). Although the charge was not made, the underlying fear
among consumers was AIDS. Used hypodermic syringes can transmit this
terminal disease. As consumers learned about the incident, the obvious
question was, "Were the syringes contaminated with the AIDS virus?"

There was such widespread fear of the AIDS virus that the very remote
possibility could plant doubts in the minds of consumers and seriously af-
fect, if not virtually halt, the sales of Pepsi products. This kind of hysteria
could be expected even though health officials maintained and made clear
early on that the acid in soft drinks would kill the AIDS virus.

Alpac felt very strongly that the tampering did not take place at its plant.
The company reviewed its quality control procedures and found no prob-
lems. It allowed television cameras to capture the canning process.
Pepsi-Cola's public relations department issued B-roll (video footage to be
used with a newscaster's voice-over) demonstrating the bottling proce-
dure. As the video showed, the cans passed under a mirror where workers
checked for foreign objects. Next the cans went up a conveyer belt upside
down; then were spun, washed, and placed directly into the machine that
filled and capped them. Finally, they were set upside down and weighed
precisely to check for leaks. An Alpac official indicated that the discovery of
dust was the worst that had ever happened in the process. Even that is rare.

"The coverage of the canning process proved very helpful in the course
of events," said Bryant. "It showed how unlikely a contamination of this
sort would be. It also, in a very real way, established what a high quality
manufacturing process was used to can soft drinks. And it bolstered con-
sumer confidence in the long run."

Bryant said that his team also shared messages with the consumer about
Alpac's excellent safety record and the limited number of consumer com-
plaints previously received.

"We also knew very early on, through laboratory analysis, that the syringe
was not contaminated," said Bryant. "The risk was limited to a chance of be-
ing stuck in the lip with a syringe, admittedly not a pleasant possibility, but
not a health risk. The FDA (Food and Drug Administration) supported this
position."

Bryant said that other calls from the media came within an hour of their
notification of the problem. "It was not a national issue at first," he said.

"We did our very best to contain it to the area, and we probably would have done so had it not been for the copycat cases. This eventually made it a national issue, but for about 4 days it was a local issue."

The crisis became a regional one when the Food and Drug Administration (FDA) issued its advisory to all Alpac distribution areas. Consumers had to be notified. Specific messages had to be tailored for certain states. For example, all Pepsi products distributed in Hawaii were also canned there, so even if there had been contamination in Seattle, Hawaii residents would not have been affected.

Handling the crisis meant being responsive not only to the needs of Alpac, but also to the FDA and to the legal counsel for Alpac's insurance company. As mentioned earlier, Pepsi-Cola was the imminent owner of the bottling company and had an enormous stake in its future. Even though Alpac would be responsible, soft-drink consumers nationwide knew little about Alpac. Furthermore, the incident happened in June, when soft-drink sales began to soar for the summer months. If the scare succeeded in causing consumers to curtail the consumption of Pepsi products, Pepsi would suffer greatly. Bryant explained how the team responded to the needs of the FDA:

> The FDA has a responsibility to investigate matters of this sort. We worked very closely with it from day one. It would have been a mistake on our part to take an adversarial stance with the government agency which, frankly, can be a mighty bear. We worked with [its people] in developing communications. We reviewed all news releases with them before they were issued. We established sort of a common point of view. The FDA maintained the weight of its authority in the matter and at the same time became our communications ally.

Because of the pending change of ownership, Alpac's attorney was scheduled to go on vacation the day after the crisis presented itself and then leave the company. The crisis team coordinated its work with Doug Hoffman, the attorney for Alpac's liability insurance company.

"He was great," recalled Bryant. "He had a wonderful understanding of PR issues and public affairs and was very sensitive to the need to communicate. He understood that communicating effectively would help maintain the company's value and limit its liability. You can run into lawyers who want to guide the entire process by solely focusing on limiting the company's liability. That can be a disaster."

The acute stage of the crisis lasted about 9 days, during which the Alpac team worked 15 to 20 hours each day. Susan Hebert and Bryant fielded as many as 200 media calls a day. Locally, it was the top news story for a week.

"Susan received calls even in the middle of the night," said Bryant. "We were constantly making decisions whenever we received new information. Fatigue became a serious factor."

An intern form the University of Washington, Erica Stone, scanned the media and wire services with help from PR Newswire and BusinessWire. "She fed us stories constantly," said Bryant. "Of course, we all tuned into broadcast news. That was easy to follow because it was always the first story."

Following is a day-to-day account of the crisis:

Thursday, June 10

Alpac's crisis communications team was assembled. The FDA was informed. The team prepared a limited number of high-ranking spokespersons to respond to the media. As noted earlier, a brief practice session was held in which media questions were anticipated and fired at the spokesperson, CEO Call.

Suggestions were made for truthful, convincing, substantial responses to the media's questions, keeping certain guiding principles in mind:

1. Treat the crisis seriously.
2. Apprize and support the FDA.
3. Demonstrate concern for the customer.
4. Communicate quickly and openly with a limited number of spokespersons.
5. Share the company's quality assurance facts.
6. Communicate the lack of health risk (this was established after it was determined there was no health risk).

Calls from the media began to come in about an hour after the Tripletts' attorney faxed a notice to Alpac. Alpac executives had not yet read the fax, so the media informed the company of the problem. Interviews were held with KING-TV, the NBC affiliate; KIRO-TV, then-CBS affiliate; and Tacoma station KSTW Channel 11, the station that made the initial call to Alpac. All newscasts contained the Alpac messages outlined by the team. Media tours of the plant were allowed that first day.

Friday, June 11

Alpac employees were advised by a bulletin board notice not to speak with the media. This was done to comply with the FDA's position of not revealing any information until the investigation was completed.

A second reported syringe-in-a-can came in to Alpac directly (see Fig. 18.1). The charges came from an unidentified person who indicated that he or she did not want to involve an attorney or the media, but merely wanted to inform Alpac.

Syringe Found in 2nd Cola Can
FDA investigates tampering

BY JERRY BERGSMAN
SEATTLE TIMES STAFF REPORTER

A syringe has been found in a second can of Diet Pepsi, this time by a Federal Way resident.

Alpac Corp., the regional Pepsi bottler, learned of the second syringe Friday night when it was called by a consumer who asked not to be identified, Carl Behnke, president of the South Seattle firm, said yesterday.

Alpac and the federal Food and Drug Administration are conducting an investigation into the apparent product tampering, a felony under federal law.

"It has to be some sort of sabotage because there is no way that type of a foreign object could enter our product in the normal course of events," Behnke said.

Preliminary testing indicated no health risk from either can, said Roger Lowell, FDA district director. Tests were made in the agency's local laboratory. Samples will go to its forensic laboratory in Cincinnati for more extensive testing.

A Fircrest, Pierce County, couple Thursday found a syringe in a can of Diet Pepsi they bought in Tacoma. No objects were found in samples of Diet Pepsi collected from stores where the cans were bought.

The Diet Pepsi was part of a case of 24 bought by Earl and Mary Triplet, 82 and 79, respectively. The rest of the case was regular Pepsi.

In the latest incident, the contaminated can was part of a 12-pack. An Alpac spokesman said the can opened Friday had been sealed six months before the first one.

Alpac produces 1.3 million beverage cans a day for King, Pierce and Snohomish counties and Alaska. It has 300 employees, including 45 on the production line.

FIG. 18.1. A news story in the *Seattle Times*, June 13, 1993, about the syringe-in-the-can crisis. (Reprinted by permission of the *Seattle Times*.)

FOR IMMEDIATE RELEASE

MEDIA CONTACT
Susan Hebert, Director of Public Affairs, (206) 326-7471

PUBLIC ADVISORY

LOCAL PEPSI BOTTLER AND FDA INVESTIGATING PRODUCT CONTAMINATION REPORTS

Reasonable precautions are advised

SEATTLE (June 12, 1993) -- Alpac Corporation, a regional Pepsi bottler, is working with the FDA to investigate two separate reports of consumers finding a syringe in a can of Diet Pepsi. The second report was received during the course of investigating the first report, according to Alpac President Carl G. Behnke.

The second report came from a resident of Federal Way, Wash. Alpac received the can yesterday afternoon and provided it to investigators from the U.S. Food and Drug Administration. Preliminary FDA laboratory tests conducted overnight revealed no chemical contamination. Additional tests are underway.

After initial testing of the second can, the FDA has told Alpac that drinking the liquid contents would not appear to present a health risk to the general public or to the consumers that reported the syringes.

Alpac and the FDA urge consumers, as a precaution, to inspect soft drink containers carefully before opening and consuming them. Consumers should gently rotate the can and listen for any non-liquid sound. As an additional precaution, consumers might prefer pouring soft drinks into a second container until this incident is resolved.

Behnke said the company's first priority is consumer safety and that he and the company are doing everything possible to assist federal investigators.

On Thursday, a couple in Tacoma, Wash. made the first report of a syringe in a Diet Pepsi can. The FDA is investigating the two complaints as separate, isolated incidents.

The FDA has not advised ALPAC that a recall is warranted at this time.

Consumers with questions should contact Pepsi's consumer hotline at 1-800-433-COLA.

FIG. 18.2. The public advisory issued by Alpac on June 12, 1993, acknowledging the crisis and the company's plans to investigate. (*Source*: Reprinted by permission of the Pepsi-Cola Company.)

Bryant said a decision was made to notify the FDA. The Alpac team said the decision was made because of its determination to be cooperative with the FDA and honest no matter what. Of course, if the person making the charge later decided to go public, Alpac would have been accused of a cover-up. The FDA conducted overnight tests that revealed no contamination of the needle.

Additional television news interviews were held with spokespersons. KOMO-TV, the ABC affiliate, joined the coverage. The newspapers basically watched to see what developed. As Bryant said, "Substantially, this was a TV news story; there was something about the visual image of a Pepsi can and a syringe that compelled news directors."

The FDA started visits to the Alpac plant. Its representatives talked to nearly all of the employees involved in production. Employees rallied on behalf of the company. The plant was inspected thoroughly. Records of quality assurance and customer complaints were reviewed.

Alpac President Carl Behnke decided to issue an advisory to consumers, urging them to pour soft drinks into a second container before drinking and to inspect containers before opening them and consuming contents.

The FDA said a public advisory should be issued, and the crisis communications team asked that Alpac be allowed to make the announcement. It wanted to take a leadership position and offer its own precautions. The suggestion from the FDA did not imply guilt by Alpac but did show concern for the public should the complaints prove legitimate. The advisory also included a consumer hotline number for the answering of questions (see Fig. 18.2).

KIRO-TV News, with a 30-minute notice, called to do a live remote to lead in its 6 p.m. newscast. The team prepared President Behnke for the experience, something he had never done. KIRO did the interview.

The rest of the media also concentrated on the advisory and the second case. CNN picked up that evening's news report from KING-TV, bringing it to national attention. The Associated Press issued a story, placing the crisis in print nationally.

Advertising was pulled in the Seattle–Tacoma market for Pepsi products that day. Said Bryant, "We wanted to avoid having people see Diet Pepsi ads and thinking 'syringe.' Also, we wanted to avoid the appearance of being callous in continuing to promote a product that some people feared might be injurious."

Sunday, June 13

The FDA issued its own advisory, thereby broadening public awareness of the crisis to all areas served by Alpac. Local Alpac managers were coached to take calls. Advisories were customized for specific markets.

There was an explosion of media calls—local, national, and international. This was the day when the number of calls peaked at 200. Among the callers were network news operations and the *New York Times*.

Another "victim," the first of several copycats, turned up in New Orleans. These copycat cases caused a national media frenzy, although some of the claims were incredible and extreme.

There was talk about a possible recall. Two Seattle television stations polled consumers asking whether they felt the company should recall Diet Pepsi. Most participants in the poll felt that the company should not recall, although reactions were mixed.

Monday, June 14

The Pepsi-Cola Co. took the lead in the national public relations effort as news of the crisis spread nationally (see chap. 19, "Pepsi and the National Syringe-in-the-Can Scare"). The FDA issued a warning against false reports of tampering and assured the public that there was no serious health risk.

At Alpac, meetings were held to advise employees of the situation. They were given a letter to distribute to retail customers to prepare them for consumer questions. The effort was successful because none of the retailers in Seattle pulled the product. Alpac employees were reminded not to speak with the media. This was done to comply with the FDA's position of not revealing any information until the investigation was completed. Following the meetings, the letters went to the retailers.

A copycat case turned up in Alaska at Carr's Supermarket. A man bought a soft drink, took it to his car, ostensibly for his daughter, and returned it to the store, creating a big emotional scene. "My daughter's been stabbed in the lip with a syringe!" the man shouted. Store personnel called the local Alpac general manager, who telephoned the crisis team, which, in turn called the FDA. The FDA asked the crisis team not to report the incident because it was suspicious. It was later discovered that the man also bought insulin syringes at the same store.

The retailer and Alpac were afraid of later being accused of a cover-up, but all concerned complied so as not to imperil the crucial relationship with the FDA. The man was eventually charged with fraud.

As the media coverage intensified, so did the fake reports.

Tuesday, June 15

Reporters started to dig deeper for what they seemed to want to be the story of the year. "They wanted intricate details about the production process. This is risky in that they would try to construct a scenario of how this *could* have happened," said Bryant. "They asked the size of the filtering

screen, how many seconds between this point and that point, who was in charge of this operation and that."

Although the crisis communications team wanted to be open, it discouraged dealing with these reporters because they were not willing to deal with "Colombos" who were trying to make a case. "We offered information," said Bryant, "that would provide a general understanding of the bottling process, but [we] did not provide technical details. To have done so would have required us to interrupt production managers who were busy assisting the FDA and trying to rule out production problems."

Wednesday, June 16

By June 16, some 65 cases of tampering had been reported. As hoaxes were uncovered, consumers, who said they thought the false charges were a mean-spirited thing to do, got angry and began to call Alpac and Pepsi-Cola expressing support for them. This provided the crisis team with an opportunity for pitching a positive story to the media.

The third Washington State report, in Mukilteo, was made. Local news reports focused on it. "Then we had a godsend," said Bryant. "A former Washington bottling inspector came to our aid unsolicited. He said, 'I've inspected this type of plant machinery for years, and I know it just couldn't happen. It's a hoax!' We couldn't have bought that kind of third party credibility, and it helped put another nail in the coffin of the crisis."

Thursday, June 17

The Mukilteo case proved by the next morning to be a hoax. More hoaxes were being uncovered than there were new cases being reported.

The hoax that topped them all was actually seen on a security camera as a woman stuffed a syringe into her can and remarked to the checker, "Look, a syringe in my can!" Pepsi linked it to a news satellite so that news programs nationwide and worldwide could download it for their newscasts.

Behnke, scheduled for final visits of the plants, was phased out as crisis spokesperson when necessity dictated that a spokesperson who would remain with the company should take the post.

The first editorial cartoons appeared. Bryant's favorite was one of a Pepsi delivery man wheeling in a case of Pepsi saying to a physician, "Doctor, the syringes you ordered are here" (see Fig. 18.3). Bryant said, "The fact that people could laugh about the crisis suggested it was no longer a serious concern and that public confidence in the reports was failing."

"I recall all of us cheering when the "CBS Evening News" announced the dismissal of the initial case," said Bryant. "Then the next day, we discovered it was a false report. The FDA apologized to the Tripletts. To this day, there has been no proven explanation of how the syringe got into their can."

FIG. 18.3. Editorial cartoon about the syringe-in-the-can scare by Chris Britt, published in the *News Tribune,* Tacoma, Washington, on June 19, 1993. (*Source*: *News Tribune,* Reprinted with the permission of Chris Britt.)

Bryant and the members of the crisis communications team considered the local media's coverage to be balanced and believed that their own determination to be open secured that balance. Cooperation with the FDA, they felt, was essential.

Alpac had a history of a corporate culture that valued its employees, which contributed to employee cooperation during the crisis. Alpac employees played a vital role in the campaign and felt a sense of being a part of both the crisis and the recovery. "Support of retailers and consumers," Bryant said, "results from a long history of positive community relations on the part of Alpac and excellent customer relations. The Behnke family had been known in the area for its philanthropy. There was a reservoir of goodwill so that people gave Pepsi and Alpac credit for telling the truth." (See the positive news story in Fig. 18.4.)

Alpac was known by the Seattle media and public as "the local Pepsi bottler," so it shared Pepsi's reputation and image. Bryant agreed that the effective handling of the 1993 crisis strengthened Pepsi's already positive image both locally and nationally.

Alpac was sold to Pepsi-Cola shortly after the crisis. Evans Group Public relations is now Publics Dialog.

Pepsi gets high marks for response
Consultants call actions a model of damage control

BY LEAH HARRISON
SEATTLE TIMES BUSINESS REPORTER

Pepsi-Cola Co.'s public-relations machinery is doing a good job handling reports of syringes and other objects found in soda cans, say professionals who work with companies facing crises.

In fact, professionals say Pepsi's handling of the situation so far is a model for minimizing damages when companies face crises—from bad earnings reports to strikes to incidents or disasters that may damage or threaten people or property.

David Marriott, a senior vice president at Elgin Syferd, a Seattle-based advertising and public-relations firm, praised Pepsi officials for seeking the advice of the Food and Drug Administration. "I don't think people will say they acted irresponsibly," he said.

"They have stressed, rightfully, that this looks more like a panic than anything else," said Larry Newman, president of The Newman Partnership, Ltd., a consulting firm in Columbia, S.C. that specializes in advising businesses in crisis.

Pepsi officials "are explaining how things really work" and showing how difficult it would be to plant syringes into cans at the company's high-speed bottling plants, Newman said.

He said statements by the FDA and local law enforcement officials amount to "third-party endorsement" that Pepsi is most likely not at fault.

Marriott, who conducts seminars on how companies should plan for possible crises, said every firm should develop a crisis-management plan.

He said the planning should include a series of "What if..." questions, such as, "What would we do if someone drove in here with a truck of explosives?"

A formal crisis-management plan should identify a team of people to handle an incident and identify each person's responsibilities. Managers should also identify "key audiences" such as employees, shareholders and the public to make sure they can reach those groups, Marriott said.

FIG. 18.4. A news story from the *Seattle Times*, June 17, 1993, praising the crisis communications team's work in the Pepsi syringe-in-the-can crisis. (*Source*: Harrison, 1993. Reprinted by permission of the *Seattle Times*.)

CHAPTER NINETEEN

Case: Pepsi and the National
Syringe-in-the-Can Scare

When Pepsi-Cola's worldwide headquarters in Somers, New York, took command of the 1993 crisis, the claims of syringes in cans of Diet Pepsi were lead stories in broadcasts and banner headlines in newspapers all over the United States (see Fig. 19.1).

Following is a chronological report of Pepsi's strategies, tactics, and results from Monday, June 14, 1993 to the end of the crisis on Friday, June 18, 1993.

Monday, June 14

On this day Craig Weatherup, president and CEO of Pepsi, had his first contact with David Kessler, commissioner of the Food & Drug Administration (FDA). It was important to Pepsi for the head of its company to communicate with the head of the FDA in a kind of merging of efforts to investigate the problem.

Weatherup also functioned as spokesperson and head of the crisis team. The team's members included the following:

Consumers shun companies in crisis

BY DENNIS CHASE
ADVERTISING AGE

PepsiCo appears to have escaped damage, but consumers say they are less likely to buy products from companies that have been involved in a public crisis over a breach in ethics or safety.

In a survey of more than 1,000 adult consumers conducted in June, just before the Pepsi scare, 80% said problems at Sears, Roebuck and Co. and 79% said problems at Food Lion made it likely they would shun those companies.

Last year, Sears was charged with making unnecessary repairs at some of its auto repair facilities, and earlier this year, Food Lion was hit with charges that it used unsanitary food safety procedures. Other companies such as Exxon Corp. and Dow Corning Corp. were also cited in the survey.

The survey, to be released by the end of the month by Omnicom Group's Porter/Novelli public relations agency, found that even crises involving simple business decisions, like layoffs, affected attitudes. About 23% said General Motors Corp.'s layoffs and plant closings would affect their purchases, and 19% said the same thing about IBM Corp.

"Companies start out in the hole," said Bob Druckenmiller, Porter/Novelli president. "People don't believe companies tell the truth."

However, PepsiCo, by responding quickly to questions about syringes allegedly found in soft-drink cans, helped itself.

"One lesson is you have to respond quickly, even if you don't have all the facts," Mr. Druckenmiller said.

The survey also found that 76% of consumes polled are most angry when companies refuse to accept blame for problems, 71% are most angry when they provide incomplete or inaccurate information, and 71% are upset when they put profits ahead of public interest.

The mail survey was done by National Family Opinion using a random sample reflecting the U.S. population. Margin of error was 3 percentage points.

Fig. 19.1. Portion of an article published in *Advertising Age* on how consumers feel about purchasing products from companies in crisis. (*Source*: Chase, 1993. Reprinted by permission of *Advertising Age.*)

237

1. The *crisis coordinator*, Rebecca Madeira, vice president of the Public Affairs Department, was instrumental in making sure the company spoke in one voice and directed the actions of the team.

2. The *Public Affairs Department* had three subteams: A *press subteam* managed media contact; the *production subteam* wrote, designed, and developed news releases (both print and video), audiotapes, charts, and photographs; and a *government affairs subteam* communicated information to 400 Pepsi bottlers.

3. *Consumer relations specialists* responded to many thousands of telephone calls, 24 hours a day (see Fig. 19.2).

4. *Scientific and Regulatory affairs* worked with the FDA in following up on each charge of a syringe in a Diet Pepsi can.

5. *Sales and marketing employees* relayed information to the management of restaurants, stores, and other retailers to assist them in keeping their businesses operable.

6. *Manufacturing experts* worked with the FDA to prepare explanations of the production processes for dissemination to the media and consumers.

7. The *Legal Department* briefed other members of the crisis team on communications issues.

All information was disseminated both externally and internally through a communications clearinghouse.

The company's and crisis team's overall goal was to avert damage to Pepsi's good name and reputation. In order to do that, the team had to consider three publics:

1. Pepsi customers, who were reached by letters and telephone calls from the sales staff. The staff used talking points, as shown in Fig. 19.2.

2. Pepsi headquarters employees, who received daily news summaries.

3. Pepsi bottlers and field employees, who received twice-a-day advisories (Pepsi-Cola, 1993a).

PHASE 1: UNDERSTANDING THE PROBLEM

Before the crisis team could communicate with publics, it had to determine what the problem was. Could there be a malicious person or persons in a plant placing syringes in cans? As Madeira said, "We had to be absolutely sure that this could not possibly have happened in our plants. We

- Yes, we've received other calls regarding alleged product tampering, and we are working with Federal authorities to verify those reports. The calls come on the heels of a much-publicized incident of an alleged tampering incident in the Seattle-Tacoma and New Orleans areas, and already we are discovering that certain of the reported incidents are hoaxes, or people reacting to perceived rather than actual problems.

- In fact, the FDA Criminal Investigation Unit has already made an arrest of an individual in Central Pennsylvania who allegedly falsely reported he found a syringe in our product. The penalty for this type of crime is a $250,000 fine and a maximum of five years in prison.

- Our first concern is consumer safety. For that reason, the President of Pepsi-Cola and the head of the FDA have been in constant communication to insure that everything humanly possible to assure consumer safety is first and foremost in our actions.

- First of all cans, as you might imagine, are the most difficult of all consumer packages to tamper with, and because our production processes are performed at such high speeds it's virtually an impossibility to introduce a foreign object.

- Canned products are produced in 140 separate and distinct locations — we produce between 20 and 30 millions cans per day. The cans themselves originate from different suppliers, and are filled at different times. It's implausible to think that these events could occur simultaneously. In fact, news reports have highlighted the safety and integrity of our manufacturing process — it's been reported that the canning process we use is probably the most tamper-proof of all manufacturing processes.

- *The FDA has not recommended a product recall.* They have issued a statement that our products are safe, and as a precaution, are encouraging consumers to pour the contents of all packages into a cup before drinking. We ask that people use their own good judgement and common sense on this matter.

- There have been no injuries, nor have our investigations found any foreign objects in any unopened cans.

- This is a criminal investigation; product tampering and false reports of tampering are criminal offenses. Therefore, in cooperation with the FDA's Criminal Investigation Unit we're unable to comment any further.

- If you see anything unusual - please don't hesitate to call us back. That's what we're here for.

FIG. 19.2. The talking points prepared for Pepsi-Cola employees responding to calls from consumers inquiring about the syringes in cans. (Reprinted by permission of the Pepsi-Cola Company.)

239

needed to develop a responsible way of talking about the situation before going public" (Pepsi-Cola, 1993b, p. 5).

PHASE 2: COOPERATION WITH THE FDA

The FDA inspected Pepsi's manufacturing process in meticulous detail. Pepsi's vice president of product safety said, "Each and every canning line at the production plants in question was studied very carefully to see if there was any way to infiltrate the line. Employee records were checked. Shipping and customer inventories were reviewed. Consumer complainants were interviewed" (Pepsi-Cola, 1993b, p. 5).

It had already been determined that the cans involved in the complaints were filled and sealed at various plants and at various times. According to Weatherup, "some of the cans were bottled six months ago, some six weeks ago, some six days ago" (Pepsi-Cola, 1993b, p. 5).

The FDA agreed that, considering the high speed and integrity of the production line as well as the constant observation of the process, it was virtually impossible for a syringe to have been placed in a can either accidentally or maliciously. Considering also that the cans came from different plants, it was determined that the syringes were placed in them after they were opened. Also, no syringes were ever found in unopened cans.

Although no injuries were reported, there was great fear of the possible transmission of AIDS through the syringes. Health officials announced that there was no risk to consumers' health from syringes in the can. Because there was no health risk and no culpability on the part of the Pepsi process, there was no need to recall the product.

Madeira said, "We were committed to putting consumer safety first, but a recall would not end the crisis or restore consumer confidence. The only thing that would stop this was to discourage—in the strongest possible terms—tampering with an opened can."

PHASE 3: DEVELOPING AND IMPLEMENTING A STRATEGY

Armed with research that vindicated the company, the crisis team set out to begin an extensive media battle.

Tuesday, June 15

The production subteam produced video footage. It was intended to be so visually persuasive as to eliminate in viewers' minds the possibility of malicious tampering in the plants. Although Weatherup and the FDA made public announcements, the crisis team knew that consumers would be more likely to believe what they could see rather than what they were told

by the company head (who could conceivably lie for economic gain). Because there was no way to take all consumers to the plants, Pepsi did the next best thing and took the plants to the consumers through videotapes of the plants in operation.

The B-roll footage showed the canning process: cans being inverted, cleaned, inverted again, filled, and sealed—all under careful inspection and all in nine tenths of a second. The footage was transmitted via satellite to television news programs all over the United States. Three other videotapes followed over the next 3 days showing more scenes of Pepsi's commitment to consumer safety (see Fig. 19.3).

"A can is the most tamperproof packaging in the food supply," said Weatherup. "We are 99.99% certain that this didn't happen in Pepsi plants" (Pepsi-Cola, 1993b, p. 6).

Madeira said, "Our strategy was to reassure the public that this was not a manufacturing crisis. What was happening with syringes was not occurring in our plants" (Pepsi-Cola, 1993b, p. 7).

In addition to the videotapes, Weatherup's interviews were aired on all the television networks on Tuesday evening. The Public Affairs Department took hundreds of calls from the print and broadcast media across the country. The

FIG. 19.3. Still photos and video footage of the rapid Pepsi manufacturing process convinced consumers that it would be extremely unlikely for syringes to be placed in cans, either accidentally or intentionally, at the plants. (*Source*: Reproduced by permission of the Pepsi-Cola Company.)

FDA's Kessler and Pepsi's Weatherup both appeared on ABC's "Nightline." Their message was that the crisis was actually a series of hoaxes by people trying to make easy money. Kessler mentioned that the first arrest had been made in Pennsylvania and that others would follow (Pepsi-Cola, 1993a).

The consumer relations members of the crisis team talked to 2,000 consumers. News releases were distributed announcing the FDA's intention to prosecute persons who filed false claims of product tampering.

Wednesday, June 16

The day began with Weatherup's appearances on CBS's "This Morning," NBC's "The Today Show," and ABC's "Good Morning America." The coverage originated from the offices in Somers, and crews were setting up as early as 4 a.m. (see Fig. 19.4). That evening, Weatherup appeared on PBS's "The MacNeil/Lehrer News Hour" and CNN's "Larry King Live." Most viewers who telephoned in during the latter show emphasized their support for the company.

Madeira said, "Wednesday was pivotal. The media understood our production integrity, and we were gaining support as the day went on. We were hopeful that the FDA would announce more arrests as reports of hoaxes and recantations poured in from police across the country" (Pepsi-Cola, 1993b, p.8).

FIG. 19.4. Pepsi CEO Craig Weatherup met with the media at a 1993 news conference. (*Source*: Reproduced by permission of the Pepsi-Cola Company.)

As far as hoaxes were concerned, on Wednesday, the crisis team had *the* hoax to end hoaxes. A surveillance camera in a Colorado convenience store had captured a woman placing a syringe in a can as she approached the checkout stand. The team prepared to broadcast the tape but held it back after the FDA requested waiting until the arrest was made.

In the meantime, tampering claims were made in four additional states. Persons who had already made claims began to confess, hoping to avoid prosecution.

Thursday, June 17

The FDA held a news conference on Thursday when FDA Commissioner Kessler was expected to announce arrests, but the Pepsi crisis team was elated when he also stated, in unequivocal terms, that Pepsi was completely exonerated, that it was a victim of the hoaxes. "The notion that there has been nationwide tampering of Diet Pepsi is unfounded," he said via satellite (Pepsi-Cola, 1993b, p. 9).

At this point, Pepsi released the Colorado surveillance tape, which team members called "the smoking gun." Weatherup made comments to go along with the silent video footage. The tape showed how simple and how fast it was to place a syringe in an open can. Pepsi couldn't have asked for a stronger tool to convince consumers of the hoaxes.

Friday, June 18

On Friday, Pepsi considered the crisis over. To certify the ending, it created an ad that ran on Monday, June 21. The ad's headline was "Pepsi Is Pleased to Announce ... Nothing" (see Fig. 19.5). The copy stated that the claims were hoaxes and, in effect, told people that Pepsi was still the refreshing drink consumers have enjoyed. It also urged consumers to participate in special offers beginning the July 4th weekend.

At headquarters, 1,200 employees attended a meeting to celebrate their victory over the crisis. They viewed the videotapes that helped end the crisis and witnessed firsthand the ad that would appear in newspapers on Monday. The videotapes and ad were also sent to the 400 Pepsi facilities so that those employees could view them.

The company, which had suffered a $30 million loss in sales as a result of the crisis, knew it was time to rebuild its market share. In a personal letter to employees, Weatherup wrote, "It's time now for us to move quickly and decisively to restore ... our business" (Pepsi-Cola, 1993b, p. 10).

With the hot summer days approaching, Pepsi's marketing department created a "Thanks America" program. A $1-off coupon appeared in newspaper ads. "Thanks America" buttons were worn by Pepsi employees, who also distributed the coupons to their friends and neighbors.

Pepsi is pleased to announce...

...nothing.

As America now knows, those stories about Diet Pepsi were a hoax. Plain and simple, not true. Hundreds of investigators have found no evidence to support a single claim.

As for the many, many thousands of people who work at Pepsi-Cola, we feel great that it's over. And we're ready to get on with making and bringing you what we believe is the best-tasting diet cola in America.

There's not much more we can say. Except that most importantly, we won't let this hoax change our exciting plans for this summer.

We've set up special offers so you can enjoy our great quality products at prices that will save you money all summer long. It all starts on July 4th weekend and we hope you'll stock up with a little extra, just to make up for what you might have missed last week.

That's it. Just one last word of thanks to the millions of you who have stood with us.

Drink All The Diet Pepsi You Want.
Uh Huh.

FIG. 19.5. The ad that Pepsi ran in newspapers nationwide in June 1993 to declare the end of the crisis. (*Source*: Reproduced by permission of the Pepsi-Cola Company.)

A week after the first hoax was uncovered, consumers bought 800,000 more cases of Pepsi products than the week before the crisis. Sales began to rebound, and they bounced back completely during the summer. The week of July 4th was Pepsi's strongest week of 1993.

The Pepsi-Cola Company won the prestigious Silver Anvil Award for businesses—bestowed by the Public Relations Society of America—for its campaign against "The Great Pepsi Hoax." The company was praised for showing to customers, the media, regulatory officials, shareholders, and its other publics that the company's manufacturing process was safe and that widespread tampering was not possible.

The Pepsi crisis team concurred that it succeeded because it was honest and open and because it had looked at the problem through the eyes of the public (Pepsi-Cola, 1993a).

CHAPTER TWENTY

Case: California State University, Northridge, and the 1994 Los Angeles Earthquake

At 4:31 a.m., on January 17, 1994, a 6.8 magnitude earthquake shook southern California for 40 seconds. Fifty-seven people died (Coffey, 1994, p. 7). Thousands were injured and many more were left homeless. Unlike the wildfires a few months before and the 1992 riots, there was no one in Southern California who was not affected by this disaster.

The city of Northridge in the San Fernando Valley suffered the worst damage. About a third of the total deaths occurred when the Northridge Meadows apartment building collapsed into its underground parking area. Northridge Meadows is located just across the street from the 353-acre campus of California State University at Northridge (CSUN).

Kaine Thompson was campus manager of public relations at CSUN; Bruce Erickson was director of public relations. Thompson lived in Santa Clarita, 30 miles from campus and usually a 45-minute ride via I-5 and the Highway 14 freeway. "Highway 14 had collapsed and no one could get in or out of the neighborhood for a couple of days," said Thompson. "There was no electricity, no water. Outgoing phone calls were impossible, but in-

coming calls did come through." Thompson used her car radio to find out what the general area damage was, but she had no idea what had happened at the university. Fortunately, it was Martin Luther King Day, a holiday for staff members, as well as winter break, the period beginning with the Christmas holidays and lasting through the month of January, when no classes are held.

Eventually, Erickson was able to get a phone call through to Thompson. He lived nearer to campus and was able to see the damage firsthand. Erickson was later quoted as saying, "In a word, it's bad. It's unprecedented. Never has a university been hit this hard by an earthquake" (Hayes & Heller, 1994, p. 22). (See Fig. 20.1.)

On that first day, the obvious damage included a completely collapsed parking structure (see Fig. 20.2), a science building burned extensively as a result of a chemical spill, and a lost roof over the majestic columns of Delmar T. Oviatt Library with its support beams unstable. Later, it was discovered that of the 58 buildings on campus, every major one was damaged or affected.

The most unstable building was South Library, which housed the recently remodeled computer center with the computer data and mainframe. The floors of the building were shifted laterally.

The public relations' office was in a trailer that had fallen off its jacks; the ramp entrance had fallen and windows were broken. Like other campus buildings not actually damaged as far as structure is concerned, its furniture, computers, books, and papers were destroyed and disheveled.

On the day of the earthquake, the media were not concerned with the campus. The lead story in the Los Angeles *Daily News*, the major newspaper in the San Fernando Valley, had two paragraphs buried in the lead story of 57 column inches that read:

> Two miles northeast of the epicenter, several buildings on the California State University, Northridge campus—where students are still on winter break—suffered serious damage, including a science building that caught fire, spewing what firefighters believed was toxic smoke.
>
> The temblor partially collapsed a year-old, four-level parking structure on Zelzah Avenue, damaged portions of the Oviatt Library and froze the clock on the Sierra Tower at 4:31 a.m. (Tranguade, 1994, pp. 1, 12)

The hot stories were about deaths, fires, collapsed freeways, homelessness, and testimonials of "What I did and where I was when the earthquake hit."

The San Fernando Valley newspapers were themselves hampered by earthquake damage. The building housing the Los Angeles *Daily News*, a paper specifically for San Fernando residents, was trashed. Two Copley newspapers offered space. Editors and reporters worked from the *Santa*

Students unsettled by quake
Northridge campus left damaged, in disarray

BY STEVEN KOSOY
STAFF WRITER

NORTHRIDGE - Passing classes and going to sporting events should have been Scott Gordon's biggest concerns during his senior year in college.

But one major earthquake later, Gordon, a 24-year-old from Glendora, had to deal with the added burden of not knowing where he would be able to finish his studies.

"Sixteen weeks away from graduating and we had to have a major earthquake," Gordon lamented. "And our campus had to be the epicenter."

When last month's 6.6 temblor rocked the Southland, one of the hardest hit victims was Cal State Northridge. Eleven on-campus structures suffered damage, as well as all 15 dorm buildings, CSUN spokesman Bruce Erickson said.

There were rumors spreading among students that the university might not re-open this year at all.

"The worst part's just not knowing," Gordon said.

Now university officials are making plans to start the spring semester on Feb. 14, about two weeks after the original date. Registration did resume on Feb. 1, Erickson said.

However, the college has not notified the students about all the changes.

"I've read it in newspapers," said Gabrielle Landau, 21, a junior. "They said they're going to send out new schedules, but I haven't got one yet."

Letters were sent out to students on Jan. 27 with registration and fee information, CSU Chancellor's office spokeswoman Colleen Bentley-Adler said.

"I think there's enough coverage in the media that students were already aware," Bentley-Adler said.

Despite the concern that the damage to the campus buildings would eliminate precious classroom space, Erickson said there should be enough room to house all of the classes.

Classes will be held in temporary buildings, Erickson said.

The university is also considering holding classes in such diverse locations as the Student Union, the Hillel house, the Satellite Student Union, the residence halls, and the new education and business buildings to make up for the lost classroom space, Erickson said.

There is also talk of holding classes at nearby community colleges - Pierce and Los Angeles Valley.

If classes are held off campus, the university may supply transportation, Erickson said.

FIG. 20.1. A news story published in the *Pasadena Star-News* on February 7, 1994, about the effects of the Los Angeles earthquake on CSUN students. (*Source*: Kosoy, 1994. Reprinted by permission of the *Pasadena Star-News*.)

FIG. 20.2. A CSUN campus parking lot shown before and after the 1994 Los Angeles earthquake. Fortunately, the earthquake occurred during a semester break, on a holiday, and very early in the morning. (*Source*: Photos by K. Fearn. Reproduced by permission.)

Monica Outlook, and printing was done at the *Daily Breeze* in Torrance. The offices of the Valley Edition of the *Los Angeles Times* were also damaged, and the staff operated from downtown Los Angeles offices.

On the day following the earthquake, the *Daily News,* in an entire first section about the earthquake, mentioned CSUN in only two paragraphs of a page-12 wrap-up story about damage in the San Fernando Valley. It was, again, a sketch of the obvious damage—the damage to Oviatt Library, the collapsed parking structure, the science building that burned, and the clock in Sierra Tower that stopped at 4:31.

On the second day, press attention turned to the university. It was and is one of the largest institutions in the Valley, with a student body of approximately 27,000 and a faculty and staff numbering 3,000 in 1994.

Erickson began the day by trying to confirm with the coroner's office whether there were any CSUN student deaths. Information was slow in coming. He relayed sketchy information about the status of campus buildings face-to-face with reporters who made their way through the city and campus rubble to find him. He was further occupied with the effort to get cellular phones to communicate with the media.

Orange County Search and Rescue set up tents to be used as the command center for the university president, Blenda Wilson, the primary spokesperson, and her executive staff.

Thompson packed as many belongings as she could in her car on the third day following the quake and drove 4 hours on an alternate route to the CSUN campus. Rather than spend 8 hours daily on freeways, she stayed weekday nights at the homes of university staff. "My office was the trunk of my car," Thompson said. "I went home on weekends and even then, it took 3 hours to go 30 miles."

In addition to the media, the CSUN public relations department was charged with communicating with the following publics, all segments of the university community: staff, faculty, visiting faculty (i.e., faculty who planned to arrive for spring semester), disabled students including hearing-impaired and deaf students, foreign students, students who lived in San Fernando Valley, and students who lived outside the area.

University President Wilson communicated with enabling publics—the regents, heads of alumni organizations, the governor, the mayor, and other officials. Normally, she would have had fact sheets and backgrounders at her fingertips. None were accessible because of the earthquake damage. Erickson and Thompson had to create new documents from memory.

"This was especially difficult," said Thompson, "because the trauma had affected everyone's ability to recall such data. During the second week, I broke into the damaged and off-limits University Relations Building and retrieved valuable information on the campus and on media sources."

Dorena Knepper, the university's director of governmental relations, was later able to compile status reports that were then put on the Internet.

Erickson and Thompson continued to research destruction, damage, and, particularly, deaths. Many CSUN students lived in the Northridge Meadows apartments and could have been among the fatalities in the building that collapsed. It was eventually revealed that two CSUN undergraduates died in the apartment collapse, one of whom had just moved into the building the day before the earthquake.

Letters were sent to the families of the two students who died, and half-page ads in the form of a letter from CSUN President Wilson were placed in the *Los Angeles Times* and *Daily News* to express sympathy, not only for families and friends of the two students, but for all who lost loved ones in the Northridge earthquake.

Assessing damage was difficult because aftershocks continued for weeks after the quake. Following each aftershock of significant magnitude, damage to buildings had to be reassessed. Damage estimates ranged from $200 million to $350 million. Most of the damage was structural.

Telephone and electric lines were down. There was no running water. Propane heaters were brought in for warmth. Books in Matador Bookstore were in 3-foot mountains; bookcases were an awesome-looking mass of twisted metal.

"We also went in search of equipment," said Thompson. "We had nothing. Not even my Rolodex, my fax numbers. We begged and borrowed whatever we could. 'Who has a functional telephone?' 'Who has a computer?' 'Who has a fax machine?' We had nothing. Then, we started working out of people's homes. We had to travel from one home to another— through earthquake-torn Northridge—and back and forth to campus."

Getting information out to CSUN students and staff members was the primary task during this period. Student questions included the following: "When will classes begin? Is the campus safe? Where will I park? Where will classes be held? Will commencement be postponed?" Many staff members did not know if they still had work. They were asking these questions: "Do I have a job? When do I report to work? Where do I report to work? Is it safe?" Many staff members were even more insecure. Some had been at CSUN for 20 to 30 years and, according to Thompson, were completely disoriented:

> The students are used to new situations, like the first day of freshman registration, but some of the longtime faculty said they felt no personal emotion about the disaster until they saw what was left of their offices. Some lost their homes, but many of them had no serious problems at their residences. The experience of not being able to find even a pencil in their offices was traumatic.
>
> Everyone was traumatized, including me. I couldn't remember names, statistics that I use all the time—like how many people work here.

There was a real dearth of information within the community around the campus. Television cables were down, so there was little television service. Electricity was out in some places. People outside the "quake zone" knew more about what was going on than the people inside the zone. Most of CSUN's publics lived inside the quake zone, in the blacked-out area.

TELEPHONES

Pacific Bell was instrumental in setting up six phone lines that first week. Publics were able to call in for information. Hotline operators—some of them volunteers—were given scripts that were updated daily with new information for students, faculty, and staff. There was information about available phone numbers and cancellation of campus events.

An additional line was set up with recorded information that was updated daily. Also, a TDD line for the hearing-impaired student population was set up. Students learned about the telephone lines after the CSUN Public Relations Department distributed news releases and public service announcements (PSAs) to the media (see Figs. 20.3 and 20.4).

For outgoing calls, cellular phones were used. The San Francisco earthquake of 1989 was a prodrome for CSUN in that San Francisco businesses, after the crisis, warned others of the importance of cellular phones.

TELEPHONE TREES

To reach various key internal publics—school deans, department heads, and others—phone trees were organized.

The president's executive staff, the vice presidents, contacted their various staffs. Provost Louanne Kennedy called the deans of the schools and, in turn, the deans contacted the department chairs, who called faculty and staff in the various departments.

"Nonessential personnel" (meaning they were not needed during the crisis, although they were quite valuable to the university otherwise) were put on administrative leave. This information was communicated through newspapers.

THE MEDIA

A backgrounder entitled "General Information Guide" was written. It included names of university officials, details and statistics of the earthquake's damage on campus, degree programs offered by the university, makeup of the student population, location and physical information about the campus, as well as the history and achievements of the university.

At first, one by one, reporters were given tours of the campus as requested by them. By the Wednesday following the Monday earthquake, me-

FIG. 20.3. A news release from CSUN's University News Bureau, written on a borrowed computer a few days after the 1994 Los Angeles earthquake. (*Source*: Reprinted by permission of California State University at Northridge.)

253

```
CALIFORNIA STATE UNIVERSITY, NORTHRIDGE

PUBLIC SERVICE ANNOUNCEMENT

To:         News Director/City Desk
From:       California State University, Northridge News Bureau

Re:         Information Lines available for
            University's Faculty, Staff and Students

NORTHRIDGE: January 27, 1994 - Due to the Northridge Earthquake, the Cal
State Northridge campus has set up several information lines for its students,
faculty and staff.

For Cal State Northridge deaf and hard-of-hearing students and personnel, a
TDD line has been set up with up-to-date information related to registration
and classes . The number is (818) 885-4900 (TDD). The information line
will be available 9 a.m. to 5 p.m., Monday through Friday. Cal State
Northridge serves hundreds of deaf and hard-of-hearing students through
its National Center on Deafness and its Deaf Studies Program.

For hearing students, the information line continues to be (818) 885-3700,
providing up-to-date information on class registration.

For faculty, information may be obtained by calling (818) 885-4700 and for
staff, (818) 885-2082.
```

FIG. 20.4. A PSA released by CSUN's University News Bureau containing
pertinent information for students. (*Source*: Reprinted by permission of
California State University at Northridge.)

dia coverage was intense and remained so until mid-February. Stories about the students who died in the apartment collapse, professors who lost years of research in the rubble, effects on students, aftershocks forcing new inspections of buildings, work crews laboring to repair buildings, rain soaking the already devastated campus, and estimates of damage were popular in numerous California newspapers, on local television and radio stations, and in the national media (e.g., television networks and newsmagazines).

The media were basically cooperative. There had been no hostility up to this point. Thompson and Erickson wanted it to remain that way. As Thompson noted:

> Sometimes the press seems to be out there to create sensation. Previously, we had had some civil unrest on campus and I was disappointed in the media's interpretation. But this time, when the sensation was created by Mother Nature, they were the public servants they are supposed to be. They did a good job of keeping the public informed. I understand the press because I was a reporter. They don't want you to stonewall them. Sometimes academics don't understand the needs or the power of the press, and I enjoy serving as a bridge between the two worlds.

The *Los Angeles Times* ran an extensive story on February 11, 1994, charging that the relatively new parking structure that collapsed was not designed to meet seismic strength standards in building codes. The fallen garage had become what one builder called "a photographic icon" for destruction wrought by the temblor.

A San Diego-based consulting firm hired by the university had claimed, even before the structure was completed, that the columns were not adequately connected to the concrete floors and beams. There was no media clamor resulting from the story. Thompson said that so many parking structures were damaged, there was no need to single out CSUN's.

Also, because of the unusual variables that caused the collapse, federal agencies reviewed the structure. Still, without a doubt, had there been deaths or injuries—as there probably would have been if the quake happened during a school day—the story would have been front-page, top-of-the-TV newscast news. It is, therefore, a prodrome for CSUN should it experience another disastrous earthquake.

On the Thursday following the quake, CSUN President Wilson held a news conference (see Fig. 20.5). The media—TV, radio, print—were led en masse to the center of the campus and Oviatt Library. The site was selected because of its visual appeal for camerapersons and wordsmiths. It was the most dramatically damaged building.

On a platform erected in front of the building, President Wilson told the media the status of the buildings, that aftershocks prevented final assess-

FIG. 20.5. Photograph of CSUN President Wilson at a January 20, 1994, news conference. Bruce Erickson, CSUN director of public relations, holds the microphone. Erickson said the photo was taken right after a serious aftershock. When the aftershock struck, two CSUN employees had gone into the badly damaged South Library by forklift to retrieve crucial backup computer files. Wilson had, seconds before, learned that they were not injured. The media never knew about it. (*Source*: Photo reproduced by permission of California State University at Northridge.)

ment of the damage, that the necessity for reassessing buildings following aftershocks made it impossible to say, "This building is okay," and that the campus was closed.

She promised, however, that classes, scheduled to begin in 2 weeks on January 31, would begin only 2 weeks later on February 14. "We were still experiencing heavy aftershocks," said Thompson. "There were those who thought we would never open again, but somehow when President Wilson announced we would open on February 14, everyone believed her. Her leadership and strength of conviction infected many of us to make the impossible possible."

President Wilson said:

People ask me how I managed to stay calm and I just laugh.

I have a deep and abiding personal faith, and I believe that you can accomplish what you need to accomplish. We just worked step by step to get the campus ready for February 14. I knew my faculty and staff would support me.

If the community at large and the campus community were to recover, we had to open. We owed it to our students to continue their education. We owed it to 7,000 students who were to graduate in Spring 1994. We owed it to the community organizations who helped us. We also owed it to our faculty and staff who needed to get back to work and find some normalcy.

After the university president had promised to return to classes on February 14, Thompson knew there was a possibility that some hostility would develop if classes did not begin on schedule. She recalled, "I knew if our president wavered, the press would eat us alive. But she's dynamic and she stuck to her position. One or two journalists were a bit nasty, but overall, coverage was balanced."

The media not at the news conference were contacted by news releases or phone calls regarding the closing of campus and the reopening date. Full-page ads were taken out in local newspapers.

STUDENT NEWSPAPER

The *Daily Sundial,* the campus newspaper, normally published a special registration issue that was mailed to new students to tell them about the campus and where services and buildings were located, and to give a general introduction to the campus.

After the earthquake, the student-run paper was published from the facilities of its sister campus, California State University, Los Angeles, some 35 miles away. The editors pooled their energies and skills, and the issue was out by the second week after the earthquake. The edition featured articles about the damage, measures being taken to ensure safety, and plans to begin the semester with all courses previously scheduled.

The *Sundial* is credited with lessening the shock of what the students would see on campus and with helping them feel connected before they came to campus.

CAMPUS RADIO

Campus radio station KCSN normally operated from the theater arts building at CSUN. This building was declared unsafe, so the staff set up a temporary headquarters in a tent on the soccer field.

Other radio stations donated thousands of dollars in equipment. A listener loaned a microdish to receive the feed from National Public Radio.

The station's operations were hampered further by rain and the noises of helicopters, of trucks transporting modular classrooms, and of horses whinnying. (In a nearby tent, there were horses being lodged by a search-and-rescue unit.) Nevertheless, the station broadcasted news updates to CSUN students. After a few weeks, the homeless station moved into a two-bedroom apartment in student housing.

The two PR practitioners set up two daily live broadcasts of interviews with various university officials, usually the president and one of the vice presidents. Sometimes they spoke themselves in the broadcasts. Radio talent also spoke from information disseminated from the public relations staff.

CAMPUS BULLETIN

The University Information Bulletin, nicknamed the "UIB," was normally disseminated weekly. With minimal phone service and subsequently little intercampus communication, it was crucial to distribute the UIB on a daily basis. "We kept the same format we had previous to the quake, but aesthetics went out the window. Printing was very limited," said Thompson.

The first issue after the crisis was distributed on February 25. It contained information about the library, mail, counseling, transportation services, cancellation of spring break, dates of final exams for spring semester, and a detailed map of the newly configured campus with shuttle routes, public transit stops, and parking.

LETTERS

A letter was mailed to CSUN faculty and staff from President Wilson. The letter reported damage sustained as well as progress and plans for restoring the campus and getting back to school.

MAKING THE DEADLINE

A detailed plan to build a temporary campus was put into effect. The success of this plan was crucial to the PR staff's desire to meet the deadline President Wilson had promised the media and thereby avoid media stories charging that "CSUN failed to open as scheduled." Meeting the deadline would also avoid calls and complaints from students and faculty displaced by the earthquake.

A sign went up at the campus entrance stating the goal of the plan and expressing the determination and spirit of the campus family: "Not Just Back, But Better."

President Wilson's plan included bringing in 400 trailers and tents for classrooms and offices as well as 29 portable bathroom trailers. The tents and trailers occupied open spaces on the campus and in parking lots.

Two weeks prior to the scheduled opening date, 22 information stations were set up in tents at every major entrance point to the campus. Each tent had two to three volunteers. Of the 350 total volunteers, many were faculty and displaced staff workers on administrative leave until they were called back to work. They just wanted to work, and to help. The volunteers arrived on Sunday, February 13, for a tour of the newly configured campus and for training to be experts in the information link.

Inside each tent was a table and two folding chairs. All the tents were supplied with schedules of classes and maps of the new campus. There were also maps of sites such as libraries, computer centers, chemistry labs, music practice rooms, and so on.

Eighty percent of the university parking space was lost because of the trailers and tents, so there was information about shuttle service to and from off-campus parking, classrooms, and resources.

A cherry picker went into the top floor of the seriously damaged computer center to retrieve computer files. The deed was heroic because, as feared, a major aftershock occurred during the rescue. There were no injuries, and the data were successfully retrieved and shipped to California State University, Fresno's computer system for registration.

During the fourth week after the quake, mail service was restored on campus. Prior to that, all mail had been put in storage. One by one, deans and heads of departments sent staff volunteers to retrieve the boxes of mail.

The PR staff worked with the *Los Angeles Daily News* to help produce a special edition informing students and campus personnel as well as the general public about the new campus and how it would operate. The edition was delivered to subscribers on Sunday, February 13. In it there were maps of the new campus and the schedule of classes. Copies of the section on the university were available in the information tents on Monday for students who did not get the Sunday edition.

President Wilson delivered on her promise. Classes began, as announced to the media, on Monday, February 14, some 4 weeks after the earthquake, 2 weeks later than originally scheduled (see Fig. 20.6). "There were minor glitches, but for the most part, things proceeded amazingly well," said Thompson. "Most students returned willing to take on the hardships in order to continue their education."

A highlight of that opening day was a phone call from President Clinton. As preparations were being made for the opening day, Melkane Benton, a community relations specialist for KABC radio talk show host Michael Jackson, telephoned Erickson asking if the popular Jackson could broadcast from the campus on that day. On Jackson's talk show, listeners call in. Erickson said his first thought was that having the broadcast on campus would present extra chaos to a naturally chaotic day. "But we always say 'Yes,' and never say 'No,' so it was approved."

Storm soaks CSUN in additional misery

BY CARMEN RAMOS CHANDLER
DAILY NEWS STAFF WRITER

NORTHRIDGE - To begin to understand the kind of day students and faculty had at CSUN Thursday, take a university campus, shake violently--and then add water.

The intense morning storm that triggered mudslides and knotted commuter traffic in the Southland forced course cancellations, turned dirt parking lots to mud and produced showers inside some portable classrooms on a campus hard hit by the Northridge Earthquake.

"What's a little rain after an earthquake?" said Bruce Erickson, a spokesman for California State University, Northridge, which opened its spring semester Monday--four weeks after sustaining as much as $350 million in quake-related damage.

Coping with disruptions has become academic at CSUN in the last month, but the rain Thursday delayed efforts by workers to finish retooling the campus for its 24,500 students.

More rain is forecast through the weekend, potentially pushing back the installation of the last 80 of 400 portable classrooms set up on the 353-acre campus.

"If the sun continues to shine Thursday and (today), then we'll be back in business and ready by Monday," Erickson said. "If it rains, then there will be more delays."

FIG. 20.6. A news story published in the Los Angeles *Daily News,* February 18, 1994. (*Source*: Chandler & Tranquada, 1994. Reprinted by permission of the Los Angeles *Daily News*.)

It was then suggested that arrangements be made to have President Clinton telephone Jackson during the broadcast. CSUN government relations staff members made the arrangements through California Assemblyman Richard Katz.

When the White House call came in, President Clinton talked about the damage to the campus and the rebuilding process and said, "You can count on us. The federal government will do its share."

"We got that on tape," said Erickson. "The federal government is going to help us. The President said so. It was documented. We documented everything. You can't have too many photographers, too many slides, too many tapes, too many photographs. We also let anybody who wanted to photograph our damage do it. We wanted people to know we were hurt badly, so when federal funds came in, no one would question our need."

Then President Clinton dropped a bombshell. He said that Vice President Gore would be on campus in 2 days. Everybody looked at somebody else. No one heard that before. Then, later that evening, "These guys in jeans showed up at our president's RV and said they were Gore's advance team," recalled Erickson. "I said to myself, 'Sure they are!' But they were; I guess that's the new White House attire."

Vice President Gore arrived on campus as scheduled. CSUN students and President Wilson greeted him. "He basically said, 'Good job!'" said Erickson, "and we got excellent media coverage from the visit" (see Fig. 20.7).

All classes originally scheduled were arranged. Even new courses were offered to take advantage of the disaster. There was a geology class that enabled students to get firsthand information about earthquakes and a social science course that dealt with counseling after a crisis. Thanks to Southern California's climate, some classes were held outside until trailers arrived.

Spring break was canceled, so classes ended only 1 week later than previously planned. Enrollment was 24,813, down about 2,000 students or 7%. Thompson said that a somewhat lower enrollment was expected anyway due to California's budget problems.

A month after classes started, CSUN was still in an emergency mode with limited access to telephones. There were about 100 workable telephones; one telephone serviced several departments housed in the same trailer. Where there once was a phonebook, there was a phone list.

Thompson said the campus had an earthquake plan:

We even had an earthquake simulation with the press invited. It was done as if school was in session and a large part of it was evacuation and treating wounds. Fortunately, that was unnecessary. If the earthquake had happened when classes were in session, there might have been significant numbers of lives lost and injuries.

Wilson hailed as force behind recovery

by CARMEN RAMOS CHANDLER
and JIM TRANQUADA
Daily News Staff Writers

NORTHRIDGE–CSUN President Blenda Wilson said her goodbyes to Vice President Al Gore on Wednesday and was dashing in her golf cart to another meeting when she spotted the FEMA officials accompanying Gore boarding a van.

She ran to them, shook their hands and thanked them for the federal agency's help since the Jan. 17 Northridge Earthquake—the nation's costliest natural disaster—crippled her 353-acre university campus.

The men smiled and exchanged business cards with Wilson.

"We're going to need their help again, and I want them to remember us," Wilson said as she climbed back into the golf cart she uses to traverse the campus's patchwork of damaged buildings, portable classrooms and tents.

"CSUN needs to be personalized in the minds of the people who have the overwhelming bureaucratic task of helping Southern California recover with thousands of needs.

"They can't forget us," she said, flashing the cards. "They won't now."

Ultimately, what they may best remember is what some people liken to the Northridge miracle: CSUN's phoenix-like rise from the devastation wrought by the magnitude 6.8 earthquake that damaged nearly all of the major buildings on campus.

The quake-delayed spring semester at California State University, Northridge, opened Feb. 14, with the campus's 24,50 students returning to attend classes at more than 400 portable trailers or at satellite locations from Thousand Oaks to Westwood.

Government and university officials credit Wilson for her ability to pull together staff and tap into an extensive network of private and public agencies—from local church to the White House—to get the campus up and running.

"What they have done at CSUN is absolutely incredible, and from what I hear, President Wilson had a large part to do with it," said U.S. Senator Barbara Boxer after a tour of the campus last week.

"You can see that she has this magnificent can-so spirit to her staff and make them believe they can reach for the stars. And they've done it."

Rep. Howard "Buck" McKeon, R-Santa Clarita, said the makeshift campus is a tribute to Wilson's leadership.

"She did something I don't think anyone thought she could do—she created an entire university campus the size of a small city within the matter of weeks," McKeon said.

For her part, Wilson credits CSUN staff and faculty, many of whom worked 12- or 16-hour days, seven days a week—sometimes using their homes as temporary offices—to get the university operating.

She also cites the assistance offered by the California State University system and local colleagues, as well as offers of help that ranged from donated computer equipment from IBM to classroom space at a Northridge church.

"I didn't pull off any miracles," Wilson said. "If anyone pulled off any miracles, it was our faculty, staff and students. They are the ones who did it … especially our physical plant staff, who gave their souls to this campus."

FIG. 20.7. A news story published in the *Los Angeles Daily News*, February 20, 1994 praising CSNU's president for leading recovery efforts. (Reprinted by permission of *Daily News*, Los Angeles.)

What was worse was that no one anticipated having no access to any buildings, no phones, no power, no supplies, no access to any tools of communication and information gathering.

Erickson and Thompson agreed that the relationships they had established with the media helped carry them through the crisis. Erickson said:

Absolutely, positively, the positive working relationships we had established with the local media helped us through the aftermath of the earthquake.

There was a core group of local reporters we had dealt with before, plus many more we had never seen—some specializing in technical subjects, like seismology, even international reporters from Japan, France. All of them just fell in and took their lead from the regular crews.

It helped, the PR professionals said, that in 1992, there was extensive media coverage of a crisis on campus in which black students charged the university's athletic department with failure to adequately advise black athletes. "I believe our effective handling of that crisis put us in good standing with the local media," said Erickson.

Asked about a crisis communications plan, Thompson responded:

There is a section in the university's *Emergency Operations Center Manual* on handling the media. It deals with phone trees, setting up a media center —all things we could not do. The phones didn't work. We had no furniture or equipment for the media center. We couldn't even get to our media guides. We're in earthquake country, so we expected an earthquake, but we never thought it would leave us without access to any materials. However, we found a way!

Kaine Thompson resigned from CSUN in June 1994 and accepted a position in Boston. She said the Southern California earthquake of 1994 had nothing to do with her decision to move.

Since the 1994 earthquake, there has been a complete turnover in the university's Public Relations Department. Richard Tyler, named assistant vice president of the Public Relations Department in 2000, said the university in mid-2000 was still recovering from the earthquake. Trailers, inflatable domes, and other temporary structures still dotted the campus. Expectations were that the campus would be completely rebuilt and restored by the end of 2000.

Staff members of the Public Relations Department moved from their wrecked quarters to temporary offices in the Education Building. They were expecting to move into the new Administration Building near the offices of the president.

Tyler said the university has "a crisis program," a crisis management manual that has been in existence for many years and was not, apparently, updated after the earthquake.

Case: Southern California Gas Company and the 1994 Los Angeles Earthquake

For Richard Nemec, manager of special communications projects for the Southern California Gas Company, the public relations problem following the 1994 Los Angeles earthquake was compounded because of three factors:

1. The earthquake struck in a densely populated area of southern California with 44,000 miles of natural gas pipeline.
2. The primary public was several million people near the epicenter and, ultimately, 16 million people who used natural gas through 4.7 million gas meters.
3. The secondary public was 9,000 employees.

Nemec lived near the Santa Monica–Los Angeles border, which is where he was when the 6.8 magnitude earthquake struck on January 17, 1994, at 4:31 a.m. "It was the most violent thing I have ever experienced," he said. "I just knew it was 'The Big One.' I thought the second story of my house was coming down, but it didn't. The phones and the power were knocked out and my wife, daughter, and I listened to a transistor radio. When they

started identifying the San Fernando Valley as the center of the earthquake, I couldn't imagine what it must have felt like there."

After about an hour and a half, Nemec's sister in Newport Beach was successful in reaching him by phone, so he realized that the phones were operational. "That' s when I started to think about the job," he said, "First, there were phone calls to make."

The Gas Company, as it was popularly called, had three departments involved in its communications department: (1) public affairs, (2) operating regions, and (3) advertising. Each department reported to a separate vice president. Nemec' s role in dealing with employee and news media communications was based in public affairs. Public affairs people in five customer regions reported to region managers, who, in turn, reported to a vice president of customer regions. Advertising reported to the vice president of marketing.

Normally, Nemec would not have been required to head the communications crisis aspect of the disaster. It just happened that the person with that responsibility, the manager of public and employee information, had resigned the Friday before the Monday temblor. Even though this manager had 2 additional weeks with the company, he was out of town and unreachable during the first 24 hours of the disaster. Nemec was a natural substitute because he had previously held the position from 1986 to mid-1992.

Nemec made phone calls to key personnel, including a news bureau representative who was on call for media purposes 24 hours a day. According to the company's disaster plan, an Emergency Operations Center (EOC) was set up in the downtown Los Angeles office within 1 hour after the earthquake. Nemec telephoned the EOC and offered to come in if necessary. Twenty minutes later he got the call that it was necessary.

Nemec described the commute to the office as "interesting." "The Santa Monica Freeway was down, so I took surface streets, principally Olympic Boulevard eastbound for about 10 miles. It wasn't as bad as it could have been because of the King holiday. Still, there were no traffic signals and a lot of traffic heading north and south at each major intersection."

Once Nemec arrived at the EOC office, he found the power out and the backup generator not working. Although telephone service was not disrupted, the personnel had been working in darkness for the first hour the EOC was open. The EOC office was located one level below the lobby in the Southern California Gas Company' s high-rise headquarters. Power for elevators and lights in the building was unavailable until around noon.

Soon after Nemec arrived, power was restored in the EOC office, but the rest of the building was still without power. Nemec was not able to access his office on the 25th floor of the 52-story building.

The EOC was equipped with all the needed supplies and equipment, but not all the necessary personnel. "We couldn't reach some people be-

cause it was a company holiday. On a regular day, they would have been here," said Nemec. "The vice president of public affairs was there a little before I was, and the news bureau on-call person was there first." All members of senior management were called through a telephone tree.

Nemec said the company had rehearsed for disasters, specifically earthquakes, once each year. He felt that the hypothetical situations in the practice exercises were more disastrous than the real quake turned out to be. "The drill," he said, "is pretty well known. It's automatic that once employees take care of their families, they report to their work location or to the company facility closest to where they live."

Other than personnel being away because of the holiday weekend, employees were also not available because they had sustained so much damage in their own homes that they could not come to the work site. Also, many people could not get to the work site because of damaged freeways.

The first task of the EOC, according to Nemec (pictured in Fig. 21.1), "was to get a sense of where the damage was concentrated, which operations were impacted, and to what extent. We didn't have a lot of information, so we just decided to dive into the task of establishing contact with [the] news media—answering and making phone calls and waiting for field operations to call in their damage assessments."

The initial concern was to determine if the Aliso Canyon gas storage facility and transmission pipeline infrastructure, the largest such underground facility in the United States, had withstood the temblor. Located 5 miles from the epicenter, it had sustained damage. It was shut down immediately after the earthquake, according to design, but was brought back to near-normal operation within 2 weeks.

Fearful of fires, thousands of Southern Californians turned off their gas, even though repair people would be required on site to restore service. Ultimately, 150,000 homes were without gas. The original estimate was 70,000 homes, but subsequent customer surveys indicated that thousands of additional customers were without gas service. Therefore, the estimate of homes without service was increased.

Only 15,000 gas services were turned off by the Gas Company for safety reasons. The rest were turned off by individuals unnecessarily. The Gas Company discovered later that some consumers managed to restore their own gas service.

In the mobilization of service crews, more than 400 volunteers from nearby gas companies—San Diego Gas and Electric, Southwest Gas, City of Long Beach Gas Department, Pacific Gas and Electric—worked out of field centers set up in tents. Beds were brought in for the visiting crews.

The crews made door-to-door calls to customers in five impacted areas to ensure that their gas service was operating safely: San Fernando Valley, Simi Valley, Santa Clarita Valley, Santa Monica/West Los Angeles/Holly-

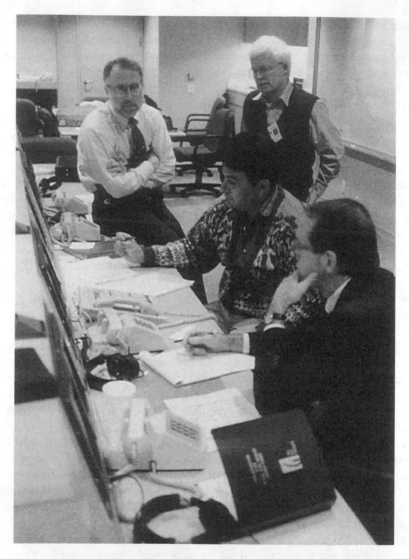

FIG. 21.1. A scene from the Southern California Gas Company's Emergency Operations Center (EOC) after the 1994 Los Angeles earthquake. Richard Nemec, manager of special community projects, sits on desk at top left of photo. Dick Friend, senior news bureau representative, stands top right. Frank Ayck, EOC manager, sits at center. Lee Steward, vice president of engineering, is at bottom right of photo. (*Source*: Reproduced by permission of Southern California Gas Company, Los Angeles.)

wood, South Central Los Angeles. These areas together were as big as the sixth largest city in the United States. Several thousand miles of pipeline were surveyed, and 1,400 distribution leaks were located and repaired. As crews searched for leaks, aftershocks continued, some so strong that pipes previously examined had to be reexamined. Only 36 transmission leaks were found in the entire system, all of them restored within 24 hours after the earthquake struck. The number of transmission leaks was low because the company had replaced many older pipes prior to the earthquake.

Transmission pipelines are larger in diameter and the gas within them flows under higher pressure than in distribution pipelines. Service pipelines running from the distribution mains to customers' homes are smaller and have lower pressure. House pipelines, on the properties of residential customers, are even smaller and of even lower pressure than service pipelines.

Forty-nine fires were traced to gas leakages resulting from the earthquake. Although there were 57 deaths attributed to the earthquake, no deaths were ever attributed specifically to natural gas fires or other gas safety problems. There were no deaths or major injuries among employees involved in the recovery effort.

Approximately 172 mobile homes were destroyed by fire. Most of them burned because water was not available to prevent the rapid spreading of fire from one home to others. The main water lines in mobile home parks were broken by the earthquake. Other mobile home fires resulting from gas leaks involved coaches that fell off foundations, broken gas risers, and appliances, mainly water heaters, that fell and broke interior gas lines.

COMMUNICATIONS

Communications during the crisis were directed to the company's major stakeholders: consumers, employees, the media, elected officials, community leaders, and state and federal government officials. Subsequently, customers and employees were each segmented into subpublics. The five subpublics for consumers were (1) customers, (2) the general public, (3) customers in impacted areas, (4) customers in outlying areas, (5) the media. The four subpublics for employees were (1) employees and their families, (2) loaned employees from other utilities, (3) employees interfacing with customers, and (4) employees in command centers (such as the EOC) and in the regions.

In the regions, staff members made initial contact with various stakeholders, including key government officials and community media. This two-way communications link continued throughout the 2-week recovery period. Except for the first 2 days, the EOC and the eight regions worked separately in the areas of public and employee communications. During the first 2 days after the earthquake, the regions concentrated on identify-

ing local problems and providing daily updates to employees. It was the re-
sponsibility of the regions to report operations issues, problems, and the
scope of damage to the EOC. Regions communicated with each other on a
daily basis about the scope of the earthquake damage through telephone,
fax, and e-mail.

Chance Williams, manager of the Pacific region, recalled that later on,
the EOC coordinated communications efforts between downtown head-
quarters and the regions: "This was done to provide consistent messages
to the public and to employees."

For advertising, radio was used along with print media, bill inserts, and
direct mail. Radio spots were found to be most effective, in both the early
part of the recovery and the wrap-up, because they could be conceived,
placed, and changed most quickly. Various print advertisements were used
to deliver thank-you and safety messages. Direct mail communications
were targeted only to consumers in the impacted areas. The regularly
staffed 24-hour service bureaus in Chatsworth, San Dimas, and Redlands
took calls from customers on a toll-free information line.

From the company's downtown headquarters, external messages were
sent to consumers during the 4 weeks following the earthquake. The exter-
nal messages were as follows:

Days 1 and 2
> "The pipeline system is intact."
> "Public safety is under control."
> "Don't shut off the gas unnecessarily."

Rest of Week 1
> "Individual customers should make safety checks."
> "Call us if there is a problem and be patient."
> "In aftershocks, don't shut off the gas unnecessarily."

Week 2
> "Safety is our first priority."
> "Call us if you have an emergency."
> "Hold off on nonemergency calls."

Week 3
> "Thank you" (sent to customers and employees).

Week 4
> "Customers may have lingering problems from appliances and vent-
> ing that shifted in the quake and aftershocks. Check. If so, call us or a
> plumber."

Internal messages included those in the preceding list as well as the following messages:

Days 1–3

"If an employee has suffered damage to his or her residence or injury to family members, the company is offering assistance in getting aid, no-interest loans, donated goods and services."

Week 1

"Employee efforts are extraordinary and they are truly appreciated by everyone: customers, top management, and shareholders, and so on."

Week 2

"Pride," "Appreciation," "Thank-you."
Recognition for loaned employees.

Week 3

"Thank you" (sent to regular employees and families).

Later (in February and March)

Reward and recognition of all company employees.

On the first day in the EOC, the following five employees concentrated on media relations and communications to other internal-external stakeholders:

Tom Sayles, vice president of public affairs
Dick Friend, senior news bureau representative
Denise King, news bureau representative
Mabel Solares, news bureau representative (the Spanish-speaking spokesperson)
Richard Nemec, manager of special communication projects

In the regions, 40 assigned community affairs specialists also concentrated on media relations and community contacts in the operating regions.

The *Los Angeles Times*, Southern California' s largest metropolitan daily newspaper, was physically knocked out itself with no power at its downtown Los Angeles offices until around noon on the day of the earthquake. Nemec recalled that his first contact with the newspaper was around 3 p.m., when he made the call to Larry Gordon, the general assignment reporter.

On the second day of the recovery effort, the company's MultiMedia Center dispatched video crews to capture employees at work. A videotape entitled *Relighting the Flame* was produced and distributed to numerous government, industry, and community groups. A longer version of the video eventually was given to all employees.

Within 48 hours of the earthquake, the company's public affairs staff was operating in normal mode. The EOC was still on the ground floor, whereas in the regular offices on the 25th floor, personnel took media calls and wrote news releases. The two offices communicated via a special phone hookup. "We used all available communications channels and determined which channels were best for the target publics [stakeholder groups] and the message," said Nemec. "For news announcements, by far, the most effective method was live broadcasts during the first 3 days. This was the best way to get timely information to customers and key stakeholders." Particularly effective were live phone-in interviews to major television and radio stations.

The staff also solicited the help of the broadcast media to disseminate key critical messages, and the stations complied willingly. Faxes to wire services and other news outlets were most effective, followed by pretaped broadcast information that was circulated routinely to all broadcast media. Later, in the chronic stage of the crisis, news advisories, news conferences, and in-the-field media contacts were most effective.

Numerous news releases were distributed. Following are the major messages they carried:

News Release	Message
January 17, 1994, 2:30 p.m.	Bills will be waived for customers in uninhabitable residences (see Fig. 21.2).
January 17, 1994, 9 p.m.	The overall system withstood the earthquake. Repair crews will work around the clock to restore service.
January 18, 1994, 11:30 a.m.	Most incoming phone lines are inoperable. Do not make nonemergency calls.
January 18, 1994, 8:30 p.m.	Most gas service will be restored by late tomorrow night. (This turned out to be an overly optimistic goal. The Gas Company was unaware that thousands of customers had shut off their service in fear of fires.) (See Fig. 21.3. Figs. 21.4, and 21.5 that show other examples of news releases and ads distributed.)
January 19, 1994	Two service restoration centers opened in the San Fernando Valley.
January 19, 1994, 4:30 p.m.	Gas service restored to 10,000 customers, a third of all customers who were estimated to be without gas at the time.
January 20, 1994	Media advisory for a news conference.

January 20, 1994, 3:30 p.m. Gas service restored to 20,000 customers; more
 outages discovered.

January 21, 1994 Service restored to 30,000 customers.

Communications directed to employees during the recovery period stage were the following:

1. The Gas Company's weekly employee newsletter, "Sendout"—both regular and special editions—kept employees up to date on the recovery.
2. The daily bulletin, "FYI," informed employees of press coverage of the company's efforts at recovery.
3. A special 14-page issue of the company's monthly tabloid, *Energy*, provided both photographs of and text about the efforts of employees in the recovery.
4. Two letters—one to employees at work locations, another to their families at home—were sent by CEO Dick Farman. They were thank-you letters for hard work, support, understanding, and dedication.
5. Four issues of *Epicenter*, a special publication in the area nearest the earthquake's epicenter, were distributed to employees involved in recovery work. It praised employees for performing quality work under extraordinarily difficult circumstances. This publication originated with the region's EOC in Chatsworth.

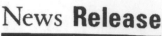

News **Release**

CONTACT: Denise King
(213) 244-3030

FOR IMMEDIATE RELEASE
2:30 p.m. Jan. 17, 1994

EARTHQUAKE REPORT FROM SOCALGAS

Southern California Gas Co. announced it will waive bills for any of its customers whose residences are uninhabitable because of damage caused by today's major earthquake. As of mid-afternoon, there was no estimate on how many customers fall into this category.

Gas Company officials are asking customers to be patient as utility workers respond to, and repair, breaks in gas lines.

The gas company reports that its overall system of 44,000 miles of pipeline has withstood today's 6.6 earthquake. As of 2:30 p.m., there were up to 5,000 customers without service, but the vast majority of the 16 million people served through 4.7 million meters were still receiving service.

Outages and damage to the gas system were concentrated in the northwest portion of Los Angeles County -- San Fernando Valley, Hollywood and West Los Angeles. Four transmission pipelines, 142 service and distribution lines sustained damage. All of these breaks are under control and repairs are under way in the impacted area. Eastern and Southeastern parts of LA County and neighboring Orange, Riverside and San Bernnardino counties sustained little or no damage to the natural gas system.

However, the overall damages were more severe than the Whittier quake in 1987 and other major quakes in recent years.

We will restore services as soon as repairs to major pipelines are completed. At this time, we don't know how many services are affected. Lack of electrical service may impact how quickly service is restored. Customers are asked to be patient. Customers in the Val Verde area may experience outages lasting up to one week. The Gas Company has 600 employees in the field performing pipeline repairs or providing service at individual customer premises. (Extra crews have been brought in from outlying area, such as Riverside and Orange Counties ties for repair work in the Los Angeles basin.)

Customers are reminded of the following:
- Don't automatically shut off your gas service.
- First, check to determine if you smell or hear a hissing gas leak.
- If you do, check to see if you can isolate the leaks at a given appliance. If you can, turn off the valve on the gas line serving that appliance.
- If you cannot do this, and you still suspect a gas leak, go to the meter an turn the valve cross-wise with the pipe to shut off service.
- Don't try to restore the service, call the gas company.
- You can call the number in the white papers of the telephone directory, the · number on your gas bill or an 800 number: 1-800-427-2200.

#

FIG. 21.2. A news release distributed by the Southern California Gas Company on the day of the earthquake. (*Source*: Reprinted by permission of Southern California Gas Company, Los Angeles.)

News Release

CONTACT: Ron Owens - (213) 244-8908

FOR IMMEDIATE RELEASE
8:30 P.M., TUESDAY, JAN. 18, 1994

GAS COMPANY HOPING TO RESTORE SERVICE

TO MOST EARTHQUAKE VICTIMS BY TOMORROW NIGHT

Southern California Gas Co. believes that most of its customers who lost gas service because of broken gas pipes will have that gas turned on by late tomorrow night. Homes that received major damage will not be restored until the house or building has been declared safe by building officials, however.

Only about 35,000 of the company's 4.7 million customers had their gas service disrupted during Monday's earthquake and aftershocks. All of these were located in the immediate quake area of the San Fernando and Santa Clarita valleys, Simi, Hollywood, Los Angeles and Santa Monica.

The utility assigned 1,700 workers to the quake area to repair pipelines and restore customer service. As pipeline breaks are repaired, employees go block-by-block, house-to-house, to restore customers' gas service. Because of this, routine service calls in most every other area of Southern California have been delayed. In addition, technical problems impaired the ability of The Gas Company's telephone lines to accommodate the large increase in the volume of customer service requests. As a result, some callers received recorded messages indicating they had reached a disconnected number.

Callers still are asked to phone only for emergencies and call 1-800-427-2200.

Customers in the earthquake area without telephone service can reach the company at two temporary walk-in stations, between 8 a.m. and 5 p.m. They are located at Santa Clarita City Hall, 23920 Valencia Blvd., and the City of San Fernando Park at 208 Park Ave. In other areas, payment offices remain open; addresses are located on the customer's bill or in the telephone directory.

The Gas Company announced that it is making a $10,000 donation to the Los Angeles County Chapter of the American Red Cross to assist in earthquake disaster relief. Also, gas company employees are volunteering to work at various community shelters.

####

FIG. 21.3. A news release distributed by the Southern California Gas Company the day after the earthquake announcing plans to restore gas service by the next night. (*Source*: Reprinted by permission of Southern California Gas Company, Los Angeles.)

Some of the most serious earthquake damage may be invisible.

Here's how to spot it.

The effects of an earthquake aren't always obvious. Carbon monoxide may build up in living spaces if gas appliances have moved or been damaged. Although colorless, tasteless and odorless, exposure to carbon monoxide can cause nausea, drowsiness, and other flu-like symptoms. Prolonged exposure can be serious. In the event of an earthquake, The Gas Company wants you to know about a few simple steps you can take to make sure your gas appliances are working safely and efficiently:

Check appliances to see if they've moved or come loose from gas connector lines.

Check venting systems on hot water heaters, furnaces and gas logs to make sure they haven't separated from the appliance, wall or ceiling. If your furnace has moved, check for gaps at the base.

If you have a forced-air unit, make sure the fan compartment door fits snugly and is tightly shut.

If you suspect your natural gas appliances are not operating properly, please have them inspected and serviced by a qualified agency. Contact The Gas Company at 1-800-427-2200, your heating/plumbing contractor or service agency.

The Gas Company‾

© 1994 Southern California Gas Company

FIG. 21.4. An advertisement circulated in newspapers by the Southern California Gas Company during the earthquake recovery period. The ad was part of the company's public service effort to provide consumers with crucial information. (*Source*: Reprinted by permission of Southern California Gas Company, Los Angeles.)

The Gas Company

News **Release**

Contact: News Bureau
 (213) 244-3030

FOR IMMEDIATE RELEASE
2 P.M., JAN.26, 1994

GAS CO. RESTORES SERVICE TO 120,000; MANY STILL WITHOUT

GAS BECAUSE WORKERS UNABLE TO ENTER CUSTOMERS' HOMES

Southern California Gas Co. has restored natural gas service to more than 120,000 customers since last week's earthquake. However, the company reported there are still several thousand customers without gas because service personnel could not gain entry into homes and businesses to check appliances to ensure they are safe to operate.

"We've almost completed restoring service to all customers, with the exception of those where we weren't able to get into the premises," said Lee Harrington, senior vice president of operations at The Gas Company. "It's important that customers who are still without service make arrangements to have someone at home, or leave a key with a neighbor, and call us at 1-800-427-2200.

"For customers whose homes have been damaged by the recent temblors, we may not be able to assist you until the building is safe," Harrington added.

The company deployed employees from throughout Southern California into the heavily damaged earthquake areas. These crews are being released from earthquake duty as restorations are completed. Within the next few days, they will be returning to their home bases.

"We hope to begin phasing into a normal work schedule next week and thank all of our customers for their patience and understanding during this emergency," he said.

#

vcedoc:quake26
94-020

FIG. 21.5. A news release distributed by the Southern California Gas Company nine days after the earthquake, when the company realized its effort to restore service was more difficult than anticipated. (*Source*: Reprinted by permission of Southern California Gas Company, Los Angeles.)

References

Most chapters in "Crisis Communications: A Casebook Approach" are based on interviews with crisis communicators by mail, e-mail, telephone, and in person.

Chapter 1: The Nature of Crises

Barton, L. (1993). *Crisis in organizations.* Cincinnati: South-Western.
Fearn-Banks, K. (1996). Crisis communications theory and ten businesses hit by news-making crises. In G. Amin & S. Fullerton (Eds.), *Global business trends: Contemporary readings.* Academy of Business Administration (pp. 847–851).
Grunig, J. E., & Grunig, L. A. (1992). Models of public relations and communications. In J. E. Grunig (Ed.), *Excellence in public relations and communication management* (pp. 285–326). Hillsdale, NJ: Lawrence Erlbaum Associates.
Grunig, J. E., & Hunt, T. (1984). *Managing public relations.* New York: Holt.
Grunig, J. E., & Repper, F. C. (1992). Strategic management, publics, and issues. In J. E. Grunig (Ed.), *Excellence in public relations and communication management* (pp. 117–157). Hillsdale, NJ: Lawrence Erlbaum Associates.
Marra, F. J. (1992). *Crisis public relations: A theoretical model.* Unpublished doctoral dissertation, University of Maryland, College Park.
Ziakas, T. (1999). Titanic and public relations: A case study. *Journal of Public Relations Research, 11,* (2), pp. 105–124.

Chapter 3: Crisis Makers

Cutting it close. (1994, September 21). Burrelles Transcripts of "Dateline NBC," No. 129.

Goleman, D. (1991, June 4). Anatomy of a rumor: It flies on fear. *The New York Times*, p. C1.

Just talk into the curtains. (1994, November 28). *Newsweek*, p. 76.

Koenig, F. (1985). *Rumor in the marketplace.* Dover, MA: Auburn House.

Roan, S. (1994, September 11). Are TV talk shows undermining America's collective psyche? *Seattle Times*, p. L4.

Rottenberg, D. (1994, May). And that's the way it is. *American Journalism Review*, 34–37.

Seitel, F. (1992). *The practice of public relations.* New York: Macmillan.

Wilcox, D. L., Ault, P. H., & Agee, W. K. (1989). Procter & Gamble fights a rumor. In *Public relations strategies and tactics* (p. 620). New York: HarperCollins.

Chapter 4: Cyber Crises

Battenberg, E. (1999, November). Dealing with cyberspace attacks. *Public Relations Tactics, 14.*

Janal, D. S. (1998). *Risky business.* New York: Wiley.

Kotcher, R. L. (1999). Surviving a crisis in cyberspace. *The Best of Tactics*, pp. 81–83.

Lucey, R. (1999, July). The truth is out there—On UTMB's web site, *Public Relations Tactics, 6.*

Noack, D. (2000, February, 25). Banana rumor called Internet terrorism. APBNews.com.

Segal, D., & Mayer, C. (1999, March 28). Sites for sore consumers; Complaints about companies multiply on the web. *The Washington Post*, p. A01.

Stiffler, L. (2000, February 4). Fraudulent donation web page is purged. *Seattle Post-Intelligencer*, p. A10.

Chapter 5: Managing a Crisis

Bernstein, C. (1994, August 9). Interview on *CBS This Morning.* New York: CBS.

Leung, M. (1999, September 7). Courting publicity, attorney makes safe food his business. *Seattle Post-Intelligencer*, pp. A1, A4.

Metzler, K. (1994, March). Shooting it out with the media. *Hemispheres Magazine*, pp. 51–53.

Spector, R., & McCarthy, P. (2000). *The Nordstrom way.* New York: Wiley.

Thompson, T., & Hess, J. (1986, November, 15). Delta accused of Jekyll-Hyde behavior in wake of crash. *Atlanta Constitution*, pp. 1–10.

Chapter 6: Case: Johnson & Johnson and the Tylenol Murders

Goodman, H. (1982, November 12). PR effort launches new Tylenol packages. *Kansas City Times*, p. A3.

Houston, J., & Griffin, L. J. (1982, October 1). 5 deaths tied to pills: Fear killer put cyanide in Tylenol. *Chicago Tribune*, pp. 1–2.

Knight, J. (1982, October 11). Tylenol's maker shows how to respond to a crisis. *The Washington Post*, p. 1.

Shanker, T., & Grady, B. (1982, October 3). Shoplifter is sought in poisoning probe: Reportedly stole Tylenol. *Chicago Tribune*, pp. 1, 4.

Chapter 7: Case: Exxon and the Valdez Oil Spill

Connelly, J. (1999, May 4). Exxon says it has paid enough for Valdez spill. *Seattle Post-Intelligencer*, p. A1.

Exxon Valdez captain finally will do community service. (1999, February 17). *Seattle Post-Intelligencer*, p. A3.

Nalder, E. (1999, March 14). Exxon Valdez captain: Was he the villain or the victim? *Seattle Times*, p. A1.

Richest merger of all time. (1998, December 1). *Seattle Times*, p. A13.

Sentence upheld over oil spill. (1988, July 5). *Seattle Times*, p. B3.

Serving time. (1999, July 12). *People*, p. 62.

Smith, C. (1992). *Media and apocalypse.* Westport, CT: Greenwood.

The big spill. (1990, February 27). Broadcast on WGBH in Boston.

The Fortune 500. (1998, April 26). *Fortune*, p. F1.

The Fortune 500. (2000, April 17). *Fortune*, p. F1.

Turning Point. (1994, June 15). Transcript of telecast of newsmagazine, p. 1.

Watson, T. (1999, February 11). Wildlife recovering from Exxon spill. *USA Today*, p. 3A.

Chapter 9: Case: Snapps Restaurant and the AIDS Rumor

Cheek, M. (1991, May 25). Student apologizes for AIDS rumor about eatery. *The Stuart News*, p. 1.

Knight-Ridder News Service. (1991, May 10). Chain denies AIDS rumors. *Denver Post*, p. 18A.

Long, P. (1991a, May 9). Store's business cut 50 percent by AIDS rumor. *The Miami Herald*, pp. 1B–2B.

Long, P. (1991b, May 25). Student apologizes for spreading rumor about restaurant. *The Miami Herald*, p. 1B.

Reeder, J. (1991, May 25). Student apologizes for restaurant rumor. *The Palm Beach Post*, p. 1.

Chapter 10: Case: Cellular Phones and the Cancer Scare

Kaye, S. D. (1993). Taking stock of cellular. *U.S. News & World Report, 114*, p. 85.

Chapter 11: Case: United Way of America and the Overspending CEO

Babcock, C. R. (1992, February 20). 3 large locals ask United Way about president's spending. *The Washington Post*, p. A6.

Shepard, C. (1992, February 16). Perks, privileges and power in a nonprofit world. *The Washington Post*, p. A1.

Teltsch, K. (1992, February 24). United Way awaits inquiry on its president's practices. *The New York Times,* pp. A7, A12.
United Way's troubles. (1991, March 3). Editorial. *Christian Science Monitor,* p. 20.

Chapter 12: Case: United Way of King County and the Overspending CEO

Harrell, D. C. (1992, February 21). United Way units withhold dues in "high living probe." *Seattle Post-Intelligencer,* p. B3.

Chapter 13: Case: They Keep Coming—Chinese Immigrants in Canada

Armstrong, J. (1999, July 21). No-name ship found crammed with Asians. *The Globe and Mail,* pp. 1-A2, 1-A3.
Communications Strategy: Boat arrivals of migrants to British Columbia, 1999.
Fennell, T. (1999, August 23). Canada's open door. *Macleans,* pp. 12–17.

Chapter 14: Case: DC Mayor Anthony Williams and Another "N" Word

Abeyta, O. (2000, January 10). Learning to be mayor. *The Common Denominator,* p. 1.
Cottman, M. H. (2000, April 16). Mayor wants inner circle to reflect city. *The Washington Post,* p. C01.
Jenkins, A. (1999, January 17). *The Washington Post,* p. B01.
Julian Bond remains critical of D.C. mayor in word flap. (1999, January 28). *Chicago Tribune,* Evening Update, News section, p. 2.
King, C. (1999, January 30). Much ado about the N-word. *The Washington Post,* Final Edition, p. A19.
Leonning, C. (2000, April 20). For district voters, a way to keep score. *The Washington Post,* p. A33.
Morin, R., & Cottman, M. H. (2000, January 13). Williams gets a big thumbs-up in poll: D.C. residents again proud of their city. *The Washington Post,* p. A1.
Weeks, L. (1999, January 29). Caught in a verbal vortex: One word leaves a lot still to be said about former D.C. official David Howard. *The Washington Post,* Final Edition, p. C01.

Chapter 15: Case: Texas A&M University and the Bonfire Tragedy

Associated Press. (1999, December 15), Photos show bonfire leaning before fall, *Waco Tribune-Herald,* p. 1.
Ball, A. (1999, December 5). 2 bonfire victims were legally drunk. *Austin American-Statesman,* p. 1.
Brown, K. (2000, January 11). Report: Bonfire ropes were cut. *Bryan-College Station Eagle,* p. 1.

Haurwitz, R. K. M., & Copelin, L. (1999, December 10). Faculty doubted bonfire's stability. *Austin-American Statesman*, p. 1.

Jones, R. L. (1999, December 19). Collapse kills 11 at Texas A&M. *The Philadelphia Inquirer*, p. 1.

Kirsch, J. (1999a, December 7). A&M refuses money. *Bryan-College Station Eagle*, p. 1.

Kirsch, J. (1999b, November 20). Bush: Bonfire should continue. *Bryan-College Station Eagle*, p. 1.

Montini, E. J. (1999, December 10). A&M can't pass buck in tragedy. *Waco Tribune-Herald*, p. 1.

Photos show bonfire leaning before fall. (1999, December 15). Associated Press. *Waco Tribune-Herald*, p. 1.

Slover, P., & Lee, C. (1999, December 3). A&M student's use of crane may have violated bonfire rule. *The Dallas Morning News*, p. 1.

Tang, I. A. (2000, March 20). *The Texas Aggie bonfire; tragedy and tradition at Texas A&M*. Austin: Morgan.

Une pyramide meutriere. (1999, November 19). *Le Matin*.

Ward, M. (2000, January 7). A&M's tab for bonfire aftermath: $292,000 and growing. *Austin-American Statesman*, p. 1.

Chapter 17: Case: The Metro Transit Accident: Driver Shot, Bus Flies off the Bridge

Fefer, M. D. (1999, January 21). King County—Too nice to sue. *Seattle Weekly*, pp. 7, 10.

McFadden, K. (1998, November 28). KOMO-TV led pack with human touches. *Seattle Times*, p. 21.

Sunde, S. (1999, November 26). A year ago today, disturbed rider set off tragic events. *Seattle Post-Intelligencer*, pp. A1, A24.

Chapter 18: Case: Alpac Corporation and the Original Syringe-in-the-Can Scare

Bergsman, J. (1993, June 13). Syringe found in 2nd Cola can: FDA investigates tampering. *Seattle Times*, p. XX.

Harrison, L. (1993, June 17). Pepsi gets high marks for response. *Seattle Times*, p. XX.

Chapter 19: Case: Pepsi and the National Syringe-in-the-Can Scare

Pepsi-Cola. (1993a). *Anatomy of a crisis: The Diet Pepsi tampering hoax* [videotape]. (Available from Pepsi-Cola Company.)

Pepsi-Cola. (1993b). *The Pepsi hoax: What went right?* Somers, NY: Pepsi-Cola Public Affairs.

Chapter 20: Case: California State University, Northridge, and the 1994 Los Angeles Earthquake

Hayes, D. W., & Heller, P. J. (1994, February 10). In a word, it's "bad": A president stands her ground. *Black Issues in Higher Education, 10,* (25), 20–23.

Coffey, S. (Ed.). (1994). *Images of the 1994 Los Angeles Earthquake, 4,* 31. Los Angeles: Los Angeles Times Syndicate.

Kosoy, S. (1994, February 7). Students unsettled by quake. *Pasadena Star News.*

Tranguade, J. (1994, January 18). 6.6 temblor cripples southland, 24 killed. [Los Angeles] *Daily News,* pp. 1, 12.

Generic Crisis Communications Plan
for a Large Company

Contents

Definitions
Communication Objective
Roles and Responsibilities
Notification of a Crisis
Communications Procedure for Handling a Minor Crisis
Communications Procedure for Handling a Major Crisis
Emergency Operations Center (EOC) Activation
Identification of a Spokesperson
Guidelines for Spokespeople
Format for Briefing Someone Identified as a Spokesperson
 for Interviews/News Briefings

News Release
 Circumstances That May Require a News Release
 Writing an Initial Statement for Release
 Information Appropriate for Release
 Information That Is NOT Appropriate for Release
 Writing a News Release

Messages for the News Media During Environmental Crises
Audiences During a Crisis
How People Receive Information During a Crisis

Tools to Use During a Crisis
 Crisis Contacts
 Key Communications/PR Contacts
 Incident Information Sheet
 Telephone Log Sheet
 Example of Initial Statement for Release
 Checklist for Establishing a News Conference Center

Definitions

Crises:

Crises are unplanned events that directly or potentially threaten our company's reputations; the environment; the health, safety, or welfare of employees; and the health, safety, or welfare of citizens in communities surrounding our plants.

Events that fall into this category include: fires, explosions, bomb threats, civil disturbances, equipment malfunctions, environmental impacts, widespread illness, hazardous material spills, and other types of incidents.

Minor Crisis:

A *minor crisis* is confined to a limited area of a building; results in minimal, if any, disruption of operations; is quickly brought under control; does not require evacuation other than by a few employees in the immediate vicinity; and causes a minor injury or none at all. Media inquiry is possible with events in this category but apt to be minimal.

Major Crisis:

A *major crisis* may involve significant injury or loss of life, prolonged disruption of normal operations, substantial property damage, or a significant environmental impact—or holds potential for any of these. Media inquiry is more likely to occur with events in this category, especially if other municipal emergency response groups have been called in for assistance.

Communication Objective

In the event of a minor or major incident on any of our sites, every effort will be made to communicate as appropriate to employees, management, surrounding communities, other target publics, and the news media promptly and accurately. The appropriate division communications staff will be the primary information source available to the news media.

When a crisis occurs, it is necessary for communications personnel to gather facts and data quickly, including the nature of our response to the crisis. The following communication efforts will strive to alleviate employees' concerns, minimize speculation by the media, and ensure that our position is presented.

It should be noted, though, that many incidents occur that are relatively minor in nature and are consequently not covered by the media. Nevertheless, it is essential to gather facts about the incidents and have them available to communicate, if necessary, to appropriate audiences.

The nature of that communication is outlined in the following plan.

Roles and Responsibilities

Each site's Crisis Committee (at the various sites) is responsible for the following: identifying, confirming, investigating crises; developing strategies for managing crises; and developing strategies for recovering from crisis incidents.

As a member of the Crisis Committee, communications personnel will:

- Provide a representative at the Emergency Operations Center (EOC) if activated
- Control the release of information to employees, surrounding communities, and to the news media
- Maintain contact with media representatives
- Establish and maintain a news conference center, if necessary

Two, and in some cases, three communicators may be required for adequate crisis communications response. Those communicators will function in the following roles: Public Relations (PR) Lead, Incident Command (IC) Interface, and PR Backup.

The responsibilities for each communication role are outlined as follows:

- PR Lead
 - Received initial notification
 - Designates staff member as IC Interface
 - Designates staff member as PR Backup (if necessary)
 - Receives initial facts and updates from IC Interface
 - Prepares initial statement for release
 - Fields media inquiries to office
 - Briefs executive identified as spokesperson
 - Joins Emergency Operations Center team, if activated
 - Provides updates to senior executives

- Incident Command (IC) Interface
 - Joins IC team
 - Gathers and documents facts as they become known
 - Share initial facts and updates with PR lead in main office
 - Prepares initial statement for release (if necessary)
 - Briefs affected organization management and employees
 - Fields media inquiries (if necessary)

- PR Back-up
 - Updates corporate personnel as necessary
 - Fields additional media inquiries to office
 - Fields employee inquiries to office
 - Conducts in-field interviews with media (if necessary)
 - Sets up media conference room (if necessary)

Notification of a Crisis

Notification is an extremely important process in managing crises and sending the right messages to all audiences. When notification goes well, it makes the rest of the crisis communications job more streamlined and effective than when it doesn't.

Notification of incidents and crises (both major and minor) have been examined by an Ad Hoc Committee to the Corporate Crisis Committee for the past year. Members of this Ad Hoc Committee included PR/Communications, Fire and Security, Facilities, and Emergency Response Coordinators.

This committee has reviewed the entire notification process from the moment a crisis begins to the point that a crisis warrants informing senior corporate executives, including the chief executive officer. This committee has endeavored to determine the most reliable notification process for each site Crisis Committee to use.

Notification Process in Brief

Notification is initiated from the area where a crisis has occurred or been identified. The person who discovers the crisis or incident calls the site emergency number, which goes to the site Fire Station Dispatch office. A senior Fire Officer is then dispatched to the incident site, evaluates the magnitude of the crisis, and then contacts the Fire Dispatch to notify additional emergency response organizations. From that point on, notification occurs according to defined call lists and through chain-of-command channels.

Site Communications personnel are now notified directly by the respective site Fire Dispatchers. Once that initial notification occurs, the Communications representative receiving the call should, in turn, notify Corporate PR offices and the company switchboard operators as soon as he/she obtains information about the incident, and then follow the procedure noted on pages 5-9.

Communications Procedure for Handling a Minor Crisis

Minor Crisis:

1. __ *Division Communications* receives notification from the Fire Dispatcher and compiles the basic facts and chronology of the event (possibly using an Incident Information Sheet).

2. __ Division Communications representative becomes the *PR Lead* and informs other communications team members.

3. __ *PR Lead* determines if more information is necessary and if a communicator should be dispatched to incident site (*Incident Command Interface*).

4. __ *PR Lead* calls Incident Commander (this is usually the senior Fire Officer at the incident site).

5. __ *PR Lead* notes more details about the incident (type of incident, when and where the incident occurred, chemical involved and potential chemical reactions, emergency response personnel on site, number of employees evacuated, any injuries, work performed in the building, what is being done to mitigate the incident, and who the appropriate contacts are and how to reach them).

6. __ On hours, **PR Lead** notifies and confers with **PR Manager** (or backup). Off hours or on weekends, **PR Lead** notifies and confers with **PR Manager** and **PR Duty Officer** when practical. If the **PR Lead** determines that the off-hour incident is likely to generate media inquiries, such notification must be made *immediately*. The **PR Duty Officer** should notify the **Switchboard Operators** (555-1000) and tell them to direct media inquiries to the person serving as **PR Lead**.

7. __ **PR Lead** and **PR Manager** agree to key messages and response to query statement.

8. __ **PR Lead** or **PR Manager** notifies **Corporate PR Manager**.

9. __ **PR Lead** prepares response to query statement, confers with division management, and obtains approval on statement.

10. __ **PR Lead** sends statement via fax to **PR Manager** and to **Corporate PR Manager**.

11. __ **PR Lead** serves as prime contact for media. **PR Manager** and **Corporate PR Manager** serve as backups.

12. __ **PR Lead** fields media inquiries and makes follow-up calls to media if necessary.

Communications Procedure for Handling a Major Crisis

==

Major Crisis:

1. __ **Division Communications** receives notification from the Fire Dispatcher and compiles the basic facts and chronology of the event (possibly using an Incident Information Sheet).

2. __ Division Communications representative becomes the **PR Lead** and informs other communications team members.

3. __ **PR Lead** determines if more information is necessary and if a communicator (**Incident Command Interface**) should be dispatched to incident site to obtain firsthand information. PR Lead also designates another person as **PR Backup**, if necessary.

4. __ **IC Interface** goes to site and obtains details from Incident Commander (type of incident, when and where the incident occurred, chemical involved and potential chemical reactions, emergency response personnel on site, number of employees evacuated, any injuries, work performed in the building, what is being done to mitigate the incident, and who the appropriate contacts are and how to reach them).

5. __ **IC Interface** calls **PR Lead** via cellular phone with details of incident. **IC Interface** should also continue to provide updates to **PR Lead** every 15–30 minutes or as circumstances change.

6. __ On hours, **PR Lead** immediately notifies and confers with **PR Manager** (or backup). Off hours or on weekends, **PR Lead** *immediately* notifies and

confers with *PR Manager* and also notifies the *PR Duty Officer*. The *PR Duty Officer* should notify the *Switchboard Operators* (555-1000) and tell them to direct media inquiries to the person serving as *PR Lead*.

7. ___ *PR Lead* and *PR Manager* agree to key messages and response to query statement.

8. ___ *PR Lead* or *PR Manager* notifies *Corporate PR Manager*.

9. — *PR Lead* prepares response to query statement, confers with division management, and obtains approval on statement.

10. — *PR Lead* sends statement via fax to *PR Manager* and to *Corporate PR Manager.*

11. — *PR Manager* informs *PR Operations Manager* and *PR-VP* (or acting PR chief) to review the incident, determine the need for additional on-site support, and decide whether the PR news bureau should be opened if it is after working hours. *PR-VP* decides at this point if executives need to be notified.

Communications Procedure for Handling a Major Crisis (continued)

12. ___ *PR Lead* or *PR Manager* informs *Internal Communications Manager* who ensures that appropriate internal communications staff will work closely with division communications personnel in collecting data for a timely report to employees.

13. ___ *PR Lead* and *PR Backup* serve as prime contacts for media. *PR Manager* and *Corporate PR Manager* serve as backups.

14. ___ *PR Lead* determines if on-site media center is needed and designates *PR Backup* to set one up.

15. ___ *PR Lead* continues to receive information from *IC Interface* and updates statements accordingly.

16. ___ *PR Lead*, in turn, provides updates to *PR Manager* and *PR Corporate Manager.*

17. ___ *PR Lead*, *PR Manager*, and *PR Operations Manager* confer on whether a press release is needed. If so, *PR Lead* writes the release, clears it with division management and *PR Manager. PR Manager* clears release with *PR Operations Manager*, *PR-VP,* and other senior officials as required.

18. ___ If incident in on-hours, *PR Lead* handles follow-up media and employee inquiries and notes incident in report, as necessary.

19. ___ *PR Manager* and/or *Division PR Lead* develops report analyzing communications aspects of the incident and lessons learned. Report is distributed to *PR Operations Manager* and *PR-VP*, *Division Communications staff*, and *Corporate PR Manager*.

Emergency Operations Center (EOC) Activation

An Emergency Operations Center (EOC) is a centralized location from which emergency response during a very severe crisis is coordinated and directed. A crisis that would force the site EOC to be engaged would be an earthquake or other incident (an act of terrorism) that causes multiple crises at once. Senior emergency preparedness personnel in the Company contend that site EOCs along with the Corporate EOC would not be fully activated for a minimum of two to three hours after the devastating event (i.e., first tremors during an earthquake).

If the site EOC is engaged, all crisis communications would be directed from that point. For adequate communication response, it is recommended that two communicators should be assigned to the center. One communicator would serve as the Communications Manager who is responsible for coordinating external and internal communications, which may include the use of a runner system, in the event all electronic means of communications are out. The other communicator would serve as the Information Officer, responsible for documenting the sequence of events in support of communications and then generating any statements for release either internally or externally.

Each site EOC will be equipped with maps, stationery supplies, white boards, flip charts, viewfoil machines, telephones, and numerous other supplies. It is recommended that communicators make sure the following items are either stored in the EOC or are available nearby:

- Pads and pencils
- Laptop computer
- Portable printer or some other printing device
- Fax machine
- Cellular phone(s)
- Radio(s)
- Division Crisis Communications Plan

The procedure for communications response should be consistent with the procedure for handling a major crisis, the only difference being that all communications would be directed from the EOC itself.

Identification of a Spokesperson

After an initial assessment of an emergency, the Division General Manager (or designee such as an outplant general manager) will identify the appropriate spokesperson for the division.

Appropriate spokespeople for most divisions are as follows:

- Division Vice President/General Manager
- Plant General Manager (for other sites under division jurisdiction)

- Division Health Manager
- Division Environmental Manager
- Division Safety Manager
- Director of Facilities
- Division Communications Manager
- Public Relations Manager
- Corporate Public Relations Manager

All releases of information outside the division and company shall be by or through the coordinated efforts of Division Communications, Group and/or Corporate public relations personnel (as noted in the *Communications Procedure for Handling Minor or Major Crises* on pages 5 through 7).

All releases of information within the Division will be coordinated by Division Communications personnel.

Guidelines for Spokespeople

1. **DO NOT SPECULATE.** Always stick to the facts. A more in-depth investigation is required to determine cause.

2. **Focus on two or three key messages to communicate and repeat them during the interview.** Keep answers short and to the point. TV reporters want "soundbites" of no more than 10 to 15 seconds. Try to bridge to your key messages throughout the interview.

3. **Use a technical expert. There is no substitute for knowledge.** If the questions are outside your area of expertise, find an appropriate technical spokesperson within the company.

4. **Speak in simple, common terms.** Avoid jargon.

5. **Remain calm.** Do not be intimidated into answering questions prematurely. You may tell a reporter that you need to clarify an important matter before you can answer questions.

6. **Do not use negative language.** Do not let reporters put words in your mouth.

7. **Consider human safety first.** When human safety or other serious concerns are involved, deal with those considerations first. You can admit concern without admitting culpability.

8. **Do not answer questions you do not understand.** Ask for clarification. Occasionally, this can be used to buy time to think.

9. **Ignore cameras and microphones.** Face the reporter. Don't look away or up at the sky. During videotaped interviews, it's all right to stop your statement and start over.

10. **Make only "on the record" statements.** There are no "off the record" statements.

11. **Avoid saying, "No comment."** If you don't know an answer, say so, then bridge to your messages.

Format for Briefing Someone Identified as a Spokesperson for Interviews/News Briefings

Executives scheduled to talk to the media should be provided a background briefing in advance of the interview. This policy should be followed *even if* the interview is only to be a brief telephone call.

The briefing should include the following eleven items:

- Date, time, and location of the interview
- Name of the reporter
- Name of the publication, wire service, station, etc.
- Our experience with the reporter or publication—to help the executive understand the degree of caution needed in this interview and to prepare for the specific reporter's approach
- Subjects/issues/questions to be covered as requested by reporter
- Our position or recommended response and the data needed to discuss these subjects
- **Top three to five messages we wish to make in the interview (not necessarily based on the reporter's suggested topics)**
- List of other executives to be interviewed during this visit, including key topics and messages you suggest the other executives cover
- Issues, if any, that the executive(s) should avoid, and recommendations on how to sidestep them
- Background information/statistics that would be useful in preparing for the interview
- Proposed length of interview

If possible, this background material should be conveyed <u>in writing</u> so the executive(s) have a chance to review it carefully. Only under exceptional circumstances should you rely on an oral briefing.

In critical situations, it is also useful to prepare a thorough set of questions and answers to define the organization's positions and to be used in rehearsing the executive.

News Release

During an emergency situation, it may be determined that a news release should be distributed to the media. The purpose of the news release is to convey written information on the incident and to avoid misinterpretation.

<u>Circumstances That May Require a News Release</u>

- An accident, fire, or explosion that results in serious injury, death, or considerable property damage
- A health or environmental incident, or discovery of a health or environmental hazard that may affect employees, the surrounding community, or the environment

- A serious traffic or air accident involving company vehicles, products, and/or personnel

- Sabotage, abduction or extortion, bomb threats, or acts of terrorism involving company personnel, products, or property

- News of an incident that is likely to be known by employees or circulated in the community and create misleading impressions

- News of an event that is unusual enough to cause concern to employees, nearby residents, or community officials

- Consistently misleading news reports

<u>Writing an Initial Statement for Release</u>

Often, reporters will call before all the facts have been gathered. In such an instance, a simple statement acknowledging the situation is useful. The short statement avoids "no comment" and acknowledges that our company recognizes the need to cooperate with media.

Examples:

"Our company is responding to the situation (or name the emergency). We have trained and experienced people on-site working on the situation."

"Our first priority is the safety of our employees and the public. We are gathering information, and as soon as details become available, we will inform the media."

<u>Information Appropriate for Release</u>

During an emergency situation, there will be information that is appropriate to release to employees and to the media. Communications personnel should do the following:

- **Tell what happened:** Give a description of the emergency situation.

- **Tell who is involved:** Report how many employees were evacuated and if any have been taken to the hospital for observation or due to injury. Report when emergency team members and/or the various city or county fire departments and police arrived on the scene (if applicable).

- **Indicate where it occurred**: Give the street address of the scene of the emergency.

- **Identify when it happened**: Give the time the incident began.

<u>Information That Is NOT Appropriate for Release</u>

Obviously, there will be a lot of information that is not appropriate for release until more is known about the nature of the crisis response and the extent of the impact.

- **Do not speculate on why the emergency occurred or what type of hazardous materials are involved**. Likewise, don't make any statement that blames any individual for the accident. (Although the cause of the incident may appear obvious, *it cannot be accurately determined* without an extensive investigation, nor can the blame be placed on an individual without a thorough investigation.)

- **Do not include "off the record" information** because there is no such information.

- **Do not overreact to or exaggerate the situation**. For instance, during a hazardous material spill, a reporter may ask for the "worst-case scenario" of what could happen with the chemicals involved in the accident. It is impossible to determine this until you have specific data regarding the hazardous chemicals involved. Bridge back to facts and messages.

- **Do not minimize the situation**. Never regard an emergency as a minor incident.

- **Do not release the names of injured individuals**, unless Human Resources authorized it following confirmation that the victim(s)' family(ies) have been notified.

- **Do not release dollar estimates concerning the extent of property damage**. Normally, there is no way to accurately determine this until extensive studies have been conducted.

- **Avoid the "no comment" response because it often leads the reporter to speculate**. If you don't know the answer to a reporter's question or if you can't discuss something, explain why in simple terms.

Writing a News Release

By following a few basic principles when writing news releases, our company stands a better chance of having reporters use the information with only minor changes. **Remember to consult the legal department as needed.**

1. **Tell the most important information in your lead paragraph**. Your "story" competes with other news and information, so the most important point should be stated clearly in the first paragraph.

2. **Answer four of the five "Ws"—Who, What, Where, and When**. Explain WHAT the emergency is. Identify WHO is involved in the emergency as well as the material and equipment involved. Tell WHERE and WHEN the emergency occurred. Explain WHAT action we are taking to mitigate or respond to the emergency. Do not explain WHY the event occurred unless complete information is available.

3. **Attribute information to a qualified source**. A news release is useful only if it conveys credible information.

4. **Write remaining information in descending order of importance**. If the media cuts off the bottom of your story, they will cut information that is least important to the public.

5. **Explain technical points in simple language**. A direct quote can add the human element to otherwise technical information and help explain a situation or event in layman's terms. Tell the real story. Avoid using language that is overly bureaucratic.

6. **Be concise**. A good news release is judged by the quality of information it communicates, not by its length. Stop writing when you've said all you need to.

Messages for the News Media During Environmental Crises

Mention of the following points during interviews may help the company communicate its position on environmental issues.

- Our primary concern is for the safety of our employees, the communities in which we operate, and the public.

- We operate a state-of-the-art safety monitoring and control system in our factories and laboratories.

- We are prepared at all times to mitigate a chemical spill or leak.

- We work continuously to reduce our use of toxic chemicals in manufacturing processes and to minimize waste.

- Our standards for "worker hazardous materials safety exposure" meet or exceed standards required by the U.S. Occupational Safety and Health Administration (OSHA).

- Our employees who work directly with hazardous materials receive special training in handling the materials safely. It is a mandatory requirement that employees attend such training.

- The company conducts periodic audits of its hazardous materials and hazardous waste installations, equipment and operating procedures to ensure they comply with environmental regulations and permits during normal and emergency conditions.

- As in the past, the company will continue to work closely with state and federal agencies to meet or exceed environmental regulations, comply with test procedures, and report results to the Environmental Protection Agency (EPA) and the Department of Ecology (DOE).

Audiences During a Crisis

To effectively communicate your message, it's essential to understand who your audience is and how you want your audience to react.

There are two key types of audiences during an emergency.

1. People directly affected by the emergency.
2. People whose attitudes about the company might be influenced by information about the emergency.

These two types of audiences are broken into seven categories. Public Relations' objectives in dealing with each of these audiences are listed below:

- **Employees**—We want employees to know that their safety is the number one priority during an emergency. Employees need information regarding the emergency as soon as possible. This must be accomplished in a manner that assures employees that the company has their best interests at heart and that it can effectively handle emergencies.

- **Community Residents**—We want to quell any unnecessary fears. We want the surrounding community residents to know that we take quick, effective steps to protect the health and welfare of community residents and the environment. This can be best accomplished by responding quickly to community concerns and need for information.

- **Top Management**—This group needs to be kept informed in the event of an emergency as well as to be accessible as a resource if necessary.

- **Government Officials**—Key members of this audience need to be kept apprised of the emergency situation, as determined appropriate by the Government Affairs Department.

- **Customers**—Customers need to know that the company is concerned about crises that impact its operating divisions and that may affect production.

- **News Media**—We want the news media to know that the company is credible, concerned, and effective at dealing with emergencies, and that we understand and meet the unique needs of each type of media.

- **Vendors, Contractors, and Suppliers**—We want these audiences to know that we operate state-of-the-art safety monitoring and control systems in our factories and laboratories and that the company takes quick, effective steps to protect the health and welfare of its employees, vendors, and suppliers.

How People Receive Information During a Crisis

In order to determine the most effective ways of communicating during an emergency, it's important to consider how each key audience potentially can receive information. The following sources of information for each audience must be considered in communications strategy for each emergency:

- **Employees**

 Direct knowledge of the event
 Other employees
 Intercom and phone systems
 Managers
 Electronic mail
 News media reports
 Fire department/police/hospital spokesperson

- **Community Residents**

 Direct knowledge of the event
 Neighbors
 News media reports

- **Top Management**

 Company Security, Communications/PR Manager
 Personal call(s) from concerned employee(s)
 News media reports

- **Government Officials**

 Government Affairs
 News media reports
 Concerned or scared citizen(s)

- **News Media**

 Public Relations representative
 Police and/or fire scanners
 Other news media
 Fire department/police/hospital spokesperson
 Eyewitnesses, including employees
 Bystanders with knowledge or hearsay
 Firsthand view of the situation
 Outside "experts"

- **Vendors, Contractors, and Suppliers**

 Direct knowledge of the event
 Employees and/or management
 News media reports

Tools to Use During a Crisis

The following documents are recommended tools that each communications group can use or adapt to specific requirements. Note that a few of the tools will definitely have to be adapted, such as Site Map(s), Building Facts and Figures, and phone lists for key emergency response contacts.

These tools can prove very useful for documenting information related to incidents and for keeping track of media inquiries:

- Emergency Response Contacts
- Key Division Directors/Managers
- Key Communications/PR Contacts
- Incident Information Sheet
- Telephone Log Sheet
- Initial Release
- Checklist for Establishing a News Conference Center
- Maps of Division Plants
- Building Facts and Figures

Incident Information Sheet

Complete using ink pen

Date: _____ Time: _____ Initial Report _____ Update _____

Describe the incident (i.e., hazardous material spill, equipment malfunction, serious injury, bomb threat, fire, etc.):

Indicate when the incident occurred and when crisis personnel first responded:

Describe which crisis groups are responding:

Indicate where the incident occurred (building number, column number, east or west side of building, etc.):

Describe the work performed in the building(s) where incident occurred (i.e., machining, office functions, mix of factory and office functions):

Estimate the number of employees evacuated:

Estimate the number of employees injured, nature of their injuries (to clarify misleading reports), and where they are being examined/treated (i.e., on-site medical, local hospital):

Describe what is being done to mitigate the emergency:

Telephone Log Sheet

Priority: _____ Date: _____ Time: _____

Call Received From:

 Name _____

 Organization _____

 Location _____

Message: _____

Call back by: _____

Date:_____ Time:_____

Notes: _____

Example of Initial Statement for Release

At approximately _____ (time) today _____ (date), a _____
(fire, explosion, etc.) occurred on the _____ site of the _____
Division.

Crisis Response personnel are now responding as well as _____ (other support
response groups or local municipalities). Our company's response groups include (list
appropriate groups such as fire and security officers, medical doctors and nurses, safety
personnel, industrial hygienists, environmental engineers, etc.).

Our major concerns are for the safety of our employees and the public and to minimize
environmental impact.

We are now involved in determining what has happened and what is being done to
mitigate the situation. As more details become available, we will pass them on to the
media.

Checklist for Establishing a News Conference Center

In a major emergency, it may be necessary to establish a news conference center. This
will be where the company can conduct briefings or news conferences, grant interviews,
and issue official statements.

Because time is of the essence during a crisis, communications teams should designate
certain locations as potential news conference centers and be prepared to carry out the
checklist before an incident occurs.

Preliminaries

1. __ Check for the best time with company spokesperson.

2. __ Notify media of time and location.

3. __ Compile list of names of reporters and editors who indicate they will attend.

4. __ Compile background information of interest to reporters.

5. __ Invite outside officials as appropriate.

6. __ Assign someone to handle the physical arrangements for the news conference.

 __ Video services to record event?

 __ Junction box for TV and radio mikes?

 __ Chairs, tables, podiums as required?

7. __ Brief staff on the subject, speaker(s), and schedule of events.

8. __ Prepare opening statement and review with lead speaker.

9. __ Review anticipated questions and answers with the speaker.

10. __ Check all sound equipment and tape recorders prior to the conference.

11. __ Place log sheet in conference room to obtain names and affiliations of
 attendees.

12. __ Place all news information and handout materials in conference room.

___ New releases

___ Background information, such as fact sheets, maps, statistics, histories, and biographical information

___ Copy of opening statement and other briefing materials

13. ___ Escort the media to the conference room.

14. ___ Use sign-in sheet.

15. ___ Distribute background materials.

16. ___ Have assigned staff member open the conference and establish the ground rules.

17. ___ Monitor questions and answers closely. Make any necessary clarifications before the end of the event.

Afterward/Follow-up

18. ___ Handle requests for follow-up information.

19. ___ Monitor coverage received; contact any news organization that has an error in its report.

20. ___ At an appropriate time, when the crisis atmosphere has cleared, contact reporters who attended and ask them what went well in terms of our handling the event and what could have been improved.

Crisis Contacts

	Office	Pager/Cellular	Fax	Home
Key Division Directors				
Jennifer Jones (South)	555-0001	C:555-4892	555-8101	555-9801
Kourtney Johnson (North)	555-0121	C:555-4241	555-8294	555-9123
Rebecca Arnold (East)	555-2127	C:555-4101	555-8711	555-9777
Jeremy Kahlil (West)	555-3122	C:555-4801	555-8222	555-9554
Key Division Manager				
Mary Bland (South)	555-0092	C:555-1121	555-8111	555-9682
John Jackson (South)	555-0013	C:555-6101	555-8221	555-9319
Sarah Yerima (North)	555-1764	N/A	555-8811	555-9276
Jonathan Kyle (East)	555-2809	N/A	555-8611	555-9211
Allison Millet (East)	555-2684	N/A	555-8314	555-9013
Nicholas Michael (West)	555-3093	N/A	555-8781	555-9901
Telephone Operators				
Mary Jackson (Supervisor)	555-2999	N/A	555-8722	555-3994
Fire Dispatch				
Adam Yerima	555-8894	C:555-8676	555-9467	555-9276
Duane Troy	555-9075	C:555-0328	555-5541	555-0101
Safety Manager				
Ron Nelson	555-1112	C:555-3434	555-6875	555-0841
Julius Jones, Jr.	555-3756	C:555-4441	555-1954	555-2395
Medical				
Ethan Floyd	555-7864	C:555-3321	555-7764	555-1346
Allyson Bernardino	555-9090	C:555-8341	555-5603	555-7651
Demetria Rudy	555-5642	C:555-2390	555-6678	555-6431
Public Relations				
Ann Davis	555-7490	C:555-4431	555-5505	555-6490
Jerry Brown	555-7456	C:555-2210	555-9898	555-7069
Corporate Public Relations				
Gina Arnold	555-8754	C:555-7890	555-2479	555-0956
	Office	*Pager/Cellular*	*Fax*	*Home*
SOUTH				
Regina Arnold	555-8754	C:555-7890	555-2479	555-0956
Blair Liggins	555-0293	C:555-7902	555-2478	555-9154
NORTH				
Kourtney Johnson	555-0121	C:555-4241	555-8294	555-9123

Myrtle Jenkins	555-2123	C:555-4545	555-9045	555-8456
EAST				
Beleria Fulks	555-2345	C:555-7690	555-3147	555-9067
Anthony Floyd	555-0789	C:555-4680	555-4896	555-3558
WEST				
Anne Burford	555-1212	C:555-0097	555-7847	555-0321
O.M. Thornton	555-9557	C:555-4502	555-5575	555-3498
Katie Marsh (Backup)	555-9057	N/A	555-0092	555-2664

Crisis Communications Plan for a Nonprofit Organization: Big Brothers/Big Sisters of America

CRISIS COMMUNICATIONS OUTLINE

I. THE CRISIS COMMUNICATIONS SYSTEM

 A. Objectives
- Contain the Crisis Events
- Reduce Risk to Agency
- Respond to Media and Community

 B. Select a Crisis Team
- Board/Public Relations Committee
- Top Management Representative
- Legal Representative
- Medical Experts
- Personnel/Human Resources
- Other

 C. Designate a Spokesperson
- Believable
- Knowledgeable
- Articulate
- Accessible

 D. Prepare a Fact Sheet
- Big Brothers/Big Sisters History
- Information on Programs and Services

 E. Prepare a Contact List
- Board President
- Attorney
- Insurance Agent
- Internal Staff and Board
- Field Managers
- BB/BSA Staff
- Government Authorities
- News Media
- Community Leaders and Supporters

 F. Training Re: Crisis Intervention
- Board
- New Board Orientation Training
- Staff

 G. Networking
- Court System
- Police
- Media
- Social Service System
- Government and CSA Protective Services
- Community Leaders (Recognition and Involvement in Agency)

 H. Select a News Site
- Accessible
- Availability of Electrical Outlets
- Telephones

 I. Get Management Approval
- Solicit Participation
- Obtain Endorsement of Plan

II. WHEN YOU KNOW IN ADVANCE

 A. Evaluate the Situation
- Analyze Options
- Anticipate Reactions
- Develop Strategy

 B. Develop the Strategy
- Include Top Management
- Inform Employees in Advance
- Notify Government Officials
- Contact the Media

III. WHEN THE CRISIS HAPPENS

 A. Assess the Situation
- Confirm the Facts
- Investigate Rumors
- Identify and Locate Witnesses
- Analyze Expert Information

 B. Mobilize
- Take Security Measures
- Adapt Crisis and Media Plans to Actual Events
- Assign Responsibilities

 C. Prepare a Statement
- Release Confirmed Facts
- Provide Background Information
- Communicate <u>Positive</u> Actions and Concerns

 D. Notify Contact List
- BB/BSA Personnel
 + Field Manager
 + Director of Marketing
 + Communications
- Attorney
- Insurance Agent (if applicable)
- Neighboring Agencies
- Government Officials
- News Media
- Community Leaders

 E. Respond to Media/Coordinate Coverage
- Alert Receptionist and All Staff
- Refer all Calls to Designated Spokesperson
- Make Press Site Available

 F. Inform Volunteers, Parents
- Changes in Operation or Programs
- Duration of Disruption
- Extent of Problem

IV. CRISIS FOLLOW-UP

 A. Follow-up Plan
- Analyze Implications/Responsibilities
 + Legal
 + Financial
- Resolve Loose Ends
- Prevent Repercussions

 + Hostile Reactions
 + Negative Actions
 • Anticipate Long-Term Effects
B. Evaluate the System
 • Monitor Responses
 • Assess and Measure Results
 • Refine System

BACKGROUND STATEMENT

Big Brothers/Big Sisters of (Agency) is affiliated with Big Brothers/Big Sisters of America, and it holds the highest affiliation ranking, that of being a Full Member Agency. The Agency's screening and service delivery policies conform to those required by Big Brothers/Big Sisters of America.

This Agency is concerned with the well-being and safety of all children, and therefore, its volunteer selection and match supervision procedures are designed to reflect that concern.

Our screening procedures require an applicant to attend an orientation session conducted by a professional staff member. Each volunteer applicant must complete an application form and provide three references. A criminal history check is conducted, and then each applicant undergoes an in-depth screening interview with a social worker. An additional interview is scheduled in the applicant's home and conducted before any match takes place. The professional staff reviews each case to determine if any applicant would be suitable as a Big Brother or Big Sister. Applicants not meeting the Agency's criteria are not accepted as volunteers in the program.

In addition to having a professional staff, the Agency's service delivery is also evaluated by the Board of Directors. This agency has served thousands of youngsters since 19(XX), and volunteers have helped these youngsters in positive growth and development.

(If EMPOWER or other child abuse prevention and education program is in place at your agency, include a sentence to that effect here.)

Our philosophy is to cooperate with agencies and authorities in their efforts to protect the children of our community. We work closely with the parents and children we serve to assure that they find the volunteer/child relationship to be enjoyable and beneficial to the child.

SAMPLE CRISIS MANAGEMENT PLAN

TABLE OF CONTENTS

RESPONSE TO POLICE INQUIRIES

INJURY OR DEATH OF CHILD OR VOLUNTEER

MISUSE OF AGENCY FUNDS

IMPROPRIETY IN A RELATIONSHIP

DISCRIMINATION/VIOLATION OF CIVIL RIGHTS

SUSPENSION OF FUNDING

SAMPLE CRISIS MANAGEMENT PLAN:
COMMUNICATION CHAIN

In the event of a crisis, this is the communications route to follow:

1. Contact Executive Director

2. Contact family in person (if applicable)

3. Executive Director contacts President of board

4. Executive Director contacts agency spokesperson

5. Executive Director contacts Field Manager for Big Brothers/Big Sisters of America

6. President of board contacts Executive Committee

7. Executive Committee members contact remaining board members

8. Executive Director contacts local and state authorities as prescribed by law

9. Executive Director and President of board deliberate and determine appropriate action

10. Executive Director contacts agency staff

11. Letters sent to parents and volunteers

12. Neighboring agencies notified

13. Agency spokesperson contacts media in certain crisis situations

14. All media inquiries routed to agency spokesperson

15. Agency spokesperson contacts Director of Marketing + Communications for Big Brothers/Big Sisters of America if members of media are extensive

SAMPLE CRISIS MANAGEMENT PLAN:
IMPLEMENTATION PROCEDURES

1. Adoption of Crisis Management Plan

2. Selection of Media Spokesperson

 A. Primary: Director of Public Relations

 B. First Alternate: Executive Director of Agency

 C. Second Alternate: President of Board of Agency

3. Staff Orientation

4. Board Orientation

5. Volunteer Orientation

6. Media Orientation

7. Annual Review

SAMPLE CRISIS MANAGEMENT PLAN:
CHILD SEXUAL ABUSE

PROGRAM OBJECTIVES IN THE EVENT OF ALLEGED SEXUAL ABUSE

1. Protect Little Brothers and Little Sisters from abuse and molestation

2. Comply fully with the law

STEPS TO BE TAKEN IN THE EVENT OF ALLEGED SEXUAL ABUSE BY VOLUNTEER

1. Executive Director (or in her/his absence the designated staff person of authority) collects all the facts available from the reporting individual (mother, child, caseworker) or agency (police department, social services department). The staff shall abide by the direction of the Executive Director, or Director's designee, in all actions regarding possible, potential, or actual child abuse cases.

2. As a general rule, the Executive Director notifies the Big Brother or Big Sister involved by telephone or in person, as soon as practical, that a report has been made

to the agency that he or she is suspected of child abuse. This verbal report will be immediately followed by a telegram. However, the Executive Director, in consultation with the caseworker and informed Board members, may, in appropriate circumstances, decide not to notify the Big Brother or Big Sister of the report until the authorities have had a reasonable opportunity to investigate the report. In the making of such a decision to do so, the following factors shall be considered:

(a) The likelihood of further abuse of the child;

(b) The likelihood of threats or actual harm to the child, the child's parent/guardian, or others;

(c) The likelihood of additional contact with the child or the child's parent/guardian pending the investigation;

(d) The likelihood of attempts to dissuade the child or others from cooperating with the investigating authorities;

(e) The likelihood of flight by the Big Brother, Big Sister or others involved;

(f) The likelihood that the police investigation will be materially hindered.

3. Executive Director, or designee, notifies the child's family in person, the Board President, agency spokesperson and the remainder of the communications chain.

4. Executive Director, or designee, and the child's caseworker contact the parent/guardian of the child in a personal visit to inquire about the child's condition, verify facts, express concern, extend support, and advise the parent and child that the match has been suspended during the investigation and neither the parent nor the child is to have any contact with the volunteer.

5. Executive Director, or designee, notifies the agency's attorney.

6. Caseworker reports the incident to the appropriate authorities, as required by federal, state, and local laws.

7. At this point, the Board President and Executive Director will determine the appropriateness of notifying all Board members of the alleged incident.

8. If any media or police authority contacts the agency concerning the alleged incident, they must be referred to the agency spokesperson, or the appropriate alternate in the spokesperson's absence. Only the agency spokesperson is authorized to make public statements. If any other staff or board members are contacted by the media or police, they are to answer no questions and immediately refer all calls to the spokesperson.

9. In the event that an attorney representing the child or the volunteer contacts the agency, no questions are to be answered and the call must be immediately referred to the Executive Director, or designee, who will refer these calls to the agency's attorney.

10. Executive Director will verbally report incident to the Big Brothers/Big Sisters of America Field Manager. Written reports will follow as needed and requested.

11. Executive Director, or designee, will call the insurance agent concerning the allegation. The Executive Director will follow up with a written notice within 24 hours.

12. Executive Director, Program Director, Caseworker, and Board President all thoroughly document their involvement in handling of the incident. The Executive Director will take possession of the Big Brother and Little Brother or Big Sister and Little Sister files. The files will include, but will not be limited to the following:

<u>Big Brother or Big Sister:</u> (a) Application
 (b) Reference letters
 (c) Interview write up
 (d) Supervision contact notes
 (e) Police check results
 (f) Federal Bureau of Investigation check results
 (g) Proof of automobile insurance
 (h) Applicant's driving records
 (i) Documentation of reasons for suspension of match

<u>Little Brother or Little Sister:</u> (a) Phone inquiry
 (b) Application
 (c) Information release form
 (d) Interview write up
 (e) Supervision contact notes
 (f) Documentation of reasons for suspension of match

13. As soon as practical, and with regard to every case of alleged child abuse, the Executive Director or designee shall give the Executive Committee of the Board a complete oral report of the case, with such analysis and recommendations for future policy as may be appropriate in light of the experience. A written report shall be prepared, with direction of legal counsel, as requested by the Executive Committee.

14. The agency shall assist the parent/guardian and Little Brother or Little Sister with referrals to appropriate professional counselors, and, if the agency determines it to be necessary, will cover reasonable costs for this independent counseling. The agency will not volunteer information concerning insurance coverage, but if asked by the parent/guardian, will respond that there <u>may</u> be insurance coverage.

STANDARD RESPONSE TO POLICE INQUIRIES CONCERNING ALLEGED INCIDENTS

"We are very concerned with the welfare of this child, as we are with all our children, and we are anxious to fully cooperate with the investigation. Because of the privileged nature of our records, it is necessary for us to request a subpoena in order to release our files."

If asked, the agency's spokesperson can verify that a particular volunteer and/or child [is] or were members of the organization and the dates of their membership. The addresses and phone numbers will also be given to the police. Upon request, the spokesperson will inform the police of the names, addresses and phone numbers of all Little Brothers or Little Sisters that the Big Brother or Big Sister in question has been matched with.

[**Editor's note**: Police will often seek agency cooperation in learning the identity of other volunteers brought into the agency by the suspect, as well as other Littles the suspect may have been matched with in the past. Local counsel should be sought for advice, but it is recommended that the agency cooperate, but only through the legal compulsory process of subpoena to better protect the agency. When the police requests the agency cooperation in not communicating the allegation to the volunteer or in not immediately suspending the match (so as to not interfere with their pending investigation), such a request should be granted. However, this request should be in writing to protect the agency from its responsibility to immediately notify the parties and to suspend the match pending investigation.]

STEPS TO BE TAKEN IN THE EVENT OF AN INJURY OR THE DEATH OF A LITTLE BROTHER/SISTER OR BIG BROTHER/SISTER WHILE INVOLVED IN AN AGENCY ACTIVITY

1. Any staff member that becomes aware of the incident is to report it immediately to the Executive Director and the Program Director. If the incident occurs at night or on the weekend, the above mentioned staff members are to be contacted at their homes.

2. The Executive Director, or the Program Director as designee, will collect all additional information from police, hospitals, family members and anyone else involved.

3. The Executive Director will report the incident to the President of the Board, or to the Vice-President in the President's absence.

4. If Executive Director and Board President deem it appropriate and necessary, Executive Director will contact the agency's legal counsel.

5. In the case of a minor injury, if the family of the victim has not been notified of the incident, the Executive Director will attempt to make this contact. In the event of serious injury or death, the agency will not give initial notification to the family; rather, that will be the task of the police authorities.

6. The Executive Director will contact the agency's insurance agent within a reasonable period of time, and will follow up in writing within 24 hours. The Executive Director, or designee, will file all necessary forms.

7. The agency will cooperate to the fullest extent with all police and medical personnel. The Executive Director, or Board President in the Director's absence, will be the only authorized spokesperson to these outside agencies.

8. In the event that the agency is contacted by the media, all questions are to be referred to the agency spokesperson.

9. The Executive Director and all agency representatives involved will thoroughly document for the case files, all their actions related to the incident.

10. The Executive Director, or designee, will follow up with the victim's family in order to offer support. Whatever resources the agency has available, or whatever community resources are available—as covered by the agency's insurance policy—will be offered to the family.

STEPS TO BE TAKEN IN THE EVENT OF MISUSE OF AGENCY FUNDS BY STAFF OR BOARD MEMBERS

1. If the alleged misuse of funds involves a staff member other than the Director or if it involves a board member, the incident must be immediately reported to the Executive Director, who will then report it to the Board President. In the absence of the Executive Director, the incident is to be reported directly to the Board President. If the alleged misuse involves the Executive Director, the incident must be reported immediately to the Board President or Vice-President in the President's absence.

2. The Executive Director will investigate the incident to the fullest extent possible and will report the findings at a special session of the Executive Committee. If the incident involves the Executive Director, it will be investigated by the Board President or designee.

3. The Executive Committee, and the Executive Director when appropriate, will determine the appropriate course of action, which may include, but not be limited to:
 (a) Suspension of employee, with pay, pending further investigation; suspension of board member.
 (b) Suspension of employee, without pay, pending further investigation.

 (c) Immediate dismissal of employee or termination of board member.

 (d) Informal agreement with employee or board member for restitution.

 (e) Formal filing of criminal charges against employee or board member.

4. The Executive Director or Board President will utilize the services of the agency attorney; the agency bookkeeper; the agency auditor; or the agency's insurance agent, as needed.

5. In the event that the agency is contacted by the police, all questions are to be referred to the person of highest authority not involved in the incident, i.e. Executive Director, Board President, Board Vice-President. No other staff member or board member is authorized to answer any questions.

6. In the event that the agency is contacted by the media, all questions are to be referred to the agency spokesperson. The agency spokesperson is the only person authorized to speak with the media.

STEPS TO BE TAKEN IN THE EVENT OF IMPROPRIETY IN THE RELATIONSHIP OF A VOLUNTEER, AGENCY STAFF OR BOARD MEMBER WITH THE PARENT OF A LITTLE BROTHER OR LITTLE SISTER

1. The alleged impropriety must be reported immediately to the Executive Director. If the director is involved in the incident or unavailable, the incident should be reported directly to the Board President.

2. The Executive Director will investigate the incident to the fullest extent possible and report the finding at a special session of the Executive Committee. If the incident involves the Executive Director, the Board President, or designee, will investigate.

3. The Executive Committee, and the Executive Director when appropriate, will determine the course of action, which may include, but not be limited to:
 (a) Suspension of employee, with or without pay, pending further investigation; suspension of board member or volunteer.

 (b) Immediate termination of employee without pay.

4. Agency's attorney and/or insurance agent will be contacted as needed.

5. Executive Director, or designee, will follow up with the parent of the Little Brother or Little Sister to give whatever agency support may be appropriate.

6. The Board President and Executive Director will determine the appropriateness of notifying all board members of the alleged incident.

7. In the event that the agency is contacted by the police, all questions are to be referred to the person of highest authority not involved in the incident, i.e. Executive Director, Board President, Board Vice-President. No other staff member or board member is authorized to answer any questions.

8. In the event that the agency is contacted by the media, all questions are to be referred to the agency spokesperson. The agency spokesperson is the only person authorized to speak with the media.

9. In the event that an attorney representing the parent of the Little Brother or Little Sister contacts the agency, no questions are to be answered and the call must be immediately referred to the Executive Director, or Board President. The Executive Director or Board President will then refer these calls to the agency's attorney.

10. The Executive Director and Board President will thoroughly document their involvement in the handling of the incident.

STEPS TO BE TAKEN IN THE EVENT OF CHARGES OF RACIAL OR SEXUAL DISCRIMINATION OR VIOLATION OF CIVIL RIGHTS BY POTENTIAL VOLUNTEERS, OR THOSE WHO HAVE APPLIED FOR, OR BEEN FIRED FROM AGENCY STAFF POSITIONS

1. Executive Director, or the Board President in the Director's absence, collects all the facts available from the reporting party.

2. Executive Director or Board President discusses the charges with the agency's attorney.

3. Board President determines appropriateness of calling a special session of the Executive Committee.

4. Executive Director discusses the situation with their Big Brothers/Big Sisters of America Field Manager.

5. In the event that the agency is contacted by the police, or an attorney for the plaintiff, all calls must be referred to the Executive Director, or Board President in the Director's absence.

6. In the event that the agency is contacted by the media, all questions are to be referred to the agency spokesperson. The agency spokesperson is the only person authorized to speak with the media.

7. The Board President will determine the appropriateness of immediately notifying all board members of the charges.

8. All agency personnel and board members involved thoroughly document their handling of the events.

STEPS TO BE TAKEN IN THE EVENT OF CHASTISEMENT OR SUSPENSION OF FUNDING BY UNITED WAY OR OTHER FUNDING SOURCES

1. The Executive Director immediately makes a verbal report to the Board President and sends a copy of any correspondence from the funding source.

2. The Board President determines the appropriateness of calling a special session of the Executive Committee.

3. The Executive Director, Board President, and—when applicable—the Executive Committee determine the course of action, which may include, but not be limited to:

 (a) The Executive Director and Board President co-author a letter to the funding source explaining the agency's position.

 (b) The Executive Director and Board President arrange a meeting with key people from the funding source.

 (c) The Executive Director prepares all materials that may be necessary for such a meeting.

4. The Board President determines the need to immediately notify all board members of the incident.

5. In the event that the agency is contacted by the media, all questions are to be referred to the agency spokesperson. The agency spokesperson is the only person authorized to speak with the media.

SAMPLE MEDIA STATEMENT

Allegation of Child Abuse

We are aware of the recent allegations against a former Big Brother in our Big Brothers/Big Sisters program. We are very concerned about anything that might harm any of our children and we are offering our full support to the family. This agency's primary concern is for the welfare of its children. Our agency is an affiliate of Big Brothers/Big Sisters of America, which sets strict standards for volunteer screening. Our agency is cooperating with the legal authorities to resolve the questions raised by these allegations. Since this is a very sensitive matter, I know that you will understand that I am not free to comment any further at this time.

Volunteer no further information. If requested, only this information can by given:

1. Verification that a particular BB volunteer and/or child is associated with your agency.

2. Historical background statement of BB/BS.

3. Confirmation that there is a screening process and what the screening process entails.

Agency Being Sued

We have been asked to comment on the recent suit brought against our agency. Because of the legal process currently underway, we have been advised not to comment on this pending litigation. We do wish to state, however, that this agency's primary concern is for the welfare of its children. We take great care to provide a safe and responsible service to our community.

Criminal Allegation Against Agency Volunteer/Staff

We are aware of the recent allegations against (a current/former volunteer/board/staff member) in our Big Brothers/Big Sisters program. We have been advised that information regarding this allegation is confidential at this time and we are not permitted to discuss the case. However, we do wish to state that this agency's primary concern is for the welfare of its children and we are cooperating with the legal authorities to resolve the questions raised by these allegations.

SAMPLE STATEMENT FOR NEIGHBORING AGENCIES

We have been asked to comment on the recent allegations in a neighboring community. Let me just say that our agency's primary concern is to provide a safe and responsible service to the children of our community. We take great care to screen all individuals who work with the children in our program. Our agency is an affiliate of Big Brothers/Big Sisters of America, which sets standards for volunteer screening. We are not, however, in a position to comment concerning matters under investigation in another jurisdiction.

SAMPLE LETTERS TO VOLUNTEERS/PARENTS/BOARD MEMBERS

Letter to Volunteers

Dear Volunteers,

You may have heard allegations made concerning a Big Brother who was previously matched in our program. Since you are a volunteer in our program, I feel it is important to communicate to you that we are very concerned and saddened by this charge.

The staff is offering its full support to this child and the family. Additionally, our agency is cooperating fully with the proper authorities in their investigation of these allegations. Because our case files are confidential, we are not able to discuss details of the case.

However, we want you to know that our main concern is to provide responsible and safe services for the children we serve. Nationwide, Big Brothers/Big Sisters is in the forefront of using screening methods with volunteers. As you know, this agency has an in-depth screening process. We believe we do as much as we can to protect the integrity of the Big Brothers/Big Sisters program and to maintain high standards of service. More than (XXX) children were successfully matched with Big Brothers and Big Sisters by the agency in the past year.

Since this is a sensitive legal matter, I am not at liberty to say any more at this time. However, please don't hesitate to call me if you have any questions or if I can be of assistance.

Be assured of our continued gratitude and support of you and the child you are matched with through our program.

Sincerely,

(Executive Director of agency)

(This letter can be adjusted for any crisis. The important thing to remember is to be honest, sincere, and supportive.)

Letter to Parents

Dear Parents,

You may have heard allegations made concerning a Big Brother who was previously matched in our program. Since your child is involved in our program, I feel it is important to communicate to you that we are very concerned and saddened by this charge.

The staff is offering its full support to this child and the family. Additionally, our agency is cooperating fully with the proper authorities in their investigation of these allegations. Because our case files are confidential, we are not able to discuss details of the case.

However, we want you to know that our main concern at Big Brothers/Big Sisters is to provide responsible and safe services for the children we serve. The children are our clients and we do everything we can to act in their best interest.

Nationwide, Big Brothers/Big Sisters is in the forefront of using screening methods to prevent entry into the program of individuals who may wish to harm children. There is an in-depth screening process that potential volunteers must go through prior to matching. The process consists of character references, an in-depth interview to gather information about personal history, a home assessment and police check. This agency also has in place EMPOWER, the child abuse prevention and education training program developed nationally to provide yet another deterrent, and a way for the children in our program to know how to handle a potentially harmful situation (if applicable). We believe our agency maintains high standards. More than (XXX) children were successfully matched with Big Brothers and Big Sisters by this agency in the past year alone.

Since this is a sensitive legal matter, I am not at liberty to say any more at this time. However, please don't hesitate to call me if you have any questions or if I can be of assistance.

Be assured of our continued gratitude and support of you and your child.

Sincerely,

(Executive Director of agency)

(This letter can be adjusted for any crisis. The important thing to remember is to be honest, sincere, and supportive.)

Letter to Board Members

Dear Board Member:

You may have heard of the recent allegation of child molestation concerning a Big Brother. As a member of the governing body, I want to assure you of our support of the family and of our full cooperation with the proper law enforcement officials. Enclosed are copies of letters sent to all volunteers and families.

There is very little more I can tell you at this time. If you have any questions or concerns that you wish to share, or if you are contacted by anyone regarding this sensitive matter, please give me a call. I may be reached at the following numbers: (phone numbers).

Sincerely,

President, Board of Directors

(This letter can be adjusted for any crisis. The important thing to remember is to be honest, sincere, and supportive.)

LEGAL TERMS: DEFINITIONS AND PROCESSES

ARRAIGNMENT—The first step in a criminal action after a person has been formally charged with a crime. The defendant is brought before a judge or magistrate and informed of the nature of the charges, his/her constitutional rights, and asked to plead either guilty or not guilty to the charges.

ARREST—The seizing of a person by the police or other law enforcement official in the belief that he/she committed a crime. A person is under arrest whenever not free to leave, and at that time must be given Miranda or constitutional rights.

ARREST RECORD—A listing of all the times a person has been picked up by the police because the police believe that he or she had violated a law. Such records are not generally available to the media or to the public, but are limited to law enforcement agencies. Also known as "rap" sheets.

ASSAULT—An attempt to unlawfully cause bodily injury to another, sometimes combined with battery to actually include an unlawful or offensive touching.

BLANK SUBPOENA—The form which is filled out by the party seeking to compel the recipient of the subpoena to either testify or produce documents. It comes in both subpoena ad testificatum and subpoena duces tecum forms, and it can be obtained from the office of the clerk of the court of whichever court the matter is to be brought before.

CIVIL SUIT—The bringing of a claim, usually for monetary damages, to try to right a wrong which has been done to a person or to settle a dispute which cannot be otherwise resolved. The end result is usually an order for someone to do or stop doing something, or to pay money to the person who brought the suit.

CONTRIBUTING TO THE DELINQUENCY OF A MINOR—Making available to a minor that which the law states is illegal for the minor to possess is contributing to the delinquency of a minor. This includes providing a minor with alcohol, drugs, and automobile and keys (if unlicensed), and in some states, cigarettes and other legal tobaccos; also, seducing a child or statutory rape.

CONVICTION—The finding by a judge or jury that the defendant is guilty of the crime or crimes with which he/she was accused.

CONVICTION RECORD—A listing of all the times a person has been convicted of committing a crime. Such records are generally available to the media and the public.

COURT ORDERED SUBPOENA—All subpoenas are issued by the court, even though the party seeking the particular testimony or documents fills them out and often has them served. However, the court may determine that a particular witness is needed in order to fully adjudicate the matter before it, and will order a court subpoena. Also used where attempts by the individual party to serve the witness have failed.

CRIMINAL SUIT—The bringing of a charge against a person who has allegedly violated one of the criminal laws of the state. The person who is the victim is the complaining witness, and the prosecuting attorney represents the state as the body which has been harmed. The person alleged to have committed the criminal act is called the defendant.

DEFENDANT—In a criminal suit, the person accused of having committed a violation of the criminal laws. In a civil suit, the person accused of having violated a promise or agreement or having done something to harm the plaintiff.

DEPOSITION—A sworn statement by a witness in either a civil or criminal suit concerning the testimony he/she will give at trial. It is often used to discover the facts of a case, or to preserve the testimony of a person who will not be available to testify at trial.

FELONY—A criminal offense defined by society to be serious, the range of punishment going from 1 year and 1 day to life or death, and/or a fine, depending on the crime, circumstances and the state's laws.

GRAND JURY—A group of 12 people selected from the surrounding community or county to sit for varying periods (average is 6 months to 1 year) and listen to the prosecutor's presentation of alleged criminal events which have occurred in the area. If the 12 people believe sufficient evidence exists to prosecute a case, an indictment is handed down. If the evidence is found to be insufficient, a "No True Bill" is issued and the case is dropped.

GROSS SEXUAL IMPOSITION—The forcing of someone to perform a sexual act while the person who is exerting the force is unclothed—usually kissing or touching, without rising to rape or sodomy.

INDICTMENT—One method of filing formal charges against a person. It is handed down by a grand jury, which has heard only the prosecutor's evidence. It simply means that the grand jury believes that there is enough evidence against the accused to merit a trial. The indictment states the time and date and place of the alleged violation of the law, and the statute that the person is alleged to have violated.

INTERROGATIONS—The questioning of witnesses or suspects concerning the facts of an incident. This can occur anywhere, but if the person is not free to leave, he/she is under arrest and must be given Miranda warnings before interrogation.

INVOLUNTARY SEXUAL BATTERY—The offense of sexual touching of another when the person who is performing the touching believes the person wants to be sexually touched, but the person really does not.

LEWD AND LASCIVIOUS ACTS—Actions which are intended to sexually excite both the actor and the recipient of the act, such as flashing, oral sex, and sexual stimulation of the actor's or another's sexual organs. Usually used in the context where one of the two (or more) participants have not voluntarily engaged in the activity, either because he/she is too young or otherwise unaware of the nature of the activities in which he/she is a participant.

LEWD ASSAULT—Attempt to cause physical harm by means of a sexual act. Usually an attempt to touch a male's or female's sexual organs, or, less frequently, attempted rape or sodomy. There need be no actual contact for an assault to have occurred—only the intent and attempt.

MIRANDA WARNINGS—Warnings to be given every time a person is under arrest; they include the right to remain silent, the fact that anything said can and will be used against them in a court of law, the right to have an attorney present, and the right to have an attorney appointed if he/she can't afford one.

MISDEMEANOR—An offense defined by society to be criminal, but not nearly as serious as a felony, punishable by from 1 day to 1 year in jail, or a fine.

MOLESTATION—The offense of touching a child's sexual organs, either through clothing or without. Most courts recognize this as always being non-consensual, especially with young children.

MOTION TO QUASH A SUBPOENA—Can be brought on behalf of the rights of the recipient of either a subpoena ad testificatum or a subpoena duces tecum; usually used with a subpoena duces tecum, where the individual or organization served with the subpoena believes that constitutional privacy rights and other rights will be violated if they are required to provide the requested documents. This is the only legal way to challenge and possibly avoid having to comply with a subpoena.

"NO TRUE BILL"—The decision returned by the grand jury when it believes the prosecuting attorney does not have sufficient evidence to prosecute a case.

ORDER FOR CLOSURE/SEAL OF RECORDS—An order by a court sealing the court file of a person so that no one can access the information contained in the court file. Often done in child abuse cases to keep the child's testimony secret, and to protect the child's identity.

PLAINTIFF—The person in a civil suit who claims he/she had been wronged either by the action or inaction of the defendant; in a criminal suit, the state is the plaintiff in the case.

PROFESSIONAL NEGLIGENCE—A wrongful action or inaction of an attorney, doctor or other professional person which thereby results in a harm or damage to the person he/she was supposed to be helping. Also called malpractice.

PROSECUTOR—The person who represents the state and all victims of crimes. Also known as the district attorney, state's attorney, or circuit attorney.

RAPE—The forcible action of sexual intercourse upon a female without her consent. In many states, it can only be performed by a male against a female to whom he is not married, although some states are now recognizing rape within a marital relationship. Rape of one male by another is called sodomy.

SEXUAL BATTERY—The offense of sexual touching of another person without his/her consent.

SEXUAL IMPOSITION—The forcing of someone to perform a sexual act, usually kissing or touching of the sexual organs, without his/her consent. This is usually done while the person being touched is fully clothed.

SEXUAL MISCONDUCT—This is similar to sexual imposition, and it is often used to replace the charge of statutory rape.

SODOMY—The performance of a sexual act termed "unnatural" upon another, or the requiring of another to perform the sexual act. This includes cunnilingus, fellatio, and anal sexual intercourse, as well as bestiality. This does not require force—it can be consensual.

STATUTORY RAPE—The act of sexual intercourse with a female who is under the statutory age for consent. In almost all states, only a female can be statutorily raped. Consent is immaterial; if the female is less than the required age, the man is guilty of statutory rape.

SUBPOENA—An official court document summoning the recipient to appear at a particular time and place to give testimony in person; it can be either for a hearing, a deposition, a trial, or other legal proceeding. Also called a subpoena ad testificatum. Failure to appear as ordered can result in the person so summoned being held in contempt of court and having to either pay a fine or go to jail.

SUBPOENA DUCES TECUM—A court order requiring that on or before a certain date, the recipient, often the custodian of records, provides specified documents to the party issuing the subpoena. This does not require the person so providing the documents to appear or testify, but merely to provide access.

SAMPLE MEDIA COVERAGE

Following are samples of publicity received by Big Brothers/Big Sisters agencies. These articles are not chosen to single out agencies having suffered through such situations, but rather to help others learn from their experiences. Some of these samples demonstrate how best to handle crisis situations; the other articles illustrate the wide range of what makes a Big Brothers/Big Sisters agency newsworthy.

TYPES OF CRISIS SITUATIONS

While many agencies feel the only kind of negative publicity generated is from child molestation allegations, there are a variety of crisis situations when an agency might find itself dealing with the media. One of the cardinal rules is to "distinguish a problem from a crisis." Take corrective action on problems and remember that both problems and crises can be controlled. Some examples of crisis situations include:

♦ Child abuse/molestation allegation

♦ Embezzlement of agency funds

♦ Sexual or racial discrimination suit/sexual harassment

- Drug related arrest of staff or youth or volunteer in program

- Major fire or explosion—wherever matches are together, e.g., at circus or sporting events, bowling centers; could also involve the destruction of the agency's office or property

- Injury or death of child or volunteer during agency sponsored activity

- Natural disaster—generally affecting agency offices

- Suspension of funding by United Way or other funding institutions

- False allegation about agency

Each of these situations has caused crisis or emergency dealings with the media for some Big Brothers/Big Sisters programs. It is important to remember that the media considers many issues newsworthy and that your agency should respond by planning *before* the need arises.

These are just some examples of crisis situations that may (but hopefully will not) befall your agency.

POSSIBLE QUESTIONS AND SUGGESTED RESPONSES

Question: **Media**: *"What do you think happened?"*

Response: **Spokesperson**: Refrain from speculation on what or why something happened. It is better to say, *"I don't know,"* unless you actually have the facts.

Question: **Media**: *"How much damage was sustained?"* or *"How large a potential suit are you facing?"*

Response: **Spokesperson**: Do not try to estimate any dollar amount. Such guesses can affect amounts of lawsuits or even insurance claims, seldom to your advantage.

Question: **Media**: *"Will you be reviewing your screening procedures after this incident?"* or, *"How will your procedures change as a result of this incident?"*

Response: **Spokesperson**: Never indicate that your current practices could in any way be considered negligent. *"We have no reason to believe our practices or procedures are in need of immediate revision"* is an appropriate response. Never instigate a program review during a time of crisis. This could be interpreted by the news media as an indication that you were at fault or negligent. Also, be especially sensitive to any staff changes or layoffs during a crisis. This, too, can be taken as an indication of wrongdoing or staff dissatisfaction, which could result in renewed or extended media coverage.

Question: **Media**: *"Will the volunteer be allowed to serve as a Big Brother or Big Sister again?"*

Response: **Spokesperson**: *"The match has been suspended pending the outcome of the allegations. However, you should know that because of the one-to-one*

nature of the Big Brothers/Big Sisters service, adults who are matched with children in our program are carefully screened. The process is thorough and comprehensive and includes references, police record checks, in-person interviews, and home assessments. The volunteer selection process is designed to assure that the matches made are as appropriate as possible, keeping the child's safety and well-being in mind at all times."

Question: **Media**: *"Have any rules or regulations been broken that you know of?"*

Response: **Spokesperson**: In answering this question, be honest, but not expansive. If it is known that rules were compromised, your answer should be that *"it appears as if that may be a possibility however, the situation is still under investigation."* At this point, most cases of wrongdoing are in the preliminary states. It is not appropriate to say that situations are more than allegations. Your interpretation of events should not be added to your message to the media—you will be held responsible for what you say if you assign guilt where legally there is none.

Question: **Media**: *"Is the issue of child sexual abuse a major problem for Big Brothers/Big Sisters agencies?"*

Response: **Spokesperson**: This is a tricky question to answer as it addresses a major issue and reflects on the entire Big Brothers/Big Sisters Movement. A suggested response to questions of this nature is *"The problem of child sexual abuse is not unique to Big Brothers/Big Sisters. That is why Big Brothers/Big Sisters has been in the forefront of requiring screening for adults who work with or volunteer to spend time with children. We also have in place at this agency EMPOWER, a child abuse prevention and education program designed to inform children to report any inappropriate behavior to a trusted adult."* Stressing your agency's prevention and education program will inform the media that you are doing as much as possible about the problem of child sexual abuse.

Question: **Media**: *"How will service be affected due to your agency's recent loss of funding?"*

Response: **Spokesperson**: *"Big Brothers/Big Sisters provides a much needed service to this community. Therefore, we do not anticipate that service will be cut back at this time. We will be looking for alternative funding sources."* If there are questions concerning the possibility of reinstatement of your funding, this could be indicated. *"We have requested a hearing to present our situation for consideration of reinstatement."*

We have previously discussed the issue of *"No comment."* It is being reiterated here in order to get across the importance of not using this phrase. This is an unwise response to any question put forth by the media, and it is generally interpreted to mean *"I know something but I'm not telling because it is damaging to me."* The media will continue to dig and pursue when confronted with this simple statement, so use of this hedge will not serve you well. It is far better to be as open and accessible as possible. The facts can be provided with greater accuracy, the story will generally become more positive as a result of your input, and the media will respect you for being cooperative and taking the initiative. You do have the right to refrain from commenting; however, you should explain why you can't comment; e.g., *"the case is in litigation and, therefore, we cannot comment on the specifics of the case."*

APPENDIX C

Crisis Communications Plan
for a Small Business

UDUB Burger Drive-In's Crisis Communications Plan for *E. coli* and Hepatitis A
Crisis Communications Plan Team
School of Communications
University of Washington
Professor Kathleen Fearn-Banks
Written March 10, 1999

Dana Anderson
Jennifer Boyeson
Sarah Doran
Meg Hemphill
Stacy Jaffe
Melissa Jones
Jaime Kennerud
David Masin
Alexandra Ootkin
Danielle Rosenow
Julie Sanders
Diva Sze

Revised May 25, 1999

Sarah Doran
Meg Hemphill
Melissa Jones
Jaime Kennerud
Danielle Rosenow

Tested: _____

Contents

Introduction: UDUB Burger's Crisis Communications Plan

Acknowledgments

Statement from Management to Employees

Purposes

Objectives

Crisis Inventory and Results

Warning Signs of a Possible Crisis

Crisis Communications Checklist* (form in Student Workbook)
> *E. coli*
> Hepatitis

Telephone log* (forms in Student Workbook)
> Media Lists*
> Local Television News Personnel
> Local Radio News Personnel
> Local Newspaper Personnel
> Local Newswire Personnel
> Public Relations Contacts

List of Key Publics*
> Internal
> External

Crisis Communications Team Directory*

The Media Spokesperson
> Criteria for Selecting
> Interview Tips
> Trick Questions

List of Emergency Personnel

Internet Sources

Materials for the Crisis Control Room

Key Messages
> *E. coli*
> Hepatitis A

Evaluation of Plan Effectiveness After a Crisis

Methods of Communication

Pregathered Information
> Generic News Release for *E. coli*

History of UDUB Burger Drive-In*
E. *coli* Fact Sheet
Hepatitis A Fact Sheet
Glossary of Food-Related Illnesses
Community Relations Programs*
Employee Relations
Employee Handbook*
Cooking Procedures*
Advertising*
Photographs and Memories*
URLs for Food Poisoning

UDUB Burger's Crisis Communications Plan

Why Is This Plan Important? With the plethora of controversy and crisis surrounding the food industry, particularly the fast-food industry, it is always advisable to be prepared for any possible emergency that could damage our establishment. UDUB's hamburger stand has a good reputation among fast-food consumers in Seattle, our target market, and we need to make sure that our reputation is not damaged.

What Could Happen If the Plan Is Not Followed? If this crisis communications plan (CCP) is not followed in the event of an emergency, the company's good name and reputation in the community could be damaged, which may result in a loss of business. Because trust and reliability are important to consumers, they must feel that they can trust that a certain problem will not reoccur and that they are safe eating at UDUB Burger Drive-In.

Has A Crisis Happened at UDUB Burger Before? Fortunately, there have not been any reports of food poisoning from our customers. However, we should always be prepared for this type of crisis because it is a common problem in the fast-food industry.

Has A Crisis Happened to Similar Companies? Yes. The E. *coli* outbreak that occurred at a Jack-in-the-Box in 1993 was a warning to all fast-food organizations. That crisis, which had a negative effect on the chain's name and reputation, serves as a good example of what not to do when dealing with the media in the midst of a crisis.

*Item is not included due to its personal nature.

Acknowledgments

By signing this statement, I verify that I have read this CCP and am prepared to put it into effect.

President and CEO

(Signature and date)

Vice President and CFO

(Signature and date)

Vice President

(Signature and date)

Office Manager

(Signature and date)

Statement from Management to Employees

There are many high-risk factors surrounding the fast-food industry, making it necessary for all food organizations to be ready for a potential public crisis at any time. Our risks are heightened by the nature of our industry: We provide quick and simple food service. Especially with meat, there is a high risk of food poisoning if the meat is not cooked properly. Because of these dangers, it is vital that UDUB's Burger's employees are prepared to deal with the media and the public quickly and efficiently in the event of a crisis.

We have worked for many years to build an impeccable reputation with the public for providing clean, quick and quality service and food to our consumers. Because the most damaging scare in the food industry, particularly with hamburgers, is food poisoning—particularly the *E. coli* virus and hepatitis A—it is crucial that UDUB Burger be prepared for any possible circumstances involving a patron of our restaurant becoming ill from our food. As mentioned earlier, the *E. coli* crisis that struck Jack-in-the-Box was a prodrome to all fast-food handlers. In order to prevent similar damage to our company, we must take very seriously what happened at Jack-in-the-Box and what Foodmaker did wrong in communicating with the media and the public.

If this CCP is not followed in the event of a crisis, irreparable damage to the reputation of UDUB Burger Drive-In is possible. The loss of trust among our consumers could also lead to a large loss of business. In dealing with this crisis plan, we must keep in mind that trust and reliability are incredibly important to consumers when choosing a place to eat, and UDUB Burger must protect its reputation as being a reliable fast-food source. We trust that all employees will keep up their outstanding work in order to protect our company from such a crisis.

Purposes

In the event of an *E. coli* or hepatitis A outbreak, we must take immediate action to inform our publics of the situation and the measures they need to take. Our open and honest transfer of information to the media and health care facilities will eliminate confusion among our publics. By being truthful and forthright, the crisis situation can be more smoothly resolved and action can be taken to eliminate any future problems.

Objectives

We will make every effort to:

1. Initiate the CCP within 2 hours of the crisis outbreak in the event of a suspected *E. coli* or hepatitis A infection from food eaten at one of our restaurants.

2. Inform all health care organizations that might be involved with the situation.

3. Inform all owners and managers within 3 hours of the outbreak.

4. Inform the media and restaurant patrons within 4 hours of the outbreak.

5. Keep the media and all publics regularly informed of updated information.

6. Maintain honesty with the media about all known information.

7. Find the source of the problem as soon as possible.

8. Distribute our findings to the media and all publics.

9. Develop ways to alleviate future problems.

10. Implement necessary changes as soon as possible and resume business as usual.

Crisis Inventory and Results

The accompanying crisis inventory graph (see Fig. C.1) analyses five possible crises that could occur at a UDUB Burger Drive-In: *E. coli* poisoning, hepatitis A poisoning, fire, injury, and violence. By studying the probability of each possible crisis and the amount of possible damage that could result if that crisis occurred, it was determined that UDUB Burger Drive-In is more vulnerable to the crises involving *E. coli* or hepatitis A outbreaks. This crisis plan was created to suit the needs of UDUB Burger Drive-In in case one of these emergencies should occur.

Warning Signs of a Possible Crisis

E. coli

- The *E. coli* crisis that occurred at a Jack-in-the-Box cost the company a large amount of customers. UDUB Burger can prevent this type of crisis by following proper food-handling instructions and by being aware of the quality of hamburger meat served to customers.

- Employees will be trained in meat-preparation techniques to ensure that the hamburgers reach a temperature high enough to kill *E. coli* bacteria.

Hepatitis A

- Warning signs of a potential hepatitis A outbreak include employee illness, failure to wash hands, and improper food handling. All employees will be educated in how to prevent the spread of hepatitis A.

- If an employee contracts hepatitis A, the individual will not be allowed to work until he or she is declared "safe" by the Department of Health.

Fire

- The 1968 kettle fire at the UDUB Burger Drive-In in Lake City was a wake-up call to all employees. Five days of business were lost. Employees could have been seriously injured. Instructions for fire prevention can be found in the *UDUB Burger Drive-In Employee Handbook.*

- Unsafe working conditions or malfunctioning equipment could lead to a potentially dangerous fire. All employees will be trained to recognize possible dangers in the preparation area.

Injury

- Whether involving employees or customers, injury in the workplace can create serious long-term problems, such as loss of business, reduced workforce, negative publicity, and legal repercussions.

- Employees will be trained to take precautions and to notice potentially hazardous areas, such as wet floors, construction areas and other unsafe areas.

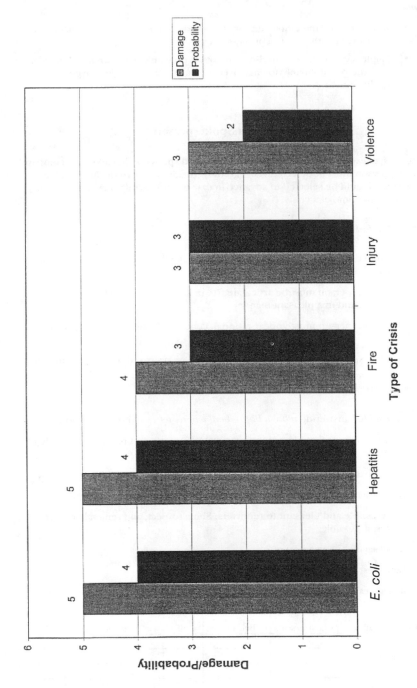

FIG. C.1. A crisis inventory graph for UDUB's Burger Drive-In.

Violence

- Whether involving employees or customers, violence in the workplace is a tragic event with serious consequences.
- Employee training, counseling, and other preventive measures will be taken to curb the possibility of violence occurring at a UDUB Burger Drive-In establishment.

The Media Spokesperson

The media spokesperson represents the company and speaks on behalf of the company. The spokesperson must be selected very carefully. In addition, two or three backup spokespeople should be selected in advance in case the primary spokesperson is unavailable at the time of a crisis.

Criteria for Selecting

- The spokesperson must have the power to make decisions and be accessible throughout the crisis.
- The spokesperson must be articulate. He or she must be able to talk clearly, concisely, and in a pleasant manner.
- The spokesperson must appear rational, concerned, and empathetic during a crisis.
- Multiple spokespersons, when used, must all be prepared to say the same thing.

Interview Tips

- Prepare for answering *who, what, when, where, why,* and *how* questions.
- Focus on two or three key messages to communicate and repeat them during the interview.
- Gather background information that may be useful during the interview.
- Be aware of subjects, issues, and questions that might be brought up.
- Be accessible and pleasant to reporters: Show respect, and remember their names, if possible.
- Avoid saying, "No comment."
- Be honest.
- Remain calm, courteous, truthful, concerned, and, if necessary, apologetic.

Primary and Backup Spokespersons	Office Phone	Cell Phone	Home Phone	E-Mail
Spokesperson 1: _____	_____	_____	_____	_____
Spokesperson 2: _____	_____	_____	_____	_____
Spokesperson 3: _____	_____	_____	_____	_____
Spokesperson 4: _____	_____	_____	_____	_____

Local Television News Personnel

Station/Channel	Address	News Director	Phone	Fax
KCTS/9	401 Mercer St. Seattle, WA 98109	Jane Seridan	206-728-6463	206-443-6691
KING/5	333 Dexter Ave. N. Seattle, WA 98109	Eric Lerner Ron Taylor (weekend)	206-448-5555 Newsphone: 206-448-3850	N/A
KIRO/7	2807 3rd Ave. Seattle, WA 98121	Bill Lord Tim Smith (assignment editor) Newsphone:	206-728-8331 206-728-8308 800-777-5476	206-441-4840
KOMO/4	100 4th Ave. Seattle, WA 98121	Joe Barnes Paula Marimon (weekend)	206-443-4141 206-443-4050	206-443-2955
KSTW/11	P.O. Box 1141 Seattle, WA 98411	Dan Ackler Keith Groteluchen (weekend editor)	206-682-7762 253-573-5789	206-272-2061
KCPQ/13	1813 Westlake Ave. N. Seattle, WA 98109	Todd Mokhtari Cory Bertman (managing editor)	206-674-1313	N/A

Local Radio New Personnel

Station	Address	News Director	Phone	Fax
KING/1090 AM	333 Dexter Ave. N. Seattle, WA 98109	Tony Iner	206-448-3651	N/A
KIRO/710 AM	2807 3rd Ave. Seattle, WA 98121	Gail Neubert	206-728-7777	206-726-7001
KPLU/88 FM	121 St. & Park Tacoma, WA 98447	Michael Marcotte	206-340-0230	N/A
KUOW/94 FM	Univ. of WA Seattle, WA 98195	Marcie Stillman	206-329-7880	N/A
KOMO/1000 AM	100 4th Ave. Seattle, WA	Jennifer Beschel	206-443-4104	N/A

Local Newspaper Personnel

Newspaper	Address	Phone/Fax	When/ Frequency
Seattle Post-Intelligencer City Editor: Kathy Best	101 Elliot Ave. W. Seattle, WA 98111	206-448-8030 Fax: 206-481-8166	a.m. daily
Seattle Times City Editor: Bill Ristow	P.O. Box 70 Seattle, WA 98111	206-464-2204 206-464-2261	p.m. daily
Morning News Editor: Tom Osborne	P.O. Box 1100 Tacoma, WA 98411	253-297-8742	a.m. daily
Everett Herald Editor: Sam Strick	P.O. Box 930 Everett, WA 98206	425-339-3428	p.m. daily
Eastside Journal	1705 132nd Ave. NE Bellevue, WA 98005	206-453-4242 Fax: 425-635-0630	p.m. daily
Eastside Week Editor: Pricilla Turner	123 Lake St. Kirkland, WA 98035	425-827-5550 Fax: 425-827-0932	a.m. weekly
Seattle Weekly Editor: Knute Berger	1008 Western Ave., Suite 300 Seattle, WA 98104	206-623-0500 Fax: 206-467-4338	a.m. weekly

Local Newswire Personnel

Name	Address	Editor	Phone	Fax
Associated Press (News and Photo Bureau)	201 Boren Ave. N., Room 5 Seattle, WA 98109	John Marlow	206-682-1812	206-621-1948
PR Newswire	1001 4th Ave., Suite 2138 Seattle, WA 98154	Derek Farley (bureau manager)	206-624-2414 1-800-367-8555	206-624-2343

Public Relations Contacts

Organization	Contact Name	Phone
King County Dept. of Public Health	Jennifer White	206-296-4755
Seattle Fire Dept.	N/A	206-386-1454
Seattle Police Dept.	Christie-Lynn Bonner	206-684-5520
Harborview Medical Center	Tina Mankowski	206-731-3000
TS McHugh's (neighboring restaurant)	Thomas "Tucker" McHugh	206-282-1910

- Face the reporter, not the camera or the microphone.

- Avoid jargon: Speak in everyday language.

- Do not speculate. Do not answer questions you don't understand. Ask for clarification.

- Be trained ahead of time, rehearsed well in advance of the crisis, and briefed prior to responding to the media.

Trick Questions

Reporters might bring you into a difficult situation by asking you trick questions. Following are examples of various types of trick questions.

1. Speculative questions that begin with *if*:

 - "If the hamburgers that were infected were served during the normal lunch hour instead of late at night, how many people would have been infected?"
 - "If the hamburgers had cooked at a higher temperature, would the *E. coli* outbreak have happened?"

2. Leading questions:

 - "You do agree that UDUB Burger could have avoided this crisis, right?"

3. Loaded questions:

 - "Isn't it true that you knew there was an *E. coli* outbreak but couldn't do anything to stop it at once, so it caused so many deaths?"
 - "Isn't it true that you knew of possible *E. coli* in the undercooked hamburgers?"
 - "Isn't it true that you knew this employee had hepatitis A and that you failed to do anything about it?"
 - "Isn't it true that the shift manager should have been aware of the warning signs of this crisis?"

4. Naïve questions:

 - "What type of food does UDUB Burger Drive-In serve?"

5. False questions (containing inaccurate details that reporters want you to correct):

 - "There were only two employees during the rush hours, right?"
 - "About 90% of your meat comes from the same plant that the contaminated meat from Jack-in-the-Box came from, correct?"
 - "More than seven people have been affected by the virus strain that started here at your restaurant, right?"

6. Know-it-all questions:

 - "We have all the facts. I just need to confirm a few things with you, okay?"
 - "I have all of the details, but could you give me some wrap-up comments about this crisis?"

7. Silence: This tactic aims to get you to "spill your guts."

8. Accusatory questions (designed to make you blame someone else):

 - "Who is actually responsible for this crisis?"

9. Multiple-part questions (designed to be intentionally confusing):

 • "What is the temperature at which you cook your meat, and is that the regulation for Washington? If it is, then how can someone contract this virus if heat is supposed to kill it?"

10. Jargon questions: Make sure to avoid using technical words that can confuse publics.

11. Chummy questions:

 • "Hey Pal, off the record, why do you think this happened?"

12. Labeling questions:

 • "Would you say that the atmosphere here at UDUB Burger is 'stressful'?"
 • "Would you call the fast-paced environment stressful enough for one to lose sight of a specified task?"

13. Good-bye questions (reporters give the impression that the interview is over before asking such questions):

 • "Good-bye. Oh, by the way, how did this crisis actually happen?"

List of Emergency Personnel

Seattle Police Department
610 3rd, Seattle 98104
911
Media Relations–684-5520
Fax: 684-8197

Fire Department
301 2nd, Seattle 98104
911
Dept. Info: 386-1400
Fax: 386-1412

Harbor View Medical Center
325 9th Ave. S., Seattle 98104
PR: 731-4199
Fax: 731-8605

Virginia Mason
925 Senaca, Seattle 98101
Communications: 583-6082
Fax: 223-6744

UW Medical Center
1959 NE Pacific St., Seattle 98105
PR: 543-3620
Fax: 685-3333

Swedish Medical Center
PR: 386-6797

King County Department of Health
206-269-4755

Materials for the Crisis Control Room

_____ Crisis Communications plan	_____ Flip charts	
_____ Press Kits	_____ Telephones	
_____ Contact lists	_____ Telephone directories	
_____ Media directories	_____ Television	
_____ Chairs	_____ Radio	
_____ Desks	_____ Map of each store	
_____ Computers	_____ Street maps	

_____	Computer printers	_____	Police radio
_____	Copy machine	_____	First-aid kits
_____	Paper	_____	Food
_____	Company letterhead	_____	Beverages
_____	Pens	_____	Camera
_____	Pencils	_____	Film
_____	Bulletin boards	_____	Cell phones
_____	Chalkboard		

Key Messages

E. coli

In the event of an *E. coli* outbreak, UDUB Burger employees' first priority is the care of its customers. Warning the public of the symptoms of *E. coli* is the first order of business. The symptoms can include one or more of the following: abdominal cramps, bloody diarrhea, and nausea. Our primary concern is with those who are infected with *E. coli*. Without knowing the exact location where the *E. coli* originated, whether from the meat distributor or inside our store, we promise the public that the source of the bacteria will be discovered as promptly and effectively as possible.

We will also restate consistently the fact that we are concerned with the *E. coli* problem and that our primary concern is for those infected. We will restate how careful and cautious UDUB Burger is in preventing diseases such as this one from occurring. We will state that our employees cook meat to the standard temperature set by the FDA and that employees follow proper cleaning procedures outlined by the FDA. We will explain that employees are required to receive a food-handler permit prior to working at UDUB Burger.

The following key messages should be stressed in the order indicated:

1. Our biggest concern is for those affected.
2. We are sorry for what happened and we take full responsibility for what happened.
3. We don't know how it happened, but we are trying to find out and we'll let you know as soon as we know.
4. We maintain a strict and thorough process on avoiding problems such as these from occurring by requiring our employees to receive a food-handler permit.

Hepatitis A

In the event of hepatitis A scare, UDUB Burger employees' first priority is the care of its customers. Warning the public of the symptoms of hepatitis A is the first order of business. The symptoms can include one or more of the following: fatigue, nausea, vomiting, fever/chills, jaundice, pain in the liver area, dark urine, light-colored stools, and/or abdominal pain. Our primary concern is with those who are infected with

hepatitis A. Without knowing the exact location where the hepatitis A originated, whether from one of the employees or an external source, we promise the public that the source of the disease will be discovered as promptly and effectively as possible.

We will also restate consistently the fact that we are concerned with the hepatitis A problem and that our primary concern is for those infected. We will restate how careful and cautious UDUB Burger is in preventing diseases such as this one from occurring. We will state that employees are required to receive a food-handler permit prior to working at UDUB Burger and that they must wash their hands before handling food.

The following key messages should be stressed in the order indicated:

1. Our biggest concern is for those affected.
2. We are sorry for what happened and we take full responsibility for what happened.
3. We don't know how it happened, but we are trying to find out and we'll let you know as soon as we know.
4. We maintain a strict and thorough process on avoiding problems such as these from occurring by requiring our employees to receive a food-handler permit.

Evaluation of Plan Effectiveness After a Crisis

After a crisis, the following steps will be followed to ensure that UDUB Burger is better prepared for the future. This evaluation is for looking at what went right and what went wrong during the crisis. It covers all aspects of the crisis, including media relations, community relations, and the crisis management team's performance. It is vital to evaluate the company's CCP while the crisis is still fresh in employees' minds. Thinking about all aspects of the crisis will help determine what we can do better next time.

1. Media relations:
 Review the media's coverage of the crisis. Were there areas in which we could have received better or more positive coverage of our company? Would the coverage have been better if we had taken more time to build strong media relationships before the crisis?
2. Community relations:
 Did the community act favorably to how we handled the crisis? If not, what can we do to build better community relations (i.e., public service donations or activities)? If we donate money or services, make sure that the public is aware of it (through media coverage or information at our restaurant locations).
3. Crisis management team:
 Did all team members perform well under pressure? Were there certain members who should have been put "behind the scenes" or on the "front lines" (speaking to the media, etc.)? Should any members be replaced by others should another crisis occur? Was the crisis control room properly stocked? Was there anything missing that needs to be ordered or created?

Pregathered Information

Generic News Release for E. coli

A UDUB Burger Drive-In customer is being treated for symptoms of *E. coli* at (*name of hospital*). His/her condition is _____. It is not known at this time if he/she contracted the illness at the UDUB Burger Drive-In location where he/she dined on (*date*).

Methods of Communication

In the event of a crisis, the following publics should be contacted in the manner indicated in the chart.

Public	Telephone	E-mail	Fax	Letter by Mail	Newsletter	Bulletin Board	Personal Visit	News Release
Meeting								
Owners	•	•						
Executive	•	•						
Employees				•	•	•		•
Electronic media		•				•		
Daily newspapers		•				•		
Weekly newspapers		•				•		
Suppliers		•	•					
Community leaders				•	•			

"We are very concerned about (*victim's name*) and we are monitoring his/her condition closely. Whether the illness came from food at UDUB Burger or other causes, we wish for his/her speedy recovery," said _____, UDUB Burger's owner and president.

According to (*whom*), (*victim's name*) ate a hamburger at the UDUB Burger Drive-In located at (*address or neighborhood*). He/She is said to be experiencing (*symptoms*).

The health department is currently investigating to see if there is a possible link between the burgers served at UDUB Burger and the victim's illness. In the 45-year history of UDUB Burger Drive-In, there have been no other reported cases of this illness.

UDUB Burger Drive-In has a strict sanitary code that requires employees to cook hamburgers to 160 degrees, 10 degrees higher than required by the U.S. Food and Drug Administration. Employees are thoroughly trained in cooking according to safety and health procedures.

E. coli Fact Sheet

Definition of E. coli. *E. coli* is an emerging cause of food-borne illness. *E. coli* are germs (bacteria) that normally live in the intestines of people and animals. There is no treatment for *E. coli*.

What Are the Symptoms? The most common symptoms are severe stomach cramps and diarrhea. Some people vomit or run a fever, but these are less common. These symptoms usually go away by themselves after 6 to 8 days. In a small number of people, this strain of *E. coli* can cause a rare but serious problem called hemolytic uremic syndrome (HUS).

What Is HUS? HUS is a disease that affects the kidneys and blood-clotting system. In severe cases, dialysis is used for a limited time to do the kidney's work. Some people also develop a bleeding problem or low red blood cell count (anemia).

Where Is E. coli Found? It lives in the intestines of healthy cattle and gets into the meat when cattle are slaughtered. The germs are killed when the meat is thoroughly cooked. Germs have also been found in raw milk, apple cider, and salami.

How Is E. coli Spread? *E. coli* must be swallowed to cause an infection. This can happen if you eat or drink something that contains these germs and is not properly cooked or pasteurized. The germs can be spread from person to person if someone who is infected does not thoroughly wash his or her hands with soap and water before preparing food for others.

How Is E. coli Prevented? Take the following steps to avoid infection:

- Do not eat nonpasteurized dairy products or undercooked ground beef.

- Do not drink raw milk or apple cider that is made from unwashed apples.

- Always wash your hands with soap and water after going to the bathroom, changing a diaper, or handling raw meat.

Hepatitis A Fact Sheet

What Is Hepatitis A? It is a highly contagious virus that attacks the liver. It is the seventh most commonly reported infectious disease in the United States (behind gonorrhea, chicken pox, syphilis, AIDS, salmonellosis, and shigellosis). Hepatitis A accounts for as many as 65% of all viral hepatitis cases in the United States each year. It is the most prevalent type of hepatitis.

What Are the Symptoms? The common symptoms of hepatitis A are fatigue, nausea, vomiting, fever/chills, jaundice, pain in the liver area, dark urine, light-colored stools, and/or abdominal pain.

How Do You Get Hepatitis A? The hepatitis A virus is transmitted by the fecal–oral route through close person-to-person contact or by ingesting contaminated food or water. Infection has been shown to be spread by:

- Close personal contact with someone infected with hepatitis A.

- Eating foods contaminated by infected food handlers.

- Contact with infected children (who do not usually show symptoms), who can then infect nonimmune children or adults at home or in child-care centers.

- Ingesting raw or undercooked shellfish (e.g., oysters, clams, mussels) from waters contaminated with the virus.

- Ingesting contaminated food or water during travel to underdeveloped areas.

- Transmission through blood transfusions or sharing needles with infected people using injectable drugs.

What Is the Course of the Disease? The incubation period for hepatitis A, which varies from 10 to 50 days (mean 30 days), is dependent on the number of infectious particles consumed. Infection with very few particles results in longer incubation periods. The period of communicability extends from early in the incubation period to about a week after the development of jaundice. The greatest danger of spreading the disease to others occurs during the middle of the incubation period, well before the first presentation of symptoms. Many infections do not result in clinical disease, especially in children. When the disease does occur, it is usually mild and recovery is complete in 1 to 2 weeks. Occasionally, the symptoms are severe and convalescence can take several months. Patients suffer from feeling chronically tired during convalescence and their inability to work can cause financial loss. Less than 0.4% of reported cases in the United States are fatal. These deaths usually occur among the elderly.

What Is the Treatment? There is currently no treatment for hepatitis A, although rest and proper nutrition can relieve some symptoms. The most important factor affecting the severity of the disease is age.

How Dangerous Is Hepatitis A? A very small percentage of people infected with hepatitis A are at risk for serious complications. An estimated 100 deaths occur in the United States each year from the virus.

Does It Come From a Specific Food? The virus has not been isolated from any food associated with an outbreak. Because of the long incubation period, the suspected food is often no longer available for analysis. No satisfactory method is presently available for routine analysis of food. Cold cuts and sandwiches, fruits and fruit juices, milk and milk products, vegetables, salads, shellfish, and iced drinks are commonly implicated in outbreaks. Water, shellfish, and salads are the most frequent sources. Contamination of foods by infected workers in food-processing plants and restaurants is common.

Glossary of Food-Related Illnesses

Botulism: A disease caused by contamination of certain foods by the botulism bacterium commonly found in the soil. The botulism toxin is produced when the bacteria grow in improperly canned foods and occasionally in contaminated seafood. Common symptoms are headaches, nausea, vomiting, constipation, and overall weakness. It progressively attacks the nervous system, causing double vision, muscle paralysis, and difficulty with breathing and speech. Symptoms appear 8 to 12 hours after eating contaminated food. Death may occur within 3 to 7 days without treatment. There is an antitoxin to treat the disease.

Campylocbacteriosis: Bacteria found in the intestinal tracts of healthy animals and untreated water surfaces. Inadequately cooked animal products and nonchlorinated water are the most common reasons for human infection. It can be easily killed by heat above 120 degrees Fahrenheit. Common symptoms are abdominal cramping, diarrhea, fever, headache, muscle pain, and nausea. Symptoms appear 2 to 5 days after eating contaminated food and may last 2 to 7 days.

Clostridium Perfringens: Bacteria found in soil, unprocessed foods, nonpotable water, and the intestinal tract of humans and animals. It is a milder form of botulism. Symptoms include abdominal pain and diarrhea. Symptoms appear 8 to 24 hours after eating contaminated food and may last 1 to 2 days.

***E. coli* Hemolytic Colitis:** Bacteria that comes in many forms; most are harmless except the *E. coli 0157:H7* strain. Abdominal cramps and bloody diarrhea are the distinctive symptoms of this strain. Other symptoms are fever, nausea, and vomiting. These symptoms appear 3 to 5 days after eating contaminated food. Symptoms may last 10 days.

Hepatitis A Virus: A highly contagious virus that attacks the liver. The virus is transmitted by the fecal–oral route, through close person-to-person contact, or by ingesting contaminated food or water. Common symptoms are fatigue, nausea, vomiting, fever, jaundice, pain in the liver area, dark urine, and abdominal pain. The disease can stay in the body for 10 to 50 days without showing symptoms. Recovery usually takes 1 to 2 weeks.

Listeriosis: Bacteria that live in humans and animals. It is usually associated with cattle and sheep having abortions and encephalitis. The elderly, newborn babies, pregnant women, and people with a weakened immune system are the most vulnerable to this infection. Possible symptoms are fever, headaches, nausea, and vomiting. Symptoms appear 3 days to a few weeks after eating contaminated food and may last several days. Death may occur in rare cases.

Salmonellosis: Bacteria spread through contact with human or animal intestinal contents or excrement, usually found in raw meat, fish, poultry, and eggs. Symptoms, which are headache, vomiting, nausea, chills, fever, diarrhea, and abdominal cramping,

appear 12 to 36 hours after eating contaminated food. The symptoms may last 2 to 7 days.

Staphylococcal Intoxication: Bacteria found on the skin and in the nose and throat of most humans. People with sinus infections and colds are high carriers. Infected wounds are rich sources of this bacterium. Sewage, raw milk, and untreated water are carriers. Symptoms are vomiting, nausea, diarrhea, and abdominal cramping. Symptoms appear 1 to 8 hours after eating contaminated food and may last 1 to 2 days.

Employee Relations

* UDUB Burger is an equal opportunity employer.

* UDUB Burger pays at least $7.00 an hour to start. A $1.00 per-hour bonus is paid to employees working between 11 p.m. and 2 a.m., and between 11 a.m. and 2 p.m.

* The opportunity to get raises in pay occurs twice a year at evaluation time.

* Benefits include the following (see the *Employee Handbook* for more information):

 Health and dental insurance plan.
 Employee scholarship plan.
 Child-care benefit program.
 Community service plan.
 401(k) tax-deferred retirement savings plan.
 Overtime hours will be paid at a rate of time and a half (based on the employee's regular hourly wage).
 Half-price food.
 Bonus program for new employee referrals.
 All employees check the "All Hands Notices" on the bulletin boards before they step onto the floor to work.

URLs for Food Poisoning

http://cdc.gov/ncidod.ncid.htm
National Center for Infectious Diseases Web Site

* Learn about the NCID
* Disease information
* Bacterial information
* Access *Emerging Infectious Diseases* (journal)

http://www.doh.wa.gov/Topics/ecoli.htm
Public Fact Sheet About *E. coli*

* What is it?
* Who gets it?
* How does it spread?
* What are the symptoms?
* How is it diagnosed?

http://www.doh.wa.gov/Topics/hepafact.html
Public Fact Sheet About Hepatitis A

- What is hepatitis A?
- How does it spread?
- How is it contracted?
- Overall history

http://www.cdc.gov/

- What the Centers for Disease Control Web Site (CDC) does
- Health News
- Hepatitis information
- Ideas for protecting oneself from diseases

http://www.doh.wa.gov/

- Washington State Department of Health Web Site
- Frequently asked questions about diseases
- Frequently called safety phone numbers in the area
- Current health issues in Washington
- General facts to keep us informed

www.jackinthebox.com
Jack-in-the-Box Web site

www.ificinfo.health.org
International Food Information Council Web site

www.odwalla.com
Odwalla Web site

Index